Luminos is the Open Access monograph publishing program from UC Press. Luminos provides a framework for preserving and reinvigorating monograph publishing for the future and increases the reach and visibility of important scholarly work. Titles published in the UC Press Luminos model are published with the same high standards for selection, peer review, production, and marketing as those in our traditional program. www.luminosoa.org

The publisher and the University of California Press Foundation gratefully acknowledge the generous support of the Joan Palevsky Imprint in Classical Literature.

TRANSFORMATION OF THE CLASSICAL HERITAGE
Peter Brown, General Editor

What Makes a Church Sacred?

For Jacq,
with gratitude for your
leadership, support, and
generosity, Mary

What Makes a Church Sacred?

Legal and Ritual Perspectives from Late Antiquity

———

Mary K. Farag

UNIVERSITY OF CALIFORNIA PRESS

University of California Press
Oakland, California

Suggested citation: Farag, M.K. *What Makes a Church Sacred? Legal and Ritual Perspectives from Late Antiquity.* Oakland: University of California Press, 2021. DOI: https://doi.org/10.1525/luminos.112

Names: Farag, Mary, author.
Title: What makes a church sacred? : legal and ritual perspectives from late antiquity / Mary K. Farag.
Other titles: Transformation of the classical heritage ; 63.
Description: Oakland, California : University of California Press, [2021] | Series: Transformation of the classical heritage ; 63 | Includes bibliographical references and index.
Identifiers: LCCN 2021012584 (print) | LCCN 2021012585 (ebook) | ISBN 9780520382008 (paperback) | ISBN 9780520382015 (ebook)
Subjects: LCSH: Church history—Primitive and early church, ca. 30–600.
Classification: LCC BR165 .F23 2021 (print) | LCC BR165 (ebook) | DDC 270.2—dc23
LC record available at https://lccn.loc.gov/2021012584
LC ebook record available at https://lccn.loc.gov/2021012585

Manufactured in the United States of America

28 27 26 25 24 23 22 21
10 9 8 7 6 5 4 3 2 1

*For my father and mother
with love and gratitude*

CONTENTS

ILLUSTRATIONS

FIGURES

CHART

ACKNOWLEDGMENTS

My work on this project began with my doctoral dissertation; after much expansion and revision, it has concluded with this book. I am grateful to many at Yale University who guided me, especially my dissertation director, Stephen J. Davis, as well as John F. Matthews, Noel Lenski, and Maria Doerfler. The project grew alongside kind, gracious, and critical engagement with many at Princeton Theological Seminary, Princeton University, and the Institute for Advanced Study in Princeton, New Jersey. To Peter Brown, Sabine Schmidtke, and Jack Tannous I owe more than I could ever repay. Wendy Mayer, Ann Marie Yasin, and the anonymous reviewers provided me with invaluable feedback. The librarians at Yale Divinity School, Princeton Theological Seminary, the Institute for Advanced Study, and Princeton University helped me access publications, and I thank them for their generous service. For their work in editing and producing this book, I am grateful to Eric Schmidt and the University of California Press at large. There are many whose names I would like to mention. I hold them dear in my heart and my gratitude to them is unabated. All shortcomings are of course my own, but I hope that this book reflects something of the love, care, support, and guidance I received all along the way from family, church communities, friends, teachers, colleagues, and even strangers.

ABBREVIATIONS

Certain texts, editions, translations, journals, and series are abbreviated according to the following list. Latin abbreviations of Greek texts of late antiquity are cited according to the list in G. W. H. Lampe, ed., *A Patristic Greek Lexicon* (Oxford: Clarendon Press, 1961), xi–xlv. Latin abbreviations of Latin texts of late antiquity are cited according to the list in Albert Blaise and Henri Chirat, *Dictionnaire Latin-Français des auteurs chrétiens* (Paris: Librairie des Méridiens, 1964), 9–29. Editions of canons are not cited in the notes but in appendix C. Translations of texts are my own unless otherwise noted.

ACO	Schwartz, Eduard, ed. *Acta Conciliorium Oecumenicorum.* 4 vols. Continued by Johannes Straub. Berlin: Walter de Gruyter, 1914–82.
BHO	*Bibliotheca hagiographica orientalis.* Brussels: Apud Editores, 1910.
c.	Canon(s)
CCH	*La colección canónica Hispana.* Madrid: Consejo Superior de Investigaciones Científicas, Instituto Enrique Flórez, 1966–.
CCSL	*Corpus Christianorum, Series Latina.* Turnhout: Brepols, 1953–.
CJ	Codex of Justinian
CMCL	Corpus dei Manoscritti Copti Letterari. https://www.cmcl.it/.
CPC	Clavis Patrum Copticorum. http://www.cmcl.it/~cmcl/chiam_clavis.html.
CPG	Geerard, Mauritius. *Clavis Patrum Graecorum.* 7 vols. Turnhout: Brepols, 1974–2018.

CSCO	*Corpus Scriptorum Christianorum Orientalium*. Leuven: Peeters, 1903–.
CSEL	*Corpus Scriptorum Ecclesiasticorum Latinorum*. Vienna: Verlag der Österreichischen Akademie der Wissenschaften, 1866–2009. Berlin: Walter de Gruyter, 2015–.
CTh	Codex of Theodosius
D.	Digest of Justinian
DOP	*Dumbarton Oaks Papers*
CVHR	Vives, José, Tomás Marín Martínez, and Gonzalo Martínez Díez, eds. and trans. *Concilios visigóticos e hispano-romanos*. España Cristiana, Textos 1. Barcelona: Consejo Superior de Investigaciones Científicas, 1963.
Edict	Edict(s) of Justinian
FC	*Fathers of the Church*. Washington, DC: Catholic University of America Press, 1943–.
GCAL	Graf, Georg. *Geschichte der christlichen arabischen Literatur*. 5 vols. Vatican: Biblioteca Apostolica Vaticana, 1944–53.
Hefele-Leclercq	Hefele, Charles Joseph. *Histoire des conciles d'áprès les documents originaux*. Translated and edited by Henri Leclercq. 7 vols. Paris: Letouzey et Ané, 1907–11.
Hess	Hess, Hamilton. *The Early Development of Canon Law and the Council of Serdica*. New York: Oxford University Press, 2002.
JECS	*Journal of Early Christian Studies*
Johannou	Joannou, Périclès-Pierre. *Discipline generale antique*. 2 vols. Rome: Grottaferrata, 1962–1964.
JTS	*Journal of Theological Studies*
Martyn	Martyn, John R. C., trans. *The Letters of Gregory the Great*. 3 vols. Toronto: Pontifical Institute of Medieval Studies, 2004.
MGH AA	*Monumenta Germaniae Historica, Auctores Antiquissimorum*. 15 vols. Berlin: Apud Weidmannos, 1877–1919.
NJust	Novels of Justinian
NMaj	Novels of Majorian
NMarc	Novels of Marcian
NTh	Novels of Theodosius
OCP	*Orientalia Christiana Periodica*
PG	Migne, Jacques-Paul, ed. *Patrologia Graeca*. Paris: n.p., 1857–66.

PL   Migne, Jacques-Paul, ed. *Patrologia Latina*. Paris: Apud Garnieri
            Fratres, 1841–55.

PO   *Patrologia Orientalis*. Paris: Firmin-Didot, 1903–68. Turnhout:
            Brepols, 1970–.

ROC   *Revue de l'orient chrétien*

Rodriguez   Rodriguez, Felix, ed. "El Concilio III de Toledo." In *Concilio III
            de Toledo: XIV Centenario, 589–1989*, ed. Felix Rodriguez, 13–38.
            Toledo: Caja Toledo, 1991.

SC   *Sources chrétiennes*. Paris: Éditions du Cerf, 1942–.

Sirm.   Sirmondian Constitutions

TTH   *Translated Texts for Historians*. Liverpool: Liverpool University
            Press, 1988–.

Introduction

"When I say 'the church,' I do not mean only a place."[1] John Chrysostom said these words in April 400.[2] Rumor had it that the bishop refused to welcome a fugitive who sought protection in his church. It was said that a certain Count John got arrested because John Chrysostom denied him asylum. John Chrysostom delivered a homily in the church that day, telling his listeners not only what happened from his perspective but also what it meant for a church to be a church. He told them that a church was not just a special shelter, a place where people could expect that they would not be assaulted no matter what their crime. He told them that the church was "faith and life" (πίστις καὶ βίος).[3] One should not just rest under the protective sacrality of the church. One should conform to the sacred "mindset" (γνώμη) of the church; one should become the church.[4]

John Chrysostom was one among many bishops who tried to define what it meant for a church to be sacred. In the homily cited above, he urges his listeners to see beyond the legal definition of a church as a *res sacra*, a "sacred thing." I will return to the story of John Chrysostom at the end of part I, but until then the topic of this book will be the very legal definition that John Chrysostom sought to transcend—the legal definition that, for John Chrysostom, governed the church as though it were a mere body without a mindset guiding it.[5] In part II, I will resume the theme of John Chrysostom's "mindset" of the church or the ritual discourse concerning "the sacred."

The making of churches into *res sacrae* occurred, legally and canonically, from Constantine to Justinian. But even though church property in many ways was already treated as a *res sacra* by Constantine and his successors, it was not until the time of Justinian that church buildings and their properties explicitly became *res sacrae*. Part I tells the story of how a definition of "the sacred" conceived for traditional Greco-Roman temples was applied to ecclesial property and expanded in scope in the process. I craft this story on the basis of two kinds of rules: the laws of emperors and the canons of bishops. A canon was an ecclesiastical statute usually promulgated as a result of a council. I use the term "law" in the broadest and most neutral sense to refer to emperors' constitutions, rescripts, *leges*, and so on. Civil and ecclesiastical authorities in late antiquity differentiated between laws and canons, even though they were not hermetically sealed sets of rules.

Imperial chanceries and episcopal synods did not act independently of one another. Emperors convoked some episcopal synods, sent officials to oversee or even preside over proceedings, and enforced certain canons by issuing corresponding laws. Bishops petitioned emperors for legislation that supported their practices, resulting in the expansion of what the designation *res sacra* entailed. While both the imperial and episcopal bodies sought to synchronize their rules, they disagreed as to the direction in which the synchronization should occur. At times, emperors refused episcopal petitions; at other times, bishops persisted in practices that civil authorities outlawed. The discursive construction of ecclesial property as a *res sacra* took place in the midst of such cooperation and tension.

Imperial and episcopal rule-making bodies from Constantine to Justinian granted ecclesial property the same characteristics that the emperor and his civil laws had. Church property became sacred things. That meant they were inviolable: they were protected by God, and in turn provided protection and safety. Just as the emperor and his laws were inviolable, divinely protected, and ensured protection and safety, so too were churches.[6] Although emperors ceased to bear the title of *pontifex maximus* ("high priest") by the end of the fourth century,[7] they nevertheless continued to wield important control over sacred things. Such is the image of ecclesial property that laws and canons paint.

I will follow the contours of this image in part I and show that familiarity with it sheds a different light on well-known episodes of ecclesiastical history. Disputes commonly considered theological in nature had as much to do with the control and administration of ecclesial property as they did with knowledge of God. For one thing, church buildings and property played no small role in the deposition of bishops such as John Chrysostom and Ibas of Edessa, among others. For another, disputes created stigmas for centuries among Christians in North Africa on account of *res sacrae*. Rules regarding ecclesial property mattered. Rule-making bodies provided the blueprint for churches by setting conceptual parameters on what could and could not be done with sacred property.

In part I, the reader will encounter three distinct but interrelated structural components: analysis of juristic pedagogy, compilation of rules from various regions of the Roman Empire, and case study. The compilation of rules does not make for light reading. I have compiled and organized rulebooks in order to make a cumulative point. No matter where one looks—north or south, east or west, canon or law—one general principle appears again and again in the late antique Roman world: sacred things are divinely protected and protecting.

It is not because copies of rules from one region migrated to another that such a general principle can be found across the Mediterranean. Rather, it is because of pedagogical practices. Even after the last western emperor died, legal practice in both East and West continued to rely on classical jurisprudence produced in the second and third centuries. The general principles outlined in such jurisprudence were taught all across the Mediterranean.[8] Nevertheless, every locale applied the general principles in its own way. Therefore, I have also included many of the specific details of the rules cataloged in part I so as not to level out the granular texture of regional particularity. However, I do not place or analyze each rule in its specific context. To do so would detract from the main point: that classical juristic principles taught in Roman law schools surface again and again in the rules produced by both imperial consistories and ecclesiastical councils. Instead, I include select case studies at the end of each rulebook. The case studies make the significance of some rules come alive through reports of bishops' trials and show how knowledge of the rules supplies us with a new reading lens by which to interpret well-known conciliar proceedings and other reports about the individuals at the highest level of ecclesiastical administration, the bishops.

It would require another book altogether to evaluate the enforcement (or lack thereof) of the rules amassed in part I.[9] This book is not about how or to what extent prescriptive ideologies affected the real lives of human persons. This book is about naming those prescriptive ideologies and noting how thoroughly they pervade the Roman Empire in late antiquity. The bottom line of part I is that, ideologically-speaking, the sacralization of things made them unowned and unownable. Scholars have sought in vain for individual or corporate owners of church property. In the late antique Roman juristic mindset, the concepts of "sacred" and "ownership" were mutually exclusive.

Whereas part I contributes to the legal turn in the study of the later Roman Empire,[10] offering a more or less comprehensive assessment of the legal status of church property, part II is not comprehensive in scope. Because jurisprudence specifies the ritual of consecration as the means by which "sacred things" are made, I turn in part II to the ritual context of the consecration of churches in order to evaluate what kind of relationship existed between the ritual discourse of consecration and the legal one. I examine select pieces of evidence: dedicatory images and inscriptions, homilies and hymns composed for church consecrations, and narratives composed to commemorate the anniversary of consecrations. I chose textual and material evidence pertaining to the ritual of consecration that a late antique audience could have likely interpreted with reference to juristic pedagogy.

I argue in part II that the discourse about church assets in dedicatory and consecratory ritual contexts is different from that of the legal one, yet not always mutually exclusive. To carve the contrast in high relief, I borrow language from social anthropologists. Legal protection of ecclesial property entailed limiting their exchangeability, a process anthropologists call "singularization."[11] Ritually, however, exchange of ecclesial property was the very means by which humans became living temples and were socialized into the celestial kingdom. In both legal and ritual contexts, ecclesial property was a "gift," but the legal discourse restricted the possibilities for regifting it, whereas the ritual one celebrated such opportunities.

"Commodity," of course, is a term foreign to the historical sources analyzed here. However, it is a useful term for describing how donors reacted to the ritual discourse. To donors, regifting amounted to the recommoditization of their singularized gifts.[12] For this reason, when bishops prioritized the ritual understanding of how to use church assets over the legal one, donors could pursue them. Sometimes bishops did suffer the juridical consequences for their ritually sound but illegal repurposing of donations.

When Christian groups did not have the law on their side and were imperially repressed, they created a ritual discourse to push back against the regulatory one in another way. Such groups resorted to the composition of pseudepigraphy about consecratory rituals to claim for their churches the status of "sacred thing" that had been denied them legally. For the pseudepigraphers, the grantor of sacrality was Christ and his agents without the intermediary of the civil government.

I distinguish ritual from law in order to indicate how the former responded to the latter. In fact, however, the two are related. It is the juridical context that authorized the ritual of consecration, making the ritual a subsidiary aspect of the law. Indeed, it is this dependence that the pseudepigraphers discussed in chapter 6 sought to undo.

The purpose of part II is not to show that such ritual discourses were somehow unique. In fact, scholars of traditional Greco-Roman ritual practices, Christian monasticism, premodern gift-giving, and still other fields will notice innumerable similarities. The purpose of part II is to show how ritual practices responded to legal strictures. Imperially endorsed bishops generated a ritual discourse surrounding *res sacrae* that, when taken to its logical conclusion, turned the legal discourse on its head. Those bishops who were not imperially endorsed created a ritual discourse that pulled the rug out from under the legal framework.

This book offers an account of how ecclesial property was socially constructed as sacred in late antiquity. It evaluates the relationship between legal and ritual views of what made church property sacred. Like tectonic plates, the perspectives "fit," but events on their colliding boundary "shook" late antique societies in discernable ways.

Chapter 1 identifies the way in which a "thing" (*res*) became "sacred" (*sacra*), by whom and how such "things" were administrated, and how others' "sacred things" were delegitimized. A case study of a dispute that Synesius of Cyrene reports shows one way by which the legal making of churches could be abused for the purpose of usurping territory outside one's jurisdiction. A case study on the trial of Crispinus of Calama demonstrates how bishops in North Africa petitioned for laws against their rival bishops in order to delegitimize them and their sacred places.

Chapters 2 and 3 examine what it meant for a thing to be sacred. Chapter 2 shows that the sacred was protected by God, while chapter 3 demonstrates that the sacred was protecting of those in need. Chapter 2 explains that ecclesial property was protected from alienation and damage. A case study on a contested early sixth-century episcopal election in Rome (the so-called "Laurentian schism") shows how the matter of churches' protection could be employed to question the validity of an election and become an opportunity for the relationship between church and state to be worked out. A case study on the problem of interests of bishops' kin demonstrates that issues of financial misconduct were as important as problems of blasphemy or heresy in trials of bishops.

Chapter 3 draws a picture of how protected places became protecting sanctuaries by analyzing three legally regulated ways in which sacred places offered protection to those in need: manumission of slaves, asylum of refugees, and ransom of captives. Although textbooks of Roman law did not teach that *res sacrae* had any protecting characteristics, bishops petitioned civil authorities for legal support of churches as places of sanctuary. The classical legal category *res sacra* was not applied inflexibly to Christian temples but rather morphed in the process of application. In particular, bishops advocated for expanding the types of sacred property exempt from the rule against alienation. Case studies on bishops accused of sacrilege for their practices of mercy bring into high relief the fine line between financial misconduct and care for the needy.

Chapter 4 examines the material remains of late antique church floors and walls, particularly images and inscriptions installed to dedicate churches to their celestial patrons. In certain ways, such material culture visually reproduced juristic rhetoric: that God and his saints protect their churches. In other ways, however, images and inscriptions invited viewers to learn that the rules governing wealth-investment strategies in the celestial realm differ from those of the terrestrial realm. Chapter 4 pairs with chapter 3 in that it resumes the topic of churches as protecting spaces.

Chapter 5 analyzes compositions produced for performance on the occasions of church consecrations. This chapter argues that orators and hymnographers ironically downplayed the significance of the church building during the festivities of its consecration. Such performers used the occasion instead to pinpoint human beings as the true temples of God and explain how humans must enter into athletic competition with church buildings and surpass their value. Chapter 5 pairs with chapter 2, showing how performances did not define ecclesial property in terms of alienability (as jurists did) but as a blueprint for the human soul's perfection.

Chapter 6 first offers a brief overview of the many ways in which consecrations were commemorated with anniversary celebrations. The chapter then focuses on one particular set of literature produced in Egypt: pseudonymous homilies for the annual anniversary of imperially repressed churches in Egypt. These homilies reframe scriptural stories to offer narratives of how the respective churches were originally built and consecrated. The chapter argues that the writers composed such stories in order to defend the sacrality of their churches despite the government's refusal to grant them the status of *res sacrae*. Chapter 6 pairs with chapter 1, analyzing ritualized responses to the juridical question, "what makes a thing sacred?"

The term "sacred" has been a difficult one to define, with most historians resorting to modern anthropological descriptions in order to make use of it. I show that there was a juridical definition of "the sacred" in late antiquity, one originally conceived for "pagan" sacred spaces but later applied to Christian temples. This legal definition of "the sacred" has far-reaching consequences for understanding why Christians fought over ecclesial property and composed pseudepigraphy from AD 312 to AD 638. Management of church wealth was a major issue—just as important as theological questions during this period of "the early church councils"—and scholars misunderstand well-known figures and events by ignoring the legalities.

The Legal Making of *Res Sacrae*

THE GOAL OF PART I IS TO TELL THE STORY of how legal practitioners conceived of ecclesial property as "sacred things." I take juristic pedagogical texts as the starting point by which and the context in which to interpret all other regulatory evidence. Chapters 1 and 2 form a tightly knit pair: pedagogical texts defined *res sacrae* (chapter 1) and detailed one of the corollaries of the definition (chapter 2): that *res sacrae* are protected places. To our knowledge, no extant pedagogical texts support a second corollary, but, as chapter 3 shows, bishops regularly petitioned for one to be added. Bishops requested legal regulation of churches as protecting places. Emperors did, to a limited extent, acknowledge this second corollary. In other words, as the legal concept of *res sacrae* was applied to Christian temples, it expanded in scope to include churches as protecting places. Part II shows that this was the most contested aspect of the legal regulation of ecclesial property as far as some bishops were concerned. Legally, the protecting capacity of churches was an extension of their protected nature, but bishops preached the opposite in ritual contexts, such as in addresses to clergy, homilies, and hagiographical texts.

1

Res Sacrae

It was an affront to Constantius II in the 350s to learn that Athanasius of Alexandria celebrated Easter in the Great Church, known as the Caesareum. How dare Athanasius consecrate the Great Church without the permission of the *pontifex maximus?*[1] Athanasius, in defense, argued that his use of the Great Church did not amount to its consecration by pointing out precedent in other regions where celebrations of the eucharist took place before the church was officially consecrated. Athanasius instead called his celebration of the eucharist an advanced purification of the place: "The place is ready [for consecration], having already been purified by the prayers which have been offered in it, and requires only the presence of your Piety."[2] Athanasius did not deny the holiness of the eucharist, but at the same time he acknowledged that it is not the eucharist alone that legally consecrates a church.

Jurists and bishops in the Roman Empire were the ones who made, identified, and controlled "sacred things" (*res sacrae*). Jurists' writings (especially laws) and bishops' decisions that were codified into ecclesiastical laws (called "canons") supply evidence for their regulatory practices. Laws and canons restricted the process by which a thing could become sacred and which things could be legally recognized as sacred. The present chapter analyzes how the regulatory discourse of the Roman Empire conceived of *res sacrae*, produced them, constructed an administrative body to manage them, and furthermore how it divested "heretics" of their *res sacrae*.

Classical Roman jurists conceived of sacred things in the context of an empire that initially did not consider Christian practices licit. Nonetheless, they established legal categories and legal precedent that would come to regulate the production of Christian *res sacrae* in the fourth century from the time of the emperor Constantine.[3] Jurists and bishops alike applied to ecclesial property definitions that had been created for "pagan" temples and associated property. As a result, imperial governance controlled which things were Christian *res sacrae* as well as which Christian administrators could be entrusted with them. Often it was at the request of Christian administrators that imperial authorities extended the arm of governmental control. Ecclesiastical administrators likewise had an apparatus of methods for controlling *res sacrae*, albeit of a different nature. Ecclesiastical administrators could control a person's ecclesiastical status and, as a result, they could impose ecclesiastical discipline, even excommunication, against those who violated their regulations.

Imperial authorities enforced laws, while ecclesiastical authorities enforced canons. Still, the two regulatory bodies did not act separately from one another. Emperors convoked some episcopal synods, sent officials to oversee or even preside over proceedings,[4] and enforced certain canons by issuing corresponding laws. Bishops petitioned emperors for legislation that supported ecclesiastical practices. Once Constantine recognized the episcopal tribunal (*episcopalis audientia*), bishops could serve as judges over legal cases, their judgments were considered legally binding, and their sentences could be enforced by imperial authorities.[5]

In their capacity as law- and canon-making authorities, jurists and bishops restricted the production, administration, and use of Christian *res sacrae*, particularly those founded on private estates. The rules that they promulgated were never created in a vacuum but were composed and enforced in response to specific problems. Sources rarely retain the detailed circumstances that led to the deliberation of canons and laws, but episcopal letters offer a window into the sorts of conflicts that arose over *res sacrae*. For instance, Synesius of Cyrene, when he was bishop of Ptolemais in the early fifth century, heard a dispute between two bishops over one church and sent a report of the hearings to Theophilus of Alexandria. Synesius's epistolary report details to Theophilus the circumstances under which the dispute arose and how Synesius temporarily resolved it. Synesius had to address the problem of an improper production of a sacred thing. He faced the following questions: Was the place still a "sacred thing" despite the ecclesiastical administrator's improper method of production? How should the ecclesiastical administrator be disciplined for his misconduct? Synesius's letter offers a concrete example of how one bishop responded to a situation that did not conform to legal and canonical conceptions of how *res sacrae* ought to be produced.

There was no legal or canonical way to deconsecrate a temple or unmake a sacred thing in the Roman Empire. In fact, *res sacrae* were unowned, so there was not even a designated legal proprietor who could desacralize the property. In effect, this left the legal decision-making about what counts as *res sacrae* and which bishops may administrate them in the hands of the highest authority: the emperor. Emperors did delegitimize the perceived sacrality of places by outlawing certain cultic practices and confiscating places where such "forbidden practices" occurred. Emperors legally divested others of their sacred things by renaming them, seizing them, giving them to imperially sanctioned administrators, and imposing debilitating penalties on nonimperially sanctioned administrators. Bishops could request of the emperor that confiscatory laws be written against their rivals. For example, at the turn of the fifth-century, bishops of North Africa petitioned imperial officials to confiscate the ecclesial property of those bishops they considered illegitimate. The writings of Augustine of Hippo offer glimpses into an effective petition against Crispinus of Calama. Other writings, such as Victor of Vita's *History of the Vandal Persecution* and Justinian's laws, show how the stigma of the penalty levied against Crispinus and other "heretic" bishops became a century-long sticking point in North Africa's religious milieus.

THE GEOGRAPHICAL AND CHRONOLOGICAL SCOPE
OF THE CANONS AND LAWS

Though I cite canons and laws produced from Constantine's accession through Justinian's tenure, I do not limit the geographical scope to the regions that they and all intervening emperors controlled. Instead, I include regions that continued to rely on classical Roman juristic pedagogy even after they no longer belonged to the Roman Empire, such as Gaul.

The sum total of canons and laws are but a small fraction of the conciliar and legislative decisions that were produced during the period between Constantine and Justinian. As Ramsay MacMullen estimates, probably no less than fifteen thousand councils were convened between AD 253 and 550, but information about only 255 of them has been transmitted to us.[6] No generalizations can be extrapolated from less than 2 percent of the data. For this reason, the account of rules that follows prefers specificity and nuance over generalization, at the cost of rapidly shifting from one time and place to another.

I examine only the laws that have been transmitted in strictly legal literature (as opposed to reports of laws in, for example, historiographies): the Codex of Theodosius, the Sirmondian Constitutions, the Codex of Justinian, and the Novels and Edicts of Justinian.[7] Although these compilations were made at specific times and places, they include prescriptions drafted for various regions both East and West. The date of each compilation's collocation is important to note, since it is from that date onward that rules originally made for specific locales became generalized and normalized for empire-wide application.

The Theodosian Codex[8] was the third of four major efforts to edit and compile imperial constitutions.[9] It was published in 438 and made a standard for both eastern and western parts of the empire, regardless of the original addressees of the constitutions cited. Conflicting decisions were juxtaposed and the most recent ones made normative. The last book of the codex was devoted entirely to ecclesiastical matters, though mention of ecclesial property is also made in the previous books as well.[10]

The name Sirmondian Constitutions is given to a small collection of eighteen constitutions issued between 333 and 425, and probably compiled by a private collector. In a number of cases, they reproduce in more complete form constitutions edited and excerpted in the Theodosian Codex. In such cases, the Sirmondian Constitutions allow one to read portions of constitutions that were edited out by the compilers of the Theodosian Codex.[11]

The Codex of Justinian, published in two editions, also collects imperial constitutions like the Codex of Theodosius II, but it differs from the latter in a number of important respects. For one thing, the book on ecclesiastical legislation did not close the codex but rather opened it as book one. For another, the compilers took a further step in the attempt to render the compilation a standard: they edited out discrepancies and conflicting decisions. The first edition, no longer extant, was published on April 7, 529. The second, updated edition superseded the first and was published five years later on November 16, 534. It is the version by which the Codex of Justinian is known today.[12]

Justinian's legislation issued after the codification project is known collectively as the *Novels*, and it consists of novels (new laws) and edicts (general laws).[13] Like the Sirmondian Constitutions, Justinian's novels and edicts were probably collected privately and, for the most part, they transmit complete laws not excerpts as the codices do. As Timothy Kearley notes, "The bulk of the novels, those of general application, were directed to the Praetorian Prefect of the [East], the Emperor's chief judicial officer, who was sometimes commanded in the law to make it widely known. This general publication often was done by writing the law on a tablet, or in stone, and displaying it in churches."[14] Although the addressee named in many of the novels is the praetorian prefect of the East, copies were also sent to other prefects and officials in many cases.

As for canons, the history of how conciliar decisions were recorded differed in the East and the West. Many acts of local councils survive from the West.[15] Much fewer do from the East. In the East, the canons of select councils of late antiquity were chosen as normative and transmitted in compilations.[16] In addition, collections of canons in the East have been transmitted, not organized by the locale of the council but by the name of the presumed president, such as the canons of Athanasius of Alexandria.[17] Much more historical work remains to be conducted before such collections, which survive in Greek, Syriac, Coptic, Arabic, and still other languages, can be used. The method of recording canons in the East adds a layer of complexity that must be addressed first in order that the canons themselves can be read critically. Therefore, I have omitted such compilations from the present study. For this reason, though the canons amassed in part I make it appear as though the West issued more than the East on the matter of ecclesial property, that is not necessarily true.

DEFINING "ECCLESIAL PROPERTY"

I use the phrase "ecclesial property" in the broadest sense. "Sacred things" included not only the church building and liturgical vessels, but also associated properties, such as revenue-producing lands or even slaves. To use legal parlance, it was not only immovable property (e.g., the church building) that counted as *res sacrae*, but also movable (e.g., the vessels) and self-moving (e.g., the slaves) property. "Ecclesial property" refers to the whole set.

My starting point for examining the legal status of ecclesial property in the Roman Empire is the pedagogical writings of jurists, who explained that sacred property has no owner, but rather falls under divine protection. This point has not escaped the attention of scholars who study Roman sacred law prior to the Christianization of the empire.[18] However, although several studies have attempted to account for the legal status of Christian sacred places, they ask the question, "Who owned ecclesial property?" and debate whether the church at large was considered a corporate legal entity or whether each individual church was a legal entity.[19] In so doing, these studies read the concept of ownership into laws and canons, instead of reading the laws and canons through the lens of Roman legal principles concerning sacred property. Other publications have focused on specific aspects of legal and canonical legislation: the topics of privileges,[20] donations,[21] alienation,[22] manumission of slaves,[23] and asylum.[24]

This chapter analyzes how imperial and ecclesiastical legal discourse conceived of the category *res sacrae* by creating a means for controlling how sacred things were made and how they were administered. At the same time, the discourse established an "othering" process to keep the category of *res sacrae* in imperially sanctioned hands. The places that "heretics" claimed as their churches or *res sacrae* were denied these designations altogether and given instead demeaning appellations, such as "feral grotto."

ROMAN JURISTIC PEDAGOGY ON *RES SACRAE*

In the three centuries that preceded the legal legitimization of the Christian cult in the time of Constantine, Roman jurists published textbooks and commentaries, among other writings, that had become classic by the time of Justinian. So as to account for temples as things (*res*) in jurisprudence that distinguished among things (*res*), persons (*personae*), and actions (*actiones*), these writings defined a legal category of "sacred things" (*res sacrae*). Such writings, in turn, became the legal platform from which ecclesial property would be made into *res sacrae*.

Jurisprudence on *res sacrae* survives in three legal texts: two textbooks and a compilation. The textbooks, both called the *Institutes*, were written by a second-century Roman jurist, Gaius, and the sixth-century quaestor under Justinian, Tribonian, along with his staff. The compilation, the *Digest*, was likewise completed by Justinian's commission, and it contains excerpts from the writings of first-through early fourth-century jurists concerning *res sacrae*. Professional jurists such as Gaius, Tribonian, and those cited in the *Digest* not only formulated legal categories and delineated the realms of legal possibility, but they also taught other jurists their trade. Jurists' studies offered frameworks to be adhered to, reinterpreted, or rejected in the composition of imperial constitutions and ecclesiastical canons.

It is important to concede from the outset that what is cited in the *Digest* cannot be divorced from its sixth-century context. Though the excerpts derive from texts written prior to the legal legitimization of the Christian cult, they were selected and arranged according to the principles of a sixth-century commission.[25] For this reason, it must be remembered that the picture of a pre-Justinianic category of *res sacrae* is colored by sixth-century choices as to which jurists should be quoted, which portion of their works should be cited, and with which citations they should be juxtaposed. In many cases, the *Digest* represents the only witness to certain jurists' otherwise lost writings.

Res Sacrae *as a Legal Category*

The jurists Gaius and Ulpian in the second and third centuries, respectively, and Tribonian in the sixth created a category of *res sacrae* foundational to the regulatory discourse of Christian sacred things. Gaius and Ulpian offer two different ways of categorizing *res sacrae* in their respective *Institutes* or legal textbooks.[26] Whereas Gaius treats *res sacrae* as separate from all other *res*, Ulpian joins the sacred together with state offices. In Justinian's codification of jurisprudence, it was Gaius's schema that was chosen to underlie the *Institutes*, but the *Digest* opened with Ulpian's.

According to Gaius, there are things subject to divine law (*res divini iuris*) and things subject to human law (*res humani iuris*).[27] They are distinguished by their relationship to "our patrimony" (*nostrum patrimonium*), which refers to the aggregate of things that are subject to ownership.[28] Things under divine law lie outside of the patrimony (*extra nostrum patrimonium*), cannot belong to anyone (*nullius in bonis*), and are further subdivided into sacred (*sacrae*), religious (*religiosae*), and sanctified (*sanctae*) things.[29] *Res sacrae* are consecrated to the gods above (*diis superis consecratae sunt*).[30] In order to be properly consecrated, the consecration must occur under the authority of the Roman people (*ex auctoritate populi Romani*), either by means of a statute (*lex*) or by a Senate resolution (*senatus consultum*).[31] In contrast, things under human law lie within the patrimony (*in nostro patrimonio*) and are further subdivided into public (*publicae*) and private (*privatae*).[32]

Ulpian, on the other hand, does not distinguish between divine law and human law. Instead, his framework divides public law from private law.[33] Each category is further subdivided into three parts. Public law covers the sacred (*in sacris*), the sacerdotal offices (*in sacerdotibus*), and the magistracy (*in magistratibus*).[34] Private law is divided into natural rules (*ex naturalibus praeceptis*), rules of all human beings ([*ex*] *gentium* [*praeceptis*]), and rules of communities ([*ex*] *civilibus* [*praeceptis*]).[35] *Res sacrae* fall under public law and are treated under the same umbrella of legal theory that the offices of the priesthood and offices of the state are treated.[36] "Private" is not as narrowly conceived as Gaius would have it, since it encompasses both personal and state rules.

TABLE 1 Division of Things according to Gaius, Ulpian, and Justinian

Gaius	Divine law, *extra nostrum patrimonium*		Human law, *in nostro patrimonio*	
		Sacred		Public
		Religious		Private
		Sanctified		
Ulpian	Public law		Private law	
		Sacred		Natural
		Sacerdotal		Human
		Magistracy		Civil
Justinian	Divine law, *extra nostrum patrimonium*		*In nostro patrimonio*	
		Sacred		Natural
		Religious		Public
		Sanctified		Communal
				Unowned
				Individual

Justinian's *Institutes* distinguish between things within the patrimony (*in nostro patrimonio*) and things outside it (*extra nostrum patrimonium*).[37] Things that lie outside the patrimony fall under divine law and are further subdivided into *sacrae*, *religiosae*, and *sanctae*, as in Gaius's schema.[38] It is here that ecclesial property is explicitly called *res sacrae*:

> Sacred are those things that are consecrated to God ritually and by the pontiffs, such as sacred buildings and gifts, which are ritually dedicated to the service of God.

> *Sacra sunt, quae rite et per pontifices Deo consecrata sunt, veluti aedes sacrae et dona quae rite ad ministerium Dei dedicata sunt.*[39]

Res sacrae are things properly consecrated to God by bishops—that is, church property. Things within the patrimony are further subdivided into five categories in Justinian's schema (see table 1 above). While Justinian's *Institutes* largely borrow from Gaius's subdivision of *res*, especially in the matter of categorizing *res sacrae*, his *Digest* begins with Ulpian's schema, and Justinian bound *res sacrae* closely with the imperial office.[40] The table above summarizes Gaius, Ulpian, and Justinian's respective divisions.

Gaius conceived of *res sacrae* as things produced as a result of a particular ritual, the consecration, provided that a statute or senate resolution authorized the performance of such a ritual. Justinian's quaestor, Tribonian, and his staff would produce a category of *res sacrae* that also identified the ritual of consecration as the method of making *res sacrae* and that placed the authority for the performance of such a ritual in particular hands: those of imperially endorsed bishops. Ulpian not only associated sacred things with the ritual agents that produced them but also with the magistracy, and, in fact, from Constantine to Justinian, imperial offices would control Christian sacred things. In part, that control consisted of authorizing certain ritual agents and outlawing others. Though Tribonian would offer the only Christian definition of the category in Justinian's *Institutes*, the regulatory discourse of Justinian's imperial predecessors had already created means for controlling ecclesial property as sacred things.

Other excerpts in the *Digest* show in more detail how Ulpian defined the process by which *res* become *res sacrae*. Ulpian specifies how a thing becomes sacred, and he even describes the transformation as a change in the nature of the thing. Ulpian explains that for a place to become sacred, it must be dedicated publicly.[41] If it is public land that is to be dedicated, the emperor or someone delegated by him should perform the dedication.[42] Ulpian stresses the fact that the consecration must be properly performed for the place to attain legal status as sacred. His explanation invokes the scenario of fulfilling a vow. If someone vows to dedicate a thing, the vow places an obligation on the person not the thing. In fulfilling the vow, the person is released from his oath, but the object is not necessarily thereby sacred because the dedication may not have been performed properly.[43]

In a discussion of the way in which partnerships can be dissolved, Ulpian shows that the ritual of consecration changes the legal nature of a thing. When a person or a thing perishes, a partnership is dissolved. A person perishes by changing civil status, from slave to freedman, for instance (one juristic person perishes, another is created by the change in civil status). Likewise, things perish when they change their nature—for example, through consecration or confiscation.[44] According to Ulpian, then, the thing perishes, receives a new nature by virtue of the consecration, and becomes a *res sacra*.

Gaius's juristic pedagogy in the *Institutes* and those of Ulpian quoted in Justinian's *Digest* show that prior to the legal legitimization of the Christian cult, Roman jurists had created a category of *res sacrae* and asserted governmental control over sacred things. Justinian's *Institutes* show that in the sixth century jurists continued to reproduce the same category but with specific reference to Christian practices and ritual agents. In pedagogical literature of the second, third, and sixth centuries, jurists identified the consecration rite as the legal means by which a thing becomes sacred. Justinian's rewriting of classical legal principles singled out bishops as the ritual agents who performed consecration rites to produce sacred things.

THE MAKING OF CHRISTIAN *RES SACRAE*

Prior to Justinian's codification project, no pedagogical literature "translated" Roman juristic principles for a Christian imperial context. Nevertheless, from Constantine's legalization of Christian practices through Justinian's codification project, jurists and bishops conceived of regulations in order to make, identify, and control Christian sacred things. Jurists composed laws, and bishops composed canons, both of which relied on classical Roman juristic pedagogy.

Bishops exercised two main forms of control: they regulated the consecration ritual as well as the administrative obligations of the ritual agents and their subordinates. Under Justinian, laws would be written to exercise the same forms of control. However, pre-Justinianic jurists primarily engaged in different methods of control: they labeled certain ritual agents as adherents of the "true faith," outlawed others, and confiscated properties that "ought not be called churches." In other words, while jurists usually engaged in practices to restrict the application of the category "sacred thing," bishops usually regulated ritual practice and the administrative duties of ritual agents.

As the following sections detail, bishops (1) outlined prerequisites for a consecration rite to occur, (2) established rules about which bishops might preside over the ritual, and (3) decided the circumstances under which churches might be reconsecrated. Though all canons (and laws) assume bishops, priests, deacons, and other clerics to be the administrators of ecclesial property, some further legislate about how they ought to administer those properties, about how to use ecclesial property as *res sacrae*, and about how to adjudicate cases of mismanagement. As for *res sacrae* on private estates, they were subject to special administrative regulations so as to ensure episcopal control of them, as will be detailed below. After the review of all the relevant laws and canons, a case study of a fifth-century church in Libya illustrates how such regulatory principles affect our interpretation of a specific conflict.

Rules on the Consecration Ritual

Bishops (and some jurists) at various times and places created two principles for the making of sacred things: (1) that only rightly authorized bishops can make churches, and (2) that once a church is made, it remains a church in perpetuity. I examine each of the rules in turn, noting general principles and any penalty schedules. Penalty schedules offer a means of assessing how grievous jurists or bishops considered any given infraction. The most severe penalty legally was capital punishment; canonically, it was excommunication and cursing.

Prerequisites for the Consecration.   Bishops of Gaul and Spain and jurists of Justinian's empire set standards for the making of churches that would enable them to remain fully functioning sacred things indefinitely. To ensure perpetuity, financial prerequisites had to be met before ecclesial property could be consecrated. For this reason, the Councils of Epaon, Gaul, in 517 and Braga, Spain, in 572 forbade the consecration of churches that lacked a sufficient endowment.[45] In 538, Justinian issued a similar regulation, but he added a means by which one might be named a "founder" without building and endowing a church from scratch.[46] Justinian established an incentive to encourage individuals to endow already built churches, since

> many people, for fame's sake, embark on the construction of most holy churches, but after having built them do not go on and see to setting aside funds sufficient for

lighting them, for the support of those serving there, and for sacred ministry; they leave them as just bare buildings, either decaying, or deprived of all sacred ministry.[47]

Even though such individuals merely endowed churches in need, they would nevertheless be considered "founders." To prevent future iterations of the same problem, Justinian ruled that no one might build a church or chapel unless (1) the bishop of the place visited the land first by going there publicly, offering vows, and affixing a cross, and (2) the founder endowed it with money for lighting the lights, the sacred ministry, maintenance of the house, and support of those engaged therein.[48] Before a church was built, the ritual agent who would consecrate it first had to grant his approval publicly by dedicating the place. A place was not to become a church unless it could remain a church in perpetuity.

The Ritual Agent.   Bishops also controlled the production of sacred things by assigning specific ritual agents to the task. The bishop of a region had to make the churches of that region; no one else could.[49] The consecration rite became a means by which bishops' jurisdictional boundaries were reified, since bishops could only produce sacred things within their own jurisdiction. A bishop was not supposed to perform a consecration on behalf of another or to widen his own jurisdiction. According to the First Council at Orange, Gaul, in 441 the bishop of the diocese in which the church was built had to consecrate it, regardless of who built the church.[50] The canon mentions two particular scenarios to which the rule applies: (1) a bishop obtains permission to build a church in another bishop's diocese; and (2) a layperson who built the church invites a bishop from another diocese to consecrate it. The responsibility for the consecration fell to the bishop of the diocese, regardless of the circumstances. In 538, the Third Council of Orleans, Gaul, added a qualification and a penalty.[51] If it so happened that a bishop consecrated a church outside his diocese, the consecration was valid, but the offending bishop would be suspended for a year for disrespecting the prerogative of the diocesan bishop. As the case study below shows, Synesius of Cyrene expressed a different opinion about the validity of consecrations improperly performed. A later council at Orleans decided that even extenuating circumstances would not affect the rule about who might produce which churches. Even if the bishop were recalled or there were no bishop for an indefinite period of time, the consecration of altars could not occur until a new bishop were installed. The bishop of a diocese had to make the sacred things of his own diocese no matter what.[52]

The Reconsecration of Churches.   In legal theory, once a sacred thing was made, it was a sacred thing for all time, and could not be "remade." While bishops adhered to this principle of production, they also faced circumstances for which they deemed reconsecration advisable. The Fourth Council of Carthage in 401 addressed the question: if it is unknown whether a church has been consecrated, should the consecration take place even at the risk of reconsecrating it?[53] To answer this question, the assembled bishops drew an analogy between churches and persons.[54] The policy regarding consecration was to follow that of baptism. A person could be baptized if it were uncertain whether he or she had been baptized; therefore, a church was to be consecrated if it was uncertain whether it had been consecrated.

More commonly, the issue of reconsecration arose when bishops acquired the churches of heretics. To consecrate the place anew would reinscribe the same principle of production named above: that only the bishop of a diocese—in this case, the only "true bishop"—could make sacred things in his diocese. Heretic churches were "never really" churches in the first place, so a consecration could be merited. While the bishops of a council at Orleans decided that a church of heretics ought to be consecrated like any other place,[55] those at Epaon chose to regard heretic churches as impure and unusable unless they had been formerly orthodox.[56] At the end of the sixth century, a council at Saragossa, Spain, required the reconsecration of certain Arian churches.[57] If a church had been consecrated by an Arian bishop prior to his reordination as a catholic, then it had to be reconsecrated by him as a catholic. These rules delegitimized the sacrality of heretics' churches by either declaring them unusable or requiring their consecration by the "orthodox" ritual agent.

Rules on Administrative Obligations to Res Sacrae

Although a bishop's production of a sacred thing was an unrepeatable one-time act, his performance of the ritual bound him to an episcopal career of obligations toward that sacred thing. As the following rules show, conciliar assemblies decided what those obligations were, constructed a subordinate administrative body to assist the bishop, and created policies and procedures for addressing allegations of administrative misconduct. Such decisions reveal how the regulatory discourse of ecclesiastical assemblies produced *res sacrae* as objects of bishops' purview even after the occasion of consecration.

The Bishop as the Chief Administrator.   Bishops were obligated to administrate *res sacrae* for pious purposes only, above all for the benefit of the poor and needy. This point is emphasized in early canons described below and likely led to the petitions discussed in chapter 3 and contributed to the conceptual framework of the ritual economy analyzed in part II.

As early as 330, a council at Antioch set forth the administrative duties of the bishop in detail.[58] The council made it incumbent on the bishop to administer ecclesial property for the benefit of the poor with discretion and the fear of God. He could use it for his needs, if necessary, and for the needs of those who received his hospitality, but he could not use it for his own ends or for those of his relatives.

He had to render account to the synod, and if he were to be accused of maladministration to the detriment of the poor, the synod would hear the case.

A reworking of the Council of Antioch's canon in the late fourth-century collection called "The Canons of the Apostles" labels the bishop, in his chief administrative duty, "oeconomus of God" (θεοῦ οἰκονόμος) and the ecclesial properties over which he exercises his administrative duty "the things of God" (τὰ τοῦ θεοῦ).[59] Such phrases echo the jurist Gaius's (and later Justinian's) teaching that sacred things are under divine law. They are consecrated to God and are therefore "the things of God." The bishop administers them on behalf of God as God's steward. Another canon from the same collection offers justification for the bishop's role as the *oeconomus* of God: if he is responsible for the precious souls of men, how much more so ought things to be in his trust?[60] Still another canon from the collection echoes the Council of Antioch's priorities for a bishop's use of ecclesial property. Bishops had to distinguish their personal property from that of the church.[61] In 589, a council at Toledo, Spain, reiterated the duty of the bishop to use ecclesial property for the benefit of the poor and strangers and in support of the clerics.[62]

Justinian would codify into law the ecclesiastical prerogative to protect ecclesial property *for* the poor and *from* the administrators and their relatives' personal needs by preventing certain kinds of individuals from becoming bishops. In 528, Justinian decreed that no one could be appointed bishop who had children or grandchildren for the following reason.[63] According to the law, donations to churches are made with hope in God, for the salvation of one's soul, to relieve the poor and needy, and for other pious purposes. Therefore, it was not right that the bishop should use them for his own sake or that of his relatives. I will return to this issue of familial interests in the administration of ecclesial property in chapter 2.

The Oeconomus as Deputy Administrator.   All clerics assisted the bishop in his administration of sacred things, but the Council of Chalcedon in 451 formally instituted the office of the *oeconomus* or steward to serve as the direct deputy to the bishop.[64] The council explained why the office of the steward ought to be established: the multiplicity of accusations against bishops concerning ecclesial property threatened the dignity of the priesthood.[65] The steward would prevent the loss of ecclesial property to both clerics and episcopal kin and assist the bishop in property administration, thereby distancing ecclesial property from the bishop's ties of kinship and the "dignity of his priesthood" from accusations. The steward would stand between bishop and property, so that accusations of administrative misconduct would affect the steward, though the bishop remained the chief administrator. The canon checked the bishop's administrative power by introducing a deputy administrator, but it also protected the bishop himself by introducing someone else who would suffer blame and penalties for administrative misconduct.

Indeed, Justinian's penalties against maladministration are usually directed against the *oeconomus,* not the bishop.

Justinian required stewards to render an account of their administration to the bishop of their own diocese on an annual basis.[66] If they died before rendering an account, their heirs would be subject to audit and responsible for making any restitutions. *Apocrisarii* (episcopal deputies at the capital), on the other hand, were legally protected under Justinian from answering suits regarding ecclesial property or being subject to exaction, unless the bishop or steward whom they represented required them to sue someone.[67]

The Administrative Duties of Clerics and Their Relationship to the Bishop.   Ecclesiastical regulatory assemblies also placed the responsibility for administrating *res sacrae* on the shoulders of other clerics, such as priests.[68] The Council of Ancyra in 314 underscored their subordinate relationship to the bishop in addressing priests' administration of ecclesial property during the vacancy of an episcopal see.[69] Priests (prior to the Council of Chalcedon's institution of the office of the "steward") were to fulfill certain episcopal administrative duties during a vacancy, but the succeeding bishop held the prerogative as chief administrator to undo the priests' legal actions.

For Justinian, one important way in which clerics were supposed to demonstrate responsibility for ecclesial property was to fulfill their liturgical duties, such as chanting. Since donations were made in order that the sacred services could be performed, the clerics had to be faithful in practicing worship.[70] Donations placed an obligation on the clerics to fulfill the kinds of duties for which the donations were made.

In sixth-century Gaul, canons were issued that leveled penalties against clerics for shirking their duties as property administrators subordinate to the bishop. A council at Arles in 554 decided that if clerics neglected the properties entrusted to them by the bishop, the junior ones were to suffer corporal punishment and the senior ones were to be regarded as murderers of the poor (*necator pauperum*).[71] The latter was a typical penalty imposed by councils in western regions for abuse of ecclesial property.[72] The sentence reinforced what previous councils in other regions had identified as the core responsibility of the bishop: to administer sacred things for the benefit the poor. The Council of Narbonne in 589 required clerics who abused their administrative duties to return ecclesial property to the trust of the bishop, excommunicated them, and imposed a period of two-year penance before they could resume their clerical position.[73] The council targeted two types of abuse in particular: stashing away property and committing fraud with it.

The Administrative Relationship of Bishops to Fellow Bishops.   Ecclesiastical regulatory assemblies established administrative bodies in such a way that bishops were independently responsible for the *res sacrae* in their jurisdiction. Bishops' relationship to other bishops primarily consisted of respecting one another's jurisdictional boundaries. Two councils adjudicated the problem of bishops appropriating ecclesial property entrusted to other bishops. First, the Council of Chalcedon in 451 allowed bishops to retain parishes they held uncontested for a prescriptive period of thirty years.[74] Second, a council at Lyons, Gaul, sometime between 518 and 523, barred bishops from annexing the parishes of another bishop.[75]

Policies and Procedures for Adjudicating Cases of Maladministration.   As mentioned above, the Council of Antioch in 330 designated the synod as the court for trying cases of episcopal maladministration.[76] In 382, the Council of Constantinople published specific policies for resolving such cases.[77] The synod cited the following reason for creating policies: too many people leveled accusations against orthodox bishops. To resolve a perceived problem of excessive lawsuits, the synod set limitations on whose accusations would be heard. The synod would only hear the cases of orthodox plaintiffs in good standing with the church. While the cases of all, without distinction, would be heard regarding personal or private accusations, ecclesiastical accusations could only be leveled by orthodox plaintiffs in good standing with the church. No heretic or excommunicated, condemned, or accused individual would be permitted as a plaintiff against a bishop or cleric. The synod also established a procedure for hearing accepted cases. Members of the provincial synod (eparchy) would hear the case first; if unresolved, then a greater episcopal assembly of the diocese would hear it. No one would be heard if he or she[78] evaded this procedure by addressing the emperor, a civil authority, or even an ecumenical council. The Council of Chalcedon in 451 would further require an examination of the plaintiff's character, regardless of whether he or she were a layperson or a cleric, before a synod could accept the accusation, let alone schedule a hearing.[79]

Justinian reiterated canonical due process for leveling a lawsuit against members of the ecclesiastical administration in a constitution of 530, but he also clarified the procedure for making appeals and he set limits on the fees that could be exacted.[80] Like the Council of Constantinople in 382, he emphasized that due process could not be bypassed. For example, an accusation against a cleric had to be heard by the local bishop first (the suit could not be brought immediately to the patriarch, for instance). The system of appeals consisted of three successive levels: the metropolitan judged a first appeal; the provincial council of bishops judged a second appeal (with the three most senior bishops as judges); and the patriarch judged a third and final appeal. As for fees, plaintiffs could be asked to pay as much as six solidi for suits against bishops, and one-sixth of a solidus for suits against any other cleric. The penalty for exacting more than the prescribed fees was that the plaintiff would receive double what he or she paid, and the cleric who imposed the excessive fee would not only be disciplined by his metropolitan or patriarch; he would also be defrocked.[81]

Rules on Res Sacrae at Private Estates

Councils created and enforced conceptions of how to make *res sacrae* and how to administrate them not only for the purpose of making and managing publicly available churches and properties. *Res sacrae* could be made on private estates, too, and such foundations were usually referred to as an "oratory" (*oratorium*) or a "place of prayer" (εὐκτήριον).[82] As the following rules show, councils emphasized the sanctity of such places and produced special regulations so as to assert episcopal control over them. Councils stretched the arm of episcopal control in three major ways: (1) by requiring the bishop's approval of the establishment; (2) by requiring the bishop's approval of the celebrants; and (3) by restricting the rites that could take place in *res sacrae* on private estates. Each of these will be discussed in turn below.

The Founding of Res Sacrae at Private Estates.   As mentioned above, Justinian would require that bishops offer their consent to the building of a new church or oratory before the construction process took place by dedicating the land publicly with vows and the installation of a cross.[83] Earlier, the Council of Chalcedon in 451 specifically required that the metropolitan (the bishop of the city) grant his consent before the construction of *res sacrae* on private estates anywhere in his jurisdiction could take place.[84] Emperor Marcian proposed this rule in the sixth session of the council, and his draft was lightly edited for inclusion in the council's canons.[85]

Just as the sixth-century councils in Gaul and Spain and Justinian's law mentioned above required churches to be sufficiently endowed before being built, a sixth-century council at Orleans imposed similar prerequisites before an oratory could be built. Whoever would build an oratory on his or her private estate also had to endow it for two reasons: for the well-being of the clerics who served there and so "that right reverence be accorded to the sacred places (*sacratis locis*)."[86] The latter reason is especially significant. Even oratories were sacred, and bishops insisted that the same method of production and management created for churches be applied to oratories as well.

Further rules bishops made for their administration and management show that the proprietors of such private estates did not always welcome the bishop's control of the oratory. In response, bishops, like those at Orleans, drew special attention to the sanctity of the place so as to justify their control, as the following section explains.

Episcopal Administration of Res Sacrae at Private Estates.   In fact, the mid-fourth-century council at Gangra, Asia Minor, asserted episcopal control by affirming respect for "all places built for the honor of the name of God," not just "the houses of God" (i.e., publicly available churches).[87] Since oratories, like churches, were sacred, the council insisted that a priest agreed on by the bishop celebrate any services held in them.[88] Two centuries later, a council at Orleans, Gaul, required the bishop's approval for itinerant clerics to serve in oratories.[89]

Landowners of estates with oratories met not only with episcopal but imperial oversight, too. In 398, Emperor Honorius acknowledged episcopal jurisdiction over oratories on private landholdings in a constitution issued to the region of Illyricum.[90] For tax purposes, however, he limited the freedom of bishops to assign clerics to oratories. So that the landholders could not avoid the capitation (or poll) tax for the clerics working on their estates, Honorius required of the bishops that the clerics they appointed to serve on such landholdings be residents of the village on which the landholding was located and not come from other municipal jurisdictions.

Permissible Ritual Practices in Res Sacrae *at Private Estates.*   Though bishops emphasized the sanctity of *res sacrae* on private estates so as to justify their oversight, bishops (and jurists, too) also undercut such claims by restricting the kinds of liturgical celebrations that could take place in oratories. The late fourth-century council at Laodicea did not permit the eucharist to be celebrated in oratories.[91] In contrast, early sixth-century councils at Agde and Clermont did allow the celebration of the eucharist in oratories built outside the region of the parish, but not on major feast days, such as Easter, Christmas, Epiphany, Ascension, Pentecost, the Birthday of John the Baptist, among others.[92] The bishops of the council threatened excommunication to anyone who would celebrate such major feasts in oratories without the express permission of the bishop. A council at Dovin, Armenia in 527 did not permit baptism to take place at private estates.[93] The Synod of Auxerre, Gaul, sometime between 561 and 605 forbade the celebration of the eucharist, nocturne vigil, and feasts of saints in particular houses.[94] It also restricted the making of vows to publicly available churches and added that they had to be made to the benefit of clerics and the poor.

Justinian enforced similar rules in two of his laws. In 537, he forbade the celebration of the mysteries in home chapels.[95] He declared that oratories on private estates could only be used for the purpose of prayer, unless the bishops provided a cleric for the celebration of a mystery there. A house that violated the rule would be confiscated to the imperial treasury, but a three-month grace period to make arrangements to accord with this law was given to those houses already in violation at the time of promulgation. Failure to enforce the law would result in a fifty-pound gold fine to the office of the prefect. By 545, the confiscation of such houses would no longer benefit the imperial treasury.[96] Instead, patrons lost their rights over their estate chapels, and bishops, stewards, and the civil magistrate could make a claim of the property for the church. If the owner was not to blame for the violation, but rather the procurators or lessees or emphyteuticaries (lessees of land), then they were to be expelled from the province and their property claimed by the church. Such laws added civil consequences to rules that bishops had already created. If patrons failed to cooperate with episcopal oversight of their oratories, they or their subordinates could face loss of property through confiscation that initially benefited the imperial treasury, but in later years enriched the bishop's diocesan landholdings.

A DISPUTE OVER A CONSECRATED CHURCH IN LIBYA

Synesius of Cyrene became metropolitan bishop of Ptolemais, Libya on January 1, 412.[97] In less than five weeks, Synesius faced some of the same issues in the production of *res sacrae* as those expressed in the canons discussed above. He traveled approximately fifty kilometers east to villages of Libya Inferior (also known as "Arid Libya") to resolve the matters.[98] Synesius offers a detailed account of his assessment and provisional resolution of a conflict between two neighboring bishops over a consecrated church in a letter addressed to his superior, Theophilus, the bishop of Alexandria.[99] From Synesius's epistolary account, one may infer Synesius's answers to the questions: What procedure should be followed to hear a case against a bishop? How ought churches to be produced? What should the consequences be if a bishop improperly made a *res sacra*? Synesius's report shows how he and a Libyan provincial synod operated with the regulatory principles observed above in order to propose a resolution suited to local exigencies.

As mentioned above, the Council of Constantinople in 382 outlined policies and procedures for the adjudication of episcopal disputes.[100] All the Libyan bishops involved followed those procedures. A provincial synod in Ptolemais had already heard the case and resolved it in favor of the prosecution, Dioscurus of Darnis.[101] The defense, Paul of Erythrum, appealed the case to Theophilus.[102] Theophilus sent the head of the provincial synod, Synesius, to investigate the matter first.

Synesius's letter to Theophilus details the results of his investigation. Synesius reported that (1) he held a hearing for the people of the villages of Palaebisca and Hydrax;[103] (2) he conducted an inspection of the disputed territory in the presence of the same provincial synod that had adjudicated the case;[104] (3) in the course of the inspection, he oversaw a negotiation between Dioscurus and Paul;[105] (4) in accord with Dioscurus's request, Synesius sent Theophilus a detailed report concerning the arbitration;[106] and (5) Synesius held a second hearing for the people of Palaebisca and Hydrax, at which time the people nevertheless submitted a petition appealing the case to Theophilus.[107] How Theophilus responded, we do not know, but Synesius and the provincial synod did not suspend Paul for overstepping his jurisdictional boundaries.[108] Synesius's temporary resolution of the conflict took place at an ecclesiastical inspection of the hill in dispute, where Synesius and the provincial synod allowed the two bishops, Paul and Dioscurus, to redraw the jurisdictional boundary. The people of Palaebisca and Hydrax, nevertheless, insisted on appealing the case to Theophilus. First, I will describe the territory in dispute. Then I will explain how Synesius provisionally resolved the conflict.

The two bishops, Paul of Erythrum and Dioscurus of Darnis, vied for control of a hill in Palaebisca and Hydrax, on which the ruins of a former fortress lay.[109] In the course of prior conflicts over the episcopal succession of Erythrum, the jurisdictional territory had been divided, then reunited, and divided again.[110] Paul consecrated a building in the fortress ruins so as to acquire the hill from Dioscurus's territory. Paul claimed to have jurisdiction of the site, but Dioscurus accused Paul of using fraudulent means to obtain that jurisdiction: Paul consecrated to God (καθοσιώσαντα [. . .] τῷ θεῷ)[111] a small aedicule (σμικρὸν οἰκίσκον)[112] in Dioscurus's jurisdiction. To resolve the dispute, Synesius and his synod inspected the locale in question, made a decision, and allowed Dioscurus and Paul to engage in a compromise.

In his defense, Paul of Erythrum made two claims: (1) that he and his predecessors had used the building as a church long before it came into the jurisdiction of Dioscurus of Darnis;[113] and (2) that he (Paul) had consecrated the building. Synesius responded to Paul's first claim much in the same way as Athanasius responded to Constantius II. Use of the site as a church does not thereby make it a consecrated church:

> The fact that a crowd of men have once prayed there by necessity, driven in by hostile attack of the enemy, does not consecrate the spot, for at that rate all the mountains and all the valleys would be churches, and no fortress would escape being a place of public worship, for in all such places, when the enemy are out for plunder, prayers and celebrations of the Holy Mysteries take place.[114]

As Athanasius had claimed to Constantius II, celebration of the mysteries in a place did not entail the consecration of that place. Synesius cited recent history as precedent. When the "enemy Arians" had the ascendancy, their opponents took flight and performed many prayers and sacred ceremonies in houses. Those houses nevertheless remained private property.[115]

Synesius not only dismisses Paul's claim to the site prior to Dioscurus's control of it, but he also dismisses the validity of Paul's act of consecration, contrary to the canons cited above. Although the canons discipline bishops who make sacred things outside their jurisdiction, they nevertheless treat the consecration itself as valid and unrepeatable.[116] Synesius, on the other hand, considered even the consecration invalid on account of bad faith on the part of the ritual agent. The two different opinions (those of the canons and that of Synesius) about weighing the relevance of good or bad faith align with opinions classical jurists had expressed centuries prior. Like Synesius, Pomponius, a second-century jurist, emphasized the importance of good faith in assessing the validity of a legal act. By contrast, Modestinus, a third-century jurist, did not think that an individual's intentions mattered for assessing the validity of an act; instead, the issue of good faith made a difference in the type of legal action the individual could pursue to redress a wrong.[117]

To evaluate Paul's intentions, Synesius asked if Paul had acquired the land from Dioscurus by gift or agreement in advance of the ritual, and he learned that Paul had in fact asked for the fort but that Dioscurus had refused his request. Despite the refusal, Paul took a small table and consecrated a small aedicule on the hill. Synesius concluded that Paul did not conduct the consecration in good faith. In fact, Synesius called Paul's consecration "a method of confiscation," and he accused Paul of using "holy things" as "weapons:"

> Clearly it had been calculated that by this manoeuvre the hill could be definitely acquired. For my own part, this whole performance seemed to me unworthy, more than unworthy, and *I was very angry at this flagrant violation of all sacred laws and civil forms of justice alike.* All things become confounded, if on the one hand a new form of confiscation is invented, and if on the other by the holiest things the most abominable should be judged, prayer, the table of the Holy Communion, and the Mystic Veil becoming instruments of a violent attack.[118]

Synesius regarded Paul's act of consecration as an act of superstition (δεισιδαιμονίαν) and therefore an illegitimate ritual, not one of piety (εὐσεβείας).[119] Synesius supported his opinion on the consecration's invalidity with two reasons: (1) "nothing [is] sacred or holy except that which has come into being in justice and holiness;" and (2) the Holy Spirit would not come to a place ruled by anger, senseless spirit, and contentious passion.[120] Not only did the wrong agent attempt to produce a *res sacra*, but his intentions in producing it were of such a sort that admitted of no sanctity. Still, Synesius did not go so far as to declare the consecration invalid. Instead, he strove to transfer the place back into the hands of Dioscurus.

Synesius and the provincial synod paid a visit to the site to conduct an ecclesiastical inspection, and it was at the inspection that Paul and Dioscurus engaged in negotiation. Since the boundary stones and the testimony of elders indicated that the fortress belonged to the jurisdiction of Dioscurus, the synod reaffirmed its decision in favor of Dioscurus.[121] The judges declared that Dioscurus had rightful claim to the hill, and Dioscurus's brother insisted that Paul's letter of appeal to Theophilus be read aloud. Synesius "read publicly the abusive paper that the blessed Paul had written in the shape of a letter addressed to your holiness, an obscene and unpleasant satire directed against his brother [Dioscurus], of which the burden of shame fell upon him who had spoken evil, not on him of whom evil had been spoken."[122] Paul "confess[ed] his error" and "gave evidence of his change of opinion more convincing than any rhetoric."[123] Since Dioscurus accepted Paul's repentance, he offered Paul concessions.

In accepting Paul's admission of wrongdoing, Dioscurus permitted Paul to purchase certain grounds of the fortress ruins in order to bring them into the jurisdiction of Erythrum: the vineyards and olive groves in addition to the hill where he had consecrated a small room.[124] Synesius and his synod judged that Dioscurus should retain his jurisdiction, even after the wrong bishop produced a *res sacra* where only Dioscurus could, but Dioscurus and Paul chose to engage in compromise. The synod honored the decision the two bishops made for their local circumstances, even though it conflicted with the synod's judgment and even with prohibitions on alienating *res sacrae*.

As a result of the compromise, Paul purchased property that he had already consecrated. As chapter 2 will demonstrate, *res sacrae* could not be objects of sale, except under specific extraordinary circumstances. It is probably for this reason that (1) Synesius expressed reasons for invalidating the consecration of the building and (2) Dioscurus insisted that Theophilus be appraised of every detail of the compromise.[125] However, as mentioned above, we do not know how Theophilus addressed the case once the documentation of Paul and Dioscurus's provisional compromise and the petition of the people of Palaebisca and Hydrax reached him.

In sum, Synesius and his synod did insist on episcopal respect for jurisdictional boundaries when it came to consecrating churches, a principle expressed in conciliar canons. However, the case also shows how local appeals could affect the situation, especially when there existed a prior history of shifting jurisdictional boundaries. Because Dioscurus was willing to compromise, he did not retain jurisdiction of certain parts of the region to which the synod declared he had rightful claim. Instead, Dioscurus made an agreement with Paul, in the presence of and with the support of the synod, to cede areas of his jurisdiction to Paul by sale, including a small aedicule that Paul ought not to have consecrated. Synesius's letter does not mention whether the synod officially repudiated the validity of the consecration and required a reconsecration; Synesius only expresses his own opinion on the matter to Theophilus (namely, that Paul's consecration of the small building was invalid). Synesius described Paul of Erythrum as one who tried to "confiscate" (δημεύειν) areas of another bishop's jurisdiction.[126] Though we cannot know how Theophilus weighed Dioscurus and Paul's provisional compromise against the appeal of the people of Palaebisca and Hydrax, it is clear that the episcopal bodies set up to administrate *res sacrae* produced and implemented policies and procedures to discipline or check bishops who created *res sacrae* outside of their jurisdiction.

On the other hand, emperors, jurists, and bishops did often acquire others' churches by renaming and confiscating them, as the following section shows. There was no legal means of unmaking or deconsecrating a *res sacra* (once a thing was consecrated, it remained a sacred thing whenever it was in the right hands), but there was a legal way to delegitimize others' sacred things: confiscation.

CONFISCATION: THE LEGAL DELEGITIMIZATION OF OTHERS' CHURCHES

Emperors, jurists, and bishops not only created sacred things; they also produced ways of identifying "faux" sacred things and eliminating them from the sacred landscape. "Faux" sacred things were produced by those who were legally recognized as "heretics" or "schismatics."[127] Legal ways to identify "faux" sacred things included (1) labeling such places "meeting places" rather than "churches," (2) confiscating places where "forbidden practices" occurred, and (3) penalizing the ritual agents who engaged in forbidden practices and the landholders or civil officials who allowed or turned a blind eye to the forbidden practices. In what follows, I review each law, noting the general principles and citing the penalty schedules (which, as mentioned above, indicate the level of severity of any given infraction). The case study focuses on one region, showing how a fine of ten pounds of gold originally issued against heretics in the prefecture of the East became a symbol of a century-and-a-half long struggle in North Africa over rival sacred spaces.

The Identification of "Faux" Churches

Theodosius I declared to the people of Constantinople in 380 that the meeting places of those who do not hold the right faith are not to be named "churches."[128] Instead, such assemblies should be called *conciliabula*, "meeting places."[129] A canon from a late fifth-century Gallic collection echoes Theodosius's refusal to acknowledge such places as churches: "The meeting places of heretics are not to be called *ecclesias* but *conciliabula*."[130] Though most constitutions did usually employ the neutral word *conciliabula* to refer to heretics' churches, some even used polemical designations. For example, a constitution issued against the Montanists in 415 calls their churches "feral grottos" (*antra feralia*)—that is, cavernous death traps.[131]

The exception proves the rule. One constitution against Manichaean churches calls them "churches."[132] When the constitution was excerpted for the Codex of Justinian, the word "churches" was rewritten. The sixth-century version replaces "churches" with "[gathering] places (*conventicula*) of heretics—which they brazenly try to call churches (*ecclesias*)."[133] In general, laws refused to ascribe any sanctity to heretics' churches. This shows that jurists controlled even the nomenclature of sacred places.

Emperor Leo I (who ruled from 457 to 474) even accused the heretics themselves of opposition to sanctity. In other words, he attributed to the heretics the legal reasoning that jurists had in fact created. In 466, Leo tried to prevent sacred things on private estates from passing into the hands of heretics through a transaction involving the entire private estate. He passed a law that "estates, properties, and immovable property, where churches or chapels of the orthodox faith are located" could not be alienated, not even by a last will, to a heretic or anyone opposed to the orthodox faith in the East.[134] If such alienation occurred, then the lands or possessions would be confiscated to the fisc (that is, the imperial treasury). Most importantly, Leo offered a rationale as to why heretics could not control sacred things: if heretics successfully gained possession of such lands, the churches would perish, because heretics "vehemently wished [they] did not exist."[135] Churches of heretics could not be churches because the heretics themselves opposed sanctity.

Jurists produced and controlled the sacred landscape, but they employed antihe-retical rhetoric to mask their control. Heretics' churches were not churches, not because the jurists made it so, Leo insisted, but because heretics opposed sanctity.

The jurist Ulpian had already composed a criterion for a valid consecration in the early third century, but the laws that confiscated heretics' churches developed more detailed measures for identifying faux sacred things. Ulpian's criterion was that a place had to be properly consecrated to be a *res sacra*. Ulpian's contempo-rary, Marcian, explained that only public authority, not private, could make a thing sacred.[136] The same principle would make its way into Justinian's *Institutes*, where faux churches are called *quasi sacrum*.[137] Confiscatory laws added that a church was not a church if "forbidden practices" took place there or "forbidden officiants" served there.

As the following section shows, the churches of heretics and sometimes schis-matics were to become imperial, fiscal, public, or sacred property.[138] When the churches of heretics were handed over to imperially recognized ecclesiastical administrators, they could become *res sacrae*. As noted above, two canons from sixth-century Gaul and Spain required such churches to be newly consecrated, but another from Gaul did not permit them to be used at all.[139]

Imperial Procedure and Policies of Confiscation

Churches could be located on two kinds of property. First, a church could be located on a wider plot of ecclesial property, in which case both the church and the associated properties were *res sacrae*. Second, a church could be located on a private landholding, in which case only the church itself was a sacred thing, but the rest of the property was not. In general, from 372 to 545, emperors would confiscate the latter kind of heretics' property to the fisc (the imperial treasury) or the public, but the former would be vindicated to imperially endorsed ("catholic") administrators. Fifteen imperial constitutions transfer the meeting places of her-etics to the ownership of the fisc, the imperial treasury, or the public;[140] twelve, to the catholic administrators of ecclesial property.[141]

The procedure of confiscation would typically occur as follows. The palatine office (*officium palatinum*) was responsible for each constitution's enforcement.[142] Various judges could impose the penalty of confiscation, while the count of the *res privata* would register and manage confiscations. Authorities were not permitted to occupy the properties before the sentence was declared, and an appeal could suspend the procedure of confiscation.[143] An inventory would take place at the ordinance of the governor who made the sentence, and a seal would be posted on the doors or on movable property to avoid property diversion prior to the inventory.[144] The procedure for taking inventory was codified in 369 by a law addressed to the count of the *res privata*, Florianus.[145]

On the basis of the laws collected in the Theodosian and Justinian Codices, the history of imperial policies for confiscating the churches of heretics can be traced.

Constitutions usually named the targeted group, the beneficiaries of the confiscated property, and a penalty schedule against those who resisted the constitution's enforcement. What follows is a detailed review of the constitutions, first those addressed to the West, then those to the East.

Imperial Policies in Western Provinces. As for the regions of Italy, North Africa, and Illyricum (when it belonged to the western empire), Valentinian I's, Gratian's, and Valentinian II's policy in 372 and from 377 to 378 divided confiscated ecclesial property. While the public churches themselves were given to the catholic administration, other landholdings associated with the churches, such as revenue-producing land (great houses and estates), were handed over to the fisc. The laws were specifically targeted against the houses and habitations of Manichaeans in Rome,[146] the churches and great houses and estates of Donatists in North Africa,[147] and anywhere heretics' altars were located in North Africa.[148]

Honorius made the largest number of confiscations in the western provinces. His initial policy was to have heretics' meeting places benefit the fisc, imperial patrimony, or public use. By the end of 407, however, he began to have confiscated places given instead to catholic administrators.

As for confiscations that benefited the fisc, in 397, Honorius confiscated Apollinarian ecclesial property in Illyricum.[149] In 404, Honorius stated that unlawful assemblies could not take place in private dwellings, and a house in which such an assembly occurred would be confiscated.[150] In 405, he confiscated Donatist ecclesial property in Italy and North Africa to the fisc.[151] In 407, Honorius had the landed estates in Rome, in which Manichaeans, Phrygians, or Priscillianists gathered, transferred to the imperial patrimony; civil officials would be fined either twenty or ten pounds of gold for failure to enforce the law, depending on the office to which they belonged.[152] In 408, Honorius had all places of assembly (*loca*) "of those who dissent from the Catholic priesthood of the church" in Italy and Illyricum appropriated for public use.[153]

Honorius's policy began to shift already at the end of 407, when he had Donatist, Manichaean, Priscillianist, pagan, and Caelicolist buildings in Italy and North Africa vindicated to the churches.[154] In 412, he had the churches, conventicles, and landed estates of the Donatists and Circumcellions in North Africa given over to the catholic churches.[155] In 414, he had the meeting places of Donatists and heretics in North Africa vindicated to catholic churches, but the penalty fines were to be deposited in the imperial treasury.[156] Chief tenants of the imperial patrimonies who would allow Donatist practices to take place on the estates would owe a fine equivalent to their rental fee, including emphyteuticaries (lessees of land). Owners of private estates were to replace any chief tenants who permitted Donatist practices to take place there; failure to do so would result in a fine equivalent to the rentals they received. As the case study below shows, once the western regions became regions ruled by non-Roman kings, the tide would turn. Former "heretics" would become the catholics, and the catholics would become heretics.

Imperial Policies in Eastern Provinces.   In the eastern provinces (including the diocese of Illyricum when it became part of the eastern empire), policies varied from region to region and from emperor to emperor.

As for Theodosius I, he had confiscated churches in Asia handed over to catholic bishops, whereas in the East, confiscations benefited the fisc. In 381, Theodosius I put the churches of Illyricum and Asia in the control of orthodox bishops by issuing two constitutions, both in the wake of the Council of Constantinople.[157] He named two criteria for determining the orthodoxy of bishops: the use of credal formulas and an alliance with specific bishops known to adhere to the right faith. Theodosius I addressed the rest of his confiscatory legislation to the East. In 381 and 383, he had churches, estates, and private landholdings of Eunomians and Arians confiscated to the fisc.[158] His actions in both years targeted Eunomians and Arians; his action of 383 also named Macedonians and Apollinarians. Likewise, in 392, he confiscated all places where "forbidden practices are attempted" to the fisc with a detailed penalty schedule against those guilty of performing illicit services there.[159] If the owner of the property were unaware of the illegal activity, the chief tenant would be held responsible and owe ten gold pounds if he were freeborn, or otherwise suffer physical torture and deportation. If the illicit practices took place in an imperial or public villa, the chief tenant and procurator each would owe ten gold pounds. Theodosius's application of the fine of ten pounds of gold against heretics in the East would have a long and tortured afterlife in the region of North Africa.

Arcadius largely continued Theodosius I's policy against heretics in the East by placing their meeting places in the hands of catholic administrators (only one constitution he addressed to the East transferred private assembly places to the imperial treasury rather than to the catholic churches), but Arcadius changed the policy in Asia. Instead of giving confiscated properties to the catholic bishops in Asia as Theodosius had done, Arcadius made them fiscal holdings. Arcadius confiscated houses and landed estates in the East, where Eunomians performed services, to the fisc in 398 and 399.[160] The constitution of 398 named not only Eunomians, but Montanists as well.[161] In 415, he confiscated houses and landholdings where Montanist "accursed mysteries" were performed in the East, along with their offertories, and gave them to the catholic churches.[162] Also in 415, he had Eunomians' conventicles in their houses or on their landholdings in the East transferred to the imperial treasury.[163]

As for Asia, Arcadius applied the same policy in place for the East. He had all heretics' places in Constantinople confiscated to the fisc in 402.[164] Arcadius imposed the most severe penalties against violators of his confiscatory laws. The procurator of the landed estate or the steward of the urban house where Eunomian rites took place in 398 were to suffer capital punishment;[165] Arcadius threatened the office of the praetorian prefect in Constantinople with a fine of one hundred pounds of gold if it failed to enforce the law of 402.[166]

Theodosius II issued only one law giving heretics' churches into the hands of the catholics. In 428, he required that the churches taken by heretics from the orthodox in the East be surrendered to the catholic church, including donations and private buildings in which assemblies took place.[167] He included a penalty schedule for complicit procurators modeled after the one Theodosius I issued in 392.[168]

In 455, Marcian adopted a policy like that of Valentinian I, Gratian, and Valentinian II in that he confiscated certain properties in Asia and Egypt to the fisc and vindicated other properties to the churches. Marcian legislated that Apollinarians or Eutychites (by which he meant those who do not adhere to definition of faith written at Chalcedon) could not construct churches or monasteries for themselves or congregate in any landholding or monastery.[169] If they did, the landholding would be confiscated to the fisc but the monastery would fall under the jurisdiction of the church of the city. If they were held without the knowledge of the owner, then the lessee/procurator/manager would be beaten publicly if of low status; if of honorable station, then he would owe ten pounds of gold. If governors or defenders of the city disregarded the constitution, they would owe ten pounds of gold to the fisc and lose their honorable status.

As mentioned above, in 466, Leo closed a loophole. Since sacred things on private estates could pass into the hands of heretics through the transaction of the entire private estate, he passed a law forbidding such transactions. The law emphasizes the same principle of later canons discussed above: that sacred things always remain sacred things. In the case of Leo's law, this meant acknowledging that sacred things would continue to be sacred things even if the larger property on which they were located were confiscated to the fisc:

> For whether these estates remain in the hands of orthodox masters or possessors (*dominos possessoresve*) or become part of Our fisc, it is imperative that the churches and chapels located on them be diligently and carefully restored. For the foresight of Our Serenity leads Us by many ways to this one end: that the temples of the Almighty God, in which the institutions of Our faith endure, shall by continuous attention be preserved through all the ages.[170]

Leo acknowledged a principle that bishops had employed to control churches and oratories on private estates: sacred things located on private property were just as sacred as publicly-available sacred things.

Justinian issued a similar law to the East in 545, but he adopted the opposite policy: instead of confiscating such property to the fisc, he allowed catholic administrators to claim the property.[171] Justinian allowed churches to claim properties on which owners allowed divine services to take place without the clergy of the bishop (or the properties of the procurators/lessees/emphyteuticaries who allowed such services to take place). Churches could also claim property on which there was a church that an orthodox person alienated or bequeathed by emphyteusis, lease, or for any other purpose to a Jew, Samaritan, pagan, Montanist, Arian, or other heretic. If the owner was aware that the lessee or the emphyteuticary was a heretic, the church could also claim the income that would have accrued in the time specified in the contract.

Episcopal Policies on Heretics' Churches

Bishops could not engage in the imperial act of confiscation, but they did issue regulations of their own to prevent their constituency from attending heretics' churches and to encourage bishops to bring heretic parishes into the catholic fold. As an example of the former type of regulation, a council that met in Laodicea in the last quarter of the fourth century forbade clerics from celebrating divine mysteries and Christians from praying in "the so-called martyria of all the heretics."[172] Canons issued thereafter addressed problems faced in the integration of catholic and formerly heretic ecclesial property. In 418, the Council of Carthage outlined policies for drawing diocesan boundaries in the event that a Donatist bishop joined the catholic communion.[173] Such boundaries could be changed or contested within a prescriptive period of three years, after which the jurisdictional boundaries were set and deemed unquestionable.[174] The episcopal assembly encouraged haste in the usurpation of Donatist diocesan territory and constituency whenever a Donatist bishop joined the catholic communion. Such bishops faced a deadline: they were to be zealous in bringing Donatist parishes that had been under their jurisdiction into the catholic fold within six months.[175] If they failed to do so, any bishop could make such an attempt and receive a jurisdictional reward: the parishes would belong to the successful bishop's jurisdiction. The Council of Toledo, Spain, in 589, on the other hand, maintained existing jurisdictional boundaries even in the face of integration. The synod decided that appropriated heretic churches would belong to the jurisdiction of the bishop of the diocese in which they were located.[176]

At Carthage and in North Africa more generally, bishops exploited the legal apparatus at their disposal to delegitimize Donatist sacred space to the point that one particular legal case became a sticking point from Honorius to Justinian. The stigma of a ten-pound gold fine leveled against the Donatist bishop, Crispinus of Calama, would not be forgotten even one century later.

THE TRIAL OF CRISPINUS OF CALAMA
AND THE STIGMA OF TEN POUNDS OF GOLD

For a century and a half, ten pounds of gold symbolized the delegitimization of ecclesial spaces and administrators in North Africa. The penalty created opportunities for bishops both to shame and patronize other bishops. It all began on

June 15, 392 when Theodosius I wrote to Tatianus, the praetorian prefect of the East, instructing him that a fine of ten pounds of gold should be applied (1) against whoever permitted the forbidden practices of heretics to take place on a landholding, be it the owner, the chief tenant, or the procurator, and (2) against the cleric who presided over the practice.[177] As mentioned above, Tatianus was to have the landholding itself confiscated to the fisc, if indeed it was the owner who had permitted the practice to take place. How the law came to be in the East and what sort of afterlife it witnessed there is unknown, but Theodosius I's decision would have a long afterlife in North Africa, enduring even through Justinian's tenure.

Bishops made three traceable efforts to have Theodosius I's law against heretics in the East applied to North Africa. Such bishops endorsed civil regulation of ecclesial property for two purposes: (1) to reclaim or delegitimize rival ecclesial property, and (2) to protect their own ecclesial property from the claims of rivals. Of all the laws issued against heretics, these petitioners chose Theodosius's law that specified a fine of ten pounds of gold so as to shame and patronize rival bishops.[178] The sum was not negligible. Ten pounds of gold equaled 720 solidi, the cost of building a city martyrion in Edessa in 504/5.[179] In the end, the bishops succeeded in petitioning Honorius for a law that he issued in 405 against their rivals.[180]

First, Augustine recounts the occasion of a petition, made around 395/6.[181] In a line-by-line rebuttal of a letter that Petilian, the bishop of Cirta, addressed to his clergy, Augustine mentioned specific cases when individuals, in his perspective, ought to have been fined ten pounds of gold. As an example, he cited an occasion when Bishop Optatus violently took over the administration of a public church.[182] Augustine said that a petition was made to Seranus, the vicar of Africa, to impose the fine of ten pounds of gold against Optatus, but Augustine admitted that the fine was never paid.[183] In all likelihood, Seranus denied the request.

Second, in the same passage, Augustine named another bishop against whom he believed a fine of ten pounds of gold should have been imposed: Crispinus of Calama. Around 402, he wrote a letter to Crispinus himself about the situation.[184] According to Augustine, Crispinus held imperial agricultural lands by emphyteusis (a type of lease) in Mapala.[185] As a bishop, Crispinus probably acquired the emphyteutic lease to produce revenue for his churches. There, on the imperial estate, Augustine says, Crispinus rebaptized eighty of his tenant farmers.[186] Since Crispinus engaged in what Augustine counted as a practice forbidden by Theodosius I's law, Augustine argued that Theodosius I's law should apply to Crispinus and that he ought to pay the fine. Augustine expressed his view first with a claim that imperial rules hold force throughout the empire, so even though Theodosius I's law was addressed to the East, it ought to apply in Crispinus's case, too.[187] Augustine's threatening letter may have served as legal evidence for Crispinus's activities at a trial.[188]

Sometime before 404,[189] Crispinus was tried and fined the penalty of ten pounds of gold. Though the fine was waived, the patronization involved in obtaining waivers shamed and subordinated Crispinus. The contentious point of the trial, according to Augustine, was whether Crispinus should be considered a "heretic," so that Theodosius I's law could apply to him.[190] Crispinus's rival bishop of Calama, Possidius, leveled the case against him, which was heard by the proconsul Septiminus and settled in Possidius's favor.[191] Possidius, in his capacity as bishop, negotiated (*intercedo*) for leniency, and Septiminus waived the fine. According to the *Life of Augustine*, written by the same Possidius of Calama, Crispinus appealed his case to Honorius, who upheld the proconsul's verdict and added the further penalty that the proconsul and his staff should be fined ten pounds of gold, too, for not enforcing their judgment.[192] Several bishops successfully interceded for the proconsul's and Crispinus's fines to be imperially pardoned. Possidius and other bishops delegitimized Crispinus by successfully petitioning for the implementation of civil regulation against him. The same bishops simultaneously patronized Crispinus by petitioning for the waiver. It is as a result of Crispinus's trial that the fine of ten pounds of gold became in North Africa a stigma and a symbol representing delegitimization and control.

The Council of Carthage in June 404 made the third petition to the emperor against the Donatists. The synod sent the bishops Theasius and Evodius to Emperor Honorius to make a number of requests. The memorandum (*commonitorium*) with which they were sent begins with an explanation of the circumstances that led to the ensuing requests.[193] Since rival bishops took over the administration of churches, the synod requested that protection be granted to the public churches both in the cities and in the suburbs.[194] One specific form of protection that the synod envisioned was that the law of Theodosius I would be confirmed: "that the law, which was promulgated by their father of religious memory, Theodosius, concerning ten pounds of gold against those heretics who ordain or are ordained and also against the proprietors [of properties] where their society is discovered, be ordered in turn to be confirmed."[195] In response, Honorius issued instructions in February 405 to Hadrianus, the praetorian prefect of Italy and Africa.[196] The law, as transmitted in the excerpts of the Theodosian Codex, does not levy Theodosius I's fine of ten pounds of gold, but nevertheless makes similar provisions. The law states that heresy has been born of schism, so the landholdings where those who rebaptize (thereby practicing "feral sacrilege") are to be confiscated to the fisc.[197] As for the landholders, if the owner granted permission for the practices to occur, then he or she would be branded with infamy, but if the chief tenant or procurator did, then his or her penalty would be corporal punishment and exile.[198] Officiating clerics would not owe ten pounds of gold, but would suffer the "penalty of poverty" through the confiscation of all their property.[199]

Despite the fact that Honorius did not name the fine of ten pounds of gold in his instructions to the praetorian prefect Hadrianus, the symbolic status that the penalty attained through the efforts of episcopal petitions and in the trial of Crispinus would not be forgotten. On February 25, 484, the Vandal king Huneric issued an edict that deliberately turned the tables and reversed the application of the Roman laws.[200] Huneric claimed that it was "necessary and very just to twist around against them [imperially supported bishops] what is shown to be contained in those very laws which happen to have been promulgated by the emperors of various times who, with them, had been led into error."[201] The former "catholics," now named "homoousians," could not possess any meeting places or build any churches anywhere; if any should be built, they would be confiscated to the fisc. Their current churches were to be vindicated to the now "orthodox" (the administrators endorsed by the king). The notorious penalty of ten pounds of gold applied to those who ordained heretic clergy and those who allowed themselves to be ordained.[202]

On August 1, 535, the tables turned yet again with Justinian's conquest of North Africa. Justinian returned all churches and ecclesial possessions to the orthodox, identified as Reparatus of Carthage and his synod.[203] The penalty of ten pounds of gold would be applied to any violators. Arians, Donatists, Jews, and any other nonorthodox were "excluded altogether from services, and from churches" and were not permitted to possess "conventicles."[204]

In the East, on the other hand, where the fine had first been levied against heretics in 392, Justinian pursued the prosecutors. He addressed Edict 2 to the praetorian prefect of the East, John, probably before 535. The edict forbids the abuse of laws that impose fines on heretics and demands the arrest of, and the imposition of fines on, those who "have gone out to various provinces to search out those who have abandoned themselves to the error of the heretics [. . .] and *have taken a very great deal of money from them by way of* sportulae [*payments or fees*]."[205] The fate of the fine in the East reinforces its symbolic status. Because individuals in the East exploited the law so as to exact enormous capital from heretics, Justinian issued an edict to curb such exploitation.

In North Africa, on the other hand, where the imposition of the fine did not in fact result in financial capital, but rather a capital of status and control, the penalty had a different history. Through episcopal petitions for civil regulation, what began in the East became in North Africa a distinct symbol of the dividing line between rival *res sacrae* and administrators.

Jurists and bishops imagined churches as sacred things that the right bishops produced and the right bishops administrated. Jurists decided which bishops were imperially-recognized bishops and therefore which sacred places were imperially sanctioned sacred places. Both jurists and bishops masked their control by treating the legal principles as unquestionable givens.

Roman jurists of the first three centuries conceived of *res sacrae* as things ritually consecrated to deities. Justinian would rewrite the legal definition with explicit reference to the Christian deity, Christian ritual practice, and Christian ritual agents, but emperors, jurists, and bishops from Constantine onward had already brought Christian temples under the control of the legal imagination about *res sacrae.* To those places that "heretics" considered churches, jurists and imperi-ally supported bishops would ascribe no sanctity. The procedure of confiscation delegitimized such places and sometimes used them to profit the jurisdictions of legally supported bishops.

Through imperially recognized rituals of consecration, churches attained the legal status of "sacred thing." This legal status came with a significant benefit: churches were thereby recognized as divinely protected. The next chapter analyzes the jurisdic pedagogy that undergirded this corollary to the definition of *res sacrae* and the legal mechanisms by which jurists and bishops produced and applied such a notion of protection. The corollary protected *res sacrae* from loss of assets and promoted their affluence.

Protected Places

As a member of a former imperial dynasty, Anicia Juliana was well-to-do. When Justinian learned of Anicia Juliana's extensive wealth, he asked her to lend it to the public treasury to fund his military activities. But Anicia Juliana avoided obliging the emperor. She hastily commissioned craftsmen to use all her gold to adorn the ceiling of a church she had founded, Saint Polyeuktos at Constantinople. Then she took Justinian to the church and said, "Most glorious Augustus, I ask that you look at the ceiling of this church and realize that my poorness is kept there in this craftsmanship. But you now do what you wish. I will not oppose you."[1] The emperor was embarrassed.

This is a story that Gregory of Tours relates in his *Glory of the Martyrs*.[2] Whether fact or fiction, the punch line of the story assumes the legal principle that jurists and bishops applied to *res sacrae:* sacred things are divinely protected. Once a thing became sacred, it could be put to no other use. It could not be sold, exchanged, bequeathed, or made the object of any transaction. Once it became sacred, it remained sacred forever. In the story, Anicia Juliana kept her wealth from funding Justinian's military activities by making it all sacred. Though she invited Justinian to avail himself of the sacred assets, she knew that legal regulations to which he had lent his own weight would prevent him from doing so. Justinian was embarrassed because Anicia Juliana found a clever way to refuse his request.

According to Synesius of Cyrene, Paul, the bishop of Erythrum, had used the process of creating *res sacrae* to claim an area of another bishop's jurisdiction. In Gregory of Tours's story, Anicia Juliana also takes advantage of the legal category of sacred things. Her goal, however, is the opposite of Paul's: to keep her territory out of another's control (whereas Paul tried to bring another person's territory into his control). She donates her extensive golden assets to a church to prevent Justinian from staking a claim to it.

This chapter will begin with an analysis of jurists' pedagogy on the divinely protected status of *res sacrae* and then turn to laws and canons formulated from the fourth through sixth centuries. According to laws and canons, it was the bishop's duty to treat ecclesial properties as divinely protected things. A case study of the trials of Ibas of Edessa shows how he was charged with the crime of sacrilege for his failure to protect ecclesial property. A case study of Dioscorus of Alexandria's trial at the Council of Chalcedon in 451 shows how a council could ratify a bishop's protective measures even while deposing the bishop.

Canons of various synods highlight the period of transition between one bishop's death and his successor's accession as a particularly vulnerable time for *res sacrae*. To guarantee the security of ecclesial property during the vacancy of the see, bishops would use their last will and testament to continue administering the property until a successor would assume office. A case study on the contested episcopacy of Symmachus of Rome offers a concrete example of how ecclesial property could be administered through the use of a legal document, the will, and how relationships between church and state were negotiated in the process.

In general, civil laws did not attempt to regulate sacred things on behalf of ecclesiastical authorities but were probably only composed in response to ecclesiastical requests for civil enforcement of canons or to maintain the integrity of civil institutions. Bishops like Symmachus of Rome nevertheless asserted the primacy of their discretion over ecclesiastical matters.

ROMAN JURISTIC PEDAGOGY ON THE PROTECTION OF *RES SACRAE*

Gaius's textbook for students of law set up two different categories of things: human and divine. The primary distinguishing feature was that whereas human things are ownable, divine things are not. "What is under divine law," says Gaius, "belongs to no one" (*quod autem divini iuris est, id nullius in bonis est*).[3] The principle that *res sacrae* belong to no one became a significant legacy of Gaius's thought. Sacred things were protected from ownership. Of course, this leaves unanswered the question of who may take responsibility for *res sacrae* when decisions must be made about them. By contrast, Ulpian's textbook categorized sacred things in a way that acknowledged what divine protection regularly meant: direct oversight on the part of the highest governmental officials. Ulpian grouped *res sacrae* with imperial offices, producing the shared characteristics of laws and churches as inviolable, and protected by God.[4] Justinian's new and updated textbook repeated the principle noted in Gaius's *Institutes* (*quod enim divini iuris est, id nullius in bonis est*), while Justinian's laws show him regularly making decisions about them.[5]

Pedagogical contexts supply easily comprehensible analogies for the purpose of teaching the concept of inalienability. Jurists likened *res sacrae* to free persons. Just as a person's status as "free" protected him or her from becoming the object of a sale, usucaption (possession of a thing through long, uncontested use), or stipulation (making a thing the condition of an agreement), so also *res sacrae* enjoyed the same protections. Paul, a jurist of the early third century, uses the same analogy to describe the act of "consecration" as a loss of possession: "There is a variety of ways in which we lose possession; [. . .] for we cannot possess a [. . .] sacred place, even though we personally spurn religion and regard the land as private; the same is true of a free man (*homo liber*)."[6] The status of consecrated land as "unowned" was no more contestable than a person's status as "free."

The analogy surfaces again in discussions of usucaption and stipulations. In Gaius's list of corporeal things that cannot be the object of usucaption, "sacred and dedicated things" stand alongside "freemen."[7] Gaius invokes the analogy to explain that stipulations are automatically invalid if the stipulation cannot be fulfilled:

> If the thing which we stipulated to be given is of such a nature that it cannot be given, it is plain that the stipulation is on natural reason invalid, for example, if a stipulation with respect to a freeman [. . .] was made between persons who were unaware that the man was free [. . .]. *The legal position is the same if someone has stipulated that a sacred or religious place be given.*[8]

In other words, a stipulation that a free man be given is just as invalid as a stipulation that a *res sacra* be given. Free persons and sacred things were by nature inalienable. Paul makes the same point except in a different context, in a discussion about stipulations that depend on a future outcome. The stipulation "do you promise to deliver him when he becomes a slave" is no more valid than "[do you promise] to convey that plot of land when it ceases to be sacred or religious and becomes secular."[9] Stipulations could not anticipate a future change in the nature of a person or thing. Paul sums up the matter as follows, "I will stipulate without effect for sacred or religious objects [. . .] or for a free person."[10] Justinian's textbook also compares sacred things to free persons. According to Justinian's *Institutes* 2.6.1, *res sacrae* could not be the objects of usucaption, the subjects of stipulations, or the objects of sale. Their monetary assets too were inalienable.[11] They could no more be objects of usucaption than a free man could be, even if they were possessed in the utmost good faith.

Justinian adds another analogy: *res sacrae* are like nonexistent things. A hippocentaur (a nonexistent thing) cannot be the subject of stipulations; the same is true of *res sacrae*.[12] Like free persons, *res sacrae* were not things at all. They were nonexistent for the purposes of stipulation as well as usucaption or sale.

It was also outside the realm of legal possibility to bequeath *res sacrae*. Ulpian treats the notion as a matter of absurdity. Only a madman would try to bequeath inalienable things.[13]

Not even disasters affected the legal status of sacred things. According to Papinian (fl. 194–212), if an *aedes sacra* (a sacred building) is destroyed by an earthquake, the land nevertheless retains its legal status as sacred. It remains inalienable and cannot be sold despite the natural disaster.[14] According to Pomponius, a second-century jurist, sacred land that was captured by an enemy would only cease to be sacred while it was in the enemy's hands. Once it was restored, the site would regain its legal status as sacred and would thereby be inalienable.[15] Again, the person-thing analogy is invoked: Pomponius says the site is restored as a kind of postliminium. Just as a citizen loses his or her rights and property as a captive, but all is restored if he or she returns to the Roman patrimony, so too *res sacrae* lose their status under captivity, but regain it on release from enemy hands.

Though *res sacrae* were inalienable, the situation could arise in which an inalienable thing were sold as though it were alienable. There are two different opinions among the jurists about the validity of such a sale. Pomponius considered such a sale to be valid, drawing the frequently used analogy of free persons to sacred things: "The purchase of a freeman or of sacred or religious land who or which cannot be held as property is considered valid, so long as the purchaser does not know."[16] The transaction was valid so long as it was made in good faith on the part of the purchaser. Modestinus (fl. 223–39), on the other hand, maintained that the transaction is invalid no matter what. Whether the purchaser could sue the vendor depended on circumstances related to the vendor. If the vendor sold the item in good faith, no action was possible, but if he did so in bad faith, then the purchaser could collect damages because of the deception.[17] Modestinus regarded the sale of sacred land as automatically invalid; Pomponius regarded such a sale as invalid only if the purchaser obtained it in bad faith.

By way of preventing such a situation in the first place, a particular clause could be included in the sale contract: "If any of the land be sacred or religious, it is not included in the sale."[18] According to Paul, if the entirety of the purchased land was sacred or religious and the contract included such a clause, the purchaser could recover what he paid by legal action.[19] According to Ulpian, such a clause allowed one to exclude particular tracts from the contract, even though they lay within the boundaries specified in the contract.[20]

Because *res sacrae* were not subject to alienation, their potential market value could not be determined. As Ulpian wrote, "A sacred thing does not receive appraisal."[21]

The Praetor's Edict prohibited damage to *res sacrae*. There were at least three interdicts in the Praetor's Edict pertaining to *res sacrae*, all intended to prevent unauthorized change in the property's condition. Ulpian cites a prohibitive interdict, "The praetor says: 'I forbid doing anything in a sacred place, or introducing anything into it,'" and comments that the prohibition does not apply to acts of embellishment, but to acts of "defacement" (*deformitatis*) and "nuisance" (*incommodi*).[22] Ulpian cites two more interdicts; these enjoin restitution. One pertains to illegal construction on sacred property: "if work has been carried out which ought not to have been, [. . .] recourse must be had [. . .] to the interdict [. . .] 'for restoration of something done in a consecrated [. . .] place.'"[23] This interdict on restoration of any illegal construction specifies consecrated property because it does not apply to public buildings. According to Ulpian, illegal construction on public property only needs to be demolished if it "obstructs public use," but in the case of sacred property it has to be demolished regardless of the circumstances:

> If someone builds in a public place and nobody prevents him, he cannot then be compelled to demolish, for fear of ruins disfiguring the city and because the interdict is for prohibition, not restitution. But if his building obstructs public use, it must certainly be demolished by the official in charge of public works. If it does not, he must impose a *solarium* (ground-rent) on it. [. . .] *The case of sacred places is different. In a sacred place, we are not only forbidden to do anything but also are ordered to make restitution: this on account of religion.*[24]

In Justinian's *Institutes*, prohibitory interdicts regarding *res sacrae* are likewise mentioned in two passages.[25]

Justinian's *Institutes* further protected *res sacrae* by guaranteeing bequests and even payments made to churches in error. Those who withheld things left "by way of legacy or trust to the holy churches and other places of veneration" would pay double the damages.[26] Payments made in error to the churches were not recoverable.[27] In these ways, students of law were taught to maintain sacred things through their inalienability and, in fact, when possible, to increase the assets of churches.

The rationale for one of Justinian's laws preventing the diminution of bequests made to churches explicitly refers to the concept that churches were under the eternal protection of God:

> For to every man there is one course of life given him by his Maker, the end of which is always death: but it is impossible to set an end to the holy houses and their congregations; *they are eternal, under the protection of God. As long as the holy houses endure (and they will endure for all time and till the end of the ages, as long as the name of Christians is among men adored)*, then righteously shall also the fortunes or revenues, bequeathed to them forever, remain undying, ever serving unceasing pious acts.[28]

The purpose of legislation was to ensure that sacred places remained under God's perpetual protection. On the basis of their eternal protection, such places would also extend perpetual protection to others by means of "pious acts."[29]

One legal and, to some extent, canonical mechanism used to propagate the notion of churches as protected places was to regulate the acquisition of ecclesial property and ensure the increase of assets in three main ways. In the first place, laws and canons added measures to support the reception of gifts (such as allowing ecclesiastical administrators an extended prescriptive period for legal action).[30] In the second place, laws and canons made churches the recipients of fines and other assets (such as the property of intestate clerics) that would otherwise accrue to civil institutions like the fisc or the imperial treasury.[31] In the third place, laws of Justinian protected churches from two specific ways of losing assets (receiving liabilities and being shortchanged in the receipt of bequests).[32]

Another, even more significant mechanism for constructing churches as protected spaces highly restricted the types of transactions for which ecclesial property could be used as currency, and it is this mechanism that I detail in what follows. I review the many laws and canons (1) forbidding or restricting the possibilities of alienating, loaning, detaining, or leasing ecclesial property, and (2) outlawing acts of violence against or on church property. As in the previous chapter, I cite penalty schedules whenever possible, since they indicate the perceived severity of infractions.

In the matter of alienation, bishops already treated ecclesial property as inalienable before laws did. However, this does not necessarily mean that ecclesial property initially was not considered legally inalienable. Both laws and canons were issued in response to specific circumstances, not as preemptive preventative measures.

RULES ON ALIENATION

What exactly counted as *res sacrae*? All consecrated ecclesial property, immovable (i.e., buildings, fields, etc.), movable (i.e., vessels, vestments, etc.), and self-moving (i.e., slaves) counted as *res sacrae*. Only the revenue produced (e.g., from vineyards) did not count. Excerpts from the writings of second- and third-century Roman jurists in the *Digest* emphasize inalienability (i.e., unexchangeability in any transaction) as the most salient characteristic of the objects that fall within the legal category of *res sacrae*. This section reviews canons and laws that address the same issue. As the following rules show, although all ecclesial property was considered *res sacrae*, exceptions to the prohibition on alienation were regularly made on a case-by-case basis.

Early fifth-century canons applied the principle of inalienability to ecclesial property. In principle, ecclesial property could not be alienated or usucapted, but any alienation that did occur had to be done by the bishop with the consent of the synod or the primate. Some canons targeted clerics who claimed ownership of ecclesial property on account of long, uncontested use (usucaption). Others were directed toward episcopal kin, so as to protect ecclesial property from conflation with personal property.

As for the laws, early and mid-fifth-century constitutions forbade the alienation of ecclesial property to non-Christians and heretics. It was not until 470 that a piece of legislation reiterated the breadth of the principle of inalienability found in the writings of classical jurists collected in the *Digest*. At the turn of the sixth century, Anastasius permitted alienation under specific circumstances. Justinian both repealed Anastasius's law and promulgated several laws to identify churches as inalienable *res sacrae*. A number of laws protected sacred things from alienation to such an extent that severe penalties were not only imposed on violators; informers were explicitly permitted to report violations without fear of defamation.

Canons and Laws on the Inalienability of Church Property

The first extant canon to ban the alienation of ecclesial property was composed at the Council of Carthage in 419.[33] Exception was made to "useless" property (property on which taxes had to be paid, but no revenue could be produced).

By contrast, the two earliest extant laws that address the alienation of ecclesial property do not forbid their alienation altogether but address the issue of their alienation to non-Christians and nonorthodox Christians. A constitution of Theodosius II in 423 suggests that consecrated churches were inalienable and could not be returned to their former legal status.[34] The law explains that since it is impossible to return to the Jews synagogues that had been converted into churches or vessels consecrated to church use, Christians must compensate Jews with places in lieu of the synagogues and money in lieu of the vessels.[35] This law assumes what later laws would reassert: that ecclesial property could not be alienated to non-Christians. It does not concern the possibility of alienating property to other Christians. Leo legislated in 466 that churches could not be alienated to heretics. According to the law, "estates, properties, and immovable property, where churches or chapels of the orthodox faith are located" cannot be alienated, not even by a last will, to a heretic or anyone opposed to the orthodox faith.[36] If such alienation occurs, then the lands or possessions are confiscated to the fisc. Since the two laws exist only as excerpts included in the Theodosian or Justinianic Codex, it is impossible to know whether the full text of either law cited a more general principle against the alienation of churches.

It is not until a piece of legislation issued by Leo and Anthemius in 470 that the principle of inalienability is described in the clearest terms. It does not include any exemption clauses as the canons at the Council of Carthage did in 419 and the Council of Agde would in 506. The justification of the law reads as follows:

> For it is proper that what belongs to the Most Blessed Church or is acquired hereafter should reverently be kept intact just like the Sacrosanct and Holy Church itself, so that just as the Church is the eternal mother of religion and faith, so her property should perpetually be kept unscathed.[37]

The imperial consistory draws an analogy here between the church as a person and a thing. Since as a person (the church personified as mother of the faith), the church is eternal, so also as a thing (ecclesial property), it should remain perpetual. The law forbids any archbishop or steward from alienating any church property received as a donation or as an inheritance, not even if all the clergy, the bishop, and the steward agree to the alienation. Anyone who attempted to acquire ecclesial property would lose all the gains, which, along with any bribes, would accrue to the church. Such property would have to be reclaimed as though no transaction had occurred at all. The officeholders implicated in the transaction would suffer the following penalties. The steward who allowed such an alienation to occur would lose the stewardship and would have to make restitution for any losses the church would incur from his own property. His death would not terminate the case nor would it render his transactions inactionable, because his heirs could be sued. The notary would be exiled. The judges or recordkeepers would lose their rank and all their property.

Anastasius, sometime during his tenure from 491 to 518, published a law that allowed for the alienation of immovable and movable ecclesial property under specific circumstances.[38] Immovable property and rights to the grain supply were inalienable, except for the discharge of debts, for profit, for the acquisition of more profitable property, for renovation, or for maintenance. Essentially, alienation was only permissible if the immovable property brought loss, not gain, and there was no movable property (aside from the sacred vessels) that could meet the expenses. For the alienation to be valid, the reason for it had to be declared under oath on the Holy Scriptures before the master of the census for Byzantium, the defenders for the provinces, and in the presence of the stewards and clerics of the church. The master of the census or the defender had to render his services free of charge, otherwise he would incur a fine of twenty pounds of gold. If any formalities were omitted, the alienation would be invalid.

It was Justinian who promulgated comprehensive laws concerning *res sacrae*. He included all pious houses (not only churches, but also hospitals, hospices, orphanages, and monasteries) under the category of *res sacrae*.[39] Justinian expresses the principle of inalienability most succinctly in a law sent in 529: "what is under divine law is not bound to human restraints" (*quae iuris divini sunt, humanis nexibus non illigari*).[40] Novel 7 of 535 was the first attempt at comprehensive legislation. It directly responded to the law of Leo and Anthemius and that of Anastasius discussed above. Novel 120 of 544 was the second attempt.

Prior to issuing comprehensive legislation regarding sacred things and alienation, Justinian issued two laws: one pertains to the alienation of donations or bequests; the other concerns alienation for the purpose of amassing funds to redeem captives. Justinian issued the first in 528 to the praetorian prefect of the East, Atarbius.[41] Though Justinian did not outlaw alienation altogether, he forbade those alienations that did not fulfill the overall purpose of donations and bequests. Donated or bequeathed property could not be alienated or diverted for the purpose of the administrator's own profit. If stewards damaged ecclesial property or converted it to their own benefit, they had to restore it. As in the case of Leo and Anthemius's law, the steward's death did not terminate the case. If a steward died before rendering an annual account, his heirs would be subject to audit and would be responsible for making restitution. The law permitted informers. The second law, issued in 529, stated the only circumstance under which particular pieces of ecclesial property could be alienated.[42] Pieces of movable property—namely, sacred and holy vessels or vestments or other votive offerings necessary for divine worship—could be sold, mortgaged, or pledged only for the ransom of captives. If they should be alienated for any other reason, bishops, stewards, and guardians had the right of recovery, while those who took them had no right of action.

After the publication of the Codex, Justinian had a law composed that was both comprehensive in scope and application.[43] In 535, he cited the inadequacies of two previous laws (that of Leo and Anthemius for having limited applicability and that of Anastasius for being imperfect) before establishing a comprehensive corrective. The law was sent to all archbishops and two praetorian prefects (John, prefect of the East, and Dominicus, prefect of Illyricum). They were not to permit the alienation of the immovable property of any church anywhere or its deliverance to a creditor by special hypothecation. Immovable property expressly included, "houses, farmlands, market gardens or anything of the kind at all, [. . .] any agricultural slave or any civic allowance" and ruins, even if the ruins were utterly dilapidated (i.e., had no recoverable buildings or building materials).[44] Alienation encompassed sale, gift, exchange, and emphyteusis in perpetuity. Monasteries "in which an altar has been consecrated" could not be alienated and transferred "into the form of a private dwelling."[45] The penalty for alienation was that which was alienated plus its equal value and right of action against the personal property of the steward who alienated the property. The quaestor and magistrates could be fined fifty pounds of gold. The law protected informers: "Such a person will escape the appellation of vexatious litigant; he will be praised for exposing an illegal act, and for being the cause of pious assistance to holy houses."[46] When Justinian took control over North Africa, he extended the applicability of the comprehensive law to North Africa.[47]

Two exceptions were made. One reiterated the law of 529 pertaining to movable property, in stating that holy vases could not be alienated at all except to redeem captives.[48] The other was significant in that it acknowledged imperial power over sacred things. The law permitted the emperor alone to exchange property with the churches, provided that he donated to them property of equal or better value than that which he took. The justification for imperial exception reads as follows: "For priesthood and sovereignty are not much different from one another, nor are sacred things from common and public things, inasmuch as wealth and structures are given to the most holy churches from continuous munificence on the part of the emperor."[49] Recall that Ulpian's schema for the division of things acknowledged a relationship between sacred things and offices of the state. Here Justinian reiterates Ulpian's perspective to justify a special imperial privilege vis-à-vis *res sacrae*.[50]

Four ensuing laws emended Novel 7 before a new comprehensive law, Novel 120, was issued in 544. The four amendments, respectively, made a further qualification to the principle of inalienability, extended the imperial right of exchange, addressed abuse of the emperor's power of exchange, and defined the metropolitan's role in the alienation of ecclesial property. They were issued over the course of three years. The first of the four amendments (issued in 536) allowed immovable ecclesial property to be alienated for the purpose of paying taxes.[51] If a debt was owed to the fisc and the fisc could not receive immovable property in payment, the immovable property could be sold for money to pay the debt. However, Hagia Sophia and its associated monasteries were excluded from the law's application. The next two amendments, both issued in 537, addressed the issue of exchange. One granted the imperial right of exchange also to all pious houses.[52] Exchanges could be made not only between the emperor and pious houses, but between one pious house and another. Property could be exchanged between pious houses without an imperial order, provided that an oath was sworn to the effect that the exchange benefited both parties. The other addressed abuse of the imperial right of exchange in Constantinople, showing that even imperially exchanged ecclesial property retained inalienable status.[53] The abuse in question took the following form: the emperor would exchange ecclesial property and give ownership of what came into his possession to a private person. To prevent exchanged ecclesial property from falling into private ownership, Justinian legislated that if property were to be exchanged with the emperor, then the emperor would retain ownership of it and it could not pass to private persons. If such a series of transactions nevertheless did occur, the steward of the church could reclaim the exchanged ecclesial property. The last amendment, issued in 538, concerned the role of the metropolitan bishop in alienations.[54] The metropolitan's presence was required for the alienation of any ecclesial property. If the metropolitan himself wished to alienate ecclesial property, then he had to do so in the presence of two bishops of his choice.

In 544, Justinian once again had a comprehensive law composed regarding the alienation of ecclesial property.[55] Ecclesial property was not to be alienated, except under the following circumstances. For the payment of debts, first movable property was to be used, and then immovable property as a last resort. To prevent churches in the provinces from retaining unprofitable land, the law permitted venerable houses in the provinces to alienate nonincome producing property. For the redemption of captives, the churches of Odessus and Tomis on the Black Sea could alienate immovable property, unless the property were expressly given on the condition that it would not be alienated. Holy vessels anywhere could not be sold or pledged except for the redemption of captives. If there were many vessels and the house was burdened by debts and there was no other movable property that could be used to pay the debt, then they could either sell the holy vessels to venerable places that needed them or melt them down and sell them. The churches of Jerusalem could sell the houses belonging to them for the purpose of purchasing another and better income, but the price of the property was not to be any less than what was collected as rental from it for fifty years.

The last extant law that Justinian issued regarding the alienation of ecclesial property returned to the same issue as the first two extant laws. Theodosius II and Leo had issued laws regarding the alienation of ecclesial property to Jews and heretics, respectively. Like Leo in 466, Justinian in 545 ruled that ecclesial property could not be alienated to heretics.[56] If it nevertheless happened, the heretic would lose the price and the property, and the steward or officeholder who effected the transaction would be removed from his post, exiled to a monastery, and denied communion for a year.

Gallic, Spanish, and North African councils throughout the sixth century also forbade the alienation of ecclesial property except under specific circumstances. Unlike Justinian, they did not even permit kings the right of alienation. The first extant Gallic canon regarding alienation of ecclesial property, composed in Agde in 506, banned the alienation of ecclesial property, citing the following reason: it is the property of the poor (*res pauperes*).[57] Like the canon issued at Carthage in 419, it contains an exemption clause: in cases of necessity, a bishop could alienate ecclesial property, provided that he had the approval of two or three colleagues. Another canon of the same council denied presbyters and other clerics the right to alienate ecclesial property (*res ecclesiae*), even the property that they held in usufruct.[58] If they nevertheless did so, the transaction would be invalid, they would have to return the property to the church, and they would be excommunicated. The first canon that cites consecration as the reason for the inalienability of ecclesial property is known as Ps-Agde canon 49 because in some collections it has been transmitted among a number of canons appended to the canons of the Council of Agde in 506. Administrators were not allowed to exchange, sell, or donate ecclesial property because they were "things considered consecrated to God" (*res sacratae Deo esse noscuntur*). Gifts of ecclesial property could not even be made to rulers, according to a council of Clermont in 535.[59] Like many Gallic canons, the canon written at Clermont declared such transactions tantamount to stealing from the poor. Toward the end of the sixth century, the Third Council of Toledo held in 589 reiterated the fact that bishops ought not alienate ecclesial property.[60]

The synod gathered at Orleans in 538 specified temporary excommunication as a penalty for the alienation of ecclesial property.[61] The excommunication would be lifted once return of the property was made. A council at Paris held sometime between 556 and 573 further specified that no bishop could receive someone excommunicated by another bishop for seizing ecclesial property.[62]

Later councils held in Orleans added that the principle of alienation applied also to ecclesial donations, as did the penalty of excommunication. In 541, the synod ruled that donations made to a parish could not be recalled or alienated without the bishop's written consent.[63] In 549, the synod stated that donations could not be sold; if one sold them, he or she would be excommunicated and considered a "murderer of the poor."[64]

Whereas the only extant law that permits churches to exchange property with one another is Justinian's Novel 54 issued in 537, a council at Hippo issued a canon already more than a century earlier permitting the same thing and a Spanish council at the end of the sixth century also allowed for the conversion of a church into a monastery. The Synod of Hippo in 427 allowed ecclesial property to be exchanged or donated between one church and another.[65] The canon does not require an oath, as Justinian's Novel 54 does. The Spanish council convened at Toledo in 589 allowed bishops to convert one pious house into another. With synodal consent, a bishop could convert a parish church into a monastery.[66]

When Gallic civic boundaries became significantly unstable during the wars between Frankish kings, canons addressed the problem of alienation of ecclesial property in no uncertain terms. While Justinian's Novel 7 issued in 535 explicitly reserved the right of exchange to the emperor, the first canon of the Council of Paris held between 556 and 573 decided that ecclesial property was not bound to civic boundaries and could not be sold or donated even by kings. Under Justinian, however, the latter was an explicit prerogative of the emperor, provided he made restitution of greater value. At Tours, a council held in 567 ruled that anyone who stole ecclesial property and refused to return it after three written requests would be declared a murderer of the poor by a procession of all the clergy reciting Psalm 108 (LXX) and that even those who associated with such a person were to be excommunicated.[67] Curses were the most severe penalty that could be imposed, more severe even than that of excommunication. While the latter is a communal act of estrangement, the former ritualizes the estrangement through chanted censure and threat. Christian interpretations of Psalm 108 identify Judas as the subject of the psalm's maledictions.[68] By virtue of chanting such a psalm in procession, the clergy ritually project the condemnation of Judas onto the offender.[69] Canon 26 of the same council refers to ecclesial property as "things of God" (*res Dei*) and adds that the possession of ecclesial property on the pretext of "protecting it" was no excuse for theft. Still further canons discussed below addressed the problem of alienation in terms of theft.

Civil laws concerned two particular issues—namely, who could not be the recipient of alienated ecclesial property (Jews and heretics) and under which specific circumstances ecclesial property could be lawfully alienated. Canons raised a number of other concerns as well, as the following section shows.

Exceptions to the Rule and Protections against Illegal Alienation

Important to bishops' meetings were questions such as how a canonical alienation might take place and how to protect ecclesial property from administrators' families and from theft, especially during vulnerable times such as the vacancy of an episcopal seat.

Alienation by Bequest or Donation.   In addition to the canons and laws cited above that claim as ecclesial property all the possessions that clerics acquire after their ordination, canons and laws also expressly forbade clerics from bequeathing ecclesial property to anyone. Canon 5 for the Council of Hippo in 427 addressed the question of whether clerics might bequeath to kin property they acquired in their own name after their ordination. The assembled bishops decided that such property would belong to the church and therefore clerics could not bequeath it to relatives. If they nevertheless did so, they dishonored the church and would be judged by the synod. It is not until Justinian a century later that a law expresses the same rule. It pertains only to bishops, however, not to all ecclesiastical administrators. Justinian's law of 528 discussed above already regarded as ecclesial property all that bishops acquired after their ordination.[70] In 545, Justinian set forth regulations regarding bishops' bequests.[71] Bishops could not donate or bequeath movable, immovable, and self-moving property (i.e., slaves) that they acquired during their episcopacy to their relatives or any other person, unless it belonged to them prior to their ordination or they inherited it from their relatives up to the fourth degree.

Several sixth-century canons from Gaul concern the same issue. The alienation of ecclesial property in the form of a bequest was simply out of the question, but some regions allowed bishops the same prerogative of exchange that Justinian had reserved for the emperor alone. Such canons require the bishop to indemnify the church for any property alienated. The Council of Agde in 506 decided that bishops could not bequeath even ecclesial property that they used for themselves.[72] On the contrary, the Council of Epaon in 517 allowed bishops to bequeath ecclesial property so long as they donated to the church something of the same worth from their private belongings.[73] Such a canon granted bishops the same right of exchange that Justinian reserved for the emperor alone.[74] Even Justinian's extension of the prerogative to exchanges between pious houses, however, did not allow an administrator's private property to supplant ecclesial property.[75] Likewise, the Fourth Council of Orleans, held in 541, required bishops to bequeath to the church the equal value of what they mortgaged, financially burdened, or sold of ecclesial property.[76] If they failed to do so, then the responsibility would fall on the heirs of the former ecclesial property to compensate the church. The council listed one exception: the bishops' freedmen could not be reenslaved for this purpose. That is to say, ecclesial freedmen could not be offered to a church as slaves to reimburse alienated property.

Alienation by Usucaption.   Aside from donations in life or death, property could also be acquired through usucaption, the long unquestioned use of property. Typically, the legal prescription period for *usucapio* was thirty years. Two sixth-century Gallic canons did not permit the laws of usucaption to transfer ownership of property from the church to another party, but a fifth-century canon did allow the prescription period to resolve jurisdictional problems. The Council of Chalcedon in 451 allowed bishops to retain possession of countryside and village parishes that they held uncontested for thirty years; any disputes that arose before thirty years had elapsed were to be resolved by the provincial synod.[77] The Council of Orleans in 511 explicitly denied that civil laws of usucaption could apply to ecclesial properties.[78] Any lands or vineyards that an ecclesiastical administrator allowed another to use belonged to the church, regardless of how long the person used it. At Epaon six years later, in 517, a council forbade clerics the usucaption of ecclesial property even if the king willed it.[79] The canons of Orleans and Epaon demonstrate that bishops of Gaul explicitly denied not only the application of a civil law to churches but, most importantly, the right of kings over ecclesial property. While Justinian reserved imperial right over ecclesial property, he nonetheless agreed that such property should not fall into private ownership even via imperial means.[80] The decision at Epaon in 517 and that of Justinian twenty years later with Novel 55 address a similar concern. Once a thing becomes sacred, its status cannot change because it is inviolable.

The Bishop's Prerogative in Matters of Alienation.   A number of canons from North Africa, Italy, and Gaul emphasize that the bishop is the sole administrator who, under specific circumstances and with the consent and witness of certain other administrators, may alienate ecclesial property. In general, canons state that no lower-ranking clerics may alienate ecclesial property, but there are specific conditions in which it was permitted. The Council of Carthage in 419 drew an analogy between the role of the presbyters relative to the bishops and that of the bishops relative to the synod. Presbyters could not dispose of the property of the church (*res ecclesiae*) without the consent of their bishop, just as bishops could not dispose of church property (*praedia ecclesiae*) without the consent of the synod or his presbyters.[81] Except in cases of necessity, even the bishop could not dispose of things from the endowment of the church (*res tituli*). At a council in Rome in 502, over which Pope Symmachus presided, it was specifically decreed that laypersons might not regulate ecclesial property, and the council anathematized clerics who signed their names on deeds that alienated ecclesial property.[82]

Gallic canons describe the consequences presbyters and other lower-ranking clergy would face for alienating ecclesial property. The Council of Epaon in 517 declared sales effected by a presbyter invalid and required that he return the property.[83] The penalty specified at Orleans about a decade later, in 538, was more severe. Presbyters and other clerics (including abbots) not only had to return alienated property; they also forfeited their office.[84] The question of donations to parishes arose in the next council at Orleans in 541; they too were ecclesial property that only the bishop could alienate.[85]

In order for the bishop himself, however, to alienate useless ecclesial property, he needed the consent of his episcopal colleagues. The Council of Carthage in 401 and that of Epaon in 517 required the consent of the primate or metropolitan of the province for any alienation to take place.[86] Almost two decades later, in 419, the Council of Carthage insisted on a decision of the synod for useless ecclesial property to be sold.[87]

Two canons further require of the bishop that he obtain the consent of the presbyters in his jurisdiction. The canon of the Council of Carthage in 419 that denies presbyters the right to alienate ecclesial property implies that bishops only have the right with the consent of not only the synod but of his presbyters as well.[88] A collection of Gallic canons made at the end of the fifth century demands the written permission of the presbyters for a bishop to donate, sell, or alter ecclesial property.[89]

There were, as always, exceptional circumstances under which a bishop did not need the consent of the synod and presbyters and under which even lower-ranking clerics could effect a valid alienation. In cases of urgent need, a bishop could alienate ecclesial property, but even so he had to gather together neighboring bishops to witness to the sale, according to the Council of Carthage in 419.[90] Likewise, the Council of Agde in 506 required the approval of two or three episcopal colleagues even in urgent cases. The same council, however, allowed small, distant patches of land or vineyards to be sold by a bishop in a poor financial situation without consulting other bishops.[91] The Council of Rome in 595 permitted one condition under which ecclesial slaves could be freed: that they might become monks.[92] As for the possibility of alienation by nonbishops, the Council of Orleans in 549 determined one scenario in which such a thing would be permissible.[93] To relieve a great need during a particular kind of episcopal vacancy (in the event that the bishop had been indefinitely recalled and no new bishop had been appointed), lower-ranking clerics could alienate (*auferre*) ecclesial property.

Legal Suits regarding Ecclesial Property.   Sixth-century Gallic canons refer to two types of legal actions: one of a church administrator to reclaim invalidly alienated property and another of any plaintiff who attempted to reclaim personal property unjustly appropriated as ecclesial property. The Council of Epaon in 517 explicitly allowed bishops to make a legal action against uncanonical sales made by abbots.[94] The Third Council of Orleans in 538 allowed a succeeding bishop to purchase back the property that the former bishop sold within thirty years and excommunicated anyone who refused to sell the property back.[95] Similarly, the Fourth Council of Orleans in 541 permitted a succeeding bishop to decide whether clerics could retain any ecclesial property they took during the vacancy of the see.[96] As for plaintiffs who attempted to reclaim their personal property from bishops, the Council of Orleans in 511 decided that they should not be excommunicated on account of taking such legal action, so long as they did not speak abusively or make criminal charges.[97]

Protections against Illegal Alienation.   Synods of fifth- and sixth-century Gaul, Spain, and Britain put measures in place to prevent or penalize theft of ecclesial property. Inventory lists or a guard would discourage theft after the death of a bishop; the requirement of episcopal kin to receive their inheritance from the church would prevent them from conflating ecclesial with personal property; and the threat of punishment offered a further means to avert theft.

Synods at Riez and Lerida set up guards to protect ecclesial property during the vacancy of a see. At Riez in 439, the synod decided that a neighboring bishop should take control of ecclesial property and report to the metropolitan.[98] The Council of Valencia less than a century later in 529 cited the decisions at Riez to forbid clerics from appropriating ecclesial property after the bishop's death and to require of the neighboring bishop that he draw up an exact inventory of the jurisdiction's property and report to the metropolitan.[99] Similarly, the Council of Orleans in 533 required, as part of the funeral preparations, that a bishop and his presbyters meet in a house of the church (*in unum domum ecclesiae*)[100] to make an inventory of church property (*res ecclesiae*) in advance and appoint a guard, so that nothing would be stolen in the course of the funeral.[101] An earlier canon from a Spanish synod at Tarragona in 516 delegated the responsibility for writing an inventory list to local priests and deacons after the funeral if the bishop died intestate.[102] Likewise, at Lerida in 546 the synod put the episcopal residence of deceased bishops in the custody of a guardian with two faithful assistants to preserve all things until the arrival of the new bishop.[103] Anyone who violated the rule would be guilty of sacrilege, be anathematized, and suffer peregrine communion (*communio peregrina*).[104]

A further provision to protect ecclesial property during the vulnerable period of a vacant see was put in place at Valencia in 529. Not only did the synod echo the earlier decision of Riez for the production of an inventory list, but it also required that the bishop's kin request permission from the metropolitan and the bishops of the province before laying claim to their inheritance.[105]

Some of the canons cited above and others too included penalties against those who unjustly acquired ecclesial property. The early fifth-century Synod of North Britain penalized monks with one year of penance and exile for a repeated offense of stealing consecrated things.[106] The Council of Agde in 506 targeted clerics who stole consecrated things from the church and penalized them with peregrine communion.[107] The Third, Fourth, and Fifth Councils of Orleans threatened excommunication against any who took ecclesial property and did not return it. In 538, the synod decided that those who took church property (*res ecclesiae*) and did not return it to the bishop would be excommunicated until the return was made; likewise, those who retained what had been bequeathed to the church or donated were excommunicated until they made restitution.[108] Similarly, in 541, the council forbade clerics and laity from having ecclesial property without the permission of the bishop.[109] Possessors of church property were to return the property at the demand of the bishop or the civil judge; those who did not would suffer excommunication until they returned the property and did penance. The council in 549 addressed the problem of bishops, clerics, and laity taking property from churches in other kingdoms.[110] Such persons would be excommunicated until restitution was made.

BISHOPS' KIN AND ECCLESIAL PROPERTY
IN ALEXANDRIA AND EDESSA

Ecclesial properties were sacred things that could not be alienated, and bishops' relatives were not exempt from the rule. Canons from the Councils of Antioch in 328, Carthage in 419, and Hippo in 427 underscore this point.[111] Kinship to the bishop did not entitle a person to any privileges or benefits. This legal and canonical context offers a lens for evaluating certain charges leveled against Ibas of Edessa and Dioscorus of Alexandria, as well as certain canons composed as a result of their trials. As for Ibas of Edessa, several clerics charged him with sacrilege against ecclesial property. In the end, Ibas's trials led to the creation of a new administrative post in every diocese for the safeguarding of sacred things. As for Dioscorus of Alexandria, a certain presbyter named Athanasius complained about his administrative conduct. Athanasius appealed legal actions that Dioscorus took actually to safeguard ecclesial property. The presbyter Athanasius's appeal was ignored; in fact, the council issued a canon to protect sacred things from clerics like him.

Before examining Ibas's and Dioscorus's cases in detail, it is important to note the nature of conciliar acts as sources.[112] To do so, it will be helpful to imagine a scene at one of Ibas's trials. It is the year 448. A council has gathered. Bishop Ibas of Edessa stands trial. Bishop Photius of Tyre presides as the main judge. Four of Ibas's clerics have accused him on many counts, including sacrilege. Photius responds to the clerics' plaint (their list of charges) by asking them to prioritize the charges. Photius says:

> First select and begin with the things that are by general agreement forbidden by both the canons and the laws and are clearly hateful to those who fear God. It is the following points that we think crucial: first, that he who has been appointed to the priesthood must be of sound faith, then that he be free from all depravity, but also that he should not betray piety especially for the sake of money.[113]

Photius lists the most egregious things a bishop could do to merit a trial. In general, a bishop could violate imperial laws, ecclesiastical canons, or both. Photius then goes on to describe two kinds of violations that are especially egregious and that are forbidden by laws and canons alike: preaching unsound faith and practicing immoral conduct, especially administrative financial misconduct, or, to quote Photius's words again, "betray[al] of piety especially for the sake of money." Photius gives voice here to the significance of administrative financial misconduct.

However, the acts of councils usually do not record proceedings pertaining to misconduct, preferring to settle them orally.[114] Conciliar acts are not verbatim transcripts of all that was said or read aloud at sessions. Instead, synods made motions to have parts of the proceedings recorded. For example, at Ibas's third trial, a presbyter gave an address to the synod, and the synod then motioned for the presbyter's account to be recorded in the acts. Why? The presbyter's account concerned matters of faith:

> The holy synod cried out: "We request that that may be stated in writing. That relates to the faith. Let it be stated in writing. It is directed against Christ. It ought to be put in writing."[115]

Transcripts of trials focus on discussions of faith, so they leave little room for historians to trace the importance of administrative financial misconduct.[116] Instead, the tracings can be found in three other places: the legal context of ecclesial property, the charges leveled by plaintiffs as recorded in retrials, and the canons issued at the end of conciliar gatherings.

Ibas of Edessa was tried four times between the years 448 and 451. At the first trial in Antioch, he was acquitted; at the second in Tyre and Berytus, he was disciplined; at the third in Ephesus, he was deposed; and at the fourth in Chalcedon, he was reinstated with discipline.[117] Charges of misconduct were leveled at all the trials, but they have only been transmitted to us because they were recorded in the third and fourth trials. The first trial took place in Antioch, where Domnus of Antioch presided. Ibas had excommunicated four of his presbyters, Samuel, Cyrus, Maras, and Eulogius, so as to prevent them from being canonical plaintiffs,[118] and only the latter two appeared before Domnus.[119] The former two went directly to Constantinople, for which reason Domnus not only excommunicated but deposed them. Since one of the charges was sacrilege, the plaintiffs expected that Ibas could be deposed on that count alone. Domnus, the judge, said, however, that "it was in [Ibas's] administrative power to act as he did."[120] According to the charge of sacrilege, Ibas melted down two hundred pounds of sacred silver vessels to amass funds to free monks and nuns from their captivity among Arabs. He received more than enough money from the treasurer but melted the vessels anyway. Justinian would allow vessels to be melted for the ransom of captives about one century later,[121] but we do not have any earlier laws or canons that address this issue.[122] The plaintiffs considered the deed sacrilege, but the judge decided that Ibas did not violate his administrative role.

The same plaintiffs appealed Domnus's decision before the Synod of Constantinople at the Church of the Holy John. There they raised the charges pertaining to the faith, and the emperor appointed the bishops Photius of Tyre, Eustathius of Berytus, and Uranius of Hemerium to hear the case at a second trial. The plaint that the four presbyters submitted to Photius of Tyre, Eustathius of Berytus, and Uranius of Hemerium is recorded in the Acts of the Council of Chalcedon. It includes the following seven charges that pertain to ecclesial property:

1. Ibas did not redeem captives (*ad redemptionem captiuorum*) with the full sum of money he received for this purpose. In fact, he melted down consecrated silver vessels (*uasis argenti sacri*) to amass funds he did not spend.

2. Ibas did not place a donated jeweled chalice (*calicem gemmatum*) in the church treasury (*inter uasa sanctae ecclesiae*).

6. Ibas alienated ecclesial revenue (*omnes ecclesiasticos reditus*) to his brother and nephews. Ibas alienated bequests and donations (*hereditates et munera*), including dedicated gold and silver crosses (*cruces positas aureas et argenteas*), to his brother and nephews. Ibas alienated the welfare of prisoners (*expensa carcerum*) to his relatives' households.

10. Ibas prevented the presbyter Pirozus from bequeathing his property to churches that had no revenue (*ecclesiis relinquente reditus nullos habentibus*).

11. Ibas did not prevent Bishop Daniel (his nephew) from bequeathing ecclesial property (*facultatem et praedia ex ecclesiasticis rebus*) to Challoa and her children. Challoa misused ecclesial property (*multis rebus ecclesiasticis abutens*) she had in usufruct by lending money at interest.

12. Abramius, a deacon and *apantetes*, bequeathed ecclesial property (*nostra ecclesia multas et innumeras res habuit, quae pro ueritate erant nostrae ecclesiae*) to Bishop Daniel, who in turn donated it to Challoa.

14. People cut wood from the ecclesial property of Edessa and used it to build on Challoa's estates (*ex ecclesiae Edessenae praedio Lafargaritas siluas caedentes portauerunt ad praedia Challoae*).[123]

In sum, the four presbyters accused Ibas of alienation of ecclesial property, obstruction of a bequest to the church, and failure to protect or reclaim ecclesial property misused by his nephew the bishop Daniel, Challoa, deacon and *apantetes* Abramius, and unnamed woodcutters. On February 25, 449, the bishops Photius of Tyre, Eustathius of Berytus, and Uranius of Hemerium reported on the hearing at which they reconciled Ibas of Edessa to his four presbyter-plaintiffs (Samuel, Cyrus, Maras, and Eulogius).

Less than two months later, Chaereas the count and judge of Osrhoene would hear the complaints of the people, archimandrites, and monks of Edessa against Ibas in the martyrium of the Holy Zachaeus on April 12, 449.[124] One of the recorded acclamations reads, "Let what belongs to the Church be restored to the Church."[125] Two days later, the same or a similar group of people approached Chaereas at the council chamber and uttered more specific acclamations: "Ibas melted down the Service of (Plate belonging to) the Church," "Ibas has plundered many Churches: the goods of the Church he now sells," "The possessions (of the Church) are ever such—Daniel and Challoa have consumed them (in pleasure). The City is ruined because of Ibas."[126]

Chaereas submitted a report to the consul Protogenes and the eparchs Albinus and Salimon, in which he described the hearings at the martyrium and council chamber and appended the petition and oath he received from Micallus, presbyter of the church of Edessa, signed by all the plaintiffs. The petition explains that the plaintiffs tried to render Ibas the honor due to a bishop, despite his maladministration of ecclesial property. Once matters regarding his faith arose, they decided that they could no longer accept him as their bishop:

> Although his [Ibas's] reputation had become sadly sullied by reason of his (mal-) administration of the property (the treasure) belonging to the Holy Church, as well as on other accounts, yet even then we still continued in this way to pay him honour, until, grievous charges being urged against him, he was arraigned on matters, relating to the Orthodox Faith.[127]

The petition quoted the following acclamations: "He has sold the Holy Thomas— he has plundered the Holy Church—he gave the possessions of the poor to his relatives"; "This man oppressed the poor. This man pillaged (made spoil of) the Church—he secreted (or appropriated to himself) the Holy Vessels—he made use of the Holy Vessels for his own purposes."[128] Ten presbyters, twenty deacons, nine subdeacons, and eleven monks signed the petition and swore the oath.

Chaereas also submitted a report to Martialis, the count and master of divine offices. It included the minutes of a hearing at which Count Theodosius was present. The latter asked Chaereas to bring an end to the tumults that arose on account of Ibas's "many acts subversive of the laws and adverse to the Christian faith."[129] Chaereas asked all those who signed the petition to come forward and confirm that they had submitted it. Then he asked the presbyters among them to state their indictment. Presbyter Samuel referred to Ibas's "habit of everywhere scattering gold abroad for the condemnation of the truth."[130]

Only charge number 8 in the four presbyters' plaint accused Ibas of unsound faith, but it is the one on which the minutes of Ibas's third (Ephesus 449) and fourth (Chalcedon 451) trials focus. Ibas was deposed at his third trial in Ephesus on the basis of that charge alone (or perhaps also in addition to the charge of sacrilege). He was rehabilitated at his fourth trial in Chalcedon on the basis of his exoneration from that charge. As part of the terms of reconciliation, Ibas promised to appoint a steward from among the clergy to administer ecclesial property and revenue.

The Council of Chalcedon issued canon 26 in response to the problems raised by Ibas and his nephew Daniel's administrative misconduct.[131] It codified into a general rule what the bishops Photius of Tyre, Eustathius of Berytus, and Uranius of Hemerium had required of Ibas so as to reconcile him to his clerical plaintiffs in 449: the appointment of an oeconomus to manage the property of the church of Edessa as was the rule in Antioch.[132] The Council of Chalcedon undid the act of deposition at Ephesus in 449 and reverted to the disciplinary decision of the second trial by issuing a canon. The twenty-sixth canon of the Council of Chalcedon generalized the discipline imposed on Ibas into a rule that all churches had to follow. The canon obliged every bishop to administrate ecclesial property through an appointed oeconomus.[133] In other words, Ibas's case led to translocal reorganization of ecclesial property administration. It would become the duty of a new staff

member, each bishop's deputy administrator or oeconomus, to prevent misconduct and ensure that sacred things were treated as sacred things.

Dioscorus of Alexandria was also tried at Chalcedon. One of the plaintiffs
was his predecessor Cyril's nephew, the presbyter Athanasius. Athanasius reacted
against the ways in which Dioscorus asserted the rights of the church over its
properties, and he presented the most detailed plaint against Dioscorus. A legal
debacle can be reconstructed from this plaint. Athanasius began by describing the
will of his uncle, Cyril, Dioscorus's episcopal predecessor:

> In the will he [Cyril] made when about to die he honoured his successor as bishop,
> whoever that might be, with many large legacies from his own estate, adjuring him
> in writing, by the venerable and awesome mysteries, to comfort his family and not
> to cause it any trouble.[134]

This statement suggests that Cyril's relatives held ecclesial properties. Cyril
bequeathed his future successor a gift so that his relatives might benefit from
ecclesial property after his death.[135]

On the basis of Athanasius's plaint and the legal-canonical context, I recon-
struct the legal battle as follows. Dioscorus took legal action to reclaim ecclesial
property from Cyril's kin. He demanded houses, adjoining buildings, porches,
and the revenue that had accrued from the properties. When the family refused,
Dioscorus confiscated the property, converted the houses into churches, and
exiled the family. Dioscorus sent a report regarding the case to a civil official, the
master of the offices. The family appealed to Constantinople, where the civil official upheld Dioscorus's decision and required the family to pay what was due. If
the property had been held unlawfully, they would have owed all the gains they
accrued during the entire term of its unlawful use. They would also owe any fines
imposed for their illegal activity. Athanasius lists enormous amounts of money
that the master of the offices required of Athanasius and his kin: 1,400 pounds
of gold from Cyril's nephews, eighty-five pounds of gold from Cyril's sisters, and
forty pounds of gold from Cyril's grandnephews.[136]

Neither an oral nor a written investigation ensued because Dioscorus refused
all three summonses to appear for trial.[137] Yet the council nevertheless put a
measure in place to ensure the sanctity of ecclesial property. The synod ignored
Athanasius's appeal and issued a canon that responded directly to the situation.
Since the presbyter Athanasius's appeal concerned properties he and his family
illegally held after Cyril's death and before Dioscorus's appointment, canon 22 pro-
hibits clerics from taking ecclesial property during the vacancy of a see.

Ibas avoided deposition at the Council of Chalcedon by making a sufficient
show of good faith and by agreeing to submit to the disciplinary action the synod
imposed. Still, the synod made an extra effort to keep sacred things inviolable. The
assembly issued a canon requiring not only Ibas but every bishop to have a deputy
assistant for the administration of sacred things. As for Dioscorus, even though

he refused to appear for trial, the synod nevertheless recognized the judiciousness of his administrative actions. The assembly issued a canon against the presbyter who appealed the actions Dioscorus took to reclaim ecclesial property. The synod wrote a rule specifying that no cleric was entitled to take ecclesial property during the vacancy of a see. Even if a bishop passed the test of faith, as Ibas did, the synod would still issue regulations to ensure proper administration of ecclesial property. Even if a bishop refused to appear for trial, as Dioscorus did, the synod would still compose rules to assert the inviolability of sacred things.

Episcopal trials were not only about theological controversy or sacred faith. The trials were also about sacred things. Photius of Tyre recognized the importance of faith, but he also mentioned conduct, especially financial misconduct. The emperors Leo and Anthemius, as mentioned above, connected the dots between faith and ecclesial property. According to their logic, faith and ecclesial property should be as eternal as the mother church herself. Late antique bishops were not only supposed to defend the faith. They were supposed to defend tangible, sacred things, too. Late antique bishops' administrative duty was to make sacred things as eternal as the faith itself.

RULES ON LOANS, DETENTION, AND LEASE

Rules on Loans (Hypothecation)

Whereas alienation resulted in an indefinite loss of ecclesial property, there were also temporary ways in which ecclesial property could be divested. Under Justinian the issue of the hypothecation of ecclesial property in Constantinople arose. Hypothecation was a kind of security deposit: property would be given to the creditor as security for the repayment of a loan. Justinian initially forbade the hypothecation of ecclesial property in a rescript to Bishop Epiphanius of Constantinople in 535.[138] The penal clause states that the creditor would be deprived of his credit and the creditor could have an action against the person who contracted the loan. Nine years later, in 544, Justinian wrote to the praetorian prefect of the East, Peter, permitting hypothecation of ecclesial property in Constantinople, but he added a condition for loan repayment.[139] If the bishop, steward, or manager received a loan, it could not be charged to the venerable house, unless they first showed that it went to the use of the venerable house. Otherwise, the creditor had no right of action against the venerable house, but rather against the person or his heirs who received the loan.

Rules on Detention and Lease (Usufruct and Emphyteusis)

Though ecclesial property could not be alienated, it could be detained (held in usufruct) or leased (held by emphyteusis). Usufruct was a temporary detention of land, by which the usufructuary could make use of the property only for his or her own needs.[140] The property itself was a *res sacra* and any revenue that exceeded the usufructuary's needs accrued to the church. Emphyteutic leases could be bequeathed over the course of one or two generations, or even permanently ("perpetual emphyteusis").[141] Laws and canons ensured that the detained or leased property remained ecclesial property, that detentions or leases were profitable to the church, and that due process was followed by all parties involved.

Usufruct.   Of the three extant laws on ecclesial usufruct, two concern the terms of the agreement and one limits the individuals eligible for the detention. The emperors Leo and Anthemius addressed a law in 470 to the praetorian prefect of the East, Armasius, regarding the usufruct of ecclesial property.[142] Ecclesiastical stewards could grant temporary usufruct of ecclesial property. Once the period agreed on expired or the usufructuary died, twice the amount of returns and the estate with its immovable property, servile tenants, and slaves had to be given to the church. Justinian reiterated the law in a rescript to Bishop Epiphanius of Constantinople in 535.[143] Ten years later, Justinian restricted the populations eligible for grants of ecclesial usufruct.[144] In a law addressed to the praetorian prefect of the East, Peter, in 545, Justinian ruled that ecclesial property could not be granted in usufruct to heretics. The penal clause stated that the heretic would lose the price and the property of ecclesial lands that he or she held in usufruct, and the contractor would be removed from his post, exiled to a monastery, and denied communion for a year.

Canons primarily regulated clerics and ecclesial freedmen's usufruct of ecclesial property. At the Council of Agde in 506, the synod permitted bishops to allow freedmen the usufruct of property that did not exceed the value of twenty gold solidi.[145] Bishops could also allow clerics and others the usufruct of useless ecclesial property. The Council of Toledo in 527 emphasized that the usufruct was not hereditary.[146] The canon states that once a cleric dies, the usufruct cannot be bequeathed; rather, the land must return to the church. The Council of Lyons in 567 ensured that succeeding bishops would honor the contracts of usufruct granted by their predecessors.[147] It stressed that any penalties imposed on usufructuaries should affect the person, not the property.

Only one known canon concerned the long-term usufruct of ecclesial property. The Council of Orleans in 541 required that the profits made on a lifetime usufruct of ecclesial property be given to the church, not alienated or given to relatives.[148]

Emphyteusis.   Like the lease of imperial property and private property, that of ecclesial property was called "emphyteusis." Justinian issued six laws on the matter of ecclesial emphyteusis, most of which loosened earlier restrictions. One law barred heretics from emphyteusis. Another required clerics to follow due procedure when entering on an emphyteutic agreement.

Around 530, Justinian began to set limits on emphyteutic leases of ecclesial property: restricting who was eligible for the lease and the temporal length of the lease.[149] Ineligible lessees were the poor, the keepers of the archives, and the prefects of the city (even by means of a third party). The penalty for noncompliant stewards was to pay out of their own pocket the same value as the property to be recovered. The penalty for prefects was the same. A fine of twenty pounds of gold applied to both the lessor and the lessee. The reason why property could only be leased to the wealthy was that it had to be restored to its former condition on return. If the property suffered damage, the lessee would be evicted and had to make restitution. As for the temporal length, a church could lease lands for up to twenty years.

In 535, Justinian expanded the temporal length of an ecclesial emphyteutic lease in a rescript to Bishop Epiphanius of Constantinople, but he also shortened the length of the grace period for unpaid rents.[150] An emphyteutic lease could be bequeathed to two heirs. Instead of the customary three-year grace period for the payment of rents, only a two-year period was granted for emphyteusis of *res sacrae*. At the end of the grace period, the church could reclaim the land held under emphyteusis. Perpetual emphyteusis (in which there was no limit to the number of generations over which the lease could be inherited) was forbidden; the penal clause lists loss of the property and perpetual payment of what would have been paid as the punishment for violators.

Only two years later, in 537, Justinian began to make exceptions to the rule against perpetual emphyteusis of ecclesial property in a rescript to Bishop Mena of Constantinople.[151] Such contracts could be made between pious houses, with the exception of Hagia Sophia.

Justinian made a second exception in 544 in a law issued to the praetorian prefect of the East, Peter.[152] Justinian permitted perpetual emphyteusis of ecclesial property in Constantinople in one case only: sacred ruins, which pious houses were unable to restore. Such places could be leased under perpetual emphyteusis, provided that the rental payment amounted to either a third of the income of the buildings when they were still standing or half the income of the buildings after their restoration. The same law allowed for similar contracts of perpetual emphyteusis in the provinces.

The same law mentioned above that excluded heretics from contracting an ecclesial usufruct excluded them from emphyteusis as well.[153] Issued in 545 to Peter, the praetorian prefect of the East, the law penalized noncompliant heretics with loss of the price and the property; the contractor would be removed from his post, exiled to a monastery, and denied communion for a year.

Justinian required clerics to follow due process in contracting an emphyteutic lease. A law issued in 546 to the master of the offices, Peter, set forth a fine schedule to be imposed on noncompliant clerics.[154] If a bishop did not follow due process in leasing ecclesial property through emphyteusis, all his personal property would be confiscated to his church. If it was a steward or other cleric who failed to follow due procedure, then he would owe a pecuniary fine determined by the bishop.[155] The law added a measure of protection to the church against legal action from lessees: anyone who received ecclesial property for the purpose of emphyteusis "[is] to have no action against the church" or any of the administrators.[156]

RULES AGAINST ACTS OF VIOLENCE

Res sacrae were, as outlined above, protected from several different forms of commercial exchanges. They were also sacred precincts in the sense that they were literally inviolable: no acts of violence could be committed and arms were not even permitted on the premises. Churches were protected from not only exterior commerce but also interior damage.

Multiple laws protected churches from acts of violence (*iniuriae*) by imposing capital punishment on perpetrators. Honorius, Marcian, and Justinian all named death as the penalty for acts of "outrage" in churches. Leo stressed proper procedure as the course of action one ought to follow rather than committing outrage in churches. One Gallic canon anathematizes those who commit outrage in churches.

Honorius issued the first extant law on outrage against churches in 409 to the praetorian prefect of Italy and Illyricum, Theodorus.[157] The law instructs that those who commit outrage against a church are guilty of sacrilege and governors in Africa are to punish them with a capital sentence. Members of the municipal council who intentionally overlooked such crimes would suffer confiscation of their property and deportation.

Two laws, one of Marcian and the other of Justinian, and one Gallic canon threatened those who disregarded the safety of churches with severe penalties. In the wake of the Council of Chalcedon, Marcian issued a general constitution exhorting all people to refrain from sedition in the sacrosanct churches and threatening violators with the supreme penalty.[158] Likewise, Justinian would also name death as the penalty for certain misconduct in churches. In 546, Justinian wrote to the master of the offices, Peter, that those who disrupted the holy mysteries or processions or inflicted harm on clerics in the course of services would suffer capital punishment.[159] A council held in Paris around 556 anathematized those who exercised violence against ecclesial property.[160]

Two constitutions of Leo that have been transmitted without dates or recipients show his emphasis on due process. One law forbids anyone who has a dispute with anyone to disturb the church; if imperial assistance should be required, he or she should seek the emperor's audience via the archbishop.[161] Another law indicates that if a disturbance is made in a church, the perpetrator loses his or her cause of action regardless of any protections under the laws; the prefect is to arrest him or her and subject him or her to punishment.[162]

Episcopal synods and imperial consistories alike issued regulations on ecclesial property for the purpose of protecting it. Laws and canons on property damage as well as acquisition, detention, and lease of property demonstrate some of the ways in which such a general principle took shape in specific contexts. Above all, regulatory practices on the matter of alienation reveal the extent to which ecclesial property received special legal and canonical protections. Ecclesial property could not be alienated, but in the event that the alienation of certain goods or lands became advantageous or even necessary for the overall increase of ecclesial assets, exceptions could be made. Even so, episcopal synods would name procedural requirements, such as the assent of multiple bishops to the alienation, to prevent misconduct and safeguard the protection of ecclesial property. The case study below highlights how a specific kind of legal document, the dying bishops' will, could play a role in the protection of ecclesial property.

A CIVIL AND ECCLESIASTICAL TUG OF WAR IN ROME

Symmachus of Rome countered the claims of his episcopal rival Laurentius in the beginning of the sixth century. To do so, Symmachus adopted the opposite strategy to that of the North African bishops described in chapter 1. Whereas the bishops of North Africa endorsed civil regulation to confront their rivals, Symmachus rejected civil rule-making pertaining to ecclesial property. While Laurentius was alive, Theodoric, the Ostrogothic king of Italy from 493 to 526, assisted Symmachus's cause.[163] Later, however, the same king would reject a conciliar decree against civil law that Symmachus promulgated. As we saw in chapter 1, ecclesiastical authorities in the fifth century actively petitioned for civil enforcement and regulation of ecclesiastical affairs. To defend himself against Laurentius's charges, Symmachus argued that there should no longer be any degree of civil governance over ecclesiastical issues and he rewrote old rules to his advantage.

One of Laurentius's charges against Symmachus claimed that the latter had violated a senate resolution issued under Odoacer (who had become king of Italy in 476) by alienating ecclesial property,[164] thereby committing sacrilege and forfeiting his episcopal position. In response, Symmachus summoned a synod to reject the resolution and to issue a new set rules against the alienation of ecclesial property in the form of a canon. The purposes of the canon were (1) to assert episcopal jurisdiction over ecclesiastical rule-making; (2) to subordinate civil law to canon in matters ecclesiastical; and (3), above all, to exonerate Symmachus from Laurentius's charge. The differences between the senate resolution of 483 and Symmachus's synodal canon of 501/2 show that Symmachus rewrote the rules so that his actions could not be considered sacrilegious.

In what follows, I first describe the charge in more detail. Then, I explain how Symmachus responded to it. Finally, I show that although Symmachus's stratagem of pushing civil authorities out of ecclesiastical matters worked in the short term, in the long term the century-long (or more) habit of negotiating ecclesiastical affairs among both civil and ecclesiastical authorities prevailed.

Symmachus's opponents leveled a complaint against him to King Theodoric in 501/2.[165] One issue they raised concerned ecclesial property. According to the entry on Symmachus in the Laurentian Fragment, Symmachus "was accused by the whole Roman clergy of squandering the estates of the church (*ecclesiastica dilapidasse praedia*) contrary to the decree observed by his predecessors, and of thereby entangling himself in the bonds of an anathema."[166] The *Liber pontificalis* suggests that the exconsuls Festus and Probinus drafted the charges.[167] A council held in several sessions from sometime in August to October 23, 501/2 vindicated Symmachus.[168] Laurentius held a synod to appeal the decision. Symmachus called a countersynod to that of Laurentius, and it is on this occasion that he specifically defended himself against the charge of maladministration of ecclesial property.

Symmachus presided over the counter-synod, which met on November 6, 501/2 at Saint Peter's Basilica. The synod undermined a longstanding procedure of operation in which bishops petitioned for civil laws to regulate ecclesiastical affairs. The synod addressed a senate resolution issued by the praetorian prefect Basilius in 483. The resolution, as cited in the synodal acts, says that it was issued in response to Bishop Simplicius of Rome's dying request regarding two issues: (1) that an election for his successor be not held without Basilius's consent; and (2) that ecclesial property be safeguarded from alienation both during the period of papal vacancy and under the tenure of all future popes. Simplicius, like many bishops before him, had sought civil enforcement of ecclesiastical regulations. Symmachus's synod, however, motioned to consider the edict void on the grounds that (1) it was written by a layperson, (2) that laypersons could not regulate the affairs of the church, and (3) that no pope or deputy metropolitan had signed it. To rephrase the council's words in terms of procedure, the council claimed that a canon ought to precede any law pertaining to ecclesiastical affairs. The synod replaced the resolution with a canon against the alienation of ecclesial property. As I will show, the canon permits more exceptions to the rule than the edict does, so as to exonerate Symmachus of sacrilege.[169]

Simplicius had given the praetorian prefect a mandate (*mandatus*) that the prefect, under penalty of oath ("by the adjuration of God" [*sub dei obtestatione*]) should ensure that no ecclesial property would be lost during the period of transition after Simplicius's death.[170] The prefect carried out Simplicius's mandate by calling a meeting of the senate and issuing a senate resolution, a law. The law stated that no ecclesial property could be alienated. Exception was made only for things that could not be kept for a long time, such as fastenings on vestments made of precious stones, gold, or silver. These things could be sold at a fair price to pay the salary of a cleric. The law anathematized anyone who violated the rule.

There are two important differences between the senate resolution and Symmachus's canon. I will explain the first here, but I will postpone discussion of the second to the end of this case study. The first lies in the exception clause. Symmachus's canon allowed urban buildings for which the cost of maintenance exceeded the property value to be alienated. These are the sorts of properties that Symmachus probably alienated and was therefore charged with sacrilege by Laurentius and his supporters. Symmachus rewrote the rule so that his actions would not be illegal.[171] Ennodius, Symmachus's apologist, does not deny the charge.[172] Symmachus avoided the penalty of the edict by undermining its validity and instituting a canon of his own in its place.

The Council of Chalcedon about half a century earlier in 451 had decided that civil mandates which violated ecclesiastical canons would be considered void. Cecropius, the bishop of Sebastopolis, made the following motion and the synod and presiding civil authorities agreed:

> So that your authority may not be saddled with receiving individual plaints, and so that we too should not be overburdened, we ask that the mandates procured by people in every province to the detriment of the canons should be incontrovertibly nullified, and that in all matters the canons should prevail—for in this way will both the faith be protected and each church have security—, and also that it should not be permitted to consecrate anyone contrary to the canons.[173]

The Council of Chalcedon effected a decision that would prevent conflict between canons and laws but that would continue to allow laws to enforce canons.

Symmachus's council went a step further from the decision of the Council of Chalcedon. Laws did not only have to be concordant with canons. Canons had to have temporal precedence over laws. In other words, laws should only reiterate what canons already state. Bishop Simplicius's testamentary mandate and the praetorian prefect's fulfillment of it violated the procedure on which Symmachus's council insisted: that ecclesiastical rules should be made in council and that civil laws should only reinforce them.

Symmachus did succeed in retaining his position as the bishop of Rome, despite Laurentius's charge, but the story does not end there. I propose reading a precept issued by King Theodoric five to seven years later as a direct response to the conflict between the senate resolution of 483 and the canon of 501/2. It is important to name at this point the second significant difference between the senate resolution and Symmachus's canon. Symmachus added a rule on usufruct: no usufruct could be granted to rural ecclesial property (only those clerics, captives, and pilgrims who were already usufructuaries prior to the synod could retain the usufruct). Around the time that the schism ended and Laurentius died, Theodoric wrote the following to the senate in 507/8. It directly addresses the same matter of usufruct:[174]

> A *suggestio* has come to our [attention], father senators, concerning a benefit announced about the church, and an *ordinatio* of your sacred assembly strikes at the pleasing hearts of our clemency. Despite the fact that, after the venerable synod, your *ordinatio* alone should suffice for such a decree of judgment, yet in response to your petition we have granted a *responsum* with this imperial pronouncement (*praesentibus oraculis*): that it is not lawful for any overseer (*antistiti*) of the church anywhere to transfer property by means of alienation. They will bestow its usufruct

on whomever they wish in fairness. The transfer of things ought to be of no effect even by the will of the pontiff alone or for the payment of clerics in any foreign place or by a statute of the church. A judgment is profane as long as it violates this part of the dispensation: while something belongs to the church and someone wishes to have it, persons claim for themselves as private a contract for the usufruct of a thing. Therefore, if someone takes forbidden things by impious attempts and wishes to take something beyond its usufruct with a bishop or cleric dispensing [it], the alienated thing in addition to its fruits are vindicated to the venerable *praesul*.[175]

If we understand *ordinatio* as a reference to the senate resolution of 483, then Theodoric not only declares valid the document that Symmachus tried to undermine. Theodoric also lends his own imperial weight to the decision because he issued the *responsum*, which forbids the alienation of ecclesial property altogether and allows episcopal discretion in the usufruct of ecclesial property. Most importantly, Theodoric does not include the major exceptions that Symmachus and his council allowed. If we read the precept in the way that I have suggested, then Symmachus's efforts to change the nature of the relationship between church and state did not succeed.

In sum, Simplicius of Rome used his will for postmortem regulation of ecclesial property. His effort succeeded and resulted in a law. Two decades later, Symmachus used procedural grounds to question the law and the relationship of church and state, though his ulterior motive was to exonerate himself from a charge of sacrilege. Symmachus's attempt to use ecclesiastical court to overrule civil law met with a response from Theodoric himself, who reinforced civil law in no uncertain terms.

As we saw earlier, Cyril of Alexandria had also used his will as a means to control ecclesial property during a period of transition: from his death to the successor's accession. Like that of Simplicius a few decades later, the legality of Cyril's will was contested. Cyril of Alexandria urged his successor with oaths on the holy mysteries to refrain from taking legal action against Cyril's family. Cyril's attempt at postmortem regulation of ecclesial property failed because Dioscorus did not heed the wish. Cyril's nephew tried first in civil court and then in ecclesiastical court to force Dioscorus's compliance but failed both times. Most importantly, the ecclesiastical court—namely, the Council of Chalcedon—agreed with both Dioscorus's decision and that of the civil official who backed him. In general, the acts of the Council of Chalcedon show efforts to maintain cooperation between church and state.

In the fifth century, dying bishops tried to facilitate administrative transition by means of a legal document: the will.[176] Such a strategy created a situation in which ecclesiastical and civil authorities faced each other's rules. Civil authorities cooperated with ecclesiastics to such an extent that new laws could not be written to overrule existing canons. But cooperation was a two-way street, so likewise new canons could not be used to overrule existing laws, despite Symmachus's assertions to the contrary.

The application of Roman legal principles on *res sacrae* to Christian conse-crated things turned churches and their associated properties into divinely pro-tected places—that is, to places that were owned by no one. The extant evidence of laws and canons shows that bishops were already treating ecclesial property as inalienable before any laws explicitly endorsed the view that Christian holy places are divinely protected.

The divine protection of ecclesial properties meant that special privileges were accorded to them. It was the bishop's responsibility as chief administrator to honor those privileges or else face the charge of sacrilege. As the laws and canons dis-cussed above demonstrate, the details of exemption clauses and the boundaries of episcopal discretion could change from decade to decade and vary from region to region. Details aside, jurists and bishops actively fashioned a concrete idea of "the sacred" and enforced regulations they created to propound and apply the idea. The cases of Ibas of Edessa and Dioscorus of Alexandria offer examples of how such regulations were enforced and new regulations were promulgated. The case of Symmachus of Rome brings to light examples of both cooperation and friction between the civil and ecclesiastical rule-making bodies over the administration of ecclesial property.

The first corollary to the legal-canonical definition of *res sacrae* was that such things were divinely protected. The next chapter turns to the construction of a sec-ond corollary: because such places were divinely protected, they might also serve as places of sanctuary—places where the needy could find and receive God's pro-tection. Juristic pedagogy did not teach this second corollary, but bishops actively petitioned for legal recognition of churches as protecting spaces.

3

Protecting Places

The Visigothic sack of Rome in 410 caused Romans to question the Christian God's protection of their city. In an effort to renew Roman confidence in Christ's triumph, Augustine of Hippo wrote *The City of God*. At the very outset of the work, Augustine argues that God did protect the city. How? All who took refuge in God's houses—that is, the churches—were spared from harm. As Augustine puts it, "Even these ruthless men, who *in other places* customarily indulged their ferocity against enemies, put a rein to their murderous fury and curbed their mania for taking captives, the moment they reached *the holy places*."[1] What a miracle, he points out, that merciless enemies, who otherwise stopped at nothing to capture prisoners of war, had mercy on all who took shelter in churches. Augustine proceeds, in the first six chapters of the work, to catalog the times in Greek and Roman history when the temples of the gods ought to have protected those who sought safety there but failed to do so. The success of asylum in churches, insisted Augustine, proves God's protection.

As we saw in the previous chapter, though episcopal synods and imperial consistories ensured the inviolability of churches in different ways, their aim was the same: to show that *res sacrae* were divinely protected. In principle, what imperially endorsed bishops consecrated remained sacred in perpetuity and therefore could not be repurposed. At the same time, one of the primary duties of bishops was to care for the needy. To fund charitable activities, bishops relied on revenue from revenue-producing lands (the land itself was sacred), donations made for the express purpose of charity, or donations that were not earmarked for any specific purpose. These sources did not suffice, especially for enormously expensive activities, such as ransoming captives. For this reason, bishops actively petitioned that ecclesial property not only be considered protected, but also protecting.

Bishops petitioned lawmakers to establish rules that made churches places where slaves could be manumitted, places of asylum for fugitives, and places that provided for the redemption of captives. In this way, the protected places would extend their protection to vulnerable members of society: slaves, fugitives, and captives. Churches would personify the protection they received and granted. The untouchable *res sacrae* would have the power to make vulnerable members of society untouchable, too, as Augustine emphasized in his opening to *The City of God*.

A law of Leo and Anthemius issued in 469 expresses this bilateral notion of a church's protection: that churches receive protection and grant it as well.[2] In the context of an explanation about how corruption of the clergy via bribes undermines the safety and protection fundamental to sacred places, Leo and Anthemius ask:

> Indeed, what place could be safe (*tutus*), and what cause defended (*excusata*), if the venerable temples of God are conquered by money? What wall shall we raise for integrity, or what rampart for honesty, if the accursed hunger for gold slithers into the innermost sanctuaries? What can be safe (*cautum*) or secure (*securum*), if uncorrupted sanctity itself is corrupted? The profane ardor of greed shall cease to loom over the altars and sinful wantonness shall be driven from the inner sanctums.[3]

The installation of an administrator by bribes prevents the church from providing safety, defense, integrity, or protection. Instead, it threatens (*imminere*) the altars themselves.[4] Administrators who accept bribes would not be likely to judge cases of asylum with integrity, for example. According to Leo and Anthemius, the altars must be protected in order for them to provide protection. The protection granted to churches translates into protection for those in need, particularly slaves, refugees, and captives.

This chapter shows how bishops petitioned for churches to be spaces offering protection to slaves, refugees, and captives. Jurists justified such legal recognition by making it an extension of the long, well-established principle that *res sacrae* are protected. As part II will show, some bishops argued that the opposite was true: *res sacrae* were protected because they were protecting, not vice versa.

MANUMISSION OF SLAVES

One way in which churches extended their protection to slaves was by serving as the public place of their manumission. As the following rules show, laws and canons set forth measures to ensure social stability among all the parties involved or interested in the public manumission of a slave in a church. In general, the rules protected the manumitted slave from challenges to his or her new social status and they protected the former master and the church itself from threats, such as expressions of ingratitude, to the honor of their patronage.

The laws on the manumission of slaves in churches state the procedure of manumission, explain the legal force of ecclesial manumission, and name specific categories of slaves who were eligible for manumission without the permission of their masters. Most of the laws were issued in response to episcopal petitions.

The canons, on the other hand, primarily concern the obligations of the church to the freedman and those of the freedman to the church. Since the manumission of ecclesial slaves (i.e., slaves that belonged to the church) could be conceived as a violation of the inalienability of ecclesial property, some canons declare that manumission is not a form of alienation.[5]

Laws on the Manumission of Slaves in Churches

Four extant laws concern the manumission of slaves in churches. Two were issued by Constantine to specific bishops; these mention the procedure for granting manumission in churches and they guarantee the legal force of the grant. The only other emperors from whom laws on the manumission of slaves in the churches survive are Honorius and Justinian, both of whom legislated about the manumission of the slaves of noncatholic masters.

The first extant law of Constantine concerning manumission in the churches was addressed as a response to a petition of Protogenes, the bishop of Serdica, in 316, explicitly allowing him to manumit slaves, since "we decreed long ago that masters could manumit their slaves in a Catholic church."[6] The law explains that the typical procedure consisted of (1) manumission in the presence of the people and bishops and (2) the composition of a legal document, which the attending bishops signed as witnesses. The second was addressed as a response to a petition from Hosius, bishop of Corduba, only five years later in 321.[7] It guarantees that the manumission of slaves in churches (via the same procedure described to Protogenes) grants the former slaves Roman citizenship.[8]

Honorius's law, issued in 405, might have been made in response to episcopal petitions planned in 401 from Carthage. It allowed slaves of Donatist masters to seek asylum and manumission in catholic churches.[9] Similarly, Justinian wrote to the praetorian prefect of the East, John, sometime between 533 and 534, allowing the slaves of Jews, pagans, and heretics to be manumitted in the catholic churches, provided that they join the church.[10] He explicitly notes that their masters may not receive any compensation for them and that the judges of the provinces, the defenders of the church, and the bishops were required to ensure their protection.

Canons on the Manumission of Slaves in Churches

As for the canons, they address four issues: (1) the need for civil recognition and support of certain manumissions; (2) the church's protection of those it manumits and the obligations of such freedmen to the church; (3) the manumission of slaves that belong to the churches; and (4) whether abbots may manumit slaves.

An anthology that the monk Dionysius Exiguus compiled in the sixth century, referred to as *Registri Ecclesiae Carthaginensis Excerpta*, collects excerpts from the acts of councils held in Carthage. According to the anthology, two councils held in Carthage in June and September 401 resolved that the emperor should be petitioned to grant churches in North Africa similar manumission rights to those of churches in Italy.[11] No laws concerning manumission in the churches addressed to Italy survive, so it is not clear what sort of precedent the bishops gathered at Carthage adduced. Honorius did, however, issue a law to North Africa four years later.[12] As mentioned above, it allowed catholic churches to manumit the slaves of Donatist masters. Perhaps Honorius issued it in response to the petitions from Carthaginian councils.

Six canons show that the grant of manumission in the church was not simply a one-time act; rather, it placed binding obligations both on the church and on the freedman. Churches had to protect the freedom of their freedmen from any threats. In return, freedmen were obligated to show gratitude to the church and to obey the church. A council at Nimes, Gaul, in 394/396 permitted the excommunication of freedmen who opposed the church (*contra ecclesia ueniunt*), citing the burden (*iniuria*) of protecting (*tuitio*) such freedmen as justification for their excommunication.[13] The Councils of Orange in 441 and Orleans in 549 stated the obligation of the church to protect its freedmen from reenslavement.[14] The Council of Orange ruled that the church had to censure those who reenslaved freedmen manumitted in the church, whether to slavery or to the colonate. A collection of canons made in Arles sometime between 442 and 506 includes one that requires accusations of a freedman's ingratitude to be heard in a civil court.[15] In 541, the Council of Orleans noted that the freedom of a bishop's freedmen was contingent on their continued service to the church.[16] A council held in Toledo in 589 guaranteed the protection of the church to those it manumitted as well as those manumitted by others at the recommendation of the bishop.[17]

Two canons affirm the fact that the manumission of slaves of the church was not tantamount to alienation of ecclesial property. The first, from the collection known as "Ps-Agde," states that ecclesial property is inalienable, but if bishops, presbyters, and deacons manumitted an ecclesial slave, the deed was considered an act of the church (*actum ecclesiae*).[18] Likewise, a canon from a council in Orleans in 541 did not permit a bishop to mortgage, financially burden, or sell ecclesial property unless he bequeathed the church equal value from his personal property.[19] The canon adds a qualification to the rule: the slaves whom he has freed remain free.

Though no canon outlines the procedure for manumission in the churches, Constantine's rescripts to Protogenes of Serdica in 316 and Hosius of Corduba in 321 suggest that only bishops could perform this legal function.[20] The problem of other leaders assuming such a role arose only, as far as the evidence of canons shows, in Epaon, where a canon from a council held 517 denies abbots the right to manumit ecclesial slaves.[21]

Finally, it is worth noting that although Gaul was not part of Justinian's empire, a canon from a council at Orleans allowed in 541 what Justinian had permitted in 533 and 534. Canon 30 states that churches may manumit the slaves of Jewish masters by purchasing their freedom.[22] Justinian's law, however, explicitly denied Jewish masters compensation for the loss of their slaves.[23]

ASYLUM OF REFUGEES

Bishops and jurists alike legislated on the matter of fugitives' asylum in churches, but their particular concerns differed. Bishops issued canons affirming the authority of churches to grant asylum to all who sought it and protecting both refugees and ecclesiastical administrators from the fugitives' prosecutors. Jurists, on the other hand, promulgated laws to limit the demographic eligible for asylum, to draw the spatial boundaries of ecclesial property on which asylum could be granted, and to hold ecclesiastical administrators responsible for bypassing civil procedure. The two rule-making bodies initially disagreed on the definition of ecclesial asylum. Ecclesiastical administrators wanted full discretion in seeking pardon for refugees. Jurists, especially in the fourth and sixth centuries, wanted to limit the scope of ecclesiastical clemency and prevent excessive proliferation of cases of appeals. The most important issue over which they were divided was the matter of forcible seizure of an unarmed refugee from the place of ecclesial asylum. The laws demanded the arrest of certain kinds of refugees, but bishops petitioned against forcible seizure altogether. There are two traceable points of interaction between the two rule-making bodies, when bishops of Carthage petitioned Emperor Honorius for a law. By the middle of the fifth century, laws civilly recognized a robust definition of the status of churches as places of asylum, but laws written during Justinian's tenure would once again place limits on ecclesial asylum.[24]

Before discussing the evidence of the canons and laws it is important to sketch an image of the motions that could take place between the defendant, the ecclesiastical administrator, the prosecutor, the judge, or other civil authorities, if the defendant sought ecclesiastical asylum. A defendant could seek asylum at a church at two possible periods of time: (1) before a trial or (2) after a civil judicial decision on the case was made.

Before a trial commenced, ecclesiastical administrators could engage in a negotiation (*intercessio*) directly with the prosecutors on the matter and indemnify the defendant from certain damages to his or her person or property by having the prosecutor swear an oath or sign a letter of security (*cautela*). If the prosecutor refused to accept the terms stipulated by the ecclesiastical administrators, then he might have the defendant forcibly seized (*abstrahere*) from the church and put on trial. The ecclesiastical administrators could in turn respond with an excommunication of the prosecutor. If the arrest were made without a judge's demand for it, the judge would have to decide whether the prosecutor was justified in making the arrest.

In the event that one or more trials already took place and the defendant pursued an appeal, the ecclesiastical administrators could help the defendant make the appeal of a former decision. If the appeal were accepted by the civil authorities, then the judge would have to sign a letter of security indemnifying the defendant from certain personal or proprietary damages in order for the ecclesiastical administrators to release the defendant. If the appeal were denied, then the civil authorities could forcibly seize the defendant. The ecclesiastical administrators could in turn respond with an excommunication of the prosecutor or the civil authorities.

Canons on Ecclesial Asylum

As for the evidence of canons, it largely stems from Gaul. Two fourth-century canons were issued in Asia Minor and North Africa regarding asylum, but the rest of the extant canonical evidence comes from fifth- and sixth-century Gaul.

That No One May Be Denied Asylum.   The Council of Serdica in 343 set forth a canon prohibiting bishops from going to the civil courts to advocate on behalf of defendants, unless expressly invited to do so by the emperor.[25] By way of qualification, the canon added that bishops could seek pardon for those who "flee to the mercy of the church" (the late antique expression for "asylum seeker" is *ad misericordiam ecclesiae confugiant*), regardless of whether the asylum seeker was a victim of wrongdoing or a condemned offender.[26] The Council of Agde in 506 and that of Macon in 585 guaranteed asylum to particular demographics: freedmen and slaves, respectively.[27] The canon produced by the Council of Macon included a rhetorical question that depended on two premises to prove the right of churches to grant asylum: (1) that church property fell under divine protection and (2) that divine law was of a higher order than human law. The synod's reasoning invoked the right of asylum at statues of the emperor: "If even worldly leaders judge in their laws that whoever should flee to their statues have asylum, how much more ought the uncondemned remain [in asylum] who have reached the protection of the immortal, celestial kingdom?"[28] The synod argued that if imperial protection affords asylum, there should be no question about whether divine protection can grant asylum or not.

That Asylum May Be Sought on Church Premises.   The Council of Orleans in 511 cited "canonical and Roman law" (*quod ecclesiastici canones decreuerunt et lex Romana constituit*) to rule that criminals, such as murderers, adulterers, and thieves, would fall under the protection of asylum if they reached the atrium of the church or even a house of the church or the bishop's residence (*ab ecclesiae atriis uel domum ecclesiae uel domum episcopi*).[29] The synod invoked the precedent of unspecified canons and laws to show that the lands on which divine protection rested consisted not only of the church building itself but of associated properties, such as the atrium and residencies. No other canons survive that prescribe the spatial limits of ecclesial asylum, but it was certainly the preoccupation of jurists to identify such boundaries, as we will see below.

That the Refugee May Not Be Forcibly Removed from the Place of Asylum or Put to Flight.   The entry in Dionysius Exiguus's anthology for the Council of Carthage held in 399 records that two bishops, Epigonius and Vincentius, were sent as conciliar delegates to Emperor Honorius to request a law forbidding the forcible seizure of any fugitive who obtained ecclesial asylum, regardless of the nature of his or her crime.[30] The law that was eventually produced as a result of this episcopal petition and a later one will be discussed below. One fifth-century and several sixth-century councils that met at Orleans, Gaul, reiterated and elaborated on the rule, for which bishops at Carthage had sought civil support. In 441, the Council of Orleans prohibited masters from removing their asylum-seeking slaves from ecclesial property.[31] In 511, another council at Orleans stated that murderers, adulterers, and thieves who found asylum in a church could not be forcibly removed.[32] Canon 3 of the same council forbade masters of refugee slaves from removing them from the precincts of asylum. Thirty years later, at the Council of Orleans in 541, penalties were added against those who violated the rule. Anyone who forcibly removed a refugee or forced him or her to flee the ecclesial place of asylum would face excommunication until the refugee was returned.[33] The council in 549 applied the same penalty specifically to masters who forcibly removed their slaves.[34]

That Prosecutors Must Make an Oath in order for the Refugee to Leave the Place of Asylum, but If the Refugee Willingly Leaves Beforehand, the Church Cannot Be Held Responsible.   Several canons required that the prosecutor swear an oath before the refugee could leave the place of asylum.[35] The canon issued at Epaon in 517 explains the purpose of the oath in detail. The oath protects the refugee from suffering two kinds of penalties as a result of his or her crime: corporal punishment and death. According to the canon, haircutting and hard labor, however, do not count as "corporal punishment," so the meting out of such punishments would not violate the oath.[36] The Council of Orleans in 511 decided that oath breakers would suffer excommunication.[37] The same council absolved clerics of responsibility for the fate of refugees who left the place of asylum of their own accord.[38]

Councils held at Orleans demanded more of non-Christian prosecutors. Jewish masters of Christian slaves had to leave a deposit (equivalent in value to the price of the refugee slave) with the bishop in order to claim their slaves from ecclesial asylum.[39] Non-Christian prosecutors had to find a Christian to make the oath on his or her behalf, since the penalty of excommunication for breaking the oath could apply only to a Christian.[40]

Appropriate Courses of Action for Specific Circumstances.   Three councils at Gaul prescribed courses of action in response to specific circumstances. At Orange in 441, the episcopal gathering ruled against masters who confiscated a cleric's slave to replace the slave protected by ecclesial asylum.[41] The Synod of Orleans in 511 decided on the punishment that kidnappers of women would face in lieu of death or corporal punishment if the kidnappers sought refuge in the church: slavery.[42] At Orleans in 541, the synod allowed churches to purchase the freedom of refugee Christian slaves from Jewish masters.[43]

Laws on Ecclesial Asylum

In the fifth century, the jurists conceded to the wishes of bishops by supporting expansions to the practice of ecclesial asylum, but in the centuries preceding and following it, jurists limited the scope. In the course of the fourth century, bakers, public debtors, heretics, Jews, disruptors of the public peace, and those convicted of particularly heinous crimes would be expressly denied asylum benefits. In the years 392 to 398, laws were issued to Egypt and the East requiring judges and ecclesiastical administrators to follow civil procedures for appeals and not to bypass them in the name of ecclesial protection. The laws of 392 concerned judges. Judges could not allow clerical intercession to sidestep civil procedure. In other words, judges were not allowed to reduce a sentence or a penalty in a negotiation with clerics that exceeded the limitations of the procedure for appeals. The purpose of ecclesial asylum was to protect refugees from extreme penalties and for clerics to negotiate for mercy toward the criminal, but negotiations had to occur within the framework of an appeal (*appellatio* or *provocatio*).[44] The law of 398 concerned ecclesiastical administrators. Just as judges could not *accept* inappropriate requests for appeals, so also ecclesiastical administrators could not *submit* inappropriate requests for appeals.

The laws directed against bakers and public debtors consider asylum to be a pretext for evading responsibility. Valentinian I addressed a law in 364 to Rome, stating that ecclesial asylum cannot protect individuals from their membership to the association of bread making.[45] The guild could recall refugee bread makers at any time. Theodosius I likewise addressed a law to the count of the sacred imperial largesse in 392 preventing public debtors from avoiding exaction of their debt through asylum.[46] Theodosius I added a penalty against clerics who nevertheless harbored public debtors: the clerics would personally be liable to pay the public debt as a punishment for offering asylum to persons to whom it was forbidden.

Heretics and Jews were denied ecclesial asylum benefits as well. In the wake of the Council of Constantinople in 381, Theodosius I issued a law to the prefect of Illyricum against those who rejected the council's rule of faith.[47] Theodosius I forbade heretics from crossing the threshold of churches (*ecclesiarum limine penitus arceantur*).[48] In 397, Arcadius wrote to the prefect of Egypt that Jews were not to be permitted asylum.[49] In fact, like the heretics, Jews were to be forced to leave (*arceantur*).[50]

In 392, Theodosius I legislated against the grant of asylum to disruptors of the public peace in Egypt and convicts of heinous crimes in the East. In Egypt, judges were not allowed to permit convicts "who by the disorder of their acts and by rebellious contumacy confound and disturb the public peace" to appeal their case as a concession to mediating clerics, otherwise the judges and office staff would face a fine of thirty pounds of gold.[51] Theodosius I similarly forbade judges in the East in 392 from waiving or reducing a penalty or sentence on account of clerical intercession or clerical hostage of the criminal, if the convict was judged guilty of a grave crime (*maximus criminis*).[52] Judges and their office staff could be fined fifteen or thirty pounds of gold, depending on the rank of the office, for granting ecclesial asylum in such cases of heinous crimes.

A law issued in 398 addressed the problem of judges and ecclesiastical administrators in the East who contravened civil procedure in the name of ecclesial protection. The grand chamberlain Eutropius petitioned Arcadius for legislation against ecclesiastical administrators in the East.[53] Two relevant excerpts of the law in the Theodosian Codex show that clerics were forbidden from offering asylum once the legal time limit for submitting a *provocatio* (appeal) elapsed and that civil authorities were obliged to forcibly seize particular kinds of individuals from ecclesial asylum. If the time limit (between the declaration of a sentence and its execution) elapsed, clerics could not "vindicate and hold by force or by any usurpation persons who have been sentenced to punishment and condemned for the enormity of their crimes."[54] Slaves (*servi*), maidservants (*ancillae*), decurions (*curiales*), public debtors (*debitores publici*), procurators (*procuratores*), collectors of purple dye fish (*mureliguli*), and anyone involved in public or private accounts (*quilibet* [. . .] *publicis privatisqve rationibus involutus*) could be forcibly seized for seeking ecclesial asylum.[55] The law penalizes ecclesiastical stewards by requiring that they pay the debts of those that clerics defended.

The laws of the fifth century expanded the limits set in the fourth century. Bishops of Carthage may have effectively petitioned for the first piece of extensive legislation issued to the entire empire by Honorius and Theodosius II. As mentioned above, a synod at Carthage in 399 sent bishops Vincentius and Epigonius to petition for legislation guaranteeing that no refugees could be forcibly seized from churches.[56] An episcopal petition with a similar cause was sent in 419, and it is possible that one law of Honorius and Theodosius II was made in order to respond to the matter. By 445, a comprehensive piece of legislation was made to fully recognize churches as places of asylum for all refugees and to permit the forcible seizure of refugees under no circumstances.

Two laws issued prior to 419 began the expansion of limits to ecclesial asylum and concerned slaves and Jews. In 405, Honorius encouraged the slaves of

Donatist masters in Italy and North Africa to seek asylum in churches in order to avoid rebaptism.[57] While Arcadius in 397 did not permit Jews asylum in churches, and even stipulated that Jews had to be clear of criminal offenses and debt before they could convert to Christianity,[58] Honorius and Theodosius II in 416 offered more leniency. In a law addressed to an otherwise unknown Annas, whose title was Didascalus (he was either the leader of a synagogue or teacher of the law),[59] the two emperors ruled that Jews would be permitted to join a church and seek asylum there. However, if those Jews did not remain faithful to the church, then judges were obliged to revoke the pardon negotiated by the clerics and enforce the original sentence.[60]

The years 419, 431, and 445 witnessed the height of legal expansiveness regarding ecclesial asylum. In 419, Honorius and Theodosius II established two new rules in response to episcopal petitions.[61] They may have responded to two Carthaginian petitions, one sent in 399 and another in 419.[62] Augustine mentions the latter petition in three of his letters.[63] His letters claim that Bishop Alypius of Thagaste had traveled to the imperial court in Ravenna to seek a decision regarding the case of refugees at a church in Carthage and that a copy of the decision had been sent to Largus, the proconsul of Africa, but that Augustine himself is still awaiting the news concerning the content of the decision. Honorius and Theodosius II's law of 419 is not addressed to Largus; in fact, it names no addressee, and it therefore may have been designated for general application. According to the first new rule established in the law, the boundary of the ecclesial space of asylum no longer ended at the doors of the church but extended fifty paces beyond it. Second, bishops were permitted to visit prisons to learn of cases and to negotiate with the relevant judge on behalf of prisoners. The matter of ecclesial asylum was so sacred (*sancta*), according to the law, that doorkeepers of prisons would be fined two pounds of gold for refusing a bishop entrance.[64]

Theodosius II addressed the first comprehensive law on ecclesial asylum to the East on March 23, 431.[65] The law was posted in Greek translation only a few weeks later in Alexandria on April 7.[66] "Those who are afraid" (*timentes*) may seek the church's protection.[67] The places of asylum included the altars, the surrounding oratory, the space in front of the outside doors of the church, any intervening space, and any space within the outer doors of the church behind the public grounds (cells, houses, gardens, baths, courtyards, colonnades). Forcible seizure of refugees was prohibited and violation of this prohibition amounted to sacrilege, except in one case only.[68] Fugitives could not bear arms into the place of asylum; but if armed fugitives were unwilling to relinquish their arms at the request of the clerics, the bishop, the emperor, or the judges could demand forcible seizure of the refugee. As further restrictions on the behavior of the refugee, the law prohibited eating or sleeping in the temple or in the altar. In fact, part of the purpose for expanding the demarcation lines of asylum was to prevent refugees from using the altar or church space for dining and overnight accommodation. The law mentions boundary marks for the extent of the protective area, and some inscriptions survive that indicate the boundaries of asylum at sacred places.[69]

One year later, Theodosius II supplemented the law of 431 with an addendum limiting the amount of time slaves could spend at the place of asylum to one day and setting forth the procedure that clerics and masters had to follow.[70] Clerics were supposed to notify the slave's master or the person from whose punishment the slave had fled. The master had to grant pardon to the slave and escort him or her out of the church. A different procedure applied to slaves who entered the church armed. Masters were to forcibly seize armed slaves from the church and were not liable for the slave's death, should the slave die in a struggle. Noncompliant clerics were to "be removed from that place which they could not protect" (*loco eo, quem tueri nequivere, submoti*), be subject to episcopal trial, and be defrocked.[71]

Leo issued the most comprehensive legislation on ecclesial asylum in 445. He legislated on the matter twice in the month of February of that year. The first law simply affirmed that all the privileges churches enjoyed as places of asylum must be respected.[72] The second detailed the most extensive rules on ecclesial asylum and procedures that applied to all regions of the East, except the city of Constantinople.[73] According to the comprehensive law, no fugitives could be expelled, delivered, or dragged from the church and the areas of asylum set forth in previous laws. In contrast to Theodosius I's law of 392 discussed above,[74] refugees' debts could not be exacted from the bishops or stewards. Refugees could not be detained or restrained to the point that they should be denied food, clothing, or rest. There were limits to the length of a refugee's stay, but the exact time frame was left to the discretion of the ecclesiastical administrators: refugees could not reside so long in the church that they would be supported to the detriment of the poor and needy. The law outlines specific procedures to be followed for dealing with refugee defendants of a civil action in connection with a private or public contract and with refugee slaves who destroyed property, stole property, or withdrew from the power of their master. The steward of the church was required to examine each refugee carefully. Violators of the rules of asylum would suffer "capital and ultimate punishment."[75]

Less than one century later, Justinian would revert to some of the limitations that had been set before the fifth-century expansions made between 419 and 445. He would also establish new limitations. In 535, Justinian instructed his provincial governors about how to carry out his policies. Regarding ecclesial asylum, Justinian summarized his overall policy as follows: "the safety of holy places has been granted by law for the benefit of those who suffer injustice, not those who inflict it. It would not be possible to assert the safety of inviolable places for them, both criminal and victim alike."[76] By contrast, Augustine argued one century earlier that if churches did not protect the unjust, then the just would find no protection either.[77] For him, it was precisely because the just rightly deserved protection that the unjust required protection as well. By allowing forcible seizure of the unjust, mistakes would invariably be made to the detriment of the just.[78] Some of Justinian's laws would explicitly name the categories of criminals who "inflict harm."

The same instruction to the governors already mentioned some of the categories of criminals who "inflict wrong" and would therefore be ineligible for ecclesial asylum: those who commit homicide, adulterers, ravishers of virgins, and public debtors. Theodosius I had excluded public debtors and convicts of heinous crimes from the benefits of ecclesial asylum in 392,[79] but no extant laws prior to those of Justinian explicitly excluded the first three categories of criminals—murderers, adulterers, and ravishers of virgins. The period for determining whether a letter of asylum should be given could not exceed thirty days. If someone brought a suit against the asylum seeker and a decision was made against him or her, he or she could either revoke the asylum and comply or receive the judgment at the sacred enclosures (τοῖς ἱεροῖς ὅροις) "with the reverence due to the pure enclosures" (μετὰ τῆς ὀφειλούσης τοῖς εὐαγέσιν ὅροις αἰδοῦς).[80] In a general law concerning the dissolution of marriages issued in 542, Justinian cited his instructions to governors to address the issue of asylum-seeking adulterers.[81] The law targets those who commit the act of adultery in the church. Justinian calls this act of sin in a church as contempt of the church and pollution of the church: "Such persons ought not to have the protection of a venerable place which they have themselves held in contempt with their uncleanness. [. . . They shall] suffer the penalties that those who dare to defile most holy places deserve (τιμωρίαν ὑπομένειν ἧς ἄξιοι καθεστᾶσιν οἱ τοὺς ἁγιωτάτους τόπους μολύνειν τολμῶντες). For where is the hope for those who commit sin in such places?"[82]

Another law of 535 would name the last explicit category of criminals excluded from the protection of the churches: violators of the Christian faith. Justinian addressed a law to North Africa in which he named "violators of the Christian faith" alongside murderers and ravishers of virgins.[83] Justinian's reasoning for the exclusion of such individuals echoes that of his overall policy cited above: "The holy church cannot both help the wicked and offer its assistance to the victims of harm."[84] Justinian considered the ecclesial protection of certain criminals and impious persons to be mutually exclusive from that of victims.

Justinian's most detailed instructions regarding ecclesial asylum concerned public debtors. As the following paragraphs show, he initially outlawed asylum for fiscal causes altogether; he then permitted asylum for setting a schedule of indemnification and providing a security. The asylum, however, would only protect the debtor from molestation, not from the penalty of exile altogether.

Edict 2, probably issued before Novel 17, "forb[ade] all most distinguished provincial governors to grant the right of asylum in fiscal cases."[85] Even asylum granted in private causes of debt had to be limited in time and nonrenewable. An edict issued in 545 addressed the provincial prefects specifically regarding their apparitors' embezzlement of fiscal funds.[86] If provincial apparitors sought asylum for embezzling money they collected for the fiscal treasury, the bishops had to receive the letter of safety, lead them out of the sacred enclosure, and deliver them to the public servants who would lead them into exile where they would live as though within sacred enclosure. Noncompliant clergy were to indemnify the fisc out of their personal property and were threatened with deposition.

In 538 or 539, when Justinian wrote to the prefect of the East to reorganize the region of Egypt, he included detailed instructions regarding asylum for fiscal causes, especially when it was sought by civil authorities.[87] In matters that pertained to the fiscal treasury, the prefect, and his staff, the bishop of Alexandria could not grant any letters of asylum, unless the asylum was requested only for the purpose of assistance (in indemnifying the fisc). The asylum seekers had to accept the grant of asylum "on condition of appearing in public and, without fail, paying what they owe to the public treasury within a stated number of days, or providing the *scriniarii* or administrators with sufficient security."[88] The civil authorities could use their own discretion in setting time limits for such letters of asylum, but the bishop of Alexandria could only set the limits that the office determined (otherwise the letter was void and the person was subject to exaction even within the sacred enclosures). The stewards and defenders of the churches would be liable to pay out of their personal pocket and that of the archbishop; then, if a balance remained, they would have to pay out of the property of the church. The significance of this cannot be underestimated, since legislation generally favored the increase of ecclesial assets and even established measures to safeguard them against diminution. If the stewards acted contrary to the bishops, they would not only be liable to the debt; they would be removed from their position as steward and would be defrocked. Civil authorities, for their dishonesty to the fisc and for making compulsion necessary, would have their property confiscated, and they would have to live in perpetual exile on the coasts of the Black Sea (the "Hospitable Sea," *Pontus Euxinus*) at Sebastopol and Pityus (cities on the modern-day Crimean Peninsula).[89]

As the foregoing analysis of laws and canons shows, ecclesial properties in the fourth through the sixth century became protecting bodies. Ecclesiastical administrators offered the church's protection to all who sought it and petitioned emperors for civil laws that defined ecclesial asylum in such a robust way. Emperors of the fourth century and, later, in the sixth century did recognize ecclesial asylum, but they limited its scope. They made certain criminals ineligible and they required both civil authorities and ecclesiastical administrators to comply with civil procedures. By contrast, in the fifth century, Theodosius II and Leo issued laws that recognized a wider definition of ecclesial asylum.

REDEMPTION OF CAPTIVES

When Honorius and Theodosius II delimited the parts of ecclesial property that legally counted as places of asylum, they justified the need for the boundary lines by claiming that refugees suffered from "imprisonment" under the then-current boundary limitations: "For when very many people flee from the violence of a cruel fortune and choose the protection of the defense of the churches, when they are confined therein, they suffer no less imprisonment than that which they have avoided."[90] While refugees willingly sought "imprisonment" in churches so that ecclesiastical administrators could intercede and negotiate on their behalf, captives were imprisoned outside the boundaries of the Roman Empire and relied on others to initiate the negotiation of their ransom and release.[91]

Only one extant canon addresses the issue of the redemption of captives.[92] The Council of Orleans in 511 decided that one permissible use of the donations of kings was for the redemption of captives.

The first extant law regarding the redemption of captives shows that churches were not only involved in the redemption of captives but were also involved in the process of rehabilitating them into their homes, and that captives were obligated to recompense their redeemers. Honorius in 408 wrote to Theodorus, the praetorian prefect of Italy and Illyricum, that ransomed captives had to restore the price of their ransom to their redeemer or render recompense through five years of service.[93] They could return to their landholdings, but if a conflict arose between a redeemed captive and an overseer, a chief tenant, or a procurator of his (the redeemed captive's) property, then the law requested that the clerics of the municipality petition the judges to enforce Honorius's law to the benefit of the redeemed captive.

Later laws regulated two specific methods for collecting ransom funds: the receipt of bequests made for this express purpose and the alienation of certain ecclesial property. Marcian and Justinian issued constitutions regarding the bequest of ransom money.[94] Justinian made exceptions to certain principles of inalienability for the sake of the redemption of captives. He allowed church construction funds to be redirected, sacred vessels to be melted down,[95] and the immovable property of certain churches to be sold. In 530, Justinian allowed funds for the construction of a church to be redirected to the redemption of captives.[96] Bishops could collect funds vowed for the construction of a church and use them instead to redeem captives. If the testator ordered a church to be built, the heirs had to provide for its completion within three years. But if that time elapsed and no church was built, the bishops were to "claim the funds left behind and [. . .] effect the construction of the most holy churches [. . .] or the ransom of captives."[97] In 535, Justinian permitted sacred vessels to be alienated for the same purpose, since inanimate utensils should not be valued over human souls.[98] In 544, Justinian gave express permission to churches in two locales to alienate immovable property for the redemption of captives.[99] The churches of Odessus and Tomis on the Black Sea could alienate immovable property for the redemption of captives, unless the property was expressly given on the condition that it would not be alienated.

The ways in which a church could serve as a protecting place were manifold, but the manumission of slaves, the asylum of refugees, and the redemption of captives were the particular acts of protection about which jurists and bishops drafted regulations, in part because these two groups of rule makers disagreed about how the church ought to protect the needy in relation to these practices. Their disagreement is particularly noticeable in the matter of asylum, since bishops advocated for expansive discretion in their capacity to offer refugees clemency, while jurists preferred to limit episcopal discretion in order to maintain the integrity of civil institutions. The manumission of slaves in churches required legal recognition for the purposes of ensuring social stability. The redemption of captives became a matter of legal concern because raising ransom funds sometimes required the exceptional alienation of ecclesial property. Though the protecting capacity of sacred things grew out of their protected nature, the case studies below show how interests in making the church a protecting space could conflict with the idea that it was a protected place.

THE USE OF ECCLESIAL PROPERTY TO PERFORM ACTS OF MERCY

In the fourth century, Cyril of Jerusalem and John Chrysostom acted on the same principle: that adherence to the rules that protected ecclesial property should not inhibit the performance of an act of mercy. Both bishops were summoned to trial for their actions; both refused to appear for trial; and both faced deposition. Their cases show that the alienation of ecclesial property was not easily justifiable, even when the welfare of the needy was at stake. The meeting of mercy and sacrilege in the alienation of ecclesial property created conflicts of interest and, in the cases of Cyril of Jerusalem and John Chrysostom, contributed to their deposition. As for John Chrysostom, he was not only accused of inappropriately using ecclesial property but also of failing to extend the protection of churches to particular refugees.

Ecclesial Textiles and the Trial of Cyril of Jerusalem

The historians Sozomen and Theodoret relate the circumstances of Cyril of Jerusalem's deposition in 357.[100] Both probably relied on Theodore of Mopsuestia's account in the fifth book of his *Against Eunomius*.[101] The historian Socrates disavows knowledge of the reasons for Cyril's deposition, but notes that Cyril refused to heed summonses for two years. After he was deposed in absentia, he became the first cleric to appeal an episcopal decision to a civil court.[102]

Sozomen describes Acacius of Contantinople's charges against Cyril, which concerned both matters of faith and ecclesial property.[103] Sozomen claims that it was the issue of misconduct that led to Cyril's deposition. He summarizes the charge of alienation of ecclesial property as follows. Cyril had to care for the poor suffering from a famine in Jerusalem and the neighboring countryside. To raise funds, he sold the vessels and sacred curtains of the church (κειμήλια καὶ ἱερὰ παραπετάσματα).[104] A donor later recognized his ecclesial gift worn by an actress. When he inquired after it, he learned that Cyril had alienated his donation to a merchant, who had in turn sold it to the actress.

Theodoret identifies the donor as Constantine and claims that the charge of maladministration of an imperial donation moved Constantius II to convoke a small synod composed of Cyril's opponents.[105] Acacius's charge, according to Theodoret, was that Constantine had donated a vestment made with golden threads to Macarius, the bishop of Jerusalem, to use for the performance of baptisms.[106] Cyril sold that garment and it fell into the hands of an actor. Theodoret does not name a purpose for the sale. Sozomen and Theodoret's accounts diverge in the details of the transaction itself.[107]

According to Sozomen, the misconduct was cause for deposition; and, according to Theodoret, it was a means of making Cyril's case personal to the emperor Constantius. If the late antique historians are correct, Cyril of Jerusalem may have been deposed for alienating ecclesial property, even for the purpose of showing mercy to the poor; and he may have been the first bishop to appeal his trial at the imperial court.

Ecclesial Protection and the Trial of John Chrysostom

Like Cyril of Jerusalem, John Chrysostom was tried and deposed in absentia. John's supporters, like Cyril's, justified his alienation of ecclesial property on the grounds that the sale supplied the means for the performance of an act of mercy. According to his accusers, John not only failed to safeguard the protected nature of churches; he also abused certain individuals' access to the protecting nature of churches. When John appealed his deposition to Innocent of Rome, he leveled accusations of his own against his opponents. John's plaint named infractions made against the sacrality of the church in the course of his own arrest.

The Trial.   The complete acts of the Synod of the Oak have not been transmitted, but the ninth-century bishop, Photius of Constantinople, summarized the acts of the synod in his *Bibliotheca*.[108] The empress Eudoxia had Bishop Theophilus of Alexandria preside over the Synod of the Oak at the Great Church of Saints Peter and Paul in the suburbs of Chalcedon. The council held thirteen sessions, the first twelve of which tried John Chrysostom. Five bishops presided as judges: Theophilus of Alexandria, Acacius of Beroa, Antiochius of Ptolemais, Severian of Gabala, and Cyrin of Chalcedon. Photius lists the accusations leveled by the deacon John and those by the monk Isaac against John Chrysostom.[109]

Deacon John named twenty-nine charges, eight of which regarded ecclesial property:

3. That John Chrysostom sold ecclesial property of value (τὰ κειμήλια πλῆθος πολὺ διέπρασε).

4. That John Chrysostom sold the slabs of marble that Nectarius had set aside for the decoration of St. Anastasia Church (τὰ μάρμαρα τῆς ἁγίας Ἀναστασίας, ἃ Νεκτάριος εἰς μαρμάρωσιν τῆς ἐκκλησίας ἐναπέθετο, οὗτος διέπρασε).

11. That John Chrysostom informed against the *comes* John in the sedition of soldiers (i.e., the coup of Gainas against the emperor Arcadius).

16. That John Chrysostom used the services of a certain Theodoulus to sell the inheritance that a certain Thecla bequeathed (τὴν κληρονομίαν τὴν ἀπὸ θέκλας καταλειφθεῖσαν πέπρακε διὰ θεοδούλου).

17. That no one knows where the revenues of the church have gone (τὰ προσόδια τῆς ἐκκλησίας οὐδεὶς οἶδε ποῦ ἀπῆλθεν).

21. That John Chrysostom handed over the presbyter Porphyrius to the grand chamberlain Eutropius to be exiled.

22. That John Chrysostom also handed over the presbyter Venerius with much force.

27. That John Chrysostom committed outrage in the Church of the Apostles by punching Memnon and offering him communion after his mouth bled (γρόνθον ἔδωκε Μέμνονι ἐν τοῖς Ἀποστόλοις, καί ῥέοντος τοῦ αἵματος ἐκ τοῦ στόματος αὐτοῦ προσήνεγκε τὰ μυστήρια).[110]

Four of Deacon John's charges name instances when John Chrysostom violated the principle that churches are protected by alienating various kinds of ecclesial property: valuable sacred vessels (τὰ κειμήλια πλῆθος), slabs of marble (τὰ μάρμαρα), a testamentary donation (ἡ κληρονομία), and revenue (τὰ προσόδια).

Another four charges were leveled at John Chrysostom, accusing him of violating the principle that churches protect. Three of them concerned the administration of churches as places of asylum. Charge 11 refers to the occasion of Count John's asylum at John Chrysostom's church. Charges 21 and 22 name two presbyters (otherwise unknown) to whom John Chrysostom failed to extend the protection of the church. In fact, he permitted the forcible seizure of one of them, Venerius. According to charge 27, John Chrysostom's physical violence created an unsafe, even bloody, ecclesial environment.

John Chrysostom was summoned four times to respond to Deacon John's charges and refused to comply. According to Photius's quotation of John Chrysostom's response to the summons, John protested the fairness of the trial and named a condition of his appearance in court: since the judges were his overt enemies, he would not comply with a summons unless a new set of judges were appointed.

The court examined four of Deacon John's charges, one of which was the twenty-seventh named above.[111] Then the synod received Isaac's *libellus*. Isaac leveled only one charge regarding ecclesial property (no. 9), which claimed that John Chrysostom granted asylum to pagans who harmed Christians.[112] While Isaac's charge admits that John Chrysostom respected the church in its protecting capacity by granting asylum, he argues that John offered such protection to ineligible individuals, who were not only non-Christian, but also committed injustice against Christians.[113]

Then witnesses were heard. In support of Deacon John's charge 3, the archpriest Arsacius, bishop Nectarius's brother, and the priests Atticus and Helpidius gave witness. They along with priest Acacius gave witness to charge 4. The fact that discussions took place and that witnesses were heard suggests that John Chrysostom was not deposed for his refusal of the canonical summonses, but for the outcome of the trial that proceeded despite his failure to appear.

Responses to the Trial.   Photius does not name the charges of which John Chrysostom was considered guilty and which led to his deposition, but three sources respond to the charges regarding the alienation of ecclesial property: two conflicting reports written by supporters and a third by an opponent. A funerary oration for John Chrysostom offers a defense regarding charges 3 and 4, as well as another charge unnamed in Photius's summary of the plaints.[114] Palladius's account of John Chrysostom's life responds to charge 3. Sixth-century sources contain information regarding a lost *liber* composed by Theophilus in defense of John Chrysostom's deposition, from which aspects of Theophilus's perspective on the accusations can be reconstructed.

The funerary oration refutes some of the charges leveled against John Chrysostom.[115] The author cites Deacon John's charges 3 and 4 as follows: "he sold some valuables and gifted others" (καὶ κειμήλια τὰ μὲν πέπρακεν, τὰ δὲ ἐχαρίσατο).[116] In response to this accusation about the alienation of inalienables, the orator says:

> And which bishop, tell me, does not have authority over the management of valuables (κειμηλίων)? In fact, he [John] gave some things to the poor bishops for their own and for the poor's sustenance, other things for the adornment of poor churches. He did not make an innovative sale, but, since those who followed the ancient custom said that they used the custom even now (namely, to gather together the surplus and make silver, due to the great number of people supported by ecclesial goods), there was no hindrance. And who is not aware of the fact that the selling and distribution of the sacred offerings of the church (τὰ ἱερὰ τῆς ἐκκλησίας) to the needy is also a practice (νόμος) among the fathers in the West? Nevertheless, the saint [John] did not even make use of such authority, but allowed things uncustomary and unnecessary for the [church] service to be administered for the support of not only the church properties, but also individuals (literally: the support of not only the material [ὑλικῶν] valuables but also rational ones [λογικῶν κειμηλίων]).[117]

The author employs three rhetorical strategies to defend the propriety of John Chrysostom's actions. First, he invokes John Chrysostom's authority as bishop to administer ecclesial property. Second, he argues that John Chrysostom's transactions used unnecessary ecclesial property for the benefit of the poor: John Chrysostom donated ecclesial property to furnish poor churches and to provide sustenance for poor bishops and poor laity. Third, he argues that there is precedent among bishops in the western provinces to make the same kind of administrative decisions that John Chrysostom did. In other words, John Chrysostom's actions were not innovative but rather consistent with customary practices.

In contrast, Palladius's account of John Chrysostom's life claims that John Chrysostom in fact did not alienate the valuables about which he was accused. Palladius relates that a presbyter called Germanus and a deacon named Cassian submitted plaints (γράμματα [. . .] ὑπομεμενηκέναι) against the actions that took place in the church during John Chrysostom's second arrest.[118] The plaint included a copy of an inventory (βρέβιον) of the church's property, signed by five civil authorities as witnesses (Studius, the prefect of the city, Eutychianus, the praetorian prefect, John, *comes* of the sacred largesse, Eustathius, the quaestor, and a *tabularius*).[119] The purpose of including the inventory copy, according to Palladius, was to exonerate John of the charge that he alienated gold, silver, and textile valuables (τὰ κειμήλια [. . .] ἔν τε χρυσῷ καὶ ἀργύρῳ καὶ ἀμφίοις).[120]

To resist his portrayal as a sacrilegious administrator, John Chrysostom and his supporters used another important rhetorical strategy: they created vivid landscapes for their audiences to visualize. As we will see, verbal images of an altar defended John from the charges relating to asylum, while the depiction of a hospice rebutted charges concerning the alienation of sacred property.

The author of the funerary oration includes a response to a charge not mentioned in Photius's résumé: that John Chrysostom used the ecclesial grain allowance set aside for disabled persons for personal ends.[121] The author's rebuttal refers to a series of events surrounding a building project mentioned in earlier sections of the funerary speech.[122] To build a large, endowed home for lepers, John Chrysostom purchased a piece of land conveniently located at a riverside, where John envisioned the lepers could wash their sores.[123] The anonymous orator took his listeners on an imagined visit to the controversial building project. John Chrysostom focused his episcopal care on those who suffered from leprosy, "a disease that drives even a soul of steel to pity, but that scares away even the most philanthropic soul."[124] John bought land with "the finest air and a river flowing by" and began to build a hospice, but before the roof was installed, the project was halted.[125] The river proved to be the most controversial aspect of the charitable building project.[126] John specifically chose a riverside location so that the lepers could easily cleanse their sores, but his opponents convinced neighbors down the river that the waters would be polluted and would fill their properties with pus and disease.[127] According to the orator, John's opponents transformed the sacred, charitable landscape that he had envisioned into an unfinished project that could have only spread pollution. The orator sought to effect a visual shift in the minds of the listeners. In John Chrysostom's hands, the landscape consisted of fine air and a river and spread mercy to those persons most shunned. In the hands of his opponents, however, the landscape turned into an unfinished, abandoned building that could only have spread disease—even if it had been finished.

How did John Chrysostom's opponents succeed in halting the project? According to the orator, they claimed that he amassed funds for the hospice by alienating ecclesial property.[128] After reviewing their charges, the orator says:

> They added to the charges that he also took the grain allowance of the disabled brothers (supplied to them of old from the church) and spent it on personal luxury. And, O men, they said these things, they who censured and obstructed that great [expenditure of his] for them [the lepers], and even pillaged the expenditure. Those who feared their [the lepers'] proximity and suspected that the running river would become a sowing of misfortune against their properties (both the land and the persons) listened and were persuaded. Their mind hated, their tongue slandered the great lover of the poor, setting a façade of philanthropy, yet subtracting the things of the poor.[129]

The author's rebuttal reproaches the prosecutors for their hypocrisy. The prosecutors dared to accuse the bishop of embezzling funds for the disabled, even though they themselves had obstructed the bishop's major building project to house and support the disabled (namely, lepers). The orator argues that the accusation is outrageous and more aptly befits the character of the prosecutors than that of the defendant.

Palladius likewise records that John Chrysostom redirected ecclesial revenue (ἀνάλωμα) to support his founding of hospitals (νοσοκομεῖα).[130] Palladius makes no mention of controversy in the affair but nevertheless rhetorically defends John Chrysostom's choice of building project by censuring bishops, such as the "lithomaniac" Theophilus, for expending ecclesial funds on unnecessary constructions.[131] Such bishops "squander money that rightly belongs to the poor in hanging walls and water cisterns three stories high and disgraceful baths for effeminate men all hidden away, or [. . .] expend their money on buildings uselessly."[132] Palladius creates a foil of a landscape by comparing John Chrysostom's charitable use of church property to Theophilus's "lithomania" in building excessively luxurious sites.

John Chrysostom's supporters rhetorically created visual landscapes to depict him as a bishop who did everything he could to fulfill his primary duty as bishop: to care for the needy. For the orator, the very same image that exonerated John Chrysostom painted his opponents in the unfavorable light of selfish motives. For Palladius, the juxtaposition of a hospice with excessively luxuriant sites put John Chrysostom in the company of the pious, while leaving Theophilus with questionable motives.

Little apologetic survives from the writings of John Chrysostom's opponents, but what does survive hints at the importance of charges regarding his administrative conduct. Facundus of Hermiane published a defense of the Three Chapters shortly after Justinian promulgated an edict condemning them in 543/4. In it, Facundus cites Jerome's Latin translation of a *liber* Theophilus composed to defend the justice of John Chrysostom's deposition.[133] According to Facundus, Theophilus said that John Chrysostom "surpassed the audacity of thieves in his crime" (*scelere suo latronum uicisset audaciam*) and was "chief among those who commit sacrilege" (*sacrilegorum principem*).[134] Facundus does not provide any further detail on Theophilus's position vis-à-vis John Chrysostom's administration of ecclesial property, but the few words quoted suggest that Theophilus addressed the charge of sacrilege in his liber.[135]

As for the charges related to churches in their protecting capacity, John Chrysostom himself preached on the asylum of the chamberlain Eutropius and the *comes* John, immediately anticipating objections to his discretionary decisions. Isaac's charge 9 and Deacon John's charge 11 fault him indeed for his actions concerning the two refugees.

Because Eutropius was not a Christian and, moreover, was instrumental in passing legislation to limit ecclesial asylum,[136] John Chrysostom expected that there would be many who would consider Eutropius unworthy of ecclesial asylum and who would object to John's reception of Eutropius in the sanctuary.[137] Even the historians Socrates and Sozomen cite resistance, like that of John's accuser Isaac, to Eutropius's asylum.[138] As Eutropius clung to the altar, John Chrysostom preached a homily. He responded to anticipated objections from the crowd by creating a vivid mental image for the audience to project over the scene at hand: Eutropius at the altar. John Chrysostom describes the church as a winged, protective creature whose embrace of Eutropius can transform him into a luminous ornament for the altar, provided that the audience joins John Chrysostom in an act of patronage. Although Eutropius had attacked the church, now that he is in need of protection the church hastens to snatch him out of the fishing net, to hold him securely under its wings and in its bosom, and to bear its shield before him.[139] With the church's power and philanthropy (τὴν δύναμιν τῆς Ἐκκλησίας καὶ τὴν φιλανθρωπίαν), Eutropius can become an ornament (κόσμος) for the altar that emits great light (λαμπηδόνα μεγάλην).[140] Despite Eutropius's faults, he would not defile the altar any more than the impure woman of Luke 23:34 defiled Jesus in grasping his feet.[141] John Chrysostom therefore invites his audience to join him so that together as patrons they might adorn the church (τὴν ἐκκλησίαν κοσμήσομεν) with Eutropius the luminous ornament by appealing (παρακαλοῦντες) to the emperor for mercy toward him.[142]

In the case of Count John, objections to John Chrysostom's actions were of the opposite nature—namely, that he did not grant asylum to a refugee.[143] John Chrysostom preached a homily in which he defended himself against the allegation that he failed to ensure the church's protection to Count John when he sought asylum during Gainas's military coup.[144] John Chrysostom argues that he did not deny Count John asylum; rather, Count John left the church premises of his own accord. Had Count John clung to the altar, he would not have been arrested.[145] John Chrysostom recycles the same evangelical image of asylum and aerial image of the church's protection he had employed in his homily on Eutropius the previous year. The sinful woman of the gospels clung to Jesus's feet and was saved as a result; likewise, Count John would have been saved had he clung to the altar. Despite attacks made against the church and despite John Chrysostom's own arrest on the occasion,[146] John Chrysostom insists that the church's protection is eternal (οὐδέποτε γηρᾷ), ascending up beyond the heavens (ὑπὲρ τῶν οὐρανῶν ἀναβέβηκε).[147] The ever-victorious church would have protected Count John had he remained in it.

Both John Chrysostom and his supporters created and disseminated depictions of his ecclesial landscapes as epitomies of divine protection. In their accounts, John Chrysostom's use of ecclesial funds helped the poorest of the poor, and he did not hesitate to give everyone the opportunity to take shelter under the protective wings of the church. And not only did John Chrysostom offer asylum to all those who sought it; he went above and beyond the call of duty. He offered refugees themselves the chance to be transformed into sacred objects, to envision themselves as luminous ornaments at God's altar.

John Chrysostom appealed his deposition to Innocent of Rome, repeating three times in the course of his letter that his accusers acted contrary to the laws and canons.[148] John makes the case that his protection at the Great Church was violated, as he was forcibly seized twice. The first time, he was arrested by the chief of the urban police from a church in the middle of the city. The emperor expelled those who attacked the church and recalled John Chrysostom "to the church from which we [John Chrysostom and his supporters] were unjustly thrown out" (εἰς τὴν ἐκκλησίαν ἧς ἀδίκως ἐξεβλήθημεν).[149] John Chrysostom pursued legal action against Theophilus of Alexandria (the first president of the synod), but Theophilus left Constantinople and made excuses to delay a court appearance. In the meantime, John Chrysostom pursued legal action against the Syrians who had supported Theophilus, but for a second time he was forcibly seized. The arrest on this latter occasion involved the use of weapons in the church. John Chrysostom complains that soldiers surrounded the sanctuary with arms (ἁθρόον στρατιωτῶν [. . .] ὅπλοις τὸ βῆμα περιεστοιχίζετο) and so much blood was spilt that the baptismal pools were reddened by it (αἵματος αἱ κολυμβῆθραι ἐπληροῦντο καὶ τὰ ἱερὰ [. . .] ἐφοινίσσετο νάματα).[150] Innocent of Rome expressed in a letter to the clergy of Constantinople that he hoped an ecumenical synod could be convened to review the case of John Chrysostom, but no such gathering ever took place.[151]

The case of John Chrysostom shows there was a fine line between mercy and sacrilege. From the perspective of his accusers, John Chrysostom practiced sacrilege toward ecclesial property by alienating it, by denying its protection to clerics and a count, and by granting its protection to ineligible persons. From the perspective of his defenders (including himself), he practiced mercy by using ecclesial property for the benefit of the disabled, the poor, and refugees. Out of these competing discourses emerges an episcopal Robin Hood: a thief in the eyes of some; a philanthropist in the eyes of others.

In general, practicing acts of mercy to the needy was considered the primary role of the bishop. The bishop's main job description, insofar as he was chief administrator of ecclesial properties, was to administer property and revenue for the benefit of the needy first and foremost. The ways in which mercy could be practiced were many and varied in late antiquity, not restricted in scope to the three discussed in this chapter. Because the manumission of slaves, the asylum of refugees, and the ransom of captives necessitated close contact between bishops and civil authorities, bishops petitioned for legal regulation of these three ways of practicing mercy. The matter of asylum, the most contested practice, caused a considerable amount of friction between bishops and jurists. Bishops preferred full discretion in their decisions to grant asylum to criminals, fugitives, and all kinds of refugees. From the bishops' point of view, judges should have always permitted bishops to intercede for mercy in all cases and at any time. Jurists, on the other hand, insisted on maintaining due process in legal trials and restricting the populations eligible for asylum, especially when the fugitive, from the perspective of the fisc, was evading taxes. Churches legally offered sanctuary to those in need, and the fisc delineated the limits of mercy's reach.

The case studies I have presented on Cyril of Jerusalem and John Chrysostom's controversial practices of mercy show how the protecting role that churches acquired could conflict with their legally protected status. Despite the exception clauses to the rule against alienation of ecclesial property, these case studies show how difficult it was to justify exceptions.[152] In the next two chapters, I show that ritual practice inverted the relative priority of these two corollaries to the definition of *res sacrae*.

The Ritual Making of *Res Sacrae*

LIKE PART I, PART II CONSISTS OF TWO CLOSELY KNIT CHAPTERS, followed by a third that challenges them. Chapters 4 and 5 form a pair, employing theories of social anthropologists to capture succinctly how ritual discourses produced in the making of *res sacrae* differed from the regulatory discourse. Chapter 4 relies on Igor Kopytoff's highly influential insights: that things have lives; that the commoditization of things is a process; and that there is in fact a process opposite to that of commoditization, which Kopytoff calls "singularization." I argue that the regulatory discourse singularized *res sacrae*. By contrast, the ritual discourse was perceived as recommoditizing *res sacrae*. This distinction explains conflicts between bishops and donors. The latter insisted on the legal singularity of their donations and resisted what they perceived as recommoditization. The former tried to convince donors that the regifting of *res sacrae* actually increased their value. Chapter 5 offers an analysis of exactly how bishops downplayed the value of *res sacrae* during the very ritual that legally singularized them, effectively "singularizing" human souls instead. By contrast, chapter 6 turns to bishops who lacked imperial endorsement and therefore used the ritual discourse to disengage *res sacrae* from the imperial clutch. The goal of part II is not to mark late antique Christian ritual practices of dedicatory, consecratory, and anniversary celebrations as somehow unique. Instead, the purpose is to highlight how they generated ideas of sacralization that were at variance with the regulatory discourse and that thereby gave rise to tensions among bishops, donors, and jurists. Ritual discourses could be deployed not only to support the legal anchors but also to destabilize them. The following chapters focus on the latter, showing how certain ritual discourses rhetorically unraveled legal knots.

4

Dedications

Do walls make Christians?[1]

In the late fourth century, Prudentius left a life of legal practice and political posts to write Christian literary works. One of them was a poem celebrating the martyr Laurentius (Saint Lawrence or Laurence), who was executed in 258 when Christian practice was illicit in the Roman Empire.[2] Prudentius imagines how the prefect of Rome and Laurentius interacted, when the prefect ordered the confiscation of the church treasury for which Laurentius was responsible.

In Prudentius's poem, Laurentius promises to perform a proper inventory in the course of three days and then to hand over the ecclesial property.[3] When the prefect arrives at the appointed time, Laurentius announces to the prefect: "Marvel at the wealth set out before you, which our exceeding rich God has in his sanctuaries. You will see the great nave gleaming with vessels of gold, and along the open colonnades course on course of precious metal."[4] With this imagined speech, Prudentius retrojects late fourth- and early fifth-century expectations of what the interior of a great church in the city of Rome would look like into the mid-third century.

When the prefect enters through the church doors, he is startled to see "crowds of poor people standing, a disfigured swarm" and to hear the loud "din" of their appeals to him.[5] Laurentius explains:

> Here then are the golden coins which a short while ago I promised, coins which tumbling walls cannot bury under burning ashes, nor thief carry away by stealth. And now I give you noble jewels also, so that you need not think Christ is poor, jewels of flashing light with which this temple is adorned. You see the consecrated virgins, and marvel at the pure old women who after the loss of their first husbands have known no second love. These are the Church's necklace, the jewels with which she decks herself; thus dowered she is pleasing to Christ, and thus she adorns her high head. There are her riches, take them up; with them you will adorn the city of Romulus and enrich the emperor's estate, and yourself be made richer too.[6]

Laurentius claims that the true wealth of the church consists of the poor and the widows. To the prefect, Laurentius offers the poor as the golden coins and the widows as the shimmering jewels. In a rage, the prefect exclaims, "We are being deceived to a stupendous extent through so many allegories!"[7]

As this chapter and the next will demonstrate, Prudentius's imagined confrontation between Laurentius and the prefect dramatically captures conflicts that occurred again and again in the fourth and fifth centuries. However, the struggles were not between ecclesiastical stewards and city prefects. Instead, bishops wishing to perform acts of mercy confronted donors who wished to protect their ecclesial donations. The inalienability of ecclesial property clashed with the bishop's primary duty to care for the poor. Some bishops used the contexts of dedication and consecration to convey allegorical lessons akin to Prudentius's Laurentius. Other bishops went a step further: they used such dedicatory and consecratory lessons to justify the alienation of *res sacrae*. This chapter concerns the context of dedication; the next chapter concerns that of consecration.

As part I showed, the legal and canonical imagination regarding *res sacrae* created mechanisms for both disciplining and preventing episcopal misconduct. By contrast, bishops and other patrons employed ritual practices to broadcast exemplary conduct. Through their installation of dedicatory images and inscriptions in churches, patrons constructed church buildings as visual and textual embodiments of sacred exchanges to be imitated by churchgoers.

Not everyone agreed, however, as to how a church should look, and the variety in types of donors' images and inscriptions attests to that. In some churches, donors were depicted in ways that marked the abundance of their offerings without direct reference to the purpose of their gift, the exchange process, the return, and so on. At the same time, a number of writers made attempts to regulate what the walls of a church ought to convey. They claimed that ecclesial images should not simply be pleasing to the eyes but should unambiguously educate viewers as to what is holy and how to become holy. In other words, ecclesial images and inscriptions were to give as little interpretive space as possible for the viewer to read them with reference to the nonsacred rather than the sacred. The purpose of church adornment was to broadcast what exactly sacred exchanges entailed. Certain types of donors' images and inscriptions did commemorate offerings in ways that directly invoked holiness and holy exchanges. Artists posed donors in gestures of pious supplication, illustrating how patronage led these donors to triumph with Christ and to receive divine largesse from him. Some donor portraits of bishops advertised such messages at focal points of church architecture: the eastern apse or the triumphal arch. Such episcopal images show how the concepts of supplication, triumph, and divine largesse, found widely among dedicatory practices, reproduce the legal-canonical imaginary on *res sacrae* explained in part I, with one important exception. In the regulatory discourse, *res sacrae* were permitted to be protecting, on the condition that this did not infringe on *res sacrae*'s status as protected. By contrast, in the ritual context of making *res sacrae*, it was the protecting role of churches that took center stage.

THEORETICAL UNDERPINNINGS

To elucidate the significance of this difference between legal and ritual discourses on *res sacrae*, it will be helpful to draw a distinction between two kinds of economies. I will borrow vocabulary about commodities and exchange processes from a theorist of material culture, Igor Kopytoff.[8] Such vocabulary will help describe the two sorts of economies of exchange in which church buildings operated, one legal and the other ritual. My focus, however, will center on how the material culture of dedicatory practices visualized the ritual economy of exchange.

The ritual of consecration turned a building and its land into a church. For both legal practitioners and ritual agents, the ritual of consecration marked a transaction; but for legal practitioners that transaction was one thing and for the ritual agents it was another. Churches participated in two economies of exchange, depending on whether one looked at churches from a legal standpoint or from a ritual one. According to legal practitioners, the ritual of consecration "singularized" churches. The ritual took churches out of the sphere of the economy, out of the sphere of commodity exchange altogether. But for ritual agents, the consecration marked one link in an endless series of exchanges between the human and the celestial realms. The church was one gift in a continuous chain of gift exchanges. The purpose of these exchanges was to mark a relationship between pious Christians and celestial beings.

Legally, a church was not exchangeable, but ritually it was. This difference created some significant tension for bishops. Because church properties were singularized legally, they could not be sold even to perform acts of mercy, though bishops did successfully petition for some exceptions.[9] And yet, acts of mercy were the most prized gifts that could be offered in the endless chain of gift exchange with the heavenly realm.

In fact, the singularization of ecclesial property effectively turned it into a person—an unexchangeable free person. Donors had the law on their side, but bishops tried to persuade them that their donations were merely things, not persons.[10] The needy were persons. Repurposing donors' gifts for the needy's sake opened a larger investment with God than did beautification of the church. In addressing donors, bishops had to reconcile an ethos that resisted the liquidation of pious investments of wealth with the need to amass funds for the redemption of captives and for other acts of mercy. Their strategy was to emphasize the *res* part of *res sacrae*. The use of sacred things to perform acts of mercy for persons actually increased the value of donors' pious investment of wealth. As chapter 5 will show, this perspective was part and parcel of a larger episcopal endeavor to spiritualize the sacrality of material things.

In what follows, I first offer examples of how types of donors' images and inscriptions varied widely and how certain writers tried to regulate the appearance of their respective local church spaces. Then, I focus on one type of dedicatory practice, one that showcased how church buildings functioned in exchanges between humans on earth and beings of the celestial realm. Finally, I show how some donors resisted the ritual economy of the "sacred," preferring instead the legal one.

HOW TO ADORN *RES SACRAE*

While certain dedicatory images and inscriptions installed in churches illustrate understandings of sanctity, others do not make explicit reference to "the sacred." When a donor is depicted in the act of engaging in his or her craft or simply states in an inscription how many square feet of a mosaic floor he or she donated, it is difficult to discern what a late antique viewer would have recognized about the sanctity of donors in such dedicatory pieces, aside from the awareness that an olive picker contributed to the adornment of God's house[11] or that a certain Januarius donated 830 feet of a mosaic pavement.[12] By contrast, some late antique writers (Nilus of Ancyra, Paulinus of Nola, Choricius of Gaza, and Anastasius of Gerasa) preferred a narrow repertoire of images and inscriptions for churches, one that unambiguously conveyed spiritual truths.

Even a cursory sample of images and inscriptions from both the East and the West attests to the multiplicity of ways churches could be adorned. Numerous mosaic programs preserved in churches of the prefecture of the East visualize how patrons' estates thrived and flourished. For example, pavement mosaics completed on August 4, 576 in the nave of a church in modern-day Kissufim near the Gaza Strip depict three patrons in the north aisle.[13] Dates, coins, and fowl attest to the abundance of these patrons' assets. One named Orbicon holds a cluster of dates in one hand and transports baskets and jars on camelback.[14] A church at Umm al-Rasas in Jordan offers further examples of how mosaics visualized patronal abundance. Most of the donors are portrayed on the nave floor conducting various agricultural activities, including plowing, hunting, slaughtering, and harvesting. All the donors were probably identified by name via a mosaic inscription beside their portrayal, but not all names survive. The figures themselves only remain in outline form.[15]

The same general observation holds of western regions. Many mosaic pavements in Italy identify the patron and the number of mosaic pavement feet he or she donated.[16] For instance, at the cathedral church of Florence, thought to date to the end of the fifth century or the beginning of the sixth, an inscription lists the names of those whose donations funded parts of the mosaic floor.[17] The Church of Aquileia (built under Bishop Theodore sometime between 304 and 325) simply depicts portraits of donors on the mosaic pavement without accompanying names.[18] Some of them are shown engaging in their occupational activity.[19] They may all have been members of one wealthy household.[20]

I do not suggest that there could be no theological interpretation of such images and inscriptions at all, only that the donors are not depicted in any immediately identifiable "holy" way.[21] Images of abundant yield and inscriptions of exact footage underscore the labor invested and the magnitude of the gift. They do not necessarily call attention to specific notions of sacrality.

In the midst of multiple, varied practices for adorning church buildings, a number of writers expressed their view that ecclesial images ought to convey the successes of spiritual athletes unambiguously. Since images of prosperity ran the risk of allowing their beholders to feast their eyes on the pleasures of earthly life, Nilus of Ancyra, Paulinus of Nola, Choricius of Gaza, and Anastasius of Gerasa all wrote in favor of ecclesial artwork that clearly expressed spiritual wealth.[22]

Nilus of Ancyra (d. 430) reacted vehemently against the idea of installing genre scenes when the prefect Olympiodorus expressed his perspective about how he wished to adorn a church built for the holy martyrs.[23] According to Nilus, Olympiodorus suggested that the eastern wall of the sanctuary be reserved for images of the martyrs, while the northern and southern wall would display scenes of animal hunts both on land and at sea. As for the nave, Olympiodorus proposed pictures of crosses, birds, beasts, reptiles, and plants. In response, Nilus distinguished images that merely delight the eyes for delight's sake from images that edify the faithful. Not only do genre scenes fail to educate the faithful; they in fact distract (περιπλανῆσαι) churchgoers from the holy lessons they ought to receive at church.[24] To emphasize the importance of spiritual edification, Nilus contrasts Olympiodorus's infantile (νηπιῶδες) and childish (βρεφοπρεπές) proposal for an ecclesial artistic program with a mature (στερρός) and adult (ἀνδρώδης) vision.[25] The latter kind of program allows no space for "unnecessary images" (περιττά), only crosses and illustrations of scenes from the Old and New Testaments,[26] so that "the illiterate who are unable to read the Holy Scriptures, may, by gazing at the pictures, become mindful of the manly deeds of those who have genuinely served the true God, and may be roused to emulate those glorious and celebrated feats."[27] For Nilus, the visual speech of church walls ought to teach churchgoers the successful practices of holy athletes.

Paulinus of Nola (ca. 354–431), on the other hand, acknowledged that it was unusual to depict saintly figures in decorative programs. Like Nilus, however, he promoted the practice of using artistic programs for pious educational purposes. Paulinus delivered an oration on the feast day of Saint Felix at the church bearing the saint's name in Cimitile, while it was still in the process of renovation and one year before it would be consecrated. In his speech, Paulinus raised a question that he expected the audience members would have in mind as they witnessed the decorative work in progress: "You may perhaps ask what motive implanted in us this decision to adorn the holy houses with representations of living persons, an unusual custom."²⁸ The motive, he explains, was educational in nature: to train formerly pagan Christians to celebrate Saint Felix's festival with Christian devotional habits, not pagan ones. Instead of feasting with food and drink, the paintings would inspire former pagans to feast with virtue:

> As the paintings beguile their hunger, their astonishment may allow better behaviour to develop in them. Those reading the holy accounts of chastity in action are infiltrated by virtue and inspired by saintly example. As they gape, their drink is sobriety, and they forget the longing for excessive wine. As they pass the day sightseeing over this quite large area, their cups are rarely filled. They have spent their time on the wonders of the place, and only a few hours subsequently remain for feasting.²⁹

For Paulinus, it was not genre scenes that risked inhibiting the attainment of virtue, but pagan feasting habits. Like Nilus, Paulinus preferred to sponsor ecclesial visual programs that would hold their audience captive toward one end: to keep viewers' eyes fixed on examples of successful holy athletes.

In one of his panegyrics for Bishop Marcianus of Gaza, Choricius of the same city (fl. late fifth or early sixth century) offers an explanation as to why artists depicted only certain types of birds in the churches Marcianus founded. The pictures of some birds would call to mind poets' stories—false fables, instead of true ones:

> The birds of the poets, nightingale and cicada, the artist has done well to reject, lest even the memory of those fables intrude upon the sacred place. Instead of them he has enjoyed depicting a host of other birds and a flock of partridges: perhaps he would have rendered the very music of their cries, had not the sound hindered the hearing of God's word.³⁰

Choricius imagines that certain images can "intrude into the pious place" (ἐν εὐσεβεῖ χωρίῳ συνεισέρχηται) and the artist that Bishop Marcianus entrusted with adorning the church avoided such intrusive subjects in his work.³¹ Since the birds of the poets ran the risk of directing viewers' attention away from the pious place and instead to poets' legends, Choricius praises Bishop Marcianus's artist for choosing to depict certain kinds of feathered creatures over others.

According to such writers as Nilus, Paulinus, and Choricius, the church should serve as a narrow, direct visual training ground for the attainment of holiness, one that provided as little room as possible for viewers to delight in earthly pleasures over celestial ones. At Gerasa, Bishop Anastasius had the inscription itself voice such a purpose. The dedicatory inscription at the Church of Saints Peter and Paul (ca. 540) speaks of "my bishop," so that the floor itself declares the founder's success in visually teaching "the faithful counsels of God." The mosaic text reads:

> Indeed, my bishop brings beautiful marvels to those who inhabit this city and land; for, *in order to teach the faithful counsels of God*, the renowned Anastasius built a house for Peter and Paul, the leading disciples (for the Savior granted them authority), and adorned it with silver and beautifully colored stones.[32]

It is the floor that declares the purpose of the church's "silver and beautifully colored stones"—namely, "to teach the faithful counsels of God."

DEDICATORY PRACTICES AND *RES SACRAE* IN ECONOMIES OF EXCHANGE

Nilus, Paulinus, Choricius, and Anastasius promoted in various ways the idea that choices regarding church adornment should be made with only one aim in view: to broadcast what it means to be sacred. While the images of donors mentioned above depict them in portrait form or in the exercise of their daily occupation with abundant yield, other pieces of dedicatory imagery portray supplicant donors requesting triumph with Christ and divine largesse. Such donor imagery creates of the church a place where viewers are invited into the same act of supplication with the hope of the same returns. The church speaks to the beholder through the nonverbal language of gestures and the verbal language of inscriptions to surround the viewer with a multitude of prayers for favor. By interacting with the images and texts, the viewer learns how to participate in an intercessory exchange that locates the church as the place where divine gifts can be sought, received, and celebrated. The exchange process visually taught on the church walls broadcasted how ritual agents understood the function of church property, which fundamentally differed from how legal practitioners understood it. Before analyzing material examples of such visual education, it will be helpful to introduce a theoretical distinction.

As mentioned at the outset, legal practitioners "singularized" church property. The anthropologist Igor Kopytoff draws a distinction between two different processes in economies of exchange: singularization and commoditization.[33] Singularization is the opposite of commoditization. The more something is exchangeable for other things, the more it is commoditized. In the United States and in many countries today, money is the most commoditized thing because almost any object can be exchanged for money. In nonmonetary economies, other objects can be commoditized. For example, Kopytoff cites the spheres of exchange among the Tiv people in central Nigeria prior to the colonial period, who are said to have had three separate spheres of exchange. In the sphere of subsistence items, yams, cereals, chickens, goats, utensils, and so on could be exchanged for each other. In the sphere of prestige items, cattle, slaves, special cloths, medicines, brass rods, and so on could be exchanged for each other. Finally, there was the sphere of rights in people—rights in wives, wards, and offspring. The item that allowed for exchanges across the three separate spheres was brass rods, which could be exchanged for subsistence items and which could also initiate transactions in the sphere of rights in people.[34] Therefore, the most commoditized things among the Tiv were brass rods. The opposite of what becomes "common" or "commoditized" is that which becomes "singular." Singularization means that something that could otherwise be a commodity is taken out of the sphere of commodity exchange altogether. One can make personal choices to singularize items like a private diary or a special heirloom—items one would never exchange. Likewise, governments can publicly singularize items. The British monarchy singularized the Star of India into the "crown jewel."[35]

Singularization is the term Kopytoff would use to describe the process that churches legally underwent in the Roman Empire. The name for the process among Roman jurists, however, was not "singularization" but *consecration*. The ritual of consecration made something a "sacred thing" (*res sacra*). Gaius, a jurist of the second century, articulated this legal principle with regard to the sacred places of Roman religion. In a textbook for students, he explained how "things" are categorized: "The main division of things is divided into two limbs; some are under divine law, others under human [law]. Under divine law, for instance, are sacred things and religious [things]. Sacred [things] are those consecrated to the gods above [. . .]. What indeed is under divine law belongs to no one."[36] In other words, only things that fall under human law are commodities. Things under divine law, such as *res sacrae*, are singular. They lie outside the spheres of exchange because they belong to no one. As part I shows, this definition of sacred things started to be applied to Christian places consecrated to God in the fourth century. Civil laws and ecclesiastical canons written in the fourth and fifth centuries make it clear that this legal principle was applied to churches. However, it would not be until Justinian issued a new and updated textbook of law in the sixth century that the principle would be rewritten with explicit reference to churches. Justinian's textbook reads: "Now, belonging to no one are sacred things [. . .]: for what is under divine law belongs to no one. Sacred are those things that are consecrated to God ritually and by the pontiffs, such as sacred buildings and gifts, which are ritually dedicated to the service of God."[37] Justinian's textbook explicitly states that churches do not belong to any human entity, whether individual or corporate.

What did it mean for ecclesial property to be taken out of the spheres of exchange? What did it mean for ecclesial property's status as a commodity to be revoked? What did it mean for ecclesial property's status to be made singular?

Or, to use the language of Roman jurists, what did it mean for ecclesial property to be made sacred? According to the jurists who wrote civil laws and the bishops who wrote ecclesiastical canons, singularization meant that churches were protected places and protecting places.[38] Ecclesial property was protected because it belonged to no one, and thus could not be the object of transactions. Ecclesial property enjoyed special privileges that favored the increase of assets. Churches were protecting places because violence was not permitted there; criminals and refugees could seek asylum there; captives could be ransomed there; and slaves could be manumitted or freed there. The legal singularization of churches made them places that were not commodities and places where protection could be sought.

In the horizontal economy—that is to say, in exchanges among humans—churches were not commodities. By contrast, the vertical economy operated under the opposite arrangement. In the vertical economy—that is to say, in exchanges between humans and celestial beings—churches were not singularized. Rather, ecclesial property was exchangeable. Dedicatory images and inscriptions installed in churches emphasize the vertical exchange of votive offerings for divine favors. Donors offered churches and church assets as gifts to Christ and patron saints. In return, donors received divine favors from Christ and patron saints. This initial exchange of gifts paved the way for a relationship between pious Christians and celestial beings.

To initiate a relationship with a celestial being, a pious Christian would offer a donation with a request for a return gift. The pious Christian—that is, the donor—would receive the return gift as divine largesse and the exchanges would continue. None of the transactions was considered a terminal one. Instead, the transactions served to initiate or mark the relationship. The final goal of all the transactions was triumph with Christ.

A good analogy is the relationship of marriage. Some cultures use gift exchanges between two families to initiate a reciprocal relationship.[39] The gift exchange is made with the expectation that the new relationship will result in a marriage between two specific members. Likewise, gift exchanges between pious Christians and celestial beings initiated a reciprocal relationship. The relationship was expected to result in triumph with Christ. A church building was one of the commodities offered as a gift to initiate or reinforce the relationship.

As both this chapter and the next will show, the dedication and consecration of a church in ritual practice contributed to the making and binding of networks of social relations among humans and celestial beings. Studies on gifts to saints have made a similar point.[40] The difference here lies in my attention to the practice of alienation. Alienating gifts that had been made to saints was an even more effective way of generating the same social bonds, according to some bishops.

Ritual practice placed no limitations on ecclesial property's social and economic function. It was not the gift that is singular. If anything was singular ritually speaking, it was the soul's triumph with Christ, the inalienable victory. Churches, crowns, and other trophies of victory merely signaled the "athletic" or "military" triumph at once assured by Christ and also attained by earthly and celestial saints. If the alienation of the trophy signaled the triumph too, then there could be no reason to object, ritually speaking.

Bishops' Donor Portraits and the Ritual Economy

Late antique mosaics of bishops as founders of church buildings illustrate vertical interactions and what those vertical interactions entailed. Each image depicts a bishop carrying a miniature of the church he founded while standing in the company of celestial beings. Interpretations of these images have usually focused on one aspect of the scene: the bishop's offer of his newly founded church to Christ.[41] However, these scenes capture much more than the bishop's offer. These scenes are snapshots of how the vertical exchange works: the donor makes a supplication and an offer to Christ via the patron saint of the church, and Christ gives the donor divine largesse in return. Most significantly, the scenes celebrate Christ's triumph, the saints' triumph with him, and the donor's expected triumph.

The images in question portray Christ as triumphant and as giver par excellence who bestows benefactions on his triumphant officials—namely, his martyrs and bishops. The late antique examples of this motif—the eastern apse mosaics of Saints Cosmas and Damian, of San Vitale, and of Saint Maurus, as well as of the triumphal arch mosaic of San Lorenzo—all come from the region of Italy and date to the sixth century. The action portrayed represents the bishops offering a church to Christ and yet receiving that church from Christ, too. The images simultaneously depict episcopal offering and divine largesse.

The mosaics share three important motifs. First, they depict Christ as the central triumphant figure. In the eastern apse of the Basilica of Saints Cosmas and Damian in Rome, Christ ascends in the clouds over the River Jordan with his right hand outstretched in a gesture of triumph (fig. 1).[42] The two figures immediately flanking Christ—Peter and Paul—raise their hands to offer acclamations in celebration of Christ's triumph. At the Basilica of San Lorenzo, also in Rome, the mosaic announces Christ's triumph in a different way. The mosaic lies not on the apse like that of Saints Cosmas and Damian but on an architectural structure that itself signifies triumph: the triumphal arch. As at the Basilica of Saints Cosmas and Damian, Peter and Paul at San Lorenzo offer acclamations to the triumphant Christ, here enthroned on a blue orb (fig. 2).[43]

Second, the mosaics juxtapose the bishop with the patron saint of the church building. At the Basilica of San Lorenzo, Saint Laurentius himself recommends Bishop Pelagius (bishop from 579 to 590) to Christ (fig. 2). In the eastern apse

FIGURE 1. Bishop's donor portrait, eastern apse mosaic, Basilica of Sts. Cosmas and Damian, Rome. Photo credit: Basilica dei Santi Cosma e Damiano, Rome, Italy.

FIGURE 2. Bishop's donor portrait, triumphal arch mosaic, San Lorenzo fuori le mura, Rome. Photo credit: Charles Barber.

FIGURE 3. Bishop's donor portrait, eastern apse mosaic, Basilica of St. Maurus, Poreč. Photo credit: Henry Maguire and Ann Terry Poreč Archive, 1990s–2000s, Dumbarton Oaks, Trustees for Harvard University, Washington, DC.

of the Basilica of Saint Maurus, Bishop Euphrasius (bishop from 539 to 553) follows the lead of Saint Maurus himself (fig. 3).[44] Likewise, at the Basilica of Saints Cosmas and Damian, Bishop Felix IV (bishop from 526 to 530) follows Saint Cosmas himself in a line toward Christ triumphant (fig. 1).[45] Finally, at the Basilica of San Vitale in Ravenna, the eastern apse mosaic (fig. 4) shows Saint Vitalis in symmetry with Bishop Ecclesius (bishop from 522 to 532).[46] Unnamed angels recommend both Saint Vitalis and Bishop Ecclesius to the triumphant Christ. Each of these mosaics thus establishes a relationship between the patron saint of the church and the bishop who founded the church. At San Vitale, the relationship is one of symmetry; at the churches of Saints Cosmas and Damian and Saint Maurus, the patron saint leads the bishop forward; and at San Lorenzo, the patron saint recommends or intercedes on behalf of the bishop.

Third, just as the bishop is juxtaposed to the patron saint, so too the church model is presented alongside the martyr's crown. At San Vitale, scholars agree that Christ extends the crown of martyrdom to Saint Vitalis.[47] The scene creates symmetry between the crown offered to Saint Vitalis and the church model in Bishop Ecclesius's hands. The triumphal arch at San Lorenzo depicts the same symmetry between Bishop Pelagius's church model and Saint Hippolytus's crown. At the Church of Saints Cosmas and Damian, Bishop Felix's church model stands in symmetry to the martyr Theodore's crown on the opposite side of the scene. At the Basilica of Saint Maurus, the symmetrical relationship is more complex. Bishop Euphrasius's church stands in symmetry to a jeweled book. Behind Bishop Euphrasius, the archdeacon Claudius's jeweled book

FIGURE 4. Bishop's donor portrait, eastern apse mosaic, San Vitale, Ravenna. Photo credit: Alfredo Dagli Orti / Art Resource, NY.

stands in symmetry to a martyr's crown. At Saint Maurus, church is to book as book is to crown. To summarize: the four mosaics (1) depict a triumphant Christ, (2) portray the patron saint of the church recommending or leading the bishop of the church, (3) and juxtapose models of church buildings with martyrs' crowns.

Unlike the other images, the mosaic in the eastern apse of San Vitale portrays the martyr Vitalis empty-handed. As mentioned above, scholars agree that while Saint Vitalis stands ready to *receive* his martyr's crown from Christ, by contrast Bishop Ecclesius *offers* his church model to Christ.[48] But the symmetry of the figures suggests rather that the actions, too, are symmetrical. In other words, if Christ awards Saint Vitalis the crown of martyrdom, then Christ also gives Bishop Ecclesius the church building. Late antique Christians could imagine Christ simultaneously receiving Bishop Ecclesius's church model and giving it back, as the following visual comparisons to imperial images show.

The *aurum coronarium*, "the golden crown," characterizes imperial images of triumph, in which citizens acknowledge the triumphant emperor as protector of the empire by giving him a crown or other offerings.[49] For example, an ivory

FIGURE 5. Ivory diptych of Justinian. Photo credit: Musée du Louvre, Dist. RMN-Grand Palais / Les frères Chuzeville / Art Resource, NY.

diptych depicts Justinian victoriously seated on a rearing horse, while a citizen in the lower zone offers him a wreath crown (fig. 5). Other citizens in the lower zone hold different kinds of offerings.[50] The obelisk of Theodosius I at the hippodrome in Constantinople presents another example.[51] The western face depicts the imperial family seated in the upper zone, as kneeling figures reverently

FIGURE 6. Obelisk of Theodosius I, Hippodrome at Constantinople, western face. Photo credit: Wikipedia Commons.

bear gifts in the lower zone (fig. 6). The worn face of the relief prevents us from identifying the types of gifts the figures offer. Christian images display homage to Christ triumphant in similar ways. At the Orthodox Baptistery in Ravenna, the dome mosaic portrays Christ's baptism in the Jordan (fig. 7).[52] Encircling the central image in the "lower zone," so to speak, are two lines of apostles, who meet to Christ's right and left. Each apostle carries a golden crown of victory for Christ on the occasion of his victory at the Jordan. The apostles offer gifts to Christ on an occasion of his triumph.

Some celebrations of imperial triumph portray the emperor *receiving* crowns and other gifts, but others depict the emperor *distributing* gifts at games held in honor of imperial triumph. For example, consuls of the Roman Empire hosted games on the occasion of their accession to office. They would hold out their insignia to indicate the start of the games but also to "provoke a theophany of Victory."[53] Victorious athletes would receive gifts, such as a crown. The eastern face of the Theodosian obelisk, opposite to the western face we saw earlier, shows Theodosius I extending the victor's wreath in the upper zone, as spectators watch the games

FIGURE 7. Orthodox baptistery, dome mosaic, Ravenna. Photo credit: Alfredo Dagli Orti / Art Resource, NY.

in the lower zone (fig. 8).[54] A golden medallion of Constantius II depicts him in the gesture of triumph standing on a chariot. The lower zone portrays the variety of gifts he distributed to victors at the games held in honor of his triumph, which includes laurel crowns among other things.[55]

Imperial visual propaganda offers precedent for both kinds of triumphant actions: the victor's reception of gifts and the victor's distribution of them. The Christian mosaics coalesce into one image both the actions celebrated in imperial triumphal propaganda—that of receiving gifts and giving them.

The wider iconographic context in which the mosaics at Saint Maurus and San Lorenzo are set point to the interpretation that Christ is the victor who distributes largesse to those worthy of his favor. Christ is the supreme benefactor from whom all good things come.[56] At Saint Maurus, if the apses to the north and south

FIGURE 8. Obelisk of Theodosius I, Hippodrome at Constantinople, eastern face. Photo credit: Wikipedia Commons.

inform one's interpretation of the central one, then one discerns the way in which reception of divine largesse took place.[57] The side apses depict divine epiphanies in which Christ awards his martyrs the crown of victory and enlists them into the heavenly ranks. In the northeast mosaic, Christ appears with each hand holding a crown that hovers over the heads of the martyrs Cosmas and Damian (fig. 9).[58] In the southeast mosaic, Christ again appears, but with each hand holding a crown directly on the heads of two martyrs, Hermacor and Severus (fig. 10).[59] The epiphanies of the side apses mirror that of the central apse (fig. 3). Just as those to the left of Christ in the central mosaic have already received their largesse, so those in the apse of the southeast side have already been crowned. Just as those to the right of Christ in the central mosaic approach to receive their largesse, so those in the apse of the northeast side await the descent of the crowns hovering over their heads.

The hands of the attendant angels in the central apse guide our vision in the same way. The angel to the left of the throne points away from Christ to those who have already received their largesse, while the angel to the right of the throne leads the pious line toward Christ. At the hippodrome that is the church, the site of spiritual athletic contests, Christ extends the gift of victory to those who participate in his triumph. For the bishops, that gift takes the form of a trust: the bishops are entrusted with the care of ecclesial property.

FIGURE 9. Northeast apse mosaic, Basilica of St. Maurus, Poreč. Photo credit: Henry Maguire and Ann Terry Poreč Archive, 1990s–2000s, Dumbarton Oaks, Trustees for Harvard University, Washington, DC.

FIGURE 10. Southeast apse mosaic, Basilica of St. Maurus, Poreč. Photo credit: Henry Maguire and Ann Terry Poreč Archive, 1990s–2000s, Dumbarton Oaks, Trustees for Harvard University, Washington, DC.

The mosaic inscriptions at San Lorenzo also support the interpretation that the bishops and martyrs receive their gifts from Christ.[60] The inscriptions announce the victories of the spiritual athletes and acknowledge divine favor. Beside Bishop Pelagius stands the patron saint of the church, Laurentius, with a book open to Psalm 111(112):9, "He has distributed freely; he has given to the poor" (*dispersit, dedit pauperibus*). The psalm verse announces that Bishop Pelagius has been faithful to the primary task of a bishop: to show mercy to the poor. In symmetry with the Laurentius-Pelagius pair, the protomartyr Saint Stephen carries a book open to Psalm 62:9 (63:8): "My soul has kept close" (*adesit anima mea*). This psalm verse announces Hippolytus's faithfulness as a martyr: his soul stayed close to Christ. Saint Laurentius and Saint Stephen intercede on behalf of Bishop Pelagius and Saint Hippolytus, recommending them with psalm verses that proclaim their faithfulness. Bishop Pelagius "has distributed freely" and "has given to the poor" and therefore receives in exchange the divine favor that brought the construction of the church to its completion. Hippolytus "kept [his soul] close" and therefore receives in exchange the divine favor of a martyr's crown. The scene depicts the distribution of divine largesse to the martyr Hippolytus and the bishop Pelagius.

In return, Christ gives Hippolytus the divine favor of a martyr's crown. The crown marks Hippolytus's triumph with Christ. Likewise, Bishop Pelagius receives the divine favor that brought the construction of the church to its completion. In fact, the inscription that Pelagius installed above the triumphal arch records the favor that Pelagius received from Saint Laurentius's intercessions to complete the church despite violent upheavals:

> The Lord drove out darkness with the creation of light. Splendor belongs to these formerly hidden places. The venerable body [i.e., the church] had narrow entrances. Now a more spacious court fascinates the peoples. Excavated level ground has returned under the mountain; for menacing ruins have been held back by means of great labor. *The martyr Laurentius resolved that his temple at that time should be given to the presider Pelagius as a precious thing.* Wonder at the faith in the midst of hostile swords and anger, that the pontiff keeps a festival with their favors. *You with the stature of the saints, whose fixed determination it was to amplify the honors, grant that the abodes consecrated for you be reverenced in peace.*[61]

The inscription does not deny that there was earthly effort involved in the restoration of the basilica under Pelagius's episcopacy; rather, it refers explicitly to "great labor" (*gravi mole*).[62] At the same time, the inscription credits the celestial favor secured by the intercessions of the patron saint Laurentius for the basilica's completion and the fulfillment of consecratory festivities. "Laurentius resolved" that Pelagius should restore his temple as "a precious thing." It was Laurentius's "fixed determination" that the consecratory festivities be fulfilled despite violent upheavals. It is Pelagius's reception of such celestial favor that the accompanying image celebrates. The scene captures several aspects of vertical exchanges—exchanges that mark relationships of patronage between humans and celestial beings: human supplication, human offering, saintly intercession, Christ's distribution of divine largesse, and the triumph of all in Christ.

Christians in late antiquity could imagine Christ simultaneously receiving Bishop Pelagius's church and giving it back to him. In the early fourth century, Eusebius of Caesarea described an imperial situation in which the moment of offering was the same as the moment of reception. Eusebius writes that he has witnessed individuals go to the imperial court to offer the emperor precious gifts, such as the *aurum coronarium*, the golden crowns. The emperor would receive each gift separately, carefully set them aside, and acknowledge them with munificent return gifts.[63] One can offer the emperor gifts, but, as the patron par excellence, the emperor responds with an even greater show of largesse. Likewise, Christ triumphant fills the center of the mosaic scene as supreme patron. Martyrs offer up their lives and receive the imperishable victor's crown in return. Bishops offer up their building and receive the same building back. By installing the mosaic, Bishop Pelagius publicly acknowledges the divine favor he received. What is more, Bishop Pelagius publicizes his relationship to the celestial patrons, Saint Laurentius and Christ.

If the mosaics celebrate the bishops' reception of divine favor, is it possible that the mosaics also celebrate the bishop as the founder offering the building to Christ? Yes. In Latin, two terms differentiated the actions of offering a building and receiving a church. *Dedicare*, "to dedicate," referred to the bishop's handing over of the building to God.[64] *Consecrare*, "to consecrate," referred to God's sanctification of the place.[65] In legal parlance, consecrated places belonged to "no one," but in theological parlance, consecrated places were thought to be God's property. Canons refer to τὸ κυριακόν, "the Lord's place,"[66] or *rerum dominicarum*, the "things of the Lord."[67] Homilies more often than not refer to churches as "God's house" or the "Lord's house."[68] For a bishop to offer a building to God meant that the bishop dedicated the building to God. For a bishop to receive a church from God meant that the bishop consecrated the church: that God sanctified the church, that God took possession of the church and entrusted the church to the bishop's care. The mosaics simultaneously depict the dedication and consecration.

Coins of the Roman imperial period supply early visual parallels to the sixth-century mosaics cited above, in which, as I have argued, bishops simultaneously offer a building and receive a consecrated church. The coins commemorate the designation of a Hellenistic city as *neokoros* (temple warden) after the city consecrated a temple dedicated to the cult of the emperor.[69] Some of the coins depict a deity, the emperor, and a small model of the newly consecrated temple. Sometimes it is the deity who holds the temple; other times it is the emperor; and still

FIGURE 11. Lesbos coin. Photo credit:
Münzkabinett der Staatlichen Museen
zu Berlin, 18271650. Photographed
by Benjamin Seifert.

FIGURE 12. Kyzikos coin. Photo credit:
Münzkabinett der Staatlichen Museen
zu Berlin, 18221354. Photographed by
Reinhard Saczewski.

FIGURE 13. Philippolis coin. Photo credit:
Münzkabinett der Staatlichen Museen
zu Berlin, 18207397. Photographed by
Reinhard Saczewski.

other times, both the deity and the emperor carry the temple model together. For example, on one coin, the island goddess of Lesbos stands to Emperor Commodus's right, holding the temple with her left hand and a scepter in her right (fig. 11).[70] Between them stands an altar. Commodus holds a spear in his left hand and probably a patera (a libation bowl) over the altar with his right hand.[71] On another coin, Emperor Caracalla stands directly in front of the city goddess of Kyzikos and with both hands carries the temple toward her right hand (fig. 12). Her left hand carries another temple.[72] On still another coin, Elagabalus stands to the left and Apollo to the right, together carrying the central temple (fig. 13).[73] Elagabalus holds the temple with both hands, while Apollo bears the temple in his right hand and an archer's bow in his left. Who offers the temple to whom? Who receives the temple from whom? The coins underscore the reciprocity between the city and the emperor. Neither one is exclusively the giver or the receiver. The city builds the temple for the emperor and offers it to him. The emperor receives it, but he gives the very same temple back to the city by granting authorization for its consecration and designating the city as *neokoros*.

Like such temples of the imperial period, churches were at once gifts given and favors received. As the emperors and deities share the temple model, offering it in each direction or holding it together, so the bishops bearing church models participate in a complex exchange in which the church model signifies at once both that which is given and that which is received. The bishop builds the church, but it is Christ and his saints who bestow the divine favor that brings the project to completion. It is Christ and his saints who entrust their house to the bishop's care.

As was mentioned earlier, Igor Kopytoff cited marriage gifts to describe exchanges that create and reinforce a relationship. In the Coptic Orthodox Christian ritual of marriage, it is the bride and groom who purchase wedding rings and give them to the celebrant, yet it is the celebrant who gives the same rings back to the bride and groom by blessing the rings and outfitting the bride and groom with the bands.[74] The couple gives the rings to the celebrant only to receive the very same objects back, blessed and ritually marked, as a result of changing hands in both directions. Likewise, mosaic depictions of miniature churches in the heavenly courts do not convey a simple act but a complex exchange process, teaching viewers how bishops succeeded in Christ's court.

Contributing Donors and the Vertical Exchange

Dedicatory images illustrated and celebrated the vertical exchange of commodities. But it was not only bishops and founders who set up such images. Contributing donors did too. At Thessaloniki, donors installed a four-part visual narrative in the Church of Hagios Demetrios.[75] The sixth-century mosaic program was severely damaged by a fire in 1917, but the documentation that W. S. George made in watercolors still allows one to study the images.[76] Spandrels D–G of the northern arcade portray a narrative sequence concerning a child Maria and her parents, the donors. By means of the gestures of the figures depicted and the text of inscriptions, the visual sequence "draw[s] the viewer into the dramatic spectacle of the scene[s]."[77] The series serves as a "practical demonstration of [Saint Demetrios's] accessibility to human prayer and intercession."[78]

In spandrel D, a mother receives a child with reverently draped hands from Saint Demetrios (fig. 14).[79] Saint Demetrios's left hand is extended upward to receive something from the figure in a medallion, probably Christ. Saint Demetrios's right hand touches the child Maria and leaves a golden cross on her forehead. To the right of the medallion stands Saint Mary, whose right hand points toward Christ and whose left hand is raised in an *adlocutio* gesture.[80] The gesture calls on the viewer to attend to her narration of what is taking place: Maria's parents supplicating Saint Demetrios, Saint Demetrios making intercessions, and Christ bestowing divine largesse.

FIGURE 14. Watercolor painting of spandrel D, northern arcade, Hagios Demetrios, Thessaloniki by W. S. George. Image from the Byzantine Research Fund Archive. Reproduced with permission of the British School at Athens.

FIGURE 15. Watercolor painting of spandrel E and apex of arch 6, northern arcade, Hagios Demetrios, Thessaloniki by W. S. George. Image from the Byzantine Research Fund Archive. Reproduced with permission of the British School at Athens.

In spandrel E, two attendant angels, Maria in her mother's draped arms, and Maria's father flank Saint Mary standing in the center (fig. 15). Saint Mary continues to guide the viewer's eyes. This time, Saint Mary gestures with her hands to the inscription on her left. The words address the viewer: "Made young again in the times of Leo, you see the church of Demetrios, previously burnt."[81] Three medallions above the inscription depict the patron saint of the church, Saint Demetrios, with two clerical founders (the bishop to his right and the deacon to his left).[82] In thanksgiving for the favor they received, Maria's parents contributed to the restoration of the Church of Hagios Demetrios.

Spandrels F (fig. 16) and G (fig. 17) depict the family making further offerings of thanksgiving to Saint Demetrios. The family uses the same reverential gesture to make offerings as that previously used to request benefaction. In spandrel F, mother and child each offer two candles to Saint Demetrios. The inscription below indicates that their offering is made also to Saint Mary. It reads: "And the lady, the holy Mother of God."[83] In spandrel G, the child Maria offers two doves to Saint Demetrios, and the parents make a final supplication for divine favor in the accompanying inscription: "And you, my Lord Saint Demetrios, aid us your servants and your servant Maria, whom you gave to us."[84]

This series of images puts Saint Mary in the role of a narrator to the viewer. Saint Mary's story is about gift exchanges between parents and Saint Demetrios. By the end of the story, the viewer learns that a couple asked Saint Demetrios for a child, and Saint Demetrios obtained a child for them from Christ. In thanksgiving, the family made donations toward the restoration of Saint Demetrios's church and

FIGURE 16. Watercolor painting of spandrel F, northern arcade, Hagios Demetrios, Thessaloniki by W. S. George. Image from the Byzantine Research Fund Archive. Reproduced with permission of the British School at Athens.

FIGURE 17. Watercolor painting of spandrel G, northern arcade, Hagios Demetrios, Thessaloniki by W. S. George. Image from the Byzantine Research Fund Archive. Reproduced with permission of the British School at Athens.

offered the artistic program, candles, and doves. Yet in the midst of thanksgiving for divine largesse already received, the parents continue to ask the patron Saint Demetrios for his help. The viewer is visually and textually guided through a lesson—a lesson about the method and efficacy of vertical exchanges, taught by Saint Mary herself.

A presbyter Leopardus supplies detailed instructions about the vertical exchange to viewers through an inscription he installed at San Lorenzo in Rome in the early fifth century. The words of the inscription address viewers directly in the second person, commanding visitors to advance peacefully through the church and behold greater and greater wonders. In particular, the inscription invites viewers to notice a hand coming down from heaven and bestowing divine largesse,

FIGURE 18. *Opus sectile* in the depression under the altar of the tomb church at Abu Mina, Egypt. DAI photo archive number L 53300–03. Photo credit: DAI Cairo.

explaining furthermore that divine largesse is awarded for "suitable achievements in the church of Christ":

> Greater wonders follow you who gaze, [wonders that] the labor of Leopardus constructed with care and vigilance. He adorned these walls of Christ with his own expenses. Look at the new sights by advancing peacefully. Behold, a hand of heaven bestows the reward of God, which you see are suitable achievements in the church of Christ.[85]

The inscription not only teaches the viewer how to walk through the space (peacefully) and what to notice (greater and greater wonders, especially the celestial hand granting God's rewards), but even how the viewer might attain divine largesse.

At a small basilica at Abu Mina in Egypt there is a simple dedicatory image as well as an inscription that succinctly summarizes the key features of the vertical exchange process (fig. 18). In the first half of the fifth century, a certain Gerōn commissioned an *opus-sectile* image of the *chi-rho* cross crowned with the laurel wreath of triumph. Below it, he inscribed: "Gerōn dedicated [it] in thanksgiving" (ΓΕΡΩΝ ΕΥΧΑΡΙΣΤΩΝ ΑΝΕΘΗΚΑ).[86] We do not know for what exactly Gerōn is thankful, but we do have his "thank-you card," so to speak, his dedication and installation of an expensive *chi-rho* cross. To make a public "thank-you card" for an unknown divine gift he received, Gerōn set up an image that acknowledges Christ's triumph: Christ's victorious crucifixion. Bishop Pelagius at Rome, the couple at Thessaloniki, presbyter Leopardus at Rome, and Gerōn at Abu Mina all made public, monumental "thank-you cards" to celebrate a gift exchange that would lead to their triumph with Christ.[87]

IS CHURCH PROPERTY A COMMODITY?

Donors' Resistance to Churches as Protecting Places

Ritually speaking, or in the vertical economy, the church building and its artistic installations were exchangeable gifts transacted to create and maintain reciprocal relationships. By contrast, the church building was not for exchange legally speaking, or in the horizontal economy. This economic discrepancy created a "Catch-22" for bishops, the chief administrators of ecclesial property. Bishops occupied a leading position in both the legal and ritual economies. On the one hand, the primary duty of a bishop was to care for the needy, to offer up gifts of mercy to the celestial realm. On the other hand, the riches lavished on churches did not result in accessible liquid wealth—wealth necessary for making gifts of mercy. Bishops were caught between a ritual system and a legal system—a system in which churches were "commodifiable" and a system in which churches were singularized.

The fact that dedicatory practices broadcasted "the holy" in the most extravagant material way conflicted with a spiritually more significant way of embodying holiness: care for the poor. A "good bishop" neither neglected the beauty of the church nor the needs of the poor. One text calls the "greatest virtue in a bishop [...] the gift of giving to the needy,"[88] but, owing to the inalienability of sacred things, bishops were generally restricted to the use of liquid donations and income from revenue-producing lands to amass assets for the needy. Exceptions were made for sacred bronze, silver, and gold *res sacrae*, which could be melted down to generate funds for the redemption of captives.[89] Donors of such objects, however, resisted their alienation, even for exceptional reasons.

From the donors' perspective, bishops were trying to recommoditize their gifts.[90] Dedicatory practices provided a means not for the "pious disposal of wealth"[91] but for the pious investment of wealth. Patrons invested their wealth in the hopes of a return, divine largesse, whether in the form of forgiveness, repose, salvation, remembrance, or other things. Dedicatory images and inscriptions often commemorated not only the investment but the anticipated return as well.

In response, bishops tried to persuade donors that their gifts would not be recommoditized at all. Rather, their gifts would increase in value. Donors' gifts could have an immediate, tangible return that increased and did not diminish the expected spiritual return. Metal objects in the Roman Empire were commonly used to store wealth for future use, since they could be melted and used for their cash value. Bishops used liturgical metal to quickly amass the large amounts of money required to redeem captives. Since donors feared that their gifts were recommoditized, that the sacred things they dedicated were no longer testimony to their desire for sanctity and victory, bishops assuaged their qualms by explaining that their investment was already producing divine largesse in the form of mercy, which in turn could only amplify the eternal spiritual return.

In persuading donors of metalware, bishops had to work around not only legal strictures, but, more broadly speaking, a late antique ethos that frowned on recycling processes that undercut or inflated the original value of an object. Ruth Leader-Newby cites hagiographical examples of donations rejected owing to their infamous *curriculum vitae* or genealogy.[92] Objects used by a prostitute were not to be refashioned into an ecclesial donation because such recycling would inflate the morality of the object. The historian Ammianus Marcellinus recounts a situation in which a banquet guest accused the host of recycling imperial *chlamydes* for use as domestic textiles, such as tablecloths.[93] Such recycling undercut the sacrality of imperial dress. Recycling objects from the nonsacred to the sacred or vice versa dishonored and defiled the sacred.[94]

It is because of this ethos that the alienation of ecclesial property was such a contested issue. Writers like Ambrose of Milan, Rabbula of Edessa's hagiographer, and Caesarius of Arles's hagiographer had an uphill battle to fight in order to oppose donors' views that their donations should not be repurposed. For donors believed that their expected return dissolved with the liquidation of their donated metalware. Ambrose and the two hagiographers argued that dissolution did not occur at all; what did (or would) occur was an amplification of the expected return. Ambrose of Milan insisted that it is "far more advantageous to preserve souls for the Lord than to preserve gold."[95] Souls matter more to the Lord than mere things (donated liturgical vessels). As for Rabbula, his efforts were not only resisted; they were also blocked; his hagiographer reports that he was prevented from alienating liturgical vessels. The *Heroic Deeds of Mar Rabbula* describes the rationale that Rabbula employed to convince his people that donations should be recycled: human souls have priority over liturgical things. Elaborate gold and silver vessels materially express the glory of God, but it is in human hearts that God's spirit dwells: "It is clear to those who know that adorned liturgical vessels of gold and silver are not especially necessary for the glory of God, but that the spirit of God rests in pure hearts."[96] As the hagiographer explains, Rabbula's rationale did not convince his people. The now deceased donors "had offered them [liturgical vessels] to God for the redemption of their spirit."[97] Rabbula was not allowed to interfere, even if his repurposing of the deceased donors' offerings would increase the spiritual value of their gifts, not reduce it. The *Life of Caesarius of Arles* justifies the recycling of donations by locating the "true church" in the human person: "when the censers, chalices, and patens had been given for the redemption of these men, the consecrated ornaments of the church were sold for the redemption of the true church."[98] As I will show in chapter 5, this rationale for using sacred things to ransom captives (in the case of Ambrose and Caesarius) or to support the poor (in the case of Rabbula) echoes a perspective preached by bishops at the consecration of churches: the sanctity of the church as a community takes precedence over the sanctity of the church as an edifice. Performances at the very occasions of church consecrations underscored this hierarchy and thereby lent support to the views of Ambrose and the hagiographers who wrote about Rabbula and Caesarius.

Donors had to be persuaded that a donation for the salvation of one's soul was not undercut by its alienation for the redemption of captives. Donors' expected return on the investment did not follow the tracks of the material object. Though the material object, the metalware, would be liquidated—literally melted down—the investment would not suffer the same fate. The investment would not be dissolved in the process. On the contrary, the investment grew as a result of the liquidation. Since the salvation of a captive was priceless by comparison to the metal liquidated to secure the ransom, the investment exponentially grew from the value of the metalware to the measureless value of the saved captive's soul. The alienation did not demote the donation but promoted it. The donation was inflated in a positive sense that furthered the original purpose of the gift rather than undercutting it. In other words, the face-value demotion of the gift actually served as a vehicle for its spiritualization. From the donors' perspective, by contrast, their singularized gifts were being recommoditized.

As this chapter has shown, the term "singularization" is helpful for describing the nature of the exchange process that took place horizontally, a process that differed significantly from the kind of exchange that took place vertically between the earthly and celestial realms. In the laws and canons analyzed in part I, churches were taken out of the sphere of commodity exchange and made singular. However, in ritual practice, the consecration of a church only marked one link in a long chain of exchanges. The consecration of a church forged a relationship with the celestial realm, a relationship that had to be cultivated and sustained through more and more exchanges that strengthened the tie between the earthly and celestial realms, such as Maria's parents' offering of candles and doves at Hagios Demetrios.

The material culture installed in churches celebrated the vertical exchange process. Dedicatory images and inscriptions portray donors as the clients of the celestial patrons—Christ and his saints. The saints recommend donors to Christ so that Christ might accept gifts from them and in return offer divine largesse. The exchange of gifts does not mark a terminal transaction. Instead, the exchange of gifts initiates and marks a relationship that is expected to culminate in donors' triumph with Christ.

Churches existed in two different economies of exchange in late antiquity: a legal economy and a ritual economy. The discrepancy in the legal and ritual possibilities of exchange caused bishops to operate within one economic system that revoked churches' commodity status, while simultaneously practicing a different economic system that celebrated churches as exchangeable things. Caught between these two systems, bishops like John Chrysostom, who prioritized the vertical economy over the horizontal one, could be tried for violating laws and canons. In late antiquity, building a church meant making a singular, unexchangeable thing as far as legal experts were concerned; but, ritually speaking, building a church meant making a nonterminal gift: the gift of a house for Christ and his cotriumphant saints—a prized gift, but not so prized as the gift of mercy.

Consecrations

Do you not know that you are God's temple and that God's spirit dwells
in you? If anyone destroys God's temple, God will destroy him. For God's
temple is holy, and you are that temple.[1]

The consecratory festival was a major celebratory occasion. Festivals for the
inauguration of a newly built or newly renovated church brought together various members of society to a context in which scripted performances took place
to honor patrons both celestial and earthly and to unveil the beauty of the new
"house."[2] Founders and visitors, young and old, men and women, individuals from
every social role and demographic attended consecratory festivals.[3] It was customary for a bishop to invite fellow bishops to the consecration of his church,[4] to the
point that the occasion of a church's dedication could double as the occasion of a
synodal gathering.[5] For the consecration of the great church of a major city, it was
necessary for the emperor not only to be invited but for him to grant his consent to
the celebration of the festival as well.[6] In addition to the presence of ecclesiastical
and civil authorities at a consecratory festival, artisans, merchants, as well as local
and trans-local visitors would attend.

These attendees participated in various modes—for example, as the audience
of performers or the customers of merchants. Homilists, poets, and orators would
perform publicly on the newly consecrated grounds. Merchants would sell their
wares in tents located in the vicinity of the church.[7] Evidence for consecratory
festivals is limited to the perspective of the orators. There are no extant accounts
composed by members of the audience. It is surely the case that material culture of
the merchants' wares survives, but locating material culture at a specific festival
of inauguration is impossible. However, such evidence does exist for anniversary
celebrations of consecratory festivals, especially the anniversary for the consecration of the Church of the Holy Sepulchre in Jerusalem.[8]

In the fourth and fifth centuries, festivities for the consecration of a church
involved processions of dignitaries carrying donations into the church, the celebration of the eucharist, and oral performances of various types (homilies,

orations, and hymns). Evidence from the writings of Ephrem the Syrian and John II of Jerusalem suggests that in Syria the altar was anointed with oil as early as the second half of the fourth century.[9] Sometimes the dedication would include the deposition of relics and therefore also a relic *adventus* ceremony (a formal welcome of the relic to its new abode).[10] It is clear that late antiquity was a formative period for the composition, redaction, and transmission of rites of consecration. There are witnesses to the fifth-century lectionary readings assigned for the consecration of a church or altar in Jerusalem and in the East Syrian liturgical tradition.[11] However, prayer texts and rubrics for such rituals are transmitted in various liturgical traditions only from the eighth century onward. Those liturgical traditions are (listed here in alphabetical order) Armenian, Byzantine, Egyptian, Roman, East Syrian, West Syrian, among others.[12]

Performances offered praises and thanksgiving in celebration of the new church. The founding bishop's performances included his ritual consecration of the church, his delivery of a homily in praise of God and the saintly patrons of the church, and his hosting of the festival as its primary organizer (ὁ ἔφορος).[13] Orators, in turn, would present encomia to the hosts (the founding bishop and any prominent civic cofounders), which could include descriptions of the church itself and comparisons of the festival to classical ones. Orators' praise of founders offered thanksgiving for the founder's beneficence and hailed founders as exemplars of contemporary virtue for posterity to emulate.[14]

In this chapter, I will show that such performances point to the sanctified space of the church building for two, interrelated reasons: (1) to present what I call a circle of sanctity (among God, patron saints, and founders both ecclesiastical and civic); and (2) to invite participants into this circle of sanctity. Most importantly, performers emphasize the insignificance of the highly ornate church by comparison with the temple that is the human soul. It is the human soul, they insist, that ought to be even more resplendent than the church building. The church building is not an end in itself. All the intense labor and pious supplication that brought the major project to completion merely resulted in a blueprint—a blueprint for what the soul should look like.

This devaluation of *res sacrae* furnished a key element in the conceptual framework of the ritual economy. Writers such as Ambrose of Milan, John Chrysostom, and the anonymous hagiographers who composed stories about Rabbula of Edessa and Caesarius of Arles argued that the human soul was of so much more value than *res sacrae* that even the holiest of church property could and should be used to save human souls. In other words, for these writers the church was a place protecting human souls above all else. The church's status as a protected thing could and should not prevent it from protecting human souls. In the ritual economy, churches were only protected because they were protecting, not the other way around.

REGIFTING

Though the word "exchange" is often taken to connote reciprocity, the type of exchange for which Ambrose of Milan, John Chrysostom, and the anonymous hagiographers (who composed stories about Rabbula of Edessa and Caesarius of Arles) advocated is not reciprocal. Reciprocity implies exchange between two agents, while three agents are always involved in ritual exchanges.

I use the term "regifting" to capture what the writers convey,[15] even though the languages of Greek, Latin, Coptic, and Syriac do not have such a word.[16] I argue (1) that there was a social taboo against regifting in late antiquity, yet (2) such writers advocated for the practice of regifting. In fact, the only method of exchange with celestial beings was that of regifting. One gives to God and the members of God's celestial court by receiving God's gifts and regifting them to others.[17]

Theoretically speaking, why not extend Kopytoff's terminology of "singularization" and "commoditization" and refer to the "regifting of *res sacrae*" as the "recommoditization of singularized things"? The difference between "regifting" and "recommoditization" is that the latter implies a former state of singularity whereas the former does not. "Recommoditization" assumes that the consecration of ecclesial property singularizes it and, therefore, prioritizes the legal concept of *res sacrae*. In this chapter, I take the ritual discourse on its own terms. Since the ritual discourse does not singularize ecclesial property, it is more appropriate to speak of regifting than of recommoditization.[18]

My theoretical construct of "regifting" depends on what Lewis Hyde calls "circular giving." Hyde distinguishes between "reciprocal giving" and "circular giving." While the former denotes only two agents involved in the exchange, the latter requires a minimum of three. Hyde explains the purport of "circle" with the following words, "when the gift moves in a circle no one ever receives it from the same person he gives it to."[19] Though there are many advantages to using Hyde's "circular giving" in lieu of "regifting," I have chosen to adopt the latter for two reasons. The primary reason is that "regifting" highlights the key difference between the legal and ritual imaginations on *res sacrae*. The secondary reason is that I use the phrase "circle of sanctity" in a technical way. Though "circular giving" would resonate well with such a phrase, the similarity may also lead to undue confusion.

The Kula exchange between the Trobriand Islands in the Pacific is the most well-known and well-studied example of circular giving.[20] Bronislaw Malinowski recounted his observations of this practice in an article published in 1920 and in a book that followed it in 1922.[21] Since then, anthropologists and sociologists have returned again and again to the topic.[22] Items for exchange among the Kula consist of shells of various degrees of value, made into and worn as armshells or necklaces. Kula "players" exchange these shells for a higher political status. Players often have to travel long distances and from island to island in order to engage in the exchange. Annette Weiner describes the path as follows: "Each player has a few partners situated geographically to the right and a few others to the left, giving each person access to necklaces coming in a clockwise direction and armshells coming from a counterclockwise direction."[23] As the shells circulate among high-ranking individuals, they increase in value. It is beyond the scope of this chapter to supply a nuanced description of the Kula in all its complexity. I offer this example of circular giving by way of analogy. As I will show, what some writers advocated in terms of gift exchange is akin to the kind of circular giving anthropologists have observed in the western Pacific.

The ritual economy differs in significant ways from what Daniel Caner, following Vincent Déroche, calls the "the miraculous economy."[24] Caner argues that late antique hagiographies show the development of a Christian idea of the pure, disinterested gift otherwise not observable in wider Greco-Roman culture. "Humans involved in charitable transactions were *mere* points of passage in a circle of gifts that emanated from God."[25] However, according to evidence for an important liturgical event in late antiquity (festivals for the consecration of a newly built or renovated church), ecclesiastical leaders in late antiquity preached not a miraculous economy but a ritual economy; not the pure, disinterested gift but the interested practice of regifting; and not humans as "mere points of passage" but as critical ones. The ritual economy identifies humans as critical "points of passage in a circle of gifts that emanate from God," because it is in the practice of regifting that humans become the church, the living temple(s) of God both individually and communally.

In what follows, I first show how both material culture and textual sources make gifts the prominent feature of the consecratory occasion. I then analyze scripted performances to define the "circle of sanctity" and how festival participants were invited to enter that circle. The invitation to enter the circle devalued the significance of *res sacrae* in order to mark the greater importance of human souls. This devaluation led some writers to advocate for the practice of regifting. Though not a term familiar to the late antique figures discussed here, my theoretical construct of "regifting" brings into high relief the latent tension between legal and ritual perspectives on *res sacrae* that sometimes gave rise to conflict when ecclesiastical administrators prioritized the ritual perspective over the legal one.

GIFTS IN CONSECRATORY FESTIVITIES
OF LATE ANTIQUITY

Three pieces of material culture and two texts offer guidance as to how one might draw a mental picture of what festivals for the consecration of churches in late antiquity looked like. They all in one way or another showcase gifts. The late antique mosaics of San Vitale in Ravenna, Italy portray a fictive consecratory procession bearing the gifts of golden vessels. A medieval ivory relief also

FIGURE 19. Justinian in procession, San Vitale, Ravenna. Photo credit: HIP / Art Resource, NY.

depicts a consecratory procession bringing the gift of a reliquary to a church, though scholars are divided as to whether the procession is fictive or not. A type of medieval manuscript illumination illustrates the bishop's consecratory gestures at the altar, the place of gift giving and gift receiving. As for texts, two orations by Choricius of Gaza offer eulogistic descriptions of the festival ambience to laud the founders for their gifts to participants. My purpose for examining the aforementioned evidence is twofold: (1) to paint in broad strokes what a typical consecratory festival might look like; and (2) to demonstrate that each of the images and texts highlights the significance of gift receiving and gift giving at consecratory festivities.

The walls north and south of the eastern apse mosaic at San Vitale, inaugurated in the mid-sixth century, depict Justinian and Theodora in procession, donating golden vessels at the consecration. Justinian and Theodora never actually visited Ravenna, but the mosaicists memorialize their gift giving by imagining the imperial couple in procession, led by Maximianus, the bishop who consecrated the church (figs. 19 and 20).[26] The entourage not only walks in the direction of the newly completed church; it also directs and guides the viewers' gaze to the large-scale mosaic of the apse, portraying Ecclesius, the bishop under whose episcopacy the construction project began, who is in a circle of sanctity with Christ and Saint Vitalis, the patron saint of the church (fig. 4).

FIGURE 20. Theodora in procession, San Vitale, Ravenna. Photo credit: Album / Art Resource, NY.

The Trier Ivory imagines the consecration of a church (fig. 21).[27] The procession portrays relics making their way to the newly built church.[28] The procession has just entered the Chalke gate of the imperial palace.[29] An emperor leads the procession.[30] The founder of the church, the empress, stands at the door of the church with a gesture of hospitality to welcome the procession.[31] The four workmen completing the rooftops convey that this is a brand-new church foundation.[32] The procession passes a three-storied arcade, in which festival participants are portrayed. The nine men visible on the second story cense and sing acclamations.[33] As was mentioned above, according to literary sources, a wide spectrum of population demographics would participate in church consecrations. However, the Trier Ivory does not depict children, elderly, or women, with the exception of the female founder. What the ivory portrays prominently are the patron saint of the church, represented by his or her relics, the founder of the church, and festival participants. The gift, in this case, consists of the relics.

Liturgical homilaries from the eleventh, twelfth, and fourteenth century include illuminations that depict a scene at the altar during a consecration. Gregory Nazianzen delivered a homily at one of the annual commemorations of the consecration of a Church of Saint Mamas near Nazianzen. Four illuminations in liturgical manuscripts that include this homily depict Gregory consecrating the

FIGURE 21. Trier Ivory. Photo credit: Hohe Domkirche Trier – Domschatz. Photographed by Ann Münchow.

church (e.g., fig. 22).[34] Gregory is portrayed prostrate before the altar base, probably anointing it with oil. As noted above, literary evidence from the second half of the fourth century in Syria suggests that consecrations at this time involved an anointing of the altar, but there is no evidence of this sort for other regions like Asia Minor. The central feature of the illuminations is the altar, the locus of gift giving and gift receiving.

These late antique and medieval images imagine crowded streets, doors, and windows, richly arrayed dignitaries, air fragrant with the scent of incense, and, most significantly, magnificent gifts at festivals for church consecrations. Golden bowls on the mosaics of San Vitale, relics on the Trier Ivory, and the table of offering (the altar) in the manuscript illuminations all evoke gift giving.

Like the material culture discussed briefly above, orations delivered at consecratory festivities can be mined for possible sociohistorical data, particularly the two orations of Choricius of Gaza (fl. ca. 527–50), master of the school of rhetoric in Gaza. Choricius's speeches at consecratory festivities fulfilled two rhetorical purposes: (1) to praise the founder for his accomplishment of building a church and receiving the divine favor that brought the construction to completion (through encomia), and (2) to take attendees on a vivid aural journey through the sacred space (through *ekphraseis*).[35] Choricius emphasizes that the spectacle of the consecratory festival consists of the gifts: the church building, especially its reliquaries (if any), artistic installations, and votive offerings.[36] In fact, Choricius says, projects that require such expenditure usually are not unveiled until the occasion of the festival for dramatic effect.[37] Choricius of Gaza's orations describe in vivid detail not only the central spectacle that is the church building but also features of the overall fair, the πανήγυρις or temporary market set up for the occasion.[38]

FIGURE 22. Bibliothèque nationale de France Grec 543 fol. 51v, Paris, France. Photo credit: Bibliothèque nationale de France.

Choricius offered orations at two consecratory festivals for churches founded by Bishop Marcianus of Gaza in the sixth century.[39] According to his oration for the consecration of the Church of Saint Sergius, participants included not only inhabitants of Gaza but visitors as well, because cities sent "the best of their citizens" to participate in the consecratory festival and view the church.[40] Prosperous citizens entertained them at the public expense.[41] As part of the festivities, stories of saints were told out loud about how "those who lived piously [. . .] exchanged piety for salvation."⁴² Other orations included encomia about the founder and epideictic speeches about the church building.⁴³ Colorful tents lined each side of the road to the church, with every other tent decorated with laurel branches.⁴⁴ Wares were sold in the tents, and the marketplace was filled with "convivial gatherings" (τὰ συμπόσια).⁴⁵ An intricate display of lights was used to wish the benefactors "many years."⁴⁶ The founder Marcianus provided a luxurious banquet.⁴⁷ Marcianus and other bishops were carried in litters in processions, as inhabitants and visitors walked alongside them.⁴⁸

Choricius's oration for the consecration of the Church of Saint Stephanus is also a combination of an encomium to Bishop Marcianus and a panegyric on the church building.⁴⁹ Marcianus, Choricius informs us, delivered speeches about the life of Saint Stephanus.⁵⁰ As for the attendees, once again they are made up not only of inhabitants of Gaza but also of visiting citizens from other cities.⁵¹ Choricius praises the quality of food for sale at the festival, mentioning Sicilian cuisine specifically.⁵² The booths are decorated with laurel branches, colors, gold, and silver.⁵³ Colorful curtains and lights in glass vessels also add to the character of the festival.⁵⁴ As at the festival for the consecration of the Church of Saint Sergius, the lamp fires shine through letters cut into the glass, so that the lights together consist of acclamations to civil and ecclesiastical authorities.⁵⁵ As at the festival of Saint Sergius, women freely roam the grounds.⁵⁶ The two main characteristics of "sacred festivals," according to Choricius, are pleasant sights and beautiful words.⁵⁷ After the festivities are over, stories are spread when the attendees are asked by others: "How was the festival of the Gazaeans? How did you enjoy the temple and the festivities?"⁵⁸ Choricius closes with reference to the votive offerings.⁵⁹

Choricius's orations include details absent from the material culture described above: the attendance of women; the consumption of food; and, most importantly, the wider context of market exchanges marked by polychrome and luminous decor. As in the images cited above, Choricius's orations place gifts on center stage—the generosity of the hosts—and highlight them as the primary spectacle of festivals.

Both texts and images corroborate the fact that festivals for the consecration of churches were extraordinarily special occasions when enormous sums were expended to host participants of every social demographic. Performers had as their captive audience the widest array of individuals. As I will demonstrate below, performers used such unique opportunities to convey two messages: (1) that the consecration of the church generated a circle of sanctity between the earthly founders, the celestial patrons, and God; and (2) that participants could join this circle of sanctity by reading the church building as a blueprint for the construction of their soul as a temple of God.

THE CIRCLE OF SANCTITY: GOD, CELESTIAL PATRON, AND EARTHLY FOUNDER

Performers at the inauguration or consecration of church buildings in late antiquity told participants at the inauguration what to see in the church and how to respond to the church. What participants had to see was a circle of sanctity. How participants had to respond was by becoming part of that circle of sanctity. The circle of sanctity consisted of (1) Christ; (2) the celestial patron to whom the church was dedicated (i.e., an angel, saint, martyr, etc.); and (3) the founders of the church. It is the exchange of gifts that generated the circle of sanctity. In other words, gift exchange constituted the key mechanism of relationship building, building a relationship between Christ, the celestial patron, and the founders. The founders offered the church building as a gift and, as a result, became relationally close to God and the celestial patron(s).[60] As for festival participants, they could join the circle of sanctity by reading in the walls of the church a blueprint for how to edify their souls. To advance this argument, I will first analyze the way in which hymns composed for the consecration of churches create a circle of sanctity consisting of God, the celestial patron, and the founders. Then, I will analyze homilies delivered at the consecration of churches to explain how the homilists invited participants to enter this circle of sanctity.

Hymnic texts name the members of the "circle of sanctity" in the context of celebrating a gift exchange within the circle of sanctity. God and the celestial patron grant the founder divine favor to build a house for them. The church founder builds the house, offers it up to God and the celestial patron, but also receives the consecrated church as a crown of piety.[61] Analysis of hymnic texts illustrates these imagined dynamics within the circle of sanctity.

One such hymnic text was written into the walls of Hagios Polyeuktos in Constantinople. Sometime between 524 and 527, Anicia Juliana founded and dedicated Hagios Polyeuktos, by far the most magnificent church in late antiquity, surpassed only by Justinian's Hagia Sophia.[62] Fragments of a monumental inscription survive. The full text of the epigram along with scholia noting where the lines were readable in the church have been transmitted in the *Greek Anthology*, a tenth-century collection of Greek epigrams composed between about 700 BC and AD 600.[63] According to the archeological reports and the manuscript scholia, the metered inscription literally wrapped around the nave entablature of the church, the atrium, and part of the outer entrance of the church.[64] Carolyn Connor estimates that if the letters of the inscription were consistently carved in the size one measures on the extant fragments, then the total length of the inscription would amount to 250 meters or one-eighth of a mile.

This inscription most likely preserves the words of a scripted performance at the consecration of Hagios Polyeuktos.[65] The epigram was composed in dactylic hexameter and consists of two parts: (1) the encomium on the church founder

Anicia Juliana, which lines the walls of the nave (lines 1–41); and (2) an ekphrasis about her pious work, the church of Hagios Polyeuktos, which could be read on five plaques at the entrance to the church and in the atrium (lines 42–76).[66] The encomium in the nave names the circle of sanctity. They are the "heavenly king," the "athletes" or "servants" of the heavenly king like the martyr Polyeuktos, and Anicia Juliana. One of the plaques at the entrance to the church characterizes Anicia Juliana herself as an "athlete" for the feat of her "divine work."[67] Anicia Juliana's "mind is full of piety" (25–26) and in return for her "blameless gifts" (18) to celestial beings, she and her family receive "protection" (39).[68]

The inscription not only declares Anicia Juliana's piety for every reader to acknowledge with his or her own voice. The inscription actually conflates Anicia Juliana's piety with the beauty and holiness of the church. What is more: the church herself speaks in praise of her maker, Anicia Juliana. The personified church asks her founder, Anicia Juliana, "What place was there that did not learn that your purpose is full of piety?" (25–26).[69] Viewers echo the voice of the church herself with each reading of these lines on the north side of the nave. The sanctity of the church—that is to say, the founder's gift—and the sanctity of the founder are literally one. The gift reflects, even gives voice to, the piety of the giver. The epigram renders the church's sacred character indistinguishable from Anicia Juliana's piety.

A Syriac hymn composed one century earlier expresses the relationship between gift and giver succinctly. Balai composed a *madrasha* to be sung at the consecration of a newly built church in Qenneshrin, Syria.[70] Balai was a *chorepiscopos* in early fifth-century Syria and served in the jurisdiction of the bishop of Beroea. Several strophes of the *madrasha* describe the relationship between the founder of the church and the church itself (the house). For example, one strophe (no. 26) reads:

> This visible house makes an announcement
> about the mind of its builder:
> Since splendid and comely is the heart within,
> its love has been given distinction by this visible [house].[71]

For Balai, the beauty of a church building depends on the beauty of the founder's heart. The invisible adornment of the founder's heart contributes to the visible glory of the building.

The epigram for Hagios Polyeuktos and Balai's *madrasha* celebrate a relationship of sanctity between a church and its founder, a sanctity accorded by the favor of God and the celestial patron. According to Balai's *madrasha* and the epigram about Anicia Juliana, because the souls of the founders are beautifully adorned with piety, the work of their soul's labor, the newly constructed churches, is likewise beautiful. Anicia Juliana's athletic crown is not a wreath but the church building. The church building is the founder's crown of piety. The church building reflects the mind of the founder and reveals the beauty of that pious mind to the faithful.

In strophes preceding the one quoted above, Balai expresses some of the theological principles that homilists and other hymnographers emphasized, as we will see below. Balai explicitly names the importance of adorning the human heart as one expects to find the church and also stresses the hierarchy of importance: that the adornment of the human heart is more valuable than that of the church.[72] Not only does Balai succinctly name what homilists expressed in many more words; he also describes a relationship between the heart of the founder of the church and the church itself (the house). It is worth citing the relevant strophes in full (nos. 21–25):

> Three [gathered] in Your name are the Church.
> Protect the thousands in Your house.
> *For they have worked the church of the heart and they have brought it*
> *to the holy temple built in Your name.*

> *May the church within be [as] comely*
> *as the church without is splendid.*
> *May you dwell in the one within and protect the one without,*
> *for sealed with Your name [are] heart and house.*

> Priests who have become the temple of Your Spirit
> succeeded in the building of Your house.
> Bless them since *heart and house*
> with labor and love they have adorned for Your name.

> The priest who built—may his tenure in office endure!
> For years may he be priest in the dwelling he adorned.
> *And may his soul surpass in hidden beauty*
> *the visible adornment the house bears.*

> For his heart bears the temple of His Lord.
> May the pure one enter the house of saints.
> And while You rest upon the understanding
> may You pay a wage for the building of walls.[73]

Though the church building does not surpass the founder's heart in splendor, the building's glory redounds to the greater glory of the founder. Of course, it was commonplace on such festive occasions to praise the founders through various kinds of encomia (hymn, homily, oration, etc.), but the theological principles thereby communicated cannot be underestimated. Praise of the founder underscored the significance of peering beyond the walls of the church to the invisible walls of the interior, human temples and of encouraging a spiritual athletic contest, the goal of which is to have the soul surpass the church walls in glory.

Paulinus of Nola's hymnic homily at the consecration of the newly renovated Church of Saint Felix in January 403 expresses the hierarchy of importance between the soul-temple and the stone temple by acknowledging that the stone temple cannot contain the uncontainable God yet by asking that God dwell in the soul-temple. This acknowledgment takes the form of a concluding prayer to the poetic homily. Paulinus asks the visiting bishop Nicetas and all those present to pray with him:

> Christ God, we build these things for you from our slight and fragile store. Yet things built with hands cannot confine (*capiunt*) You, highest Creator, for the universe with its entire frame cannot confine You. For You, heaven is small and the earth is a pinpoint. But by paying devoted service to Your perennial saints, with paltry homage we revere those great men. We hope that by their intercession You will perfect our completed works, and that as Lodger You will dwell here in the edifice of our hearts (*extructis habitator mentibus adsis*).[74]

Paulinus, like the homilists described below, invites all festival participants to request Christ's presence in their soul-temples by doing what Paulinus as patron did to enter the circle of sanctity of Christ and his saints: paying homage to the saints and receiving divine largesse.

Other homilists and hymnographers detail the method by which festival participants may enter the circle of sanctity and secure themselves welcome in the house of God. The method in question is that of contemplating the church edifice. To my knowledge, only Paulinus of Nola asks, "How, then, can this structure furnish for me a pattern by which I can cultivate, build, and renew myself inwardly, and make myself a lodging for Christ?";[75] but the performers described below were all engaged in answering this question. However, it is important to call attention briefly to the wider religiophilosophical context of festivals, from the time of Plato to the Christian *panēgyreis*, since Christian consecratory festivals of late antiquity belong to a long history of contemplation at religious festivals for soul-edifying ends.

FESTIVALS, *THEŌRIA*, AND THE JOURNEY OF THE SOUL

The Christian homilies and hymns selected for analysis below are not the first pieces of literature to use the spectacle of festivals for a pedagogical purpose: to model the ascent of the soul. Andrea Nightingale has shown how Plato in the fourth century BC defined "philosophy" as not simply the "search for wisdom" but more specifically as the practice of *theōria* that leads the soul up to the divine realm.[76] At the time, *theōria* was the word to describe the practice of spectating in which an individual engaged when he or she traveled to a festival, viewing and gazing on the special spectacles set up for the occasion. The individual would return home with a report about what he or she saw.[77] Plato bookends the *Republic* with the setting of a religious festival. The *Republic* begins with Socrates departing from a religious festival at which he "theorized the spectacle" (θεωρήσαντες) and begins to report what he saw.[78] The *Republic* ends with another religious festival. A certain Er goes on a pilgrimage to attend a religious festival (πανήγυρις), as it were, with the souls of the dead in the underworld. Plato employs the experience of a religious festival to model what the philosopher does.[79] "Plato identifies the philosopher as a new kind of *theōros*, an intellectual ambassador who makes a journey to a divine world to see the spectacle of truth and then brings a report of his vision to the people at home."[80] Vision of the glory of the divine realm trains the eye of the soul to recognize the light of truth and relate that truth to others.[81]

Christian homilists also used religious festivals as a pedagogical context in which to model the practice of *theōria*.[82] The significance of the philosophical *Sitz im Leben* for these homilies delivered at consecratory festivals does not end with Plato. Jeremy Schott compares Eusebius of Caesarea's understanding of the pedagogical purpose of beauty in the homily examined below to aesthetic theories developed by Philo of Alexandria, Plotinus, and Porphyry of Tyre, showing how all these writers identified vision of beauty as the first step in the practice of *theōria*, the practice of the soul's ascent to and unity with God.[83] It is beyond the scope of this chapter to catalogue all the late antique sources that assume *theōria* as the purpose of ecclesial material culture, but it is worth noting two.

First, the contemplative function of pious viewing is named in an epigram composed to accompany a painting of the archangel Michael, attributed to the sixth-century historian Agathias:

> Oh, greatly daring was the wax that molded the invisible chief of the angels, incorporeal in the appearance of his form. And yet it is not without grace, *for a mortal looking on the image directs his heart to a higher contemplation* (ἐπεὶ βροτὸς εἰκόνα λεύσσων θυμὸν ἀπιθύνει κρέσσονι φαντασίῃ); he no longer has a wavering respect, but, engraving the image in himself, he reveres him as though he were present. The eyes coax the intellect out of its depths; by colors can skill transport the mind's apprehension.[84]

The eyes' perception of a corporeal image of an incorporeal being leads the eyes of the soul to perceive spiritual truths.

Second, the *Miracles of Saint Demetrios* attribute a similar function to a silver cross on the dome of a ciborium: "At the very summit flashes forth the trophy that is victorious over death: by its silver composition it amazes our corporeal eyes, while by bringing Christ to mind, it illuminates with heavenly gifts *the eyes of the intellect*—I mean the life-giving and venerable cross of God our Saviour" (87).[85] This description of the process of viewing a cross explicitly names the causative effect corporeal visual perception has on the soul's incorporeal eyes.

Christian homilists speaking *in* a newly consecrated church *about* a newly consecrated church engage in the practice of *theōria*. Four homilists (Eusebius of Caesarea, Shenoute of Atripe, Augustine of Hippo, and Caesarius of Arles) and two anonymous hymnographers took the visual context of the surroundings, i.e., the newly constructed and highly ornate church building, as a starting point for leading the audience to contemplate higher and higher forms of beauty.[86] Performers used the spectacle of the church at a consecratory festival to sketch a pedagogical map for Christian souls to follow. The enjoyment of the glorious beauty of a newly built church was not an end in itself, they would argue, but rather a means of leading the Christian soul to see the kind of beauty with which it ought to be adorned.

INVITING FESTIVAL PARTICIPANTS INTO THE CIRCLE OF SANCTITY

As mentioned at the beginning of this chapter, festivals attracted large numbers of attendees from a great variety of demographics: old and young; rich and poor; local inhabitant and visitor. How were these participants invited into the established and celebrated circle of sanctity? Homilies and other scripted performances on these occasions offer an answer. Extant homilies delivered at the consecration of churches urge the gathered faithful to imitate and surpass the beauty of the church building. In other words, participants are invited to compete in a contest with the founders of the church, to strive in mimetic rivalry to outdo the piety of the church founders, the piety expressed on the visible walls. However, the pious responses to which participants are urged are different from the founder's piety of establishing a magnificent church. Participants are not encouraged to found more churches. Instead, participants' pious responses consist of the practice of virtues, such as the giving of alms.

At festivals that celebrated specific celestial patrons of church buildings and shrines, such as saints and martyrs, homilies often took the form of a panegyric on the individual's life and deeds. Homilists glorify the deeds of the saint or martyr as worthy of imitation.[87] When the relics of the celestial patron were present at a consecratory festival, homilists, such as Ambrose of Milan and Gaudentius of Brescia, would construct their orations focusing on the presence of the celestial patron(s) and how the patron conducted his or her life in a praiseworthy manner.[88]

If a newly constructed church, however, were not dedicated to a saint or martyr or if there were no relics, then homilists, such as Eusebius of Caesarea, Augustine of Hippo, Shenoute of Atripe, and Caesarius of Arles, and hymnographers, like the anonymous composers of the *sogitha* on the Church of Edessa and the *kontakion* on Hagia Sophia in Constantinople, employed a different rhetorical strategy for exhorting listeners to imitate certain behaviors and states of being. These performers used the double meaning of "ecclesia" as "church building" and "church community" to urge the audience to respond to the model example of what it means to be "church" that the newly consecrated building furnishes. Performers urged their audience to peer beyond the church as a "body" to perceive the church as a "soul," a role model for the spiritual edification of the audience.

Eusebius of Caesarea on the Cathedral of Tyre

At the Cathedral of Tyre in 315, Eusebius draws a one-to-one correspondence between the cathedral's architectural features and the types of souls out of which God constructs God's living temple. "Everywhere and from every place [God] has selected the living and firmly set and solid stones of souls. In this manner he builds the great and royal house of all, bright and full of light, both the inner and the outer parts."[89] This living temple shares the same architectural features as the cathedral. Just as the cathedral is divided into parts, so too are the souls divided according to their "powers."[90] Most souls constitute the outer enclosure because they are "incapable of bearing a greater structure."[91] Those who guide others to enter the church form the vestibules. In the rectangular hall beyond the vestibules, the pillars or columns are also guides. These columns bear up the weight of the souls above who are being initiated into the four gospels of the four walls in the rectangular hall. The catechumens are the stones of the walls flanking the basilica along the north and south, looking inward toward the divine things. Some of the catechumens become illumined by receiving light from the windows and are supported by the pillars within the basilica, the "innermost mystical doctrines of the Scriptures."[92] The thrones, seats, and benches represent the souls on which the Holy Spirit sits as a tongue of fire and to whom the Holy Spirit imparts gifts.[93] As for the altar, Eusebius asks, "of what nature would the consecrated and great and unique altar be than the pure and holy of holies of the common Priest of all?"[94] The altar, in other words, represents the soul of Jesus.[95]

Visual perception of the cathedral should lead the Christian soul to contemplate its place in God's eternal house. Visual perception of each inanimate stone should result in meditation on the more important animate stone, the soul. Eusebius explicitly names this hierarchy: the human soul is more important than the inanimate stones that signify it. Eusebius employs superlatives when describing the temple visible to God alone, the invisible temple constructed of souls. Eusebius asks,

> This living temple, then, of a living God, formed out of yourselves—I speak of the greatest and truly holy sanctuary whose innermost shrine is not to be seen by the many and verily is holy and holy of holies—who, if he should see it, would dare describe? Who is able even to look within the sacred enclosures save only the

great High Priest of the universe, for whom alone it is right to search through the mysteries of every rational soul?"[96]

Later in the homily Eusebius says, the church building is "a very great wonder, indeed," but there is another temple "more wonderful" than "wonderful things."[97] What is this more wonderful temple? "The renovation of the divine and rational building in our souls."[98]

Eusebius turns the church building into a mirror for his listeners. When viewing the church, the Christian soul ought to see a reflection of itself. If anything falls short of beauty, it should be the inanimate church building, not the soul. The newly consecrated church is a wonder, but more wonderful than the wonder should be the soul of every Christian, building up the eternal house of God.

Anonymous on the Church of Edessa

A Syriac *sogitha* composed for the consecration of the Church of Edessa around AD 543–54 models the practice of *theōria*, the sight of the visible religious festival leading to contemplation of invisible, edifying realities.[99] The anonymous composer does not delineate relationships between the church edifice and the contemporary souls of the founders and the faithful in the way Eusebius does. Instead, the composer draws one-to-one correspondences between architectural features of the church and significant beings and places of what the hymn calls "the Savior's dispensation," relying primarily on numbers to reveal the meaning of the architectural allegory. The three open windows of the sanctuary reveal the Trinity (13). The many lights call to mind the many apostles, prophets, martyrs, and confessors (14); the eleven columns supporting the bema, the eleven apostles in the upper room (15); the columns behind the bema, Golgotha (16); the five doors, the five virgins (17); the ten columns, the ten apostles that fled from Golgotha (18); the nine steps to the altar, the nine ranks of angels (19).[100] Throughout, the hymn underscores a concept of the temple as a place that reveals divine mysteries. In fact, the third strophe captures the result of practicing *theōria*: "Clearly portrayed in [the temple] are the mysteries / of both Your Essence and Your Dispensation. / He who looks closely / will be filled at length with wonder."[101] Those who contemplate the temple learn from the temple edifice about who God is and what God has done.

Shenoute of Atripe on the Great Church of the White Monastery

According to a twelfth- or thirteenth-century inscription in the north apse, the White Monastery Church was consecrated in the 106th year of Shenoute's long life.[102] In Shenoute's homily on this occasion, he capitalizes on building imagery to comment on the need for purity of soul and, by the same token, avoidance of what pollutes the soul.[103] Shenoute produces out of the architecture of the church a piety of moral living, carrying out one's life in a way that is worthy of God's household.

The soul in which the Lord resides is impact resilient. Like the well-built edifice of the church, pure souls cannot be shaken. Shenoute cites Psalm 45:6: "The Lord is in its midst and she [the soul] will not be shaken."[104] He interprets the notion of stability in the psalm to indicate the soul's refusal to be drawn toward ungodliness and unnatural acts. By contrast, souls that ally themselves with what God hates will have no part in such stability. Instead, they share the same fate as the plastered wall in Ezekiel 13. While such souls claim that their "wall will stand firm," God himself promises in Ezekiel 13:11 that their wall shall fall.[105] In Shenoute's exegesis, the plastered wall refers to a soul that commits evil yet receives honor and commendation in return. The soul corresponds to the wall and the plaster corresponds to the undue praise. Shenoute assures such souls that they will surely tumble down like an unstable wall. With sarcasm, he responds to the praise accorded to such unworthy souls: "where now is your plaster, O wall, and where is the benefit of those who plastered you?"[106] The soul tumbles down like a wall, and the plaster, the undue praise, offers no shield from ruin.

The newly consecrated church offers a visual example of the resistance to ruin that should characterize the soul-temple. The attendees are to see that the walls of the church before their eyes are well constructed and, through the help of Shenoute's exegetically informed commentary on the church, learn that the soul-temple must be a place of God's habitation to have comparable sturdy walls. The beauty of the church building can supply a helpful blueprint, but it is the spiritual temple of the soul and its beauty that matters more.[107]

Augustine of Hippo on Unknown Churches

Shenoute's contemporary Augustine of Hippo also uses the occasion of a church's dedication to characterize the community as the temple of God. The visible building supplies the metaphors, the image of what the community ought to look like. In Augustine's words, "the building which we ourselves are is being constructed for God to live in spiritually."[108]

The construction materials for the spiritual edifice are good works. Faith, hope, and love fashion, make firm, and cement the good works. Humility creates an even floor. Prayers, sermons, and teaching build up the walls. So long as Christ remains the cornerstone, the house will be structurally sound. It cannot "collaps[e] when the rain pours down, nor b[e] swept away when the river floods, nor overthrown when the winds blow."[109]

The most distinctive aspect of Augustine's sermon is the way in which he speaks of God as the head of the household. Augustine turns the eschaton into the day of dedication performed by the head of the household. It is then that God will take possession of the ecclesial body and dwell in it. Augustine exhorts his audience to let themselves be built a spiritual house, "so that the Lord our God may [. . .] *take possession of you* forever as his perfected and dedicated dwelling."[110] More important than the consecration of the earthly basilica taking place in the moment is the future dedication of souls on the last day.

Caesarius of Arles on Unknown Churches

Caesarius of Arles's homilies offer some specific examples of how the soul can advance in athletic training. Caesarius became bishop in 502.[111] During his episcopacy, he delivered three sermons for the consecration of unknown churches.[112] Within the first two sentences of each sermon, Caesarius urges his audience to recognize that the consecration of a church visualizes what ought to be occurring in the "true temple," the Christian heart. Each Christian heart is a house. Gift giving invites God into the house of the heart. In particular, practices of mercy, like generous almsgiving, are the types of gifts that invite God's presence.[113] Caesarius explains that failure to practice mercy damages the house of the heart, evicts Christ, and instead invites the devil. By contrast, almsgiving does to the heart what windows and glittery, reflective, shining surfaces do to the church building. Almsgiving brightly illumines the temple of the heart.[114] Through gifts of mercy, the soul engages in the etiquette proper for hosting Christ as a guest. In Caesarius's words, the soul "invite[s] Christ our Lord in faith, feed[s] Him with hope, and give[s] Him to drink with charity."[115] The Christian who offers him or herself as a "vessel of mercy" (*vasa misericordiae*) receives Christ as he ought to be received and offers him the gifts that are his.[116] The value of these gifts, Caesarius says, exceed the value of the gifts of church buildings. Churches, yes, are "holy," but "much more precious in the sight of God," is the temple of the heart.[117]

Eusebius and Augustine's emphasis on the community together as the temple of God, making one-to-one correspondences between architectural features and individual Christian souls, might appear to contrast with Shenoute's and Caesarius's focus on individual Christian souls as temples. Caesarius, however, shows that the two are not mutually exclusive. Caesarius makes the point that all the individual temples come together to make one temple: "Notice, brethren how beautiful is the temple which is constructed from temples; just as many members form one body, so many temples form one temple."[118] In fact, like Augustine, Caesarius points to the eschaton as the true day of consecration, the day when the many individual temples will be consecrated as one temple.

Anonymous on Hagia Sophia in Constantinople

Eusebius of Caesarea and Caesarius of Arles both noted the effects of luminosity in churches. Eusebius saw the stones of the Cathedral of Tyre on which the light of the windows shines as representative of illuminated baptismal candidates. Caesarius called almsgiving the windows of the soul, since it is via almsgiving that one's soul may be illumined. A *kontakion* composed for the rededication of the Great Church of Hagia Sophia in Constantinople in AD 562 emphasizes how the church building supplies the visual environment for mystical visions to occur through special attention to the performance of light.[119]

Since the festival for the reconsecration of Hagia Sophia began on Christmas Eve, the primary theme of the hymn is that of the incarnation.[120] However, the portions of the poem in which the composer describes the luminosity of the church building capture the principles of interest here. Although the composer does not draw an explicit connection between the human soul as a temple and the reconsecrated building, the theme of luminosity makes the link apparent.

The composer draws a triple analogy between the "ceiling" of the soul, the ceiling of the church, and the "ceiling" of the cosmos (the firmament). The Christian, as a habitation (οἰκητήριον) for the Word, should be covered or "thatched with *luminous* virtues."[121] In other words, virtues do to the ceilings of the soul-temple what gold and jewels do to the ceilings of the stone temple: they create a performance of light.[122] Vision of the church's ceiling leads to "spiritual thoughts" about the cosmic firmament, which in turn result in "a mystic vision of holy waters" (8).[123] The church ceiling spiritually interprets the stars of the cosmic firmament as "spiritual luminaries," such as prophets, apostles, and teachers, who can be seen "flashing with the lightning of their doctrines" (9); it is these spiritual luminaries who "enlighten in the night of life those drifting about on the ocean of sin" (9).[124] The *kontakion* evokes the moisture of the heavenly firmament (7) in naming the "ocean" and "clouds" of the mind (8–9).[125] The "firmament" of the mind, though it contains "clouds of human failings," becomes luminous like the ecclesial ceiling and cosmic firmament when "prayers of fervent repentance" and "tears [. . .] as reinforcements" clear the soul's sky (8).[126] The firmament of the soul rains tears and itself becomes a luminous, starry sky when the mind receives the church ceiling's spiritual teaching on the cosmic firmament: the stars of the cosmic firmament interpreted as the luminous teachings of spiritual luminaries flashing in the ceiling of the church.[127] The anonymous hymnographer used the luminosity of the church building (itself analogous to cosmic light) to create a concrete image of how a soul can become virtuous. Like the homilists named above, the hymnographer treats the completed church building as a blueprint for the construction of the soul-temple.

These homilies and hymns model the practice of *theōria* for festival participants. The performers offer a contemplation of the church building that allows the inner eye of the soul to see invisible, divine truths through the perceiving eyes' vision of a church building. What do these invisible divine truths mean for the ritual economy? To answer this question, I will first argue that regifting was taboo in late antiquity. Then I will explain how the homilists' emphasis not just on the soul's contemplation of the church but on the soul's pursuit of surpassing the church building in beauty contributed to a larger conceptual framework. This broader conceptual framework allowed certain writers to advocate for regifting as a ritual practice, even though regifting was otherwise taboo in late antique culture.

REGIFTING AS TABOO IN LATE ANTIQUITY

A story recorded in Caesarius of Arles's *Vita* demonstrates how countercultural it was to repurpose gifts. According to the story,

> When Caesarius had taken a room at an inn, the king [Theodoric] sent him a silver dish (*discum*) as a gift for use at his table. It weighed about 60 pounds [. . .]. [With the gift] he made a request: "Take this, holy bishop. Your son, the king, asks that your blessedness worthily accept this vessel (*uasculum*) as a gift and use it in his memory." But Caesarius, who never used any silver at his table except spoons, had the dish (*discum*) appraised by his attendants and on the third day sold in public. With its proceeds he started to free many captives. Soon, they say, the king's retainers announced to him, "Behold, we saw your lord's gift put up for sale in the market-place. With its price the holy Caesarius is ransoming crowds of captives. Indeed, so many poor people were crowded into his lodgings, and the entrance hall of his house was so congested, that it was hardly possible to approach him to say hello because of the sheer number of poor men making their requests to him. We also saw countless groups of unfortunate people running about the streets and going to him repeatedly." When he learned of this action, Theodoric admired and praised it so much that all the senators and leading men in attendance at his palace competed in wishing for the blessed man to distribute the price of their gifts with his right hand.[128]

Theodoric gave Caesarius a silver dish of sixty pounds as a gift, asking him to "use" it in his memory.[129] The story plays on the word "use" (*in usum*) to explain why Caesarius repurposed the vessel: Caesarius never "used" silver dishware for his meals. The word that refers to the dish (*discus*) implies that it was a piece of flat-ware. A *discus* of sixty pounds was more likely a decorative piece—literally memo-rabilia, as Theodoric's request suggests. The famous Missorium of Theodosius, for example, was recorded with a weight of fifty pounds.[130] According to the story, Caesarius has the plate sold publicly and uses the proceeds to ransom captives. The ensuing narrative suggests that Caesarius's act of regifting was unexpected, countercultural, and would probably have incurred the ill will of the gift giver, Theodoric. Contrary to expectation, Theodoric expressed pleasure in Caesarius's work, which alone was enough to encourage senators and "other leading men" to "compete" with one another "in wishing for the blessed man [Caesarius] to distrib-ute the price of their gifts with his right hand."[131]

Theodoric gives the gift to Caesarius. Caesarius receives the gift. Caesarius then regifts the dish. The twist of the story is that Caesarius repurposes the king's gift yet does not incur the wrath of the king for doing so. On the contrary, the king praises him. In fact, Caesarius's act of regifting successfully persuades other wealthy individuals to value regifting as a practice in an economy that regards regifting as taboo. The point of this story is to celebrate Caesarius's enculturation of a counter-cultural value: regifting.

Another hagiographical story, set more than a century later in Northumbria, describes how Bishop Aidan regifted a horse that King Oswine had given him. According to Bede's story,

> [King Oswine] had given Bishop Aidan an excellent horse so that, though he was normally accustomed to walk, he could ride if he had to cross a river or if any other urgent necessity compelled him. A short time afterwards Aidan was met by a beggar who asked him for alms. He at once alighted and offered the horse with all its royal trappings to the beggar; for he was extremely compassionate, a friend of the poor and a real father to the wretched. The king was told of this and, happening to meet the bishop as they were going to dinner, he said, "My lord bishop, why did you want to give a beggar the royal horse intended for you? Have we not many less valuable horses or other things which would have been good enough to give to the poor, without letting the beggar have the horse which I had specially chosen for your own use?" The bishop at once replied, "O King, what are you saying? Surely this son of a mare is not dearer to you than that son of God?"[132]

As in the account related of Caesarius, Aidan receives a kingly gift and almost immediately regifts it. In this story, the king directly broaches the subject with the bishop, asking why, of all the many horses available, Aidan regifted the one that Oswine gifted to him. Aidan responds with words reminiscent of those used by Ambrose. Recall that Ambrose had argued that the souls of captives were more valuable than the gold of sacred vessels.[133] Similarly, Aidan defends his counter-cultural action by calling attention to the fact that a "son of God" has greater value than a "son of a mare." Like the story concerning Caesarius, the surprise lies in the performance of a taboo: regifting. In each case, kings (and other high officials in Caesarius's story) learn the unexpected lesson that God values regifting.

Gift giving in late antique societies, like in many societies today, singularizes a former commodity. This is a one-way process in theory, but in practice a singularized commodity may become recommoditized, sliding in the wrong direction of the implied hierarchy on the scale.[134] Recommoditization was taboo and, in the case of *res sacrae*, was expressly forbidden by law. Legally, the ritual of consecration singularized ecclesial property, making *res sacrae* as singular as singular could get, since consecrated ecclesial property was not subject to ownership at all. Ritually, however, the consecration was merely one of many ways that humans regave God's gifts.

REGIFTING IN THE RITUAL ECONOMY

The homilies analyzed above noted the greater value of soul-temples over stone temples. The combination of this point with King David's declaration on his endowment of the first temple gave theologians the conceptual framework to justify regifting as a valued practice in the ritual economy. Of course, this conceptual framework (drawn here on the basis solely of consecratory practices) relates to the shift from classical euergetism to Christian care for the needy.[135] The point here, however, is that the ritual discourse clashes not only with classical euergetism but also with the legal notion of *res sacrae*. I will sketch the conceptual framework by enumerating three interrelated claims.

First, God is the giver of all things. According to 1 Chronicles 29:14, King David acknowledged God as the giver par excellence when he offered an endowment for the building of the first temple: "For all things are yours and we have given you of your things" (LXX: ὅτι σὰ τὰ πάντα, καὶ ἐκ τῶν σῶν δεδώκαμέν σοι).[136] Chapter 4 demonstrated how this message was conveyed via epigraphy and imagery. The second and third claims are made in the scripted performances analyzed above.

Second, humans' return gifts to God benefit humans. The church building—a gift given to God from God's own things—is a site for humans to learn divine truths. The giver of the church building or of votive offerings is the one who benefits from the gift. Eusebius, Shenoute, Augustine, Caesarius, and the anonymous hymnographers each in their own way emphasize that the Christian soul should mirror all that is laudable about the church building—God's house.

Third, there is an explicit hierarchy of value. The gift of a church building is valuable, but more valuable still is the gift of the human temple. The church building visibly represents what the invisible human temple ought to look like. Eusebius, Shenoute, Augustine, and Caesarius each in the own way urge their audiences to let the human temple surpass the inanimate temple in laudable qualities. The human temple is more wonderful and precious than the church building and ought to be treated that way. In short, humans' gifts to God instruct humans on how to give even more valuable gifts to God.

When it came to church property, regifting was illegal.[137] It was illegal to take consecrated church property and repurpose that property. Moreover, the cultural context generally did not value regifting as a practice. The stories about Caesarius and Theodoric's sixty-pound silver dish, as well as Aidan and Oswine's royal horse, have only been recorded and transmitted because of their surprising outcome. The ritual economy, by contrast, did value regifting as a practice. In fact, because God is the giver of all things, the entire ritual economy is based on regifting. The legal regulations on *res sacrae* and the ritual economy could nevertheless coexist, so long as consecrated church property was never repurposed to perform an act of mercy.

Homilists at church consecrations preached the basic principles that underwrite the ritual economy, an economy that makes the repurposing of church property for the sake of performing mercy an acceptable, even virtuous, practice. Eusebius, Shenoute, Augustine, and Caesarius do not explicitly argue this point, but they, among others, set forth the theological framework on which the ritual economy is based. To find voices that explicitly argue that sacred things should be repurposed to practice mercy, it is necessary to look beyond festivals for church consecrations.

Rabbula was the bishop of Edessa in the fifth century. The writer of Rabbula's hagiography tells the following story about him:

> [Rabbula] straightaway ordered that many silver vessels, which had been fashioned with care for the serving of ten tables of clerics, be sold. He distributed equitably the price they fetched for the use of the needy. He gently persuaded the clerics to use clay vessels. He also determined to sell the liturgical vessels of silver and gold which the churches had and to give the prices they fetched to the poor, as he said, "It is clear to those who know that adorned liturgical vessels of gold and silver are not especially necessary for the glory of God, but that the spirit of God rests in pure hearts." Yet his order was neglected because of their contempt. At the request of many, he was restrained from doing this because the vessels were the offering of their earlier, now deceased, fathers, who had offered them to God for the redemption of their spirit.[138]

The character in this story, Rabbula of Edessa, did not himself dine with silver dishes (recall the same custom mentioned in connection with Caesarius above).[139] Rabbula preferred the use of less expensive, ceramic vessels because he did not believe that gold and silver were necessary for expressing or communicating the glory of God.[140] In fact, Rabbula is said not to have engaged in any ecclesial building projects except to repair a damaged nave.[141] Rabbula advocated for the alienation of gold and silver liturgical vessels in order to raise funds for the support of the needy. Rabbula argued that God does not need silver or gold dishes either because, as scripted performances at consecrations emphasized, the more valuable temple and place of God's dwelling is that of pure hearts. So Rabbula tried to repurpose consecrated silver and gold vessels to support the poor, but his effort was thwarted. According to the hagiographer, Rabbula's opponents thought the act of regifting liturgical vessels in the service of the poor would interfere with the deceased donors' exchange with God. The deceased donors gave the vessels "to God for the redemption of their spirit." Regifting the vessels, the opponents imagined, would interfere with this ritual exchange. So Rabbula was not permitted to repurpose the sacred things.

John Chrysostom's homilies on 2 Corinthians and the Gospel of Matthew show how this fourth-century priest of Antioch and later bishop of Constantinople would have responded to Rabbula's opponents. John Chrysostom would have asked, "What does it mean for the deceased donors to have given the golden vessels for the redemption of their souls?" John Chrysostom says in a homily on the Gospel of Matthew: "Let us not consider offering golden vessels only, but [let us also offer] righteous labors. [. . .] It is necessary for us to offer souls, since God in fact accepts [vessels] for the sake of souls."[142] For John Chrysostom, the fact that precious things are offered for souls only underscores the value of souls. Therefore, using precious liturgical vessels to help other souls makes the original donor's offering even more valuable to God. Regifting does not interfere with the exchange process; on the contrary, it enhances the exchange; it brings the exchange to whole new level of value. To use an analogy from today's system of banking, imagine the deceased donor had opened up a certificate of deposit and placed $1,000 in a bank to accrue a fixed amount of interest. Rabbula's opponents claim that taking that certificate of deposit and using it to support the poor interferes with the deceased donor's interests. John Chrysostom would respond that, far from interfering with the deceased donor's interests, using the money to support the poor is like depositing $100,000 in place of the original $1,000. In general, John Chrysostom advocated so much for the prioritization of mercy toward the needy over the adornment of churches that one can speak of a "liturgy of the poor" preached in his works.[143]

In a homily on 2 Corinthians, John Chrysostom captures with one image what homilists and hymnographers expressed in many words. John Chrysostom says the priest stands at the altar in church and invokes the Spirit. Likewise, Christians ought to stand at the altar of others' souls and invoke the Spirit by doing good deeds toward others. "Whenever you see a poor believer," John Chrysostom says, "think that you are looking at an altar."[144] In the ritual economy, there are altars everywhere, visible altars of churches and invisible altars of souls. Gifts at both types of altars are valuable, but the gifts of higher value in the ritual economy are the ones offered on the altars of souls.

In the second century AD, an orator named Lucian spoke in a beautiful hall.[145] The topic of his speech was whether the hall was a help or a hindrance to the speaker.[146] For the first half of the speech, Lucian makes the case that the hall helps the speaker make a good speech. For the second half of the speech, Lucian makes the opposite case—namely, that the hall hinders the speaker from making a good speech.

Christians in late antiquity struggled with a similar question. Are lavishly bedecked church buildings a help or a hindrance to Christians' spiritual edification? The answer that orators provide on the very occasion of church consecrations and on other occasions, too, is that the church buildings are a help. Other writers, like Ambrose and John Chrysostom, would add the following qualification: so long as Christians are encultured to value regifting as a practice in the ritual economy. Responding rightly to the beauty of a church building means learning the values of the ritual economy—that is, learning that God is the only one who gives, that all Christians do is regift, that all Christian regifting is actually for Christians' own benefit, and therefore that intangible gifts of mercy are more valuable than the tangible offerings made in church buildings. Homilists at church consecrations use the church building as a help in their efforts to guide the audience to recognize the glory and protection of God that surpasses that of the hall and to urge the audience to build themselves up as spiritual matches to the building's material display. The edification process, though spiritual in its *telos*, consists of building a relationship with the celestial realm through the exchange of gifts.

Conversely, the church building could be a hindrance because it could prevent the faithful from ascending to the spiritual meaning of the place and because it could prevent funds from being used for showing mercy to the needy. In addition to the story of Rabbula recounted above, a story told of Pachomius and Ambrose's response to charges illustrate how the beauty of the church may be a hindrance to the faithful.

As we saw, Balai's wonder at the beauty of the church of Qenneshrin led him to even greater wonder at the heart and soul of the founder. By contrast, we are told that Pachomius, the fourth-century Egyptian monastic leader, had the opposite reaction to a church. The *Paralipomena* records the following story:

> The blessed Pachomius built [a chapel] and he made porticos for it and set up pillars of bricks, and he furnished it very well. He was pleased with the work, because he had built it well. Then he thought that it was through a diabolic activity that he was marveling at the beauty of the house. Therefore he took ropes and tied them to the pillars; then he made a prayer in his heart, ordered the brothers to pull and bend all the pillars so they remained crooked. And he said to the brothers, "I pray you, brothers, do not make great efforts to adorn the work of your hands. But whatever may enter into the work of each one of you by the grace of Christ *and from his gift*, take great care that your mind may not stumble through the praise given to the art, and become a prey to the devil."[147]

Pachomius received the gift of building a chapel from Christ. He performed the task in such a fine manner that he began to admire his own work. Because he lost sight of Christ and Christ's gift, he taught himself a lesson by defacing his fine work.

This story captures the idea that the gift of God (the chapel) that humans (Pachomius) give to others (the brothers) ought to lead humans to God and not away from God. Because Pachomius's soul was not in fact worthy of the beauty of the chapel, Pachomius had the place defaced. Pachomius went so far as to damage the newly erected chapel, in order to prevent its beauty from distracting liturgical participants.

Ambrose of Milan's justifications for alienating ecclesial property reiterate the same theological principles named above. Ambrose cites the hierarchy of importance of the soul-temple over the stone temple to celebrate the alienation of ecclesial property as the morally appropriate course of action for a Christian leader.[148] In his treatise *On Duties*, Ambrose both identifies the primary responsibilities of church leaders and offers a defense for melting down consecrated golden chalices to amass funds for the redemption of captives, to build more churches, and to buy land for cemeteries. Ambrose says the following about the duties of ecclesiastical administrators:

> Here is what is appropriate for a priest (*sacerdos*) in particular: to deck out the temple of God with a splendor that is suitable, making the courts of the Lord resplendent

by giving them a particular finery; to make sure that money is always being spent in accordance with the obligations that mercy imposes; to give strangers what they genuinely require, not sums that are unnecessary but amounts that are suited to their actual needs, so that things do not go beyond what humanity demands but are in keeping with its constraints.[149]

Although Ambrose names the beautification of churches before acts of mercy in his summary of the obligations of church leaders, he nevertheless justifies his own choice to prioritize an act of mercy over the sacrality of church property. In the same book, Ambrose later defends his own decision to melt down golden vessels for charitable purposes and explains to his intended clerical readers that they may do the same "without doing anything irreverent."[150] Ambrose argues that the "real treasure of the Lord," "the gold of Christ," lies not in golden vessels but in Christian souls.[151] He prioritizes acts of mercy over the glory of temples. Like John Chrysostom's fiftieth homily on Matthew, Ambrose claims that ecclesial gold only has value because it is for Christian souls. With a play on the words *redemptor* and *redimo*, Ambrose says, "This was the very function for which the gold of the Redeemer deserved to be of value—ransoming those in danger."[152]

As the writings of Ambrose and others show, Eusebius, Shenoute, Augustine, and Caesarius were not the only ecclesiastical leaders to prioritize the consecration of the temple of the soul over that of newly built or renovated ecclesial structures.[153] However, the significance of their words lies less in what they said than in the occasion on which they chose to say it—at the very event that, legally, constituted the moment when the church became a *res sacra*, a gift offered in perpetuity to God that in principle could not be regifted under any circumstances. It is at this moment that the homilists Eusebius, Shenoute, Augustine, and Caesarius devalue *res sacrae* as mere *res*, focusing instead on the importance of making human souls holy.

Festivals for the consecration of churches celebrated relationships within the circle of sanctity: God, the celestial patron, and the church founder. Participants could join the circle of sanctity through the following steps. First, by entering the newly built house of God, participants would be surrounded by the example of the church founder's piety visually expressed in the beauty of the church building. Second, by responding piously to the church building (in other words by responding piously to the church founder's piety expressed on the walls), participants could be welcomed into the circle of sanctity. Responding piously to the church building meant offering the gift of oneself as a vessel of mercy—either by imitating the soul of Christ, as Eusebius would say, or by giving alms generously, as Caesarius would say. Exchanges within the circle of sanctity operated according to the rules of the ritual economy, an economy that valued regifting or what Hyde calls "circular giving." The operation and effect of regifting in the ritual economy can be schematized by the diagram below. As gifts circulate from one person or group to another and the circle of sanctity enlarges, the glory that redounds to previous givers multiplies.

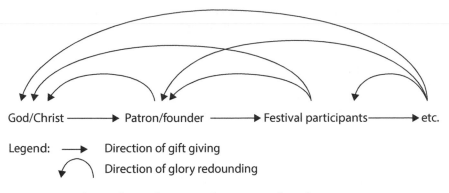

God/Christ ──────▶ Patron/founder ──────▶ Festival participants──────▶ etc.

Legend: ──▶   Direction of gift giving
         ↙   Direction of glory redounding

CHART 1. Regifting in the ritual economy of consecratory festivals.

An altar cloth described by Paul the Silentiary vividly captures the core message of the ritual economy. Paul the Silentiary delivered an ekphrastic poem on the
renovated Hagia Sophia during the festivities for the rededication of the church
between December 24, 562 and January 6, 563.[154] The altar cloth, he says, depicts
Christ flanked by Peter and Paul within a temple enclosure in the main register.[155]
The lower register, the hem, portrays pious foundations, such as churches and
hospitals, alongside illustrations of the miracles of Christ.[156] The Silentiary does
not offer further commentary on the altar cloth, but in the context of the ritual
economy described above, the textile speaks volumes. The historical merciful acts
of Christ are placed side by side with the places where Christ's mercy can presently
be found—at churches and at hospitals (legally, "pious foundations" since the time
of Justinian). The altar cloth itself, a consecrated textile, depicts merciful acts as the
greatest offerings or return gifts or regifts one can lift up to Christ and his saints.
The textile juxtaposes Christ's acts of mercy with the places in which his mercy
may continue to be sought, and that juxtaposition happens on the altar itself,
the place of gift giving and gift receiving.[157] What is a church for? According to the
implied ritual economy of performers at festivals for church consecrations: gifts of
mercy for human souls.

6

Anniversaries

It is not the place that commends man, but it is man who commends
the place.[1]

The previous four chapters have shown how the main corollary to the definition
of *res sacra* differed depending on whether the primary context was legal or ritual.
Legally, the corollary that a church is protected took precedence; ritually, the corollary that a church is protecting did. This chapter shows how non-Chalcedonian
writers used the ritual context to completely override civil authorization of the
concept of *res sacrae*.

Recall that Augustine and others had petitioned to have the Donatist bishop,
Crispinus of Calama, penalized in Africa on the basis of a law promulgated against
heretics in the Roman prefecture named the East.[2] All our information regarding
this particular dispute comes from members of the prosecution. We will never
know how Crispinus defended himself. By contrast, we do have the voices of
opposition that non-Chalcedonian writers transmitted in response to their Chalcedonian rivals' legal upper hand. The objections were not recorded in the form
of legal literature. Instead, such defensive voices were raised in ritual contexts celebrating anniversaries of church consecrations.

The historical evidence analyzed here is of a different nature from the foregoing chapters. It is shrouded by the strategy of pseudepigraphy.[3] Two homilies
produced in the late sixth or early seventh century tell stories about how churches
were consecrated. One is attributed to Basil of Caesarea, the other to Theophilus of
Alexandria. They have been difficult to interpret, considered at best "pious fic-
tions" and at worst "apocrypha" among scholars. I will show that these pseudepi-
graphic homilies respond to the issue of which churches are sacred. The writers
assume a great deal of contextual knowledge on the part of the implied audience.
The wider legal and ritual discourse of late antiquity, coupled with ongoing debates
over the administrative decisions made at the Council of Chalcedon, provide the
interpretive keys to these cryptic homilies. The shrouded stories respond to
the question of what counts as *res sacrae*.

On the anniversary celebrations of churches' consecration, these pseudonymous writers offered a reason independent from the juristic one for why their churches were sacred—not because they were legally consecrated but because Christ's very own hands sanctified them. Of course, the bishops and other writers and artists cited in chapters 4 and 5 would not have denied the presence and authorization of Christ and his saints at fourth- and fifth-century consecrations, but they did not detach the significance of such celestial authorization from its civil intermediaries. Recall that Justinian and Theodora's depictions stood right alongside episcopal depictions at San Vitale in Ravenna (figs. 4, 19, and 20). The sixth- and seventh-century writers discussed in this chapter did detach celestial authority from civil intermediaries. Christ and his saints directly governed and enforced the sacrality of churches and the protection of churches. The sixth- and seventh-century need to override the law arose in the long aftermath of the Council of Chalcedon in 451.

The Council of Chalcedon in 451 led to a deep rift between Chalcedonians and non-Chalcedonians.[4] By the late sixth and early seventh centuries, the church was geographically divided. For the most part, non-Chalcedonians dominated the Roman regions of Egypt and Syria, while Chalcedonians largely held Asia Minor and Palestine. Chalcedonian churches were legally recognized. Non-Chalcedonian ones were not.

Non-Chalcedonian writers would use church building and consecration as a narrative topos for defending the sanctity of their places of worship and responding to Chalcedonian claims. Dispossessed of legal status and exiled from the sacred topography of Palestine, non-Chalcedonian writers deployed a ritual conception of "the sacred" to insist on the sanctity of their holy places despite the law, to de-stress the significance of *res sacrae* in Jerusalem, and to create a new Holy Land.

Since the imperial government did not recognize the episcopacy of non-Chalcedonian bishops, the church consecrations they performed were, therefore, not legally valid and did not generate *res sacrae*. To bypass the imperial authorization that they lacked, non-Chalcedonian writers appealed to the authorities of the heavenly realm, Christ the King par excellence and his agents, the holy ones. The consecration of churches, according to these non-Chalcedonian narratives, took place at the very hands of Christ, as well as the patron saint of the church. The celestial agents who performed the liturgy indisputably bore authority for Chalcedonians and non-Chalcedonians alike. There was no need for recognition from the emperor, no need for an intermediary government. Christ and his court governed non-Chalcedonians directly.

However, the narratives do not appeal solely to the authority of the agents performing the ritual, in accordance with legal stipulations. The stories also claim sacred status as defined in the ritual sphere. Their holy places promoted practices of mercy. The narratives praise those who expend their assets on those in need and they denounce the wealthy who fail to practice mercy in such ways. These stories were composed as homilies to be read at the respective church's annual anniversary of consecration. Yearly, festival participants would gather to hear the story of how the church was originally built and consecrated by Christ himself and his saints.

Because the non-Chalcedonian stories offer ritualized responses to legal issues concerning the consecration of churches, this chapter makes them the centerpiece of an analysis of anniversary celebrations. Many other types of anniversary practices, however, arose in late antiquity. Though they will not be the focus of study, the next section offers a brief overview of them in order to situate the specific anniversaries to which this chapter is devoted within the broader context of anniversary celebration.

ANNIVERSARY CELEBRATIONS

Of all church consecrations, one stood out, and in retrospect it became significant throughout the East: the dedication of the Church of the Holy Sepulchre in Jerusalem in 335.[5] The church's imperial founder, Constantine, did not attend the consecration, and none of the performative elements of the occasion were published in antiquity.[6] So we do not know what was heard and seen at the festivities of the inauguration in 335. This fact stands in stark contrast to the mass of evidence that survives of anniversary celebrations for the inauguration of the Church of the Holy Sepulchre, not only at the church itself, but elsewhere across the Mediterranean as well. The first known pilgrim to attend an anniversary of the Church of the Holy Sepulchre's consecration is Egeria. Like the *theoroi* described in the previous chapter, the nun wrote a report for her fellow ascetics at home in Hispania. She places the importance of the festival on par with the great feasts of Epiphany and Easter and describes where and how each day of the octave was spent.[7] The feast, as Egeria and the historian Sozomen note, could be referred to simply as the *encaenia*, the feast of "renewal."

The *encaenia* coincided with the feast for the finding of the cross, and this dual celebration migrated far beyond Jerusalem and its environs, spreading into every eastern Christian liturgical calendar. At these anniversary celebrations, homilists often addressed the theme of the resurrection (on account of the name of the church commemorated) or the cross (on account of the proximity of the feast day to the feast of the cross and the coordinated theme of the passion). In the West, the feast of the cross migrated without its concomitant celebration of the *encaenia*, since, by the seventh century, the importance of the *encaenia* came to be eclipsed by that of the cross. In the East, the relationship between the *encaenia* and the cross became so obscure that even Sophronius of Jerusalem could confess that he did not understand why the resurrection was celebrated as a prefeast to that of the cross.[8] It is during this time that the feast of the cross made its way into Western calendars without the *encaenia*.[9]

In the West, as in the East, however, the anniversaries of other specific churches would become so important that their celebrations would spread beyond the locale of the church building. The festivals for the anniversaries of the Lateran, of Saints Peter and Paul, of the Liberian Basilica, and of the Archangel Michael spread throughout the West.[10] In Armenia, the celebration of the anniversary of the Church of Etchmiadzin, "mother of all the churches of the world," spread.[11] Like saints, churches had birthdays, too, and they were celebrated in similar ways. Though the birthday celebration of the Church of the Holy Sepulchre became most widespread in late antiquity, locally the birthdays of nearby churches would be celebrated year after year, and sometimes these festivities migrated beyond the locale of the church itself too.

In Syria, a general birthday of "the Church" and all church buildings developed. This feast would be celebrated for two to five weeks to launch the start of the liturgical year in West Syria, but it was celebrated to mark the end of the year in East Syria. The length of the feast varies (two, three, four, or five weeks), depending on the calendar.[12] The same set of lections are prescribed in both West and East Syrian four-week-long periods.[13] This period has two names in East Syrian liturgical books: "renewal of the Church" (*ḥuddāt 'ēdtā*) and "dedication of the Church" (*quddāš 'ēdtā*).[14]

A survey of all the evidence for retrospective practices would create a dizzying array. A large amount of historical evidence survives for anniversary celebrations in late antiquity, relative to the amount of evidence for the inaugurations. This chapter analyzes only select anniversaries celebrated in the region of Egypt in order to show how homilists deployed anniversaries as occasions for defending the sanctity of illegal churches.

NON-CHALCEDONIAN HOMILIES ON THE FIRST CHURCH OF MARY

For the unknown homilists of this chapter, the church building is not an exemplar of beauty that human souls must surpass, as the known homilists discussed in chapter 5 maintained. The church building is actually held to an even higher standard than human souls. Materials used for church construction must be perpetually spotless. This exceptionally high standard for the "life cycle" of church construction materials—a theological perspective at odds with the principles analyzed in chapter 5—developed not in conversation with fourth- and fifth-century homilies and hymns but in defense of non-Chalcedonian causes. Because non-Chalcedonian churches were not consecrated by imperially endorsed bishops, because their places of worship were denied the legal status of *res sacrae*, non-Chalcedonian writers defended the sanctity of their holy sites by claiming that they were sanctified by the very hands of Christ and his saints. One narrative goes so far as to claim that a part of the church was *acheiropoiētos*, not made by human hands. The composers of two homilies concerning the very first church built in the name of Saint Mary insist that the respective churches were completely virginal. The homilists produce a high standard for the church building, one that the listeners must rise up to meet in order to gain entry into the church, but one that would be difficult to surpass.

In Copto-Arabic literature, three different stories claim to commemorate the first church built and consecrated in the name of the Virgin Mary. One story claims that this church is in Philippi; another claims it is in Koskam; and still a third claims it is in Athribis.[15] The stories evince no awareness of each other's claims to primacy. The feast days of each consecration coexist on Egyptian liturgical calendars despite the fact that the stories of Philippi, Koskam, and Athribis make mutually exclusive claims.[16] One Ethiopic collection of the miracles of Mary juxtaposes the stories about Athribis and Koskam—again despite their mutually exclusive claims.[17]

In what follows, I focus on the accounts concerning Philippi and Koskam. At the end, I return to the story concerning Athribis. I argue that the anonymous writers who assumed the pseudonyms of "Basil of Caesarea" (for Philippi) and "Theophilus of Alexandria" (for Koskam) hypervalorized the sacrality of their churches to the following ends: (1) to claim for their churches the status of "sacred thing" (*res sacra*) despite imperial repression; and (2) to respond to their dispossession of *res sacrae* in Palestine. The stories offer two-pronged, non-Chalcedonian responses to Chalcedonian possession of churches in Palestine, particularly Jerusalem. I will first analyze the special status claimed for the churches of Philippi and Koskam. Then I will propose political subtexts related to the aftermath of the Council of Chalcedon in 451 and explain how the compositions address the trauma of ecclesial dispossession and consolidate the identity of a non-Chalcedonian opposition.

The Ps-Basilian and Ps-Theophilan stories have been difficult to place historically, though by all accounts scholars consider them late antique compositions.[18] I argue that they belong to the period of the late sixth and early seventh centuries. Like most Coptic literary productions of this period, the texts respond to the Chalcedonian Byzantine Empire's claims.[19] They do so, however, in subtle ways, and their concern lies not in doctrinal matters but in *res sacrae*, in churches.

Witnesses to Ps-Basil and Ps-Theophilus's homilies survive in multiple languages: Coptic, Arabic, and Ethiopic. Ps-Theophilus's homily (*maymar*) also survives in Syriac. The earliest witness to Ps-Basil's homily ("catechesis") dates to the tenth century, and it is possible that the earliest witness to Ps-Theophilus does, too. A late-tenth century manuscript that originally belonged to the library of the Monastery of Saint Macarius in Wadī al-Natrūn, Egypt transmits Ps-Basil's homily in Bohairic Coptic.[20] Sahidic Coptic fragments of Ps-Theophilus's homily that may date to the tenth or eleventh centuries originally belonged to the White Monastery in Sohag, Egypt.[21] The two texts circulated widely in Arabic translation and redaction, sometimes occupying the same volume.

WHY THE FIRST CHURCH OF MARY IS SACRED

Both stories claim that their respective churches were the first ever to have been built and consecrated in the name of the Virgin Mary. For this reason, they are irrefutably sacred, even if they are not legally *res sacrae*. In addition to the personal involvement of Christ, angels, saints, and the Virgin Mary herself, the stories emphatically underscore the sacrality of the church in still other ways.

According to Ps-Basil of Caesarea, the foundations of the first church in Philippi were miraculously and effortlessly drawn, having been laid by the hands of the apostles Peter and Paul and led by the hands of Christ himself. During the ritual of consecration, Christ laid hands on Peter and ordained him patriarch of the apostles. The church is irrefutably sacred because Christ himself, his mother, and the apostles conducted the entire affair, and that included the choice of location, the demarcation of foundation lines, the construction, and the consecration. In fact, the first patriarchal ordination in Christian history occurred in it just after the church was consecrated.

Whereas Basil learned all these details by finding a letter written by the hand of Luke the doctor of Antioch, Theophilus heard about the first church built in Koskam firsthand in a personal revelation from the voice of Mary herself. Mary told Theophilus that before Christ ascended to heaven, he took her and the apostles to Koskam and consecrated the very first church ever built in her name.[22] The ritual practice observed at that service became the model that every church consecration thereafter would follow.[23] The church is irrefutably sacred because Christ himself, Mary, and the apostles consecrated it not only before Mary died but even before Christ ascended to heaven. What is more: it was at Koskam that Christians first learned how to consecrate a church.

The first churches of Mary were so sacred that they served as the church of the first patriarchal ordination and the church of the first consecration ritual, respectively. Legally, however, non-Chalcedonian churches were not *res sacrae*. Roman and Byzantine law and ecclesiastical canons designated only churches consecrated by imperially endorsed bishops as *res sacrae*. Because the non-Chalcedonian ecclesiastical hierarchies did not have an imperial stamp of approval, they resorted to authorization beyond the realm of the law. No mere bishop, legally recognized or not, consecrated non-Chalcedonian churches. Christ the King himself consecrated them. Yet the stories do not stop there. The special construction materials and the saints' protection of the churches testify to a sacrality *intrinsic* to the material churches.

Special Building Materials

The Construction of the Churches at Philippi. The "catechesis" of Ps-Basil of Caesarea recounts the construction of not just one but two churches: the original church of Mary built by Christ, Peter, and Paul and a new public Great Church constructed under the patronage of Bishop Basil and a civil official, the *praepositus*

Eumenius.[24] The story mirrors the two construction processes by means of a narrative doublet. In the course of each construction—that of the original church and that of the new church—the narrative juxtaposes the privileged sight of the clergy with the obstructed view of the marveling people. During the construction of the original church, only the apostles and the few disciples see Christ pour water into the foundation lines and command columns to set themselves up. The crowd of people watch and marvel at the spectacle without seeing Christ.[25] During the construction of the new church, Mary tells Basil how to find an *acheiropoiētos* ("not made by hands," ⲁⲟⲛⲉⲭⲓⲝ ⲛ̄ⲣⲱⲙⲓ) mosaic of her.[26] Basil finds the mosaic covered with a silk cloth, uncovers it, and sees the face of Mary depicted on it. After he and the clerics accompanying him bring the mosaic and set it down in front of the sanctuary, the crowd marvels at the size of the slab and its covering, without seeing the mosaic image.[27] The privileged seers see Christ on the first occasion and they see the depiction of Mary on the second occasion; the crowds in each case marvel at an obstructed vision. This narrative trope of privileged sight amplifies the sacrality of the building materials at both moments of construction. The more sacred the sight, the more restricted its viewing becomes.

The building materials are specially chosen by Christ or Mary. This feature is particularly pronounced in the story of the Basilian foundation. Basil had already acquired precious materials, itemized three times in the narrative as a slab of hyacinth (ⲡⲗⲁⲝ ⲛ̄ⲣⲓⲁⲕⲩⲛⲑⲓⲛⲟⲛ), gold (ⲛⲟⲩⲃ), precious stones (ⲡⲓⲱⲛⲓ ⲙ̄ⲙⲏⲓ), pearls (ⲡⲓⲱⲛⲓ ⲙ̄ⲙⲁⲣⲅⲁⲣⲓⲧⲏⲥ), and white lead (named only in the third list, ⲡⲓⲩⲓⲙⲓⲑⲓⲛⲟⲛ).[28] Basil had requested the hyacinth-stone slab from a "merciless rich man" (ⲣⲁⲙⲁⲟ ⲛ̄ⲁⲑⲛⲁⲓ), who refused to supply it, uttered blasphemies, and died as a result.[29] The man's family donates the slab, plus all the other expensive materials itemized above, to secure forgiveness on his behalf. Mary appears to Basil in a vision, however, and informs him that he must not allow the donated materials to be used to make an image of her. The materials were acquired violently, she says, and the oil of sinners may not anoint her head.[30] Mary's mosaic must be made of materials with the purest lineage, to the point that the image's production must not have involved human hands at all. The acceptable adornment of the new church of Mary required materials of the utmost sacrality.

The icon is not only *acheiropoiētos*; it is also personified as a living being. When Basil hesitates to carry the large-scale mosaic from the site of its discovery to the church under construction, the mosaic speaks to Basil, asking him why he delays in picking it up and promising that its burden is light.[31] The *acheiropoiētos* icon testifies to its own exceptionality.

The Virginal Space of the Church at Koskam.   The story of the church at Koskam does not attribute to it any luxury; nor does it mention any icons, yet the church at Koskam, too, is made of the most sacred of building materials. The church does not contain an *acheiropoiētos* mosaic or a speaking one, but simply consists of natural, pure, rock landscape never previously occupied before the Holy Family's sixth-month stay there. According to the story, Mary and Joseph disagree about where to stay after they have met with tribulation after tribulation throughout their three-year journey south. Joseph proposes staying in an inhabited place, but Mary insists on going into the mountainous wilderness. Joseph's resistance underscores Mary's choice to go to a never-inhabited place. In fact, as darkness descends and they still have found no place to rest, Joseph reprimands Mary for failing to heed his advice. The child Jesus in turn defends his mother, telling his earthly father Joseph that it is the will of his heavenly Father that they dwell in an uninhabited house.[32] The Father himself selected a virginal landscape as the place of a long-term abode for the Holy Family, which would later become the place for the consecration of the first church. The text does not use the term *acheiropoiētos* or any near equivalent, but the emphasis on a never-inhabited, pure, wilderness implies divine creation unsullied by human involvement.

Special Protection from Acts of Outrage

Pure and Inviolate Koskam. Both irrefutably sacred spaces also withstand threats of violation.[33] Mary narrates to Theophilus a long catalog of abuses that she, the child Jesus, Joseph, and Salome endured after their entry into Egypt from the northeast and throughout their journey southward. At Koskam, however, the family enjoys a long respite with angels serving them throughout their stay. A threat of an attack occurs, however, when Satan appears to Herod for a second time, informs him of the Holy Family's exact location in the mountains west of Koskam, and instructs him to send ten soldiers to kill Jesus. Joseph's nephew Mūsās learns of Herod's new plan and travels ahead of the soldiers to warn Joseph in advance. The plan becomes divinely thwarted somehow. The family remains undisturbed in the previously uninhabited house for a total of six months until an angel appears to Joseph and instructs him to return to Israel because Herod has died and the ten soldiers he had sent are now in Gehenna.[34]

Not only does the house in the mountain of Koskam remain pure and inviolate despite the king's threats; Theophilus does not renovate or renew the house. Before arriving at Koskam, Theophilus had traveled throughout Egypt to expend an imperial donation of pagan temple spolia on the poor, the monasteries, the buildings in the mountains, and the building and restoration of churches in Egypt.[35] Theophilus intends to return to Alexandria when he is told about Koskam and is invited to celebrate the feast of Mary there on 21 Tūbi.[36] Theophilus prays for a revelation regarding the church of Koskam, and Mary appears to him to tell him the full story herself. Theophilus merely recounts what Mary told him; the story makes no mention of any embellishments or changes to the existing structure that result from Theophilus's visit.

Policing Access to the Sacred at Philippi.   At Philippi, the very materiality of the church protects it from any form of outrage. When a woman guilty of three egregious sins (betrayal, sororicide, and adultery) anoints herself with oil issuing from the *acheiropoiētos* mosaic, she becomes leprous. When a spring of water issues from one of the columns supporting the mosaic, she and other sinners come to wash but, instead of receiving healing, an abyss opens at the foot of the column and swallows them. According to the story, the waters are healing waters, but the narrative provides no concrete account of how an individual received mercy through the icon or the springwater.[37] The materiality of the church is so sacred that it can police its own boundaries, permitting access only to the pure, unarmed with any grievous sins.[38]

For both stories, the churches are sacred for all the same reasons stipulated in Roman and Byzantine law: they are consecrated and divinely protected, especially from acts of outrage. However, there is one legal stipulation from which they must excuse themselves: consecration at the hands of an imperially endorsed bishop. They therefore resorted to claims of celestial consecration, explicitly marking the superiority of celestial royalty's festivals over those of earthly royalty.

Earthly versus Celestial Festivals of Consecration.   Ps-Basil and Ps-Theophilus preface their main stories with a comparison of earthly versus celestial rulers' choices. According to Ps-Basil,

> It is not a consecration like the consecration of the former time when our forefathers and the kings who ruled on the earth celebrated consecrations. If the kings of the earth, when they have founded palaces or temples, slay calves/bulls on the foundation as well as he-goats and wild animals (for they do such things), and once they have ceased building the palace, the friends of the king gather in it and bring expensive things, gold, silver, wood, and many costly stones to complete the palace, and they recline and bring the players of the *kithara* and the *kitharas*, drums, cymbals, and flutes and make abominable songs in the midst, which draw the souls who do such things to the Gehenna of fire—for if they do so in sensuous deeds in impious dwelling places, then they perform otherwise [in] the temple of the queen and her palace, the dwelling place of angels, the church of the faithful, the frequent gathering place of all the holy ones.
>
> For I see a crowd of kings gathered in this holy place today who are *not of the earth*. And I see a crowd of strong powers in full regalia gathered with us who are *not of these times*. I see crowds of trumpeters and horn-blowers who are *not of the flesh* gathered with us celebrating joyfully in full regalia in the palace of the Queen of all women, the holy Virgin, the Mother of God, the holy Mary.[39]

Ps-Basil replaces imperial consecratory festival participants with heavenly ones, not of the earth or of time or of the flesh. He even criticizes the excesses of imperial festival practices.

As for Ps-Theophilus, he explicitly names Christ "the lawgiver," with the unstated implication that this appellation does not belong to the emperor.[40] Ps-Theophilus also stresses how starkly different the kind of abode Christ chose is from the abodes of rulers: "Truly God preferred this mountain (and descended to it with his Mother the Virgin) over all the cities of Egypt, and he did not wish to live in the house of an *archon*, nor did he choose the houses of the rich, but rather he desired the abode of this deserted house uninhabited by any human."[41] God rejects the residencies of the powerful, selecting to live instead in the natural wilderness, where no human had ever lived. Furthermore, Ps-Theophilus employs Herod's kingship as a foil to that of Christ. While King Herod's most trusted adviser is the devil, the Father is the one who guides Christ the King's actions in the story.

This general contrast between what Christ the King and Lawgiver and his mother Queen Mary do versus what "kings of the earth," "friends of the king," "archons," "the rich," or "King Herod" do constitutes the only explicit means by which Ps-Basil and Ps-Theophilus suggest a political context. As I will argue below, the texts otherwise respond in implicit or cryptic ways to major issues that followed in the wake of the Council of Chalcedon. The stories assume knowledge on the part of the implied audience of broader political subtexts. They do not respond to political circumstances by trying to persuade outsiders of their causes but by consolidating the insider identity of the opposition. In other words, they are stories written by non-Chalcedonians for non-Chalcedonians (not for Chalcedonian rivals or powers that be).

THE AFTERMATH OF THE COUNCIL OF CHALCEDON

Like all ecclesiastical councils, the Council of Chalcedon in 451 considered administrative matters, not just theological issues, and these were also quite controversial. Among non-Chalcedonians, Juvenal of Jerusalem would be remembered as the bishop who betrayed doctrinal orthodoxy in exchange for the elevation of his episcopal seat to patriarchal status. Jerusalem had formerly fallen under the jurisdiction of the metropolitan see of Caesarea. As a result of the decision at Chalcedon, however, Caesarea lost a large amount of jurisdictional territory, ceding it to the see of Jerusalem, which had henceforth been promoted to the status of patriarchate of all Palestine.[42] It was not only the opposition to Chalcedon in Palestine, Syria, and Egypt that criticized this decision; even the Chalcedonian Pope Leo of Rome voiced his dissent.[43]

By all accounts, both Chalcedonian and non-Chalcedonian, Juvenal used every means, fair and foul, to elevate the position of his episcopal seat. Non-Chalcedonians initially succeeded in installing one Theodosius as the non-Chalcedonian bishop of Jerusalem and keeping Juvenal out of the city. However, Juvenal would arrive twenty months later with imperial troops to subdue the opposition and assume his patriarchal position.[44] For a century, the fate of Palestine—the region of *res sacrae* par excellence—remained unclear: would it fall into Chalcedonian or non-Chalcedonian hands? By the end of Justinian's imperial tenure in the sixth century, however, Palestine's Chalcedonian identity would be secured.[45] There would be almost a three-century long vacancy in the non-Chalcedonian hierarchy of Jerusalem after Theodosius's exile and Juvenal's reinstallation.[46] Non-Chalcedonians no longer administered the most celebrated of *res sacrae*, such as the Church of the Holy Sepulchre.

It was also in the aftermath of the Council of Chalcedon that Mary's role came to be politicized on a much grander scale than heretofore. By the mid-sixth century, she would become the official protectress of the city of Constantinople.[47] Juvenal would be remembered as the one who found Mary's funeral garment in the Church of Mary in the Valley of Josaphat in Jerusalem and gave it to the regents Pulcheria and Marcian at their request, who proceeded to enshrine it as a contact relic in the Marian Church of Blachernae in Constantinople.[48] Byzantine troops would carry Mary's girdle and icons in battle against the Avars in 626.[49]

By the mid-sixth century, not only the Marian shrines but all the *res sacrae* of Palestine fell squarely and firmly into the hands of Chalcedonians. For one century (the mid-fifth to the mid-sixth century), Palestine was the primary battleground over which Chalcedonians and non-Chalcedonians fought.[50] While Palestine became uncompromisingly Chalcedonian, the regions of Egypt and Syria, by contrast, remained strongholds of opposition to Chalcedon. Egypt even became a place of exile for some Palestinian and Syrian non-Chalcedonians.[51]

The non-Chalcedonian writer of Ps-Theophilus's story has a distinctive perspective on Mary's role and interprets non-Chalcedonian experiences of exile, travail, and ecclesial dispossession by imagining hers. The non-Chalcedonian writer of Ps-Basil's story responds in another way to ecclesial dispossession—by imagining an all-powerful Mary in full support of Caesarea's primacy over Jerusalem. Though the strategies they employ differ, the writers of both stories downplay the importance of *res sacrae* in Jerusalem.[52]

NON-CHALCEDONIAN PERSPECTIVES ON MARY

Mary in Ps-Theophilus's Homily: A Non-Chalcedonian Response to the Loss of Palestine's Res Sacrae

The *maymar* of Ps-Theophilus relates in detail Mary's sadness, tears, and agony throughout her three-and-a-half years as a refugee in Egypt. The *maymar* does not dive directly into a narration of Mary's exile but first supplies the reader with an apocalyptic interpretive lens. The initial paragraphs claim that Koskam has become more significant than the mountains of Jerusalem and Sinai. The *maymar* quotes Isaiah 2:2–3 as a proof text and employs the passage as a hinge, opening the door to an exegesis of Revelation 12. When Isaiah spoke of the mountain of the Lord in the last days, he meant Mount Koskam:

> "*In those last days, the mountain of the Lord* will appear with signs and it will be renowned and *elevated over all the mountains* and become higher than the mounts and hills, and every nation and all the peoples will come to it, saying to one another, 'Come, let us go to the mountain of the Lord, to the house of the God of Jacob, so He may inform us of the way to follow.' For the law comes from Zion and the word of God from Jerusalem" [Is 2:2–3]. You [Koskam] are truly *the mountain of the Lord* and the house of the God of Jacob because the one who gave the law and laid down the law and his mother the Virgin dwelt in you. You are the new, upright, smooth path that everyone follows easily.[53]

The *maymar* identifies the mountain that would appear in the last days as the mountain of Koskam on the grounds that the one who set forth and issued the law (Christ) and his mother both came to dwell in the mountain of Koskam. Mary appears in this interpretation not directly linked to the passage cited from Isaiah, but as the one who accompanied the lawgiver in his abode on the mountain.

The *maymar* then turns from the "last days" as described by Isaiah to the book of Revelation, particularly the woman described in chapter 12. The *maymar* supplies an allegorical interpretation. After quotations from Revelation 12:1, 5, and 13–17, the *maymar* then names the allegorical key. The woman is the queen of all women, Mary. The sun with which she is clothed is "our Savior Jesus." The moon under her feet is John the Baptist. The twelve stars on her head are the twelve disciples. The dragon is the devil. The flooding water is Herod. The desert to which the woman fled is "this house," the church of Koskam.[54]

The ensuing story of Mary's exile details at length what Revelation 12 described in veiled terms. Mary offers personal testimony of her journey with her son (Jesus), betrothed (Joseph), and midwife (Salome). Mary explains how the devil twice advised Herod to pursue them and how she endured the fatigue of carrying her son in her arms over long distances, the bitterness of the rejection of even a cup of water, the theft of her and her family's belongings, and the threat of a violent death in her exile from Jerusalem. She says that she wept many a tear and complained to her son regularly of the tribulations she endured over the course of three-and-a-half years.[55] Even decades later, Mary continued to weep about her exile. The resurrected Christ asks,

> My pure mother, why are you weeping and despondent? You have unending joy, cheer, and rejoicing. Do not be despondent about my crucifixion and death; for by my death I have given life to all of my creation. *If you are despondent about your trials, flight from place to place, and your stay in a deserted house where there was no human, I will now consecrate it with my divine hand before any church is consecrated on the earth in my name.*[56]

Koskam becomes the consolation of all Mary's tears and trials, the end of her weeping and the beginning of her joy.

The text does not explicitly refer to Chalcedonians or late antique political exigencies, but I propose reading the *maymar's* identification of Koskam with the mountain in Isaiah 2 and Mary with the woman of Revelation 12 as strategic. Mary's trials become an exemplar through which the audience might read their own current experience of ecclesial dispossession and exile.[57] That Mary in this text may represent a non-Chalcedonian experience of exile in Egypt I will argue by juxtaposing Ps-Theophilus's *maymar* with two other texts—Rufus of Shotep's *Homilies on Matthew* and Stephen of Heracleopolis Magna's *Panegyric on Apollo, Archimandrite of the Monastery of Isaac.*

Nothing is known of Stephen, the bishop of Heracleopolis Magna, except two works he wrote, one of which is a panegyric on the archimandrite Apollo, probably composed by the turn of the seventh century.[58] To criticize the Chalcedonian ascendency of the sixth century, Stephen offers an allegorical interpretation of Revelation 9:1–2 and follows it with an extended reflection on the theme of lament.

> "I saw," said John in his Apocalypse, "a star that had fallen from heaven" [Rev 9:1a]. "The pit of the abyss was opened. Smoke of a great fire went up. The sun and the air became dark though the smoke of the pit" [Rev 9:2], the pit of the impiety which the rulers had gathered up who had come together to Chalcedon. This very pit of the abyss was opened again in the days of the Emperor Justinian. [. . .] The bad weed grew again in the kingdom of Justinian like a hidden fire in chaff which continues to produce smoke.[59]

Stephen interprets imperial endorsements of Chalcedon as openings and reopenings of "the pit of the abyss" of Revelation 9. The panegyric then brackets recollections of the non-Chalcedonian orthodox's lamentable experiences at the hands of the Chalcedonians with the imperative, "Let the people weep" at the outset, and then the rhetorical question, "What lament then is not for the orthodox at that time?" at the end.[60] The panegyric attests to the fact that at least one bishop in Upper Egypt read part of Revelation as a prophetic depiction of the turmoil that would afflict the church in the wake of the Council of Chalcedon. The panegyric underscores the tears and despondency that accompany non-Chalcedonian plight.

Another Coptic writer, Rufus of Shotep, delivered homilies on the Gospel of Matthew in the last quarter of the sixth century.[61] Rufus provides a witness of how one non-Chalcedonian bishop in Egypt interpreted the flight of the Holy Family into Egypt narrated in Matthew 2:13–18. Rufus allegorically interprets Herod as a heresiarch, and the blood of the executed children as the blood of the martyrs. Matthew 2:18 cites Jeremiah 31:15, which describes Rachel weeping over the loss of her children. Rufus explains that the name Rachel means "lamb," and the lamb weeps because "the wolf has destroyed her children."[62] "What is the lamb?" Rufus asks, "Rachel is the church."[63] This exegesis places a heresiological and martyrological lens on the Holy Family's exile. The story becomes one of a her-esiarch pursuing the innocent orthodox, resulting in the spilling of martyrs' blood and the church's weeping. As far as we know, Rufus does not pinpoint any particular heresiological context. However, Rufus's contemporary context of the sixth century witnessed the first accession of an unbroken line of Chalcedonian emperors, beginning with Justin I in 518. His audience may well have had current political affairs in mind as they heard his interpretation of the Holy Family's flight. Pursued by the heresiarch (Justinian or other Chalcedonian emperors), the Holy Family (non-Chalcedonians) flee to Egypt, while children (non-Chalcedonians) suffer martyrdom, and Rachel (the non-Chalcedonian church) weeps.

If one reads Rufus of Shotep's interpretation of Matthew 2 and Stephen of Heracleopolis Magna's exegesis of Revelation 9 alongside Ps-Theophilus's under-standing of Revelation 12 and first-person Marian testimony of the Holy Family's exile, one discerns a subtle political valence to the pseudepigraphon. Faced with the reality that Palestine belongs uncompromisingly to Chalcedonians, dispos-sessed of the *res sacrae* in Palestine, Ps-Theophilus creates a new, local Holy Land. Ps-Theophilus designates Mount Koskam as the mountain of the last days that rivals and exceeds the significance of Mounts Zion, Sinai, Horeb, and the Mount of Olives. Koskam is where Christ and his Father chose to build the first church of Mary. The preascended Christ personally took Mary and the disciples there before Mary died. Christ consecrates the church of Koskam to console his weep-ing mother, to lift her up from her unending despondency. At the very end of the narrative, Christ returns to Jerusalem with Mary and his disciples and he ascends to heaven. Therefore, Christ's final deed on earth, before his ascension to heaven, is to return to Koskam with his still-living mother and generate the first site of the Holy Land by performing the first consecration of a church.

Non-Chalcedonians weeping over their loss of *res sacrae* in Palestine were to find encouragement at Koskam. Just like non-Chalcedonians, Mary was expelled from Palestine; Mary suffered; and Mary wept. Her tribulations resonate all too well with the non-Chalcedonian plight. Just as Mary herself was given Koskam as her solace, non-Chalcedonians should be consoled by Egypt's Holy Land, which surpasses the *res sacrae* of Palestine.[64]

It is telling that in the history of the interpretation of Revelation 12, non-Chalcedonian interpreters identify the woman with Mary, but Chalcedonian ones are reluctant to do so. In fact, a thirteenth-century Chalcedonian exegete even interprets the woman as the "anti-Theotokos."[65]

Mary in Ps-Basil's Homily: A Non-Chalcedonian Response to Jerusalem's Ecclesiastical Elevation

It is possible that Ps-Basil also evokes the woman of Revelation 12, at the very outset of the "catechesis" and when describing Mary's appearance. The first evoca-tion lines up the words of Revelation 12:1 with a portrayal of the catholic church as a mother. The "catechesis" opens with this invitation, a call to the children of the church: "Come to us today, O people beloved of Christ, children with whom the catholic church was in travail and bore."[66] The words for "travail" (ϯⲛⲁⲕⲣⲓ) and "bore" (ⲙⲓⲥⲓ) are exactly the same as those of extant Bohairic translations of Revelation 12:2.[67] Additionally, when Mary appears to Basil, she "shines like the sun as though her clothes were spun with shining lightning."[68] These details of Mary's illuminating clothing may have evoked Revelation 12:1.

However, the Mary of Ps-Basil never weeps. She is not despondent or sad; she is powerful and patiently teaches Basil to stop worrying and to trust in her support. She berates Basil once for his ignorance and twice for his negligence. In her first appearance, she greets Basil with the question, "Master Basil, don't you know who I am?"[69] She instructs him to find her *acheiropoiētos* icon, but Basil objects on the grounds that he will also need two columns for the icon. She promises to provide these as well, so Basil goes to find the icon. On finding it, Basil and the clergy accompanying him are at a loss as to how they will carry such a long and broad mosaic. The mosaic berates Basil, asking him, "Why do you neglect to carry me?"[70] Mary later appears to Basil in a second vision and greets him with the question, "Why are you worried and have become neglectful of everything?,"[71] since Basil has not begun the task of retrieving the two columns she had promised him. In this story, Mary plays the part of the all-powerful leader and Basil that of the worried, neglectful, and reluctant servant. Mary teaches Basil to trust her and demonstrates her unwavering support of him.

The Primacy of Caesarea. This Mary, I argue, belongs to a story with the larger project of insisting on the primacy of Caesarea. Mary ratifies the primacy of Caesarea by personally superintending the construction of her new church there. The story either erroneously or intentionally conflates three different geographical locations with Caesarea, Palestine. Caesarea Philippi in Syria, Caesarea in Cappadocia, and the harbor city of Philippi in Macedonia are all merged into one place: the harbor city of Caesarea, Palestine. The writer draws together three important persons and events that take place in locales named either Caesarea, Philippi, or both. (1) Christ's apostolic elevation of Peter at Caesarea Philippi (Matt 16); (2) the apostolic sailing from the harbor city of Philippi (Acts 20); and (3) Basil's episcopacy in Caesarea are all imagined to take place in the harbor city of Caesarea, Palestine.

Caesarea Philippi figures in only one context in apostolic history: Peter's confession of Jesus as Christ the son of God; Peter's naming as the rock (πέτρα) on which Christ will build his church; and Peter's receipt of the keys to the kingdom of heaven (Matt 16:13–20).[72] There is no mention of Caesarea Philippi in the Acts of the Apostles; in fact, there is no mention of any Caesarea in the book of Acts. The harbor city of Philippi, however, does figure into the stories, and is mentioned three times. One of these instances includes the apostolic companion

Aristarchus of Thessalonica (Acts 20). According to the Lukan letter that Basil quotes, the apostles gather in the house of Aristarchus in Thessalonica. From Aristarchus's house, Christ takes them to Philippi to construct the very first church and to ordain Peter patriarch of the apostles in that first church. Since no post-ascension apostolic story portrays the apostles in Caesarea Philippi or any other Caesarea, for this reason Philippi in Macedonia becomes conflated with Caesarea Philippi in order to produce a context in which Matthew 16 may resonate with the narrative of Peter's ordination as patriarch. The strictures of the canonical apostolic stories cause the intentional or erroneous identification of Caesarea Philippi in Syria with Philippi in Macedonia.[73]

A geographical problem remains in that Basil of Caesarea constructs the new church, but Basil was neither the bishop of Caesarea Philippi in Syria, nor was he the bishop of Philippi in Macedonia. What is Basil doing consecrating a church far beyond his jurisdiction? The issue of episcopal jurisdictional boundaries arose often between neighboring or coterminous jurisdictions, and these resulted in large-scale disputes and juridical trials. It would transgress the limits of late antique plausible imagination to have Basil of Cappadocia consecrating a church in Syria or Macedonia. I believe that the writer actually imagines Basil as bishop of the harbor city of Caesarea, Palestine, and conflates this harbor city with that of Philippi. As a result, Basil is bishop of the very location where Christ and the apostles had consecrated the first church in the name of Mary.

Two pieces of evidence show that Cappadocia and Palestine were conflated in Coptic literature. In his second panegyric on Claudius of Antioch, Constantine, the bishop of Sioout, provides biographical information about himself and Rufus of Shotep. He claims to have found a letter in the "library of Cappadocia" in the course of a journey undertaken with Rufus to venerate the cross in Jerusalem.[74] This has rightly caused scholars to wonder how Rufus and Constantine could have possibly been going through Cappadocia while en route to Jerusalem.[75] It simply does not make geographical sense for travelers departing from Egypt. In addition, no other writers in antiquity speak of a "library of Cappadocia," but there was a well-known library in Caesarea, Palestine. The rise of the cult of Saint George may have played a role in the conflation of Cappadocia and Palestine. George was said to have had a Cappadocian father and a Palestinian mother, and he was known interchangeably as "George of Cappadocia" and "George of Diospolis/Lydda (Palestine)." An encomium attributed to Theodotus of Ancyra of Galatia calls George's grandfather "eparch of Melitene and all Palestine" (επαρχοс ϩιχεν ΜελιτΗΝΗ Νεм †ΠαλιϹτΙΝΗ ΤΗΡϹ), even though Melitene belonged to Cappadocia, never to Palestine.[76] Also, George is said to identify himself as "George the Melitene [Cappadocia] from Diospolis [Palestine]" (ΓεωΡΓιοϹ ΠΙΜελιΤωΝ ΝͰρεΜ†οϹΠολιϹ).[77] In any event, Constantine speaks of being in Cappadocia en route to Jerusalem, which only makes geographic sense for a traveler setting sail from Egypt, if Constantine's "Cappadocia" in fact refers to Palestine. There are also indications that the Caesareas of the two provinces (Cappadocia and Palestine) were conflated even in early Greek hagiographical literature.[78]

If the "Basil of Caesarea in Cappadocia" was thought to be the bishop in fact of Caesarea, Palestine, and if the harbor city of Philippi in Macedonia was identified as the harbor city of Caesarea, Palestine, then the geographical conundrum of the Ps-Basilian narrative may be solved.[79] Basil consecrates a church in his very own city and cites an apostolic narrative about the very first church that had been built in that very same city. The authoritative, uncontroversially orthodox voice of Basil of Caesarea would thus be co-opted to insist on the primacy of Caesarea over all Palestine in the face of Jerusalem's elevation to the status of a patriarchal see and the concomitant diminution of Caesarea's status and jurisdiction.

To restate the proposition another way: imagine the pseudepigrapher, whose goal is to employ Basil of Caesarea, Jesus's elevation of Peter, and postascension apostolic travel in tandem to underscore the primacy of Caesarea over Jerusalem. The pseudepigrapher conflates Palestine with Cappadocia, and therefore, when he says, "Basil of Caesarea, Cappadocia," he means in fact the Caesarea in Palestine. Basil's authority must also be combined with apostolic memory of Petrine authority established at Caesarea Philippi (in Syria) and with accounts of postascension apostolic travel to Philippi (in Macedonia). So, Caesarea Philippi and Philippi are interpreted as referring to the same place. Finally, the harbor cities of Philippi and Caesarea, Palestine are interpreted as the same place. The writer appears to refer to three different places (Caesarea, Cappadocia; Caesarea Philippi, Syria; and Philippi, Macedonia), but in fact means only one—Caesarea, Palestine. Why?

The bishops of Jerusalem had a long, documented history of demeaning the status of Caesarea, Palestine. Bishops of Jerusalem regularly attempted to have bishops of Caesarea prosecuted for their unorthodox faith, to the point that there is no bishop of Caesarea, Palestine who was celebrated in the sixth century for his orthodoxy.[80] In fact, the most famous of all the bishops of Caesarea, Palestine, Eusebius, would come to be remembered as an "Arian." For any writer seeking to defend Caesarea's place in the episcopal rankings by adopting a pseudonym, an uncontroversially orthodox bishop with great postpatristic authority would have to be chosen. For this reason, I believe, the anonymous composers of the Ps-Basilian text adopted Basil of Caesarea, Cappadocia as the spokesperson for Caesarea, Palestine on the basis of either an erroneous or an intentional conflation of the two regions of Cappadocia and Palestine.

For anyone acquainted with the historical Basil of Caesarea, his curriculum vitae aligns all too well with circumstances that non-Chalcedonians faced in Palestine. Basil of Caesarea had a large episcopal jurisdiction until Emperor Valens divided Cappadocia into two parts. Caesarea became the capital of only Cappadocia Prima, while Tyana became the capital of Cappadocia Secunda. Ecclesiastical jurisdiction as a rule followed civil lines; so, as a result of Valens's measure, Basil lost half of his metropolitan jurisdiction to Anthimus of Tyana. In response to the territorial diminution he faced, Basil consecrated many subordinate countryside bishops in an attempt to expand his jurisdiction.[81] So, Basil, too, suffered territorial diminution and protested it. Basil was also remembered for refusing to comply with Emperor Valens's wish that he endorse a heretical doctrinal position, and Basil almost faced exile as a result.[82] Basil—uncontrovertibly orthodox; known for suffering territorial diminution; known for resisting imperial pressure to subscribe to a heretical doctrine—made the perfect choice for a spokesperson on behalf of the non-Chalcedonian cause in favor of Caesarea. Recall that it is in Jerusalem that Basil finds Luke's letter about the first church and Peter's patriarchal ordination. Jerusalem itself testifies to the primacy of Caesarea.

Echoes of Justinian's Nea Ecclesia.   It is possible that Justinian's construction of a massive church of Mary in Jerusalem may also underly the political issues to which the Ps-Basilian narrative responds. Since there was already a church of Mary in the Valley of Josaphat, Justinian's church acquired the designation "new church" (Nea Ecclesia).[83] Justinian had political reasons for founding this new Marian church-and-monastery complex in Jerusalem. Susan Graham states them well: "The presence of an imperially established monastery at the Nea, populated with 'orthodox' (Chalcedonian) monks and dedicated to the Theotokos, surely sent an implicit imperial message to non-Chalcedonians in Jerusalem and the Judean desert, for the monastic community in Jerusalem and the nearby desert was acutely divided theologically and ecclesiastically in the sixth century."[84] The Chalcedonian emperor Justinian built the largest, most lavish church of Mary in Jerusalem for Chalcedonians, a monumental sign of the exclusion of non-Chalcedonians.

A feature common to both Procopius's description of Justinian's Nea in Jerusalem and Ps-Basil's account of the construction of the new church of Mary is the miraculous story of how two exceptionally large stone columns of fire-red hue were discovered to support the sanctuary. According to Procopius, the Nea was built on such a large scale that finding stones from which to fashion the columns became a problem with only a miraculous solution. The stones that were discovered were of fire-red hue.[85] Archaeologists have shown that the only place where two exceptionally large columns needed to be installed in the Nea was at the triumphal arch leading into the sanctuary.[86] Because the columns in the portico of the Jewish temple were also said to have been of fire-red hue, one scholar suggested that the construction of the Nea involved the spoliation of the temple portico.[87] Ps-Basil's story describes the miraculous spoliation of a temple to produce two columns, so large that they were made in the time of the giants (ⲓⲥϫⲉⲛ ⲡⲥⲏⲟⲩ ⲛ̄ⲛⲓⲁⲫⲱⲫ), to support the sanctuary and the fire-red stone (ⲡⲗⲁϩ ⲛ̄ⲁⲟⲩⲁⲛ ⲛ̄ϫⲉⲃⲥ) on which Mary's mosaic icon lay.[88] The resonance of such minute details—spoliation of two exceptionally large fire-red stone columns to install a triumphal arch in a church of Mary—render it plausible that stories of Justinian's Nea Ecclesia serve as political subtexts of the Ps-Basilian story. In response, Ps-Basil claims that Mary herself oversaw the construction of a new church in her name and that the project took place not in Jerusalem but in Caesarea, and not in the sixth century but in the fourth during Basil's episcopacy.

As in Ps-Theophilus's homily, the Mary of Ps-Basil's offers consolation to non-Chalcedonians. Mary ratifies the primacy of Caesarea. Indeed, she herself directly oversaw the construction of her own church there in Caesarea, not in Jerusalem.

NON-CHALCEDONIAN *RES SACRAE*

According to the Chalcedonian writer Anastasius of Sinai, control of *res sacrae* or "the holy places" (οἱ ἅγιοι τόποι) was the marker par excellence of orthodoxy.[89] God showed his favor toward orthodox Christians by allowing them long-term control of sacred things. To make his point, Anastasius quotes a debate that took place in Alexandria, Egypt, in the early sixth century between the followers of various non-Chalcedonian leaders and a Chalcedonian uneducated in the art of rhetoric. The uneducated Chalcedonian draws a comparison between how God acts and how emperors act by posing the following rhetorical question: "If the Emperor owns certain treasuries and honoured dwellings where his essential secret business [lit. "mysteries"] is despatched, to whom will he confide these places, to those who are faithful to him or to those who are unfaithful?"[90] Analogously, the Chalcedonian argues, God has demonstrated his support of Chalcedonians by granting them long-term administration of the holy places, even though "the barbarians now control the land of the Holy Places."

Whether a real or imagined debate between Chalcedonians and non-Chalcedonians, Anastasius's story echoes what we already heard from Augustine concerning the sack of Rome: protection of *res sacrae* is a sure sign of God's favor.[91] Even after the Arab takeover of Palestine, Chalcedonians continued to hold the *res sacrae*, not non-Chalcedonians. Non-Chalcedonians had an uphill battle to fight in defending their exclusion from Palestine and the sacrality of their churches. They resorted to the production of pseudepigraphy to render the sacrality of their holy places unassailable and make them preeminent over the *res sacrae* of Jerusalem.[92]

Non-Chalcedonian homilists used the anniversary celebration to address the fundamental question of what makes a thing sacred. At anniversary celebrations of church consecrations in Egypt, unknown writers implicitly claimed that it did not matter whether an imperially recognized bishop consecrated the place. Therefore, the question of the bishop's legal recognition was irrelevant. It was Christ the King and Lawgiver and his agents who personally consecrated their churches. What made a thing sacred was not the emperor or the emperor's recognition of a bishop. What made a thing sacred was Christ himself and his court. As for the two corollaries of the legal definition, non-Chalcedonians in Egypt claimed that the saints protected their churches, not the law. Non-Chalcedonians in Egypt used the ritual context of anniversary celebrations of consecrations to place the legal discourse on *res sacrae*, both the definition and the two corollaries, under the direct and unmediated purview of Christ.

Yet a third church claimed primacy as the first church of Mary. Arabic, Garshuni, and Ethiopic manuscripts dating from the fifteenth to the nineteenth centuries transmit a story set in the early ninth century, during the caliphate of al-Ma'mūn, son of Harūn al-Rashīd (813–833).[93] According to this story, al-Ma'mūn orders the destruction of all churches of Egypt, but the first church of Mary located in Athribis makes a stand against the decree. In the end, Mary, "the mother of mercy," commands the commander to annul the order; the first church of Mary's stand protects all the churches of Egypt from destruction; and the caliph even enriches the church in Athribis and builds a church of Mary near his palace in Baghdad.

Though the story presents no account of the original construction or consecration of the church, two aspects resonate with the other stories of the first church of Mary. Like Ps-Basil's story, that of Athribis also features a mosaic Marian icon. The protagonist of the story, John the monk-priest of Athribis, ceaselessly prays for three days before the mosaic icon of Mary. On the third day, the mosaic speaks to John, assuring him of the church's protection. Like the stories of both Ps-Basil and Ps-Theophilus, the church is impervious to threats of outrage. Mary protects her first church from harm, and it is the political resistance of her first church that prevents all other churches in Egypt from suffering destruction.

Though it is beyond the scope of this chapter to analyze the story of Athribis in detail and place it in historical context,[94] it is important to note here the story's resonance with those of Philippi and Koskam. The writer of the story of Athribis sets it in an overtly political situation, one in which the threat of ecclesial dispossession is at stake. As in the stories of Philippi and Koskam, the first church of Mary in Athribis serves as the antidote to ecclesial dispossession. Somehow the primacy of a Marian church makes it capable of responding to the issue of ecclesial dispossession.

Non-Chalcedonians repeatedly made recourse to claims of ecclesial primacy to cope with ecclesial dispossession and to consolidate an identity resistant to the politically endorsed one.[95] The powers that be may have denied non-Chalcedonian holy places the status of *res sacrae*, but non-Chalcedonians possessed incontrovertible reasons for recognizing the sacrality of their holy places: Christ himself and his saints authorized them by their own hands. In fact, non-Chalcedonians would denigrate the value of imperial authorization in comparison to that of the celestial realm: "You [Chalcedonians] submit to the abominable ordinance of the *autocrator* [i.e., the emperor]; we [non-Chalcedonians] obey the *Pantocrator* [i.e., the Ruler of All, God]."[96] The powers that be may have elevated Jerusalem, but Mary stands by Caesarea. The powers that be may usurp the *res sacrae* in the Holy Land; non-Chalcedonians create a new Holy Land, authorized by the prophecies and revelations of scripture and the voice of Mary herself. The powers that be may threaten non-Chalcedonian churches; Mary guards them. Mary plays the most prominent role in these stories, since it is the first church built in her name that comes into question. Why is Mary's church at stake? Why do not the writers speak of the very first church of Christ?

As mentioned above, the Council of Chalcedon and its aftermath politicized Mary in ever-increasing ways. What is more: in the cultural memory of non-Chalcedonians, it was at an early church of Mary in Jerusalem[97] where Juvenal, who betrayed the non-Chalcedonian cause in exchange for the elevation of his epis-copal seat, was forcibly reinstalled after a twenty-month-long non-Chalcedonian stronghold over the city. It was at a church of Mary in Jerusalem where non-Chalcedonians were brutally massacred during the celebration of the eucharist on her feast day.[98] A text known as the *Panegyric of Macarius of Tkōou* includes the story of this massacre. According to the story, as non-Chalcedonians are being martyred, Mary says, "My Lord and my God and my Son, behold, my sacrifice. I have offered it up to you upon your holy altar today, the day of my feast. Accept it unto yourself."[99] In stark contrast to the stories about Philippi, Koskam, and Athribis, Mary does not protect her church.[100] She allows non-Chalcedonians to be sacrificed (i.e., martyred). The imperial soldiers violently enter the church, kill the men, and violate the women, with the exception of only two virgins.[101] Can it be that non-Chalcedonians tried three times to rewrite their cultural memory? Can it be that non-Chalcedonians tried three times to remember a Mary who *did* guard them from outrage at her church? This remains a matter of conjecture. Taken together, the evidence analyzed above does show one thing: how texts that appear fantastic at face value convey in fact the apologetic voices of marginalized communities coping with ecclesial dispossession and defending their *res sacrae*.

In the ritual contexts of dedication, consecration, and anniversary celebrations, bishops did not preach jurists' principles and guidelines. Just as bishops petitioned emperors for adjustments to the laws on *res sacrae*, so they used the ritual context of what was seen and heard in churches to proclaim responses to the law. Legally recognized bishops, like Ambrose of Milan and John Chrysostom, inverted the relative priority of the juridical corollaries. Writers lacking legal authorization, like the non-Chalcedonians in Egypt, overturned the imperial basis of the law. Non-Chalcedonians claimed that Christ and his saints governed them directly without the intermediaries of Christian emperors and their agents.

Conclusion

> Those who either out of ignorance confuse or out of negligence violate and
> offend the sanctity of divine law commit sacrilege.[1]

What made a church sacred in late antiquity? In both legal and ritual prescriptive contexts, the answer was ostensibly the same: the rite of consecration produced *res sacrae*. But method of production is one thing and the way the product functions is another. For legal practitioners, the status of *res sacrae* ensured the perpetuity, stability, and wealth of divine institutions. Even legally, the needy could participate in such institutional stability and wealth but only under limited circumstances. A church's protected status took precedence over its protecting capacity. After all, churches only became protecting because they were protected.

This is not the logic evident in Christian ritual practices of dedication and consecration. According to (1) the orations of bishops who spoke on such occasions, (2) the images that were installed to commemorate the dedicatory and consecratory events, and (3) still other pieces of evidence, churches were protected because they were protecting. Though the difference appears slight, this inverse relationship between legal and ritual views had profound ramifications. Liturgically, the only limitation to a bishop's performance of an act of mercy was his and his fellow clerical colleagues' discretion. Nothing was to hinder practices of mercy, not even the law. The church itself was not supposed to interfere with a soul's salvation. If one donor's gift for the sake of his or her soul were repurposed to save still another soul, then the number of saved souls multiplied. And that was what the church was for.

Like tectonic plates, the legal and ritual discourses of the sacred fit, but their colliding boundary—the practice of mercy—generated charges of sacrilege. It is at the colliding boundary that ritual mercy and legal sacrilege became indistinguishable. Some bishops, like Ambrose of Milan, would be celebrated for their mercy and not penalized for their sacrilege.[2] Other bishops, like John Chrysostom, would suffer the trauma of exile for their sacrilegious act of mercy.[3]

Ironically, sacrilege could only take place at legally recognized sacred places. Imperially recognized bishops were the only agents whose rite of consecration legally produced a sacred thing. Therefore, sacrilegious acts could only take place with reference to such things. Consecrations performed by imperially repressed bishops could not legally produce sacred things. The question of sacrilege, therefore, could never be posed about such things. Yet the law had ways of demeaning the alleged status of others' sacred things. Legally speaking, the churches of "heretics" were "feral grottos," according to a law targeted against Montanists.[4] In the eyes of non-Chalcedonians, however, non-Chalcedonian churches were certainly not "feral grottos." Their churches were not cavernous death traps. Their churches were founded on the pure, uninhabited, rocky landscape that the Father himself had chosen for Christ, for Mary, and for their true followers.[5] Just as mercy and sacrilege met at a juncture, so too did the inviolable sacred and the violating feral.

There did come a time and a place when authorities would try to neutralize the difference between the legal and the ritual perspectives on the sacred. In the late eleventh century, jurists and bishops of the Byzantine Empire found a way to remove the colliding boundary, to fuse the two tectonic plates, so to speak. In 1081, a synod allowed Emperor Alexios I Komnenos to alienate *res sacrae* in order to fund his military activities. Leo, the metropolitan of Chalcedon, opposed the synod's decision and spent much of the 1080s voicing and defending his position against the emperor and members of the synod.[6] By then, the iconoclastic controversies of the eighth and ninth century had produced theories about sacred materiality. Leo and other bishops revisited these theories to ascertain whether Alexios's alienation of ecclesial property was in fact legal.

Another synod took place in 1091 at the Blachernae in Constantinople. The synod argued that it was the intangible, abstract form of icons that was sacred, not the matter ($ὕλη$). Therefore, the alienation of *res sacrae* to fund military activity was justifiable. "The emperor [Alexios] asked, 'Tell [me], what are icons? Are icons matter ($ὕλας$) or the likenesses that are made known in it [i.e., the matter]?' Everyone responded, 'The likenesses that are made known in the matter.'"[7] The synod argued that sacrality pertained only to form, not matter, so no sacrilege occurred in the alienation of the matter, even if the purpose of the alienation had nothing to do with practicing mercy.

Leo of Chalcedon had charged Emperor Alexios I Komnenos on counts that would have convicted an emperor in late antiquity. But Alexios used some claims of the iconoclastic controversies in his favor, to allow for the repurposing of sacred things. Ironically, the spiritualization of sacred materiality in this case allowed sacred things to be repurposed to wage war. By contrast, Gregory of Tours' story about Anicia Juliana celebrated the clever solution Anicia Juliana had found to rebuff Justinian's attempt to borrow her wealth to wage war.[8] Anicia Juliana used that wealth to furnish a gilded ceiling for a church she had founded. As a result, Justinian would have had to violate his own laws to borrow her assets. In the posticonoclastic context of the eleventh century, Anicia Juliana would not have been able to protect her wealth from Justinian's military pursuits by consecrating it.

With Constantine's legalization of Christian practice in the fourth century, Christian holy places began to be slotted into a preexisting legal category of *res sacrae*. This process came with benefits: the stability and enrichment of ecclesiastical institutional structures, legal support for ecclesiastical administrators and their work, and so on. By the sixth century, the process was complete. In 533, Justinian had a new textbook on Roman law published by rewriting textbooks produced centuries prior. This new textbook explicitly stated that *res sacrae* were gifts to the Christian God consecrated by bishops.

The application of Roman jurisprudence to Christian holy places was by no means without controversy. All along the way, negotiations took place, stories and counterstories were told, and violence occurred. In general, bishops petitioned for increased legal support of churches in their protecting capacity with limited success. Jurists, by contrast, worked to maintain the integrity of civil institutions. Donors took a vested interest in their transactions with the celestial realm. Donors, jurists, and bishops engaged in nuanced discourses over what it meant for church property to be "sacred" in late antiquity. What may appear to be legal minutiae make all the difference for appreciating the significance of controversies over the sacred in late antiquity.

The Sources of Justinian's
Institutes 2.1.pr–10

Justinian's *Institutes* are usually said to be a rewritten version of Gaius's *Institutes*, but 2.1.pr–10 is made up largely of verbatim excerpts from D. 1.8.2–9. See table 3 below for a synopsis of 2.1.pr–10 with its proposed sources. The first two sentences of 2.1.pr quote Gaius's *Institutes* 2.1 (a pericope not excerpted in the *Digest*), but the rest of the section hardly relies on Gaius's *Institutes*. The next sentence of 2.1.pr through 2.1.1–2 quote Marcian's *Institutes* found in D. 1.8.2 and 1.8.4. This section creates the categories of what is *in nostro patrimonio* and begins to elaborate on them. Whence the sentence 2.1.3 derives is unknown. The continued elaboration in 2.1.4–5, with the exception of the last sentence, quotes Gaius's *Everyday Matters or Golden Words* as recorded in D. 1.8.5. The last sentence of 2.1.5 quotes neither Gaius's *Institutes* nor the *Digest*; the source is unknown. Section 2.1.6, a further elaboration on the five-part division, uses Marcian's *Institutes* again, as recorded in D. 1.8.6.1. Sections 2.1.7–8 turn to *divini iuris*, especially *res sacrae*, and quote Marcian's *Institutes*, as recorded in D. 1.8.6.3 with some additions from unknown sources. Marcian's *Institutes* are once again cited to explain *res religiosae* in 2.1.9, taken from D. 1.8.6.4, with two additions from unknown sources. To explain *res sanctae*, the compilers return to Gaius's *Institutes* (2.8 = D. 1.8.1.pr) and, perhaps, to Ulpian's *Edict*, recorded in D. 1.8.9.3. The last sentence of 2.1.10 derives from an unknown source. The following table summarizes these observations.

TABLE 2 Sources of Justinian's *Institutes* 2.1.pr–10

Justinian's *Institutes*	Sources	Nature of the reliance
2.1.pr	Gaius, *Institutes* 2.1	Verbatim
2.1.pr–2	Marcian, *Institutes* 3 = D. 1.8.2, 4	Verbatim
2.1.3	Unknown	n/a
2.1.4–5	Gaius, *Everyday Matters or Golden Words* 2 = D. 1.8.5	Almost verbatim
2.1.5	Unknown	n/a
2.1.6	Marcian, *Institutes* 3 = D. 1.8.6.1	Verbatim
2.1.7–8	Marcian, *Institutes* 3 = D. 1.8.6.3	Reworking
2.1.9	Marcian, *Institutes* 3 = D. 1.8.6.4	Reworking
2.1.10	Gaius, *Institutes* 2.8 = D. 1.8.1.pr	Verbatim
2.1.10	Ulpian, *Edict* 68 = D. 1.8.9.3	Reworking?
2.1.10	Unknown	n/a

In the following table, underlined words, phrases, and sentences mark differences between Justinian's *Institutes* and the proposed source text. The texts of Justinian's *Institutes* and *Digest* are taken from Paul Krueger and Theodor Mommsen, eds., *Corpus Iuris Civilis*, vol. 1 (1867–1870; repr., Berlin: Apud Weidmannos, 1962). The text of Gaius's *Institutes* is taken from Francis de Zulueta, ed. and trans., *The Institutes of Gaius*, vol. 1 (Oxford: Clarendon Press, 1946).

TABLE 3 Synopsis of Justinian's *Institutes* 2.1.pr–10 and Proposed Sources

Source	Source Text	Justinian's *Institutes*
Gaius, *Institutes* 2.1	Superiore commentario de iure personarum exposuimus; modo videamus de rebus: quae vel in nostro patrimonio sunt vel extra nostrum patrimonium habentur.	(pr) Superiore libro de iure personarum exposuimus: modo videamus de rebus. quae vel in nostro patrimonio vel extra nostrum patrimonium habentur.
Marcian, *Institutes* 3 (D. 1.8.2)	Quaedam naturali iure communia sunt omnium, quaedam universitatis, quaedam nullius, pleraque singulorum, quae variis ex causis cuique adquiruntur. Et quidem naturali iure omnium communia sunt illa: aer, aqua profluens, et mare, et per hoc litora maris.	Quaedam enim naturali iure communia sunt omnium, quaedam publica, quaedam universitatis, quaedam nullius, pleraque singulorum, quae variis ex causis cuique adquiruntur, sicut ex subiectis apparebit. (1) Et quidem naturali iure communia sunt omnium haec: aer et aqua profluens et mare et per hoc litora maris.

TABLE 3 *(Continued)*

Source	Source Text	Justinian's *Institutes*
Marcian, *Institutes* 3 (D. 1.8.4)	Nemo igitur ad litus maris accedere prohibetur <u>piscandi causa</u>, dum tamen villis et aedificiis et monu- mentis abstineatur, quia non sunt iuris gentium sicut et mare: idque <u>et divus Pius piscatoribus Formianis et Capenatis rescripsit</u>. Sed flumina paene omnia et portus publica sunt.	Nemo igitur ad litus maris accedere prohibetur, dum tamen villis et monumentis et aedificiis abstineat, quia non sunt iuris gentium, sicut et mare. (2) Flumina autem omnia et portus publica sunt: ideoque <u>ius piscandi</u> omnibus commune est in portubus fluminibusque.
Unknown	N/A	(3) Est autem litus maris, quatenus hibernus fluctus maximus excurrit.
Gaius, *Everyday Matters or Golden Words* 2 (D. 1.8.5)	Riparum usus publicus est iure gentium sicut ipsius fluminis. Itaque navem ad eas appellere, funes ex arboribus ibi natis religare, retia siccare et ex mare reducere, onus aliquid in his reponere cuilibet liberum est, sicuti per ipsum flumen navigare. Sed proprietas illorum est, quorum praediis haerent: qua de causa arbores quoque in his natae eorundem sunt. In mare piscantibus liberum est casam in litore ponere, in qua se recipiant.	(4) Riparum <u>quoque</u> usus publicus est iuris gentium sicut ipsius fluminis: itaque navem ad eas appellere, funes ex arboribus ibi natis religare, onus aliquid in his reponere cuilibet liberum est, sicuti per ipsum flumen navigare. Sed proprietas earum illorum est quorum praediis haerent: qua de causa arbores quoque in isdem natae eorundem sunt. (5) <u>Litorum quoque usus publicus iuris gentium est, sicut ipsius maris</u>: et ob id quibuslibet liberum est, casam ibi imponere, in qua se recipiant, sicut retia siccare et ex mare deducere.
Unknown	N/A	Proprietas autem eorum potest intellegi nullius esse, sed eiusdem iuris esse cuius et mare, et quae subiacent mari terra vel harena.
Marcian, *Institutes* 3 (D. 1.8.6.1)	Universitatis sunt, non singulorum, veluti quae in civitatibus sunt theatra et statia et similia et si qua alia sunt communia civitatium.	(6) Universitatis sunt, non singulorum, veluti quae in civitatibus sunt, ut theatra statia et similia et si qua alia sunt communia civitatium.
Marcian, *Institutes* 3 (D. 1.8.6.3)	Sacrae res et religiosae et sanctae in nullius bonis sunt. Sacrae autem res sunt hae, quae publice consecratae sunt, non private: si quis ergo privatim sibi sacrum constituerit, sacrum non est, sed profanum. Semel autem aede sacra facta etiam diruto aedificio locus sacer manet.	(7) Nullius autem sunt res sacrae et religiosae et sanctae: <u>quod enim divini iuris est</u>, id nullius in bonis est. (8) Sacra sunt, <u>quae rite et per pontifices deo</u> consecrata sunt, <u>veluti aedes sacrae et dona, quae rite ad ministerium dei dedicata sunt, quae etiam per nostram constitutionem alienari et obligari prohibuimus, excepta causa redemptionis captivorum</u>. Si quis vero auctoritate sua quasi sacrum sibi constituerit, sacrum non est, sed profanum. Locus autem, in quo sacrae aedes aedificatae sunt, etiam diruto aedificio, adhuc sacer manet, <u>ut et Papinianus scripsit</u>.

(Contd.)

TABLE 3 *(Continued)*

Source	Source Text	Justinian's *Institutes*
Marcian, *Institutes* 3 (D. 1.8.6.4)	Religiosum autem locum unusquisque sua voluntate facit, dum mortuum infert in locum suum. In commune autem sepulchrum etiam invitis ceteris licet inferre. Sed et in alienum locum concedente domino licet inferre: et licet postea ratum habuerit quam illatus est mortuus, religiosus locus fit. Cenotaphium quoque magis placet locum esse religiosum, sicut testis in ea re est Vergilius.	(9) Religiosum locum unusquisque sua voluntate facit, dum mortuum infert in locum suum. In communem autem locum purum invito socio inferre non licet: in commune vero sepulcrum etiam invitis ceteris licet inferre. Item si alienus usus fructus est, proprietarium placet, nisi consentiente usufructuario locum religiosum non facere. In alienum locum, concedente domino, licet inferre: et licet postea ratum habuerit quam illatus est mortuus, tamen religiosus locus fit.
Gaius, *Institutes* 2.8 (D. 1.8.1.pr)	Sanctae quoque res, velut muri et portae, quodam modo divini iuris sunt.	(10) Sanctae quoque res, veluti muri et portae, quodammodo divini iuris sunt et ideo nullius in bonis sunt.
Ulpian, *Edict* 68 (D. 1.8.9.3)	Proprie dicimus sancta, quae neque sacra neque profana sunt, sed sanctione quadam confirmata: ut leges sanctae sunt, sanctione enim quadam sunt subnixae. Quod enim sanctione quadam subnixum est, id sanctum est, etsi deo non sit consecratum: et interdum in sanctionibus adicitur, ut qui ibi aliquid commisit, capite puniatur.	Ideo autem muros sanctos dicimus, quia poena capitis constituta sit in eos qui aliquid in muros deliquerint.
Unknown	N/A	Ideo et legum eas partes quibus poenas constituimus adversus eos qui contra leges fecerint sanctiones vocamus.

TABLE 4 Chronological List of Roman Legislation on Ecclesial Property

=	(indicates extracts of the same constitution)
CRP	*comes rei privatae* (Count of the Privy Purse)
CSL	*comes sacrarum largitionum* (Count of the Sacred Largesses)
mag. off.	*magister officiorum* (Master of the Offices)
PPO	*praefectus praetorio* (Praetorian Prefect)

Blank columns indicate that the information is unknown.

Date of Issue[a]	Constitution[b]	Issuer(s)[c]	Place of Issue	Recipient[d]	Topic(s)[e]
June 8, 316	CJ 1.13.1	Constantine		Protogenes, Bishop	Manumission of slaves
April 18, 321	CTh 4.7.1	Constantine		Hosius, Bishop	Manumission of slaves
July 3, 321	CTh 16.2.4= CJ 1.2.1	Constantine	Rome	The People	Bequest to churches
September 25, 326	CTh 16.5.2	Constantine	Spoleto	Bassus, Prefect of the City	Novatian churches and burial places
September 27, 364	CTh 14.3.11	Valentinian and Valens	Aquileia	Symmachus, Prefect of the City	Asylum of breadmakers
March 2, 372	CTh 16.5.3	Valentinian and Valens	Trier	Ampelius, Prefect of the City	Confiscation
April 22, 376/378	CTh 16.5.4	Valens, Gratian, and Valentinian	Trier	Hesperius, PPO Italiae et Galliae	Confiscation
October 17, 377	CTh 16.6.2= CJ 1.6.1	Valens, Gratian, and Valentinian	Constantinople	Florianus, Vicar of Africa[f]	Confiscation

(*Contd.*)

TABLE 4 *(Continued)*

Date of Issue[a]	Constitution[b]	Issuer(s)[c]	Place of Issue	Recipient[d]	Topic(s)[e]
February 28, 380	CTh 16.1.2	Valens, Gratian, and Valentinian	Thessalonika	People of Constantinople	Definition of churches vs. *conciliabula*
January 10, 381	CTh 16.5.6= CJ 1.1.2	Gratian, Valentinian, and Theodosius	Constantinople	Eutropius, PPO Illyrici (CJ); Hesperius, PPO (CTh)	Right of assembly; Vindication to churches; Asylum of heretics
July 19, 381	CTh 16.5.8	Gratian, Valentinian, and Theodosius	Constantinople	Clicherius, Count of the Orient	Right to build churches; Confiscation
July 30, 381	CTh 16.1.3	Gratian, Valentinian, and Theodosius	Heraclea	Auxonius, Proconsul of Asia	Vindication to churches
December 3, 383	CTh 16.5.12	Gratian, Valentinian, and Theodosius	Constantinople	Postumianus, PPO Orientis	Confiscation
June 20, 383	CTh 16.5.10	Gratian, Valentinian, and Theodosius	Constantinople	Constantianus, Vicar of the Diocese of Pontus	Right of assembly
July 25, 383	CTh 16.5.11	Gratian, Valentinian, and Theodosius	Constantinople	Postumianus, PPO Orientis	Right of assembly; Oratories of heretics
January 23, 386	CTh 16.1.4	Valentinian, Theodosius, and Arcadius	Milan	Eusignius, PPO Italiae et Illyrici	Right of assembly
March 10, 388	CTh 16.5.14	Gratian, Valentinian, and Theodosius	Thessalonika	Cynegius, PPO Orientis	Right of assembly; "Private churches"
June 21, 390	CTh 16.2.27	Valentinian, Theodosius, and Arcadius	Milan	Tatianus, PPO Orientis	Bequest of deaconesses
August 23, 390	CTh 16.2.28	Valentinian, Theodosius, and Arcadius	Verona	Tatianus, PPO Orientis	Bequest of deaconesses
March 13, 392	CTh 9.40.15	Theodosius, Arcadius, and Honorius	Constantinople	Tatianus, PPO Orientis	Asylum of those accused of a great crime and sentenced

TABLE 4 *(Continued)*

Date of Issue[a]	Constitution[b]	Issuer(s)[c]	Place of Issue	Recipient[d]	Topic(s)[e]
April 9, 392	CTh 11.36.31	Theodosius, Arcadius, and Honorius	Constantinople	Hypatius, Augustal Prefect	Asylum of convicted persons or those who have confessed to crimes
June 15, 392	CTh 16.5.21	Gratian, Valentinian, and Theodosius		Tatianus, PPO Orientis	Confiscation
October 18, 392	CTh 9.45.1	Theodosius, Arcadius, and Honorius	Constantinople	Romulus, CSL	Asylum of public debtors
March 30, 395	CTh 16.5.26	Arcadius and Honorius	Constantinople	Rufinus, PPO Orientis	Right of assembly
March 3, 396/402	CTh 16.5.30	Arcadius and Honorius	Constantinople	Clearchus, Prefect of the City	Confiscation
April 1, 397	CTh 16.5.33	Arcadius and Honorius	Constantinople	Eutychianus, PPO Illyrici	Confiscation
June 17, 397	CTh 9.45.2= CJ 1.12.1	Arcadius and Honorius	Constantinople	Archelaus, Augustal Prefect	Asylum of Jews with debts or criminal charges
March 3, 398	CTh 16.5.34	Arcadius and Honorius	Constantinople	Eutychianus, PPO Orientis	Confiscation
April 25, 398	CTh 16.2.31= Sirm. 14	Arcadius and Honorius	Milan	Theodorus, PPO Italiae, Illyrici, et Africae	Outrage against churches
July 27, 398	CTh 9.40.16= 9.45.3, 11.30.57; 16.2.33 and CJ 1.4.7	Arcadius and Honorius	Constantinople	Eutychianus, PPO Orientis	Asylum of those sentenced and condemned
July 27, 398	CTh 9.45.3= 9.40.16; 11.30.57; 16.2.33 and CJ 1.4.7	Arcadius and Honorius	Constantinople	Eutychianus, PPO Orientis	Asylum of those who evade duties or debts
July 6, 399	CTh 16.5.36	Arcadius and Honorius	Constantinople	Eutychianus, PPO Orientis	Confiscation
September 11, 404	CTh 16.2.37	Arcadius and Honorius	Constantinople	Studius, Prefect of the City	Right of assembly; Confiscation

(Contd.)

TABLE 4 *(Continued)*

Date of Issue[a]	Constitution[b]	Issuer(s)[c]	Place of Issue	Recipient[d]	Topic(s)[e]
November 18, 404	CTh 16.4.6	Arcadius, Honorius, and Theodosius	Constantinople	Eutychianus, PPO Orientis	Right of assembly
February 12, 405	CTh 16.6.4	Arcadius, Honorius, and Theodosius	Ravenna	Hadrianus, PPO Italiae et Africae	Confiscation; Asylum of the slaves of Donatists; Manumission of the slaves of Donatists
February 22, 407	CTh 16.5.40= CJ 1.5.4	Arcadius and Honorius	Rome	Senator, Prefect of the City	Confiscation
November 25, 407	Sirm. 12=CTh 16.2.38; 16.5.43; 16.10.19; 16.5.41	Honorius and Theodosius	Rome, posted at Carthage	Curtius, PPO	Vindication to churches
November 27, 408	CTh 16.5.45	Arcadius and Honorius	Ravenna	Theodorus, PPO Italiae, Illyrici, et Africae	Confiscation
December 17, 408	Sirm. 16	Honorius	Ravenna	Theodorus, PPO Italiae, Illyrici, et Africae	Redemption of captives
January 15, 409	Sirm. 14=CJ 1.3.10	Honorius and Theodosius	Ravenna	Theodorus, PPO Italiae, Illyrici, et Africae	Outrage against churches, Forcible seizure
April 1, 409	CTh 16.8.19=CJ 1.9.12, CJ 1.12.2, Sirm. 12, and CTh 16.5.43	Honorius and Theodosius	Ravenna	Jovius, PPO Italiae	Asylum and forcible seizure
June 26, 409	CTh 2.4.7=CTh 16.5.47	Honorius and Theodosius	Ravenna	Jovius, PPO Italiae	Legal suits regarding the church
June 24, 411 or May 25, 412	Sirm. 11=CTh 16.2.40 and CTh 16.11.16	Honorius and Theodosius	Ravenna	Melitius, PPO Italiae	Outrage against churches
January 30, 412	CTh 16.5.52	Arcadius and Honorius	Ravenna	Seleucus, PPO Africae	Vindication to churches

TABLE 4 *(Continued)*

Date of Issue[a]	Constitution[b]	Issuer(s)[c]	Place of Issue	Recipient[d]	Topic(s)[e]
June 17, 414	CTh 16.5.54	Arcadius and Honorius	Ravenna	Julianus, Proconsul of Africa	Vindication to churches
August 30, 415	CTh 16.10.20=CJ 1.11.5	Honorius and Theodosius	Ravenna		Vindication to churches
October 31, 415	CTh 16.5.57	Arcadius and Honorius	Constantinople	Aurelianus, PPO Orientis	Right of assembly; Vindication to churches
November 6, 415	CTh 16.5.58	Arcadius and Honorius	Constantinople	Aurelianus, PPO Orientis	Confiscation
September 24, 416	CTh 16.8.23	Honorius and Theodosius	Ravenna	Annas, Didascalus, and the Elders of the Jews	Asylum of Jews
November 21, 419	Sirm. 13	Honorius and Theodosius	Ravenna		Asylum
July 14, 421	CTh 16.2.45	Honorius and Theodosius		Philippus, PPO Illyrici	Canons
February 15, 423	CTh 16.8.25	Honorius and Theodosius	Constantinople	Asclepiodotus, PPO Orientis	Alienation
May 30, 428	CTh 16.5.65= CJ 1.5.5 and CJ 1.6.3	Theodosius and Valentinian	Constantinople	Florentius, PPO Orientis	Right of assembly; Right to build churches; Vindication to churches
March 23, 431	CTh 9.45.4= CJ 1.12.3	Theodosius and Valentinian	Constantinople	Antiochus, PPO Orientis	Weapons; Asylum
March 28, 432	CTh 9.45.5= CJ 1.12.4	Theodosius and Valentinian	Constantinople	Hierius, PPO Orientis	Asylum of slaves; Forcible seizure of slaves
December 15, 434	CTh 5.3.1= CJ 1.3.20	Theodosius and Valentinian		Taurus, PPO Orientis	Bequests; Legal suits
August 3, 435	CTh 16.5.66=CJ 1.5.6	Theodosius and Valentinian	Constantinople	Leontius, Prefect of the City	Right of assembly
January 31, 438	NTh 3.1.5= CJ 1.9.18	Theodosius and Valentinian	Constantinople	Florentius, PPO Orientis	Vindication to churches

(Contd.)

TABLE 4 *(Continued)*

Date of Issue[a]	Constitution[b]	Issuer(s)[c]	Place of Issue	Recipient[d]	Topic(s)[e]
February 11, 445	CJ 1.3.22	Theodosius and Valentinian	Constantinople	Florentius, PPO Orientis	Asylum
July 13, 451	CJ 1.12.5	Marcian	Constantinople	The People	Outrage against churches
November 12, 451	CJ 1.2.12	Valentinian and Marcian	Constantinople	Palladius, PPO Orientis	Canons
April 22, 455	NMarc 5=CJ 1.2.13	Valentinian and Marcian	Constantinople	Palladius, PPO Orientis	Bequests of women
August 1, 455	CJ 1.5.8	Valentinian and Marcian	Constantinople	Palladius, PPO Orientis	Right to build; Confiscation
456	CJ 1.3.25=CJ 1.4.13	Marcian		Constantine, PPO Orientis	Legal suits
November 6, 458	NMaj 7.1	Leo and Majorian	Ravenna	Basilius, PPO Italiae	Asylum
	NMaj 10	Majorian			Bequests
February 28, 466	CJ 1.12.6=CJ 1.3.27 and CJ 9.30.2	Leo	Constantinople	Erythrius, PPO Orientis	Asylum; Forcible seizure
466	CJ 1.5.10	Leo		Erythrius, PPO Orientis	Alienation; Confiscation
	CJ 1.12.7	Leo			Outrage against churches; Legal suits
	CJ 1.12.8	Leo			Outrage against churches
August 18, 468	CJ 1.3.28	Marcian	Constantinople	Nicostratus, PPO Orientis	Bequests for the redemption of unnamed captives
March 8, 469	CJ 1.3.30	Leo and Anthemius	Constantinople	Armasius, PPO Orientis	Asylum; Redemption of captives
470	CJ 1.2.14	Leo and Anthemius	Constantinople	Armasius, PPO Orientis	Alienation; Usufruct; Bequests
April 4, 472	CJ 1.3.32=CJ 1.3.33	Leo and Anthemius		Erythrius, PPO Orientis	Alienation; Legal suits
476	CJ 1.2.15	Zeno			Oratories
484–524	CJ 1.3.38				Donations
491–518	CJ 1.2.17	Anastasius			Alienation
November 19, 524	CJ 1.3.40	Justinian	Constantinople	Archelaus, PPO Africae	Bequests

TABLE 4 *(Continued)*

Date of Issue[a]	Constitution[b]	Issuer(s)[c]	Place of Issue	Recipient[d]	Topic(s)[e]
527	CJ 1.5.12	Justin and Justinian			Right of assembly
528	CJ 1.2.19	Justinian		Menas, PPO Orientis	Donations
March 1, 528	CJ 1.3.41	Justinian	Constantinople	Atarbius, PPO Orientis	Alienation; Donations; Bequests
March 1, 528	CJ 1.3.42	Justinian	Constantinople	Epiphanius, Archbishop of Constantinople	Legal suits
529	CJ 1.2.21	Justinian		Demosthenes, PPO Orientis	Alienation
529	CJ 1.2.22	Justinian		Demosthenes, PPO Orientis	Donations
530?	CJ 1.2.24	Justinian			Emphyteusis
March 28, 530	CJ 1.2.23	Justinian		Julian, PPO Orientis	Donations; Bequests; Legal suits
October 14, 530	CJ 1.2.25	Justinian		Julian, PPO Orientis	Bequests
October 18, 530	CJ 1.3.44	Justinian	Constantinople	Julian, PPO Orientis	Donations; Bequests; Canons
October 18, 530	CJ 1.3.45	Justinian	Constantinople	Julian, PPO Orientis	Bequests; Redemption of captives
October 18, 530	CJ 1.4.29	Justinian	Constantinople	Julian, PPO Orientis	Legal suits
November 22, 530	CJ 1.5.20	Justinian	Constantinople	CRP	Right of assembly; Confiscation
August 23, 531	CJ 1.3.48	Justinian	Constantinople	John, PPO Orientis	Bequests; Redemption of captives
November 17, 533	CJ 1.3.53	Justinian	Constantinople	Hermogenes, mag. off.	Vindication to churches
533–534	CJ 1.3.54	Justinian		John, PPO Orientis	Vindication to churches; Manumission of slaves
September 12, 534	CJ 1.3.55	Justinian	Constantinople	John, PPO Orientis	Bequests
Before 535?	Edictum 1	Justinian		All the bishops	Informers

(Contd.)

TABLE 4 *(Continued)*

Date of Issue[a]	Constitution[b]	Issuer(s)[c]	Place of Issue	Recipient[d]	Topic(s)[e]
Before 535?	Edictum 2	Justinian		John, PPO Orientis	Asylum of debtors
April 15, 535	NJust 7	Justinian	Constantinople	Epiphanius, Archbishop of Constantinople	Alienation; Exchange; Usufruct; Emphyteusis; Hypothecation; Donations; Redemption of captives
April 16, 535	NJust 17	Justinian		Provincial Governors	Asylum; Legal suits
August 1, 535	NJust 37	Justinian		Salomon, PPO Africae	Asylum; Donations; Vindication to churches
August 18, 536	NJust 46	Justinian	Constantinople	John, PPO Orientis	Alienation
September 1, 537	NJust 54	Justinian	Constantinople	John, PPO Orientis	Exchange
October 18, 537	NJust 55	Justinian	Constantinople	Mena, Archbishop of Constantinople	Exchange; Emphyteusis
November 3, 537	NJust 58	Justinian	Constantinople	John, PPO Orientis	Oratories; Confiscation
May 1, 538	NJust 67	Justinian	Constantinople	Mena, Archbishop of Constantinople	Alienation; Oratories; Donations
538/539	Edictum 13	Justinian		John, PPO Orientis	Asylum of debtors
December 18, 542	NJust 117	Justinian			Asylum
May 9, 544	NJust 120	Justinian	Constantinople	Peter, PPO Orientis	Alienation; Emphyteusis; Loans; Hypothecation; Redemption of captives
545	Edictum 10	Justinian		Prefects	Asylum of provincial apparitors

TABLE 4 *(Continued)*

Date of Issue[a]	Constitution[b]	Issuer(s)[c]	Place of Issue	Recipient[d]	Topic(s)[e]
March 18, 545	NJust 131	Justinian	Constantinople	Peter, PPO Orientis	Alienation; Usufruct; Emphyteusis; Donations; Bequests; Oratories; Confiscation; Redemption of captives Canons
May 1, 546	NJust 123	Justinian	Constantinople	Peter, mag. off.	Emphyteusis; Oratories; Legal suits; Vindication to churches; Outrage against churches; Redemption of captives
	CJ 1.5.14				Right of assembly
	NJust 111 (=Edictum 5)	Justinian			Legal suits

[a] See the important note by Noel Lenski, "Note on the Dating of Constitutions," in *The Codex of Justinian: A New Annotated Translation, with Parallel Latin and Greek Text, Based on a Translation by Justice Fred H. Blume*, ed. Bruce W. Frier (Cambridge: Cambridge University Press, 2016), xciv–xcvi.

[b] In some cases, the same constitution is attested in both the Codex of Theodosius and that of Justinian.

[c] Constitutions were issued in the name of all the *augusti*, regardless of the recipient's jurisdiction.

[d] Recipients' jurisdictions are taken from A. H. M Jones, J. R. Martindale, and J. Morris, eds., *Prosopography of the Later Roman Empire*, 3 vols. (Cambridge: Cambridge University Press, 1971–92).

[e] The "Topic(s)" column contains my brief annotation to each constitution. "Vindication to churches" means that the constitution puts churches of those deemed heretics into the hands of those considered catholic or orthodox.

[f] CJ 1.6.1: "Asiae." Cf. SC 497:341n4.

APPENDIX C

TABLE 5 Chronological List of Ecclesiastical Canons on Ecclesial Property

Year[a]	Location	Canon no.[b]	Topic(s)	Edition[c]
314	Ancyra	15	Alienation	Joannou 1.2:66–67.
330	Antioch	11	Legal suits	Joannou 1.2:113.
		24	Administration	Joannou 1.2:123–24.
		25	Administration	Joannou 1.2:123–24.
ca. 340[d]	Gangra	Anathema 5	Contempt of churches	Joannou 1.2:91.
		Anathema 6	"Private" churches	Joannou 1.2:91–92.
		Anathema 7	Donations	Joannou 1.2:92.
		Anathema 8	Donations	Joannou 1.2:92.
343	Serdica	7 (8)	Asylum; Legal suits	Joannou 1.2:169–70. Hess 2002, 217.
		8 (9a)	Legal suits	Joannou 1.2:170. Hess 2002, 217.
		9 (9b)	Legal suits	Joannou 1.2:171. Hess 2002, 217.
375–400	Laodicea	9	Martyria of heretics	Joannou 1.2:134.
		58	"Private" churches	Joannou 1.2:153.
382	Constantinople	6	Legal suits	Joannou 1.1:49–53.
394/396	Nimes	7	Manumission of slaves	CCSL 148:51.
399	Carthage	Envoy	Asylum; Forcible seizure	CCSL 149:194.
ca. 400	Canons of the Apostles	38	Administration; Alienation	Joannou 1.2:26.
		40	Administration	Joannou 1.2:27.
		41	Administration	Joannou 1.2:28–29.
401	Carthage	8 (64)	Manumission of slaves	CCSL 149:198.

(*Contd.*)

TABLE 5   *(Continued)*

Year[a]	Location	Canon no.[b]	Topic(s)	Edition[c]
401	Carthage	7 (72)	Consecration of churches	CCSL 149:201–2.
		16 (81)	Bequests	CCSL 149:204.
		17 (92)	Manumission of slaves	CCSL 149:204.
404	Carthage	Envoy	Confiscation	CCSL 149:211.
407	Carthage	5 (99)	Administration	CCSL 149:216.
410	Carthage	Envoy	Donatists and the Edict of Toleration	CCSL 149:220.
418	Carthage	10	Jurisdiction	CCSL 149:103.
		11	Prescriptive period	CCSL 149:104.
		12	Legal suits	CCSL 149:104.
		13	Jurisdiction	CCSL 149:104.
419	Carthage	26	Acquisition of property	CCSL 149:109.
		32	Alienation	CCSL 149:110.
		33	Alienation	CCSL 149:110–11.
427	Hippo	4	Exchange	CCSL 149:251.
		5	Acquisition of property; Bequests	CCSL 149:251.
		9	Consecration of churches	CCSL 149:252–53.
438	Carthage	4	Alienation	CCSL 149:356.
		6	Consecration of churches	CCSL 149:357.
		14	Bequests	CCSL 149:358–59.
439	Riez	6	Interim administration	CCSL 148:69
441	Orange	5	Asylum of slaves; Manumission of slaves	CCSL 148:79.
		6	Manumission of slaves	CCSL 148:79.
		9	Consecration of churches	CCSL 148:80–81.
442	Vaison	4	Bequests	CCSL 148:97.
451	Chalcedon	3	Administration	Johannou 1.1:71–72.
		8	Jurisdiction	Johannou 1.1:75–76.
		17	Prescriptive period	Johannou 1.1:82–83.
		25	Interim administration	Johannou 1.1:88–89.
		26	Administration	Johannou 1.1:89–90.
475	Statuta Ecclesiae Antiqua	Ch. 31	Administration	CCSL 148:169.
		Ch. 32	Alienation	CCSL 148:174.
		Ch. 95	Bequests	CCSL 148:182–83.
501/2	Rome		Alienation, Usufruct	MGH AA 12:448–51.

TABLE 5 *(Continued)*

Year[a]	Location	Canon no.[b]	Topic(s)	Edition[c]
442–506	Arles	30	Asylum of slaves; Manumission of slaves	CCSL 148:120.
		32	Manumission of slaves	CCSL 148:120–21.
		34	Legal suits	CCSL 148:121.
		36	Consecration of churches	CCSL 148:121.
		37	Consecration of churches	CCSL 148:121–22.
		47	Bequests	CCSL 148:123.
506	Agde	4	Bequests	CCSL 148:194.
		5	Alienation	CCSL 148:194.
		6	Donations	CCSL 148:194–95.
		7	Alienation	CCSL 148:194–95.
		14	Consecration of altars	CCSL 148:200.
		21	Oratories	CCSL 148:202–3.
		22	Alienation	CCSL 148:203.
		26	Diminution of assets	CCSL 148:205.
		29	Asylum of ecclesial freedmen	CCSL 148:206.
		45	Alienation	CCSL 148:211.
	Ps-Agde	48	Bequests	CCSL 148:225.
		49	Alienation	CCSL 148:225.
		51	Bequests	CCSL 148:225.
		56	Alienation; Manumission of slaves	CCSL 148:226.
		59	Usucaption	CCSL 148:226.
511	Orleans	1	Asylum; Forcible seizure	CCSL 148A:4–5.
		2	Asylum	CCSL 148A:5.
		3	Asylum of slaves	CCSL 148A:5–6.
		5	Donations; Ransom of captives	CCSL 148A:6.
		6	Legal suits	CCSL 148A:6–7.
		10	Consecration of churches	CCSL 148A:7–8.
		14	Administration	CCSL 148A:9.
		15	Donations	CCSL 148A:9.
		17	Jurisdiction	CCSL 148A:9.
		23	Usucaption	CCSL 148A:9.

(Contd.)

TABLE 5 *(Continued)*

Year[a]	Location	Canon no.[b]	Topic(s)	Edition[c]
516	Tarragona	8	Donations; Repairs	CCH 4:276–77.
		10	Donations	CCH 4:277–78.
		12	Interim administration	CCH 4:278–79.
517	Epaon	7	Alienation	CCSL 148A:26.
517	Epaon	8	Acquisition of property; Alienation; Manumission of slaves	CCSL 148A:26.
		12	Alienation	CCSL 148A:27.
		17	Bequests	CCSL 148A:28.
		18	Usucaption	CCSL 148A:28–29.
		25	Foundation and consecration of churches	CCSL 148A:30.
		26	Consecration of altars	CCSL 148A:30.
		33	Use of heretics' churches	CCSL 148A:33.
		39	Asylum of slaves	CCSL 148A:34.
518–523	Lyons	4	Jurisdiction	CCSL 148A:40.
527	Dovin, Armenia	1	Donations	Hefele-Leclercq 2.2:1078.
		2	Donations	Hefele-Leclercq 2.2:1078.
		3	Loans	Hefele-Leclercq 2.2:1078.
		14	Donations	Hefele-Leclercq 2.2:1079.
		15	Sacred vessels	Hefele-Leclercq 2.2:1079.
		16	"Private" houses	Hefele-Leclercq 2.2:1079.
		23	Donations	Hefele-Leclercq 2.2:1079.
527	Carpentras		Administration	CCSL 148A:48–52.
527/531	Toledo	4	Bequests	CCH 4:351–52
529	Valencia	2	Interim administration	CCSL 148A:78–79.
		3	Interim administration	CCSL 148A:79.
533	Orleans	6	Interim administration	CCSL 148A:99–100.
533	Massilia		Alienation	CCSL 148A:85.
535	Clermont	3	Proper use of ecclesial property	CCSL 148A:106.
		5	Alienation	CCSL 148A:106.
		8	Proper use of ecclesial property	CCSL 148A:107.
		14	Bequests	CCSL 148A:108–9.
		15	Oratories	CCSL 148A:108–9.
		Letter	Jurisdiction	CCSL 148A:111–12.

TABLE 5   *(Continued)*

Year[a]	Location	Canon no.[b]	Topic(s)	Edition[c]
538	Orleans	5	Donations	CCSL 148A:116.
		13	Alienation; Restitution	CCSL 148A:116.
		14	Asylum of slaves of Jews	CCSL 148A:120.
		16	Consecration of altars	CCSL 148A:120.
		25	Alienation; Bequests	CCSL 148A:123–24.
		26	Alienation; Stipulation	CCSL 148A:124.
541	Orleans	7	Oratories	CCSL 148A:133–34.
		9	Alienation; Manumission of slaves	CCSL 148A:133–34.
		11	Alienation; Donations	CCSL 148A:134–35.
		14	Legal suits	CCSL 148A:135.
		18	Alienation	CCSL 148A:136.
		19	Bequests	CCSL 148A:136–37.
		21	Asylum; Forcible seizure	CCSL 148A:137.
		24	Asylum of slaves	CCSL 148A:138.
		25	Alienation	CCSL 148A:138.
		30	Asylum of slaves of Jews; Manumission of slaves	CCSL 148A:139–40.
		33	Oratories	CCSL 148A:139–40.
		34	Usufruct; Alienation	CCSL 148A:141.
		35	Interim administration; Usucaption	CCSL 148A:141.
		36	Usufruct	CCSL 148A:141.
546	Lerida	3	Consecration of churches	CCH 4:300–301.
		16	Interim administration	CCH 4:306–9.
549	Orleans	7	Manumission of slaves	CCSL 148A:141.
		8	Interim administration	CCSL 148A:141.
		13	Alienation; Donations	CCSL 148A:141.
		14	Jurisdiction	CCSL 148A:141.
		16	Bequests	CCSL 148A:153–54.
		22	Asylum of slaves	CCSL 148A:156.
551	Eauze	6	Bequests	CCSL 148A:164.
554	Arles	6	Diminution of assets	CCSL 148A:164.

(Contd.)

TABLE 5 *(Continued)*

Year[a]	Location	Canon no.[b]	Topic(s)	Edition[c]
556–573	Paris	1	Alienation; Restitution; Legal suits	CCSL 148A:205–6.
		2	Damage, Restitution	CCSL 148A:207.
		7	Alienation	CCSL 148A:208.
561–605	Auxerre	3	Private houses	CCSL 148A:265.
		14	Interment of corpses on church grounds	CCSL 148A:267.
		15	Interment of corpses on church grounds	CCSL 148A:267.
561	Braga	19	Consecration of altars and churches	CVHR, 75.
567	Tours	25	Alienation; Restitution	CCSL 148A:192–93.
		26	Alienation; Restitution	CCSL 148A:193–94.
567	Lyons	2	Bequests	CCSL 148A:201.
		5	Usufruct	CCSL 148A:201.
572	Braga	5	Foundation of churches; Consecration of churches; Donations	CVHR, 83.
		6	Purpose of founding churches	CVHR, 83.
581	Macon	4	Bequests	CCSL 148A:224.
583	Valencia		Donations	CCSL 148A:235.
585	Macon	8	Asylum	CCSL 148A:242–43.
589	Narbonne	8	Alienation	CCSL 148A:255.
589	Toledo	3	Administration; Alienation	Rodriguez, 29.
		4	Change of status	Rodriguez, 30.
		6	Manumission of slaves	Rodriguez, 30.
		9	Jurisdiction	Rodriguez, 30.
		15	Foundation of churches	Rodriguez, 31.
		19	Administration	Rodriguez, 32.
		21	Ecclesial slaves	Rodriguez, 32.
592	Saragossa	3	Reconsecration of churches	CVHR, 154.
595	Rome	3	Acquisition of property	Martyn, 388–92.
		6	Ecclesial slaves	Martyn, 388–92.

[a] Some of the years given are an approximation only.

[b] "Envoy" indicates that the council sent representatives to petition the emperor. "Letter" refers to a letter sent from the council to the emperor/king.

^c This column cites an edition for each canon, except for those of Dovin, Armenia, for which I consulted only the translation and notes provided in Hefele-Leclercq.

^d Timothy Barnes argues that the Synod of Gangra probably took place around 355, but Avshalom Laniado offers evidence from Syriac sources that points to the widely accepted period of the 340s and more specifically to 343. See T. D. Barnes, "The Date of the Council of Gangra," *JTS*, n.s., 40 (1989): 121–24; Avshalom Laniado, "Note sur la datation conserve en syriaque du Concile de Gangres," *OCP* 61 (1995): 195–99.

Late Antique Lections for the Consecratory Ritual

As mentioned briefly in chapter 5, two lectionaries offer a window into fifth-century selections of scriptural passages for the consecration of a church or altar: one a witness to the practices of Jerusalem; the other to those of East Syria. An Armenian manuscript witness to a fifth-century lectionary of Jerusalem (known by the siglum P for Paris, BnF Armenian 44, tenth century) includes the following note between the Feast of Saint Andrew on November 30 and the Feast of Saint David on December 25:

> For the dedication of all the altars constructed, the following canon is performed:
> Psalm: *I will enter before the altar of God, to God* (Ps 42:4).
> From the letter to the Hebrews: *As for us, we have an altar from which those who serve the tabernacle have no right to eat . . . for God is pleased with such a sacrifice* (Heb 13:10–16).
> Alleluia 25: *Judge me, O Lord, for, as for me, I have walked in my innocence* (Ps 25:1).
> According to Matthew: *Whoever exalts himself will be abased . . . and he who swears by heaven swears by the throne of God and he who sits upon it* (Matt 23:12–22).[1]

No other Armenian lectionary witness to the practices of Jerusalem includes this entry.[2] In addition, no other such witness includes prescriptions for feasts that can take place throughout the liturgical year, as the following lectionary does.

A fifth-century manuscript containing an East Syrian lectionary includes, at the end, lessons for occasions that can take place throughout the liturgical year: the tonsure of a man to be a *Bar Kyāmā*; the commemoration of martyrs; the commemoration of bishops; the ordination of a priest. The final two prescribe the lections for the dedication of a church and an altar:

Lesson for the dedication of a Holy Church:

    1 Ps 84, resp. vv. 3b, 4a ("My King and my God, blessed are they that dwell in Thy House").

    2 Heb 9:1–28

    3 Halluliah, Ps 147, resp. ver. 12a (ver. 1a Syr.).

    4 John 10:22–42.

Lesson for the dedication of an Altar:

    1 Ps 43, resp. ver. 4a.

    2 1 Kings 8:1–53.

    3 Heb 12:28–end.

    4 Halluliah, Ps 26, resp. ver. 1a.

    5 Matt 23:12–22.[3]

These two lectionaries offer a window into fifth-century selections of scriptural passages for the consecration of a church or altar—the first in Jerusalem and the second somewhere in East Syria.

These lectionaries have been discussed, however, in relation to the general dedication days of the West and East Syrian calendars. Because the Armenian lectionary cited above names the prescribed readings for the consecration of an altar in between prescriptions for November 30 and December 25, Bernard Botte (and many scholars following him) have interpreted the entry to refer to a general dedication day that took place sometime in December in fifth-century Jerusalem—a precursor to the general dedication days observed in later West and East Syrian calendars.[4] However, it is more likely that the scribe of the Armenian manuscript P mistakenly began to copy down a list of entries for feasts that can fall throughout the liturgical year. The scribe completed the entry for the dedication of an altar, but did not continue the list, because (like the other Armenian witnesses) the lectionary was to contain only feasts that took place on a particular day of the year (whether moveable or immoveable). The Armenian lectionary (P) and the East Syrian lectionary both attest to fifth-century lections assigned for the festival of the consecration of a church or altar, whenever such a festival would take place. They do not attest to a fifth-century general dedication day.

NOTES

INTRODUCTION

1. John Chrysostom, *Homily on the* Comes *John* 1. PG 52:397: Ἐκκλησίαν δὲ λέγω, οὐ τόπον μόνον. John Chrysostom does not name the individual in question, but Alan Cameron makes the case for identifying him with Count John. Alan Cameron, "A Misidentified Homily of Chrysostom," *Nottingham Medieval Studies* 32 (1988): 34–48. According to Sever Voicu, only the first two sections of the homily are compatible with the corpus of John Chrysostom's writings that is considered authentic (Sever Voicu, "La volontà e il caso: La tipologia dei primi spuri di Crisostomo," in *Giovanni Crisostomo: Oriente e occidente tra IV e V secolo, XXXIII Incontro di studiosi dell' antichità cristiana, Roma, 6–8 maggio 2004,* vol. 1, Studia Ephemeridis Augustinianum 93 (Rome: Institutum Patristicum Augustinianum, 2005), 111–12. My argument here relies on this portion.

2. Because Alan Cameron (in "A Misidentified Homily") identifies the individual in question with Count John, he dates the homily's delivery to the year 400. Sever Voicu dates it to sometime between the Synod of the Oak in 403 and John Chrysostom's death (Voicu, "Spuri di Crisostomo," 112).

3. John Chrysostom, *Homily on the* Comes *John* 1; PG 52:397.

4. John Chrysostom, *Homily on the* Comes *John* 1; PG 52:397.

5. John Chrysostom uses γνώμη to refer to a faculty or power of the soul. Raymond Laird, *Mindset, Moral Choice and Sin in the Anthropology of John Chrysostom*, Early Christian Studies 15 (2012; repr., Sydney: SCD Press, 2017), 1–2. Here, John Chrysostom underscores the significance of this critical faculty of the Church's soul.

6. "By the early 3rd century, imperial documents came routinely to be referred to as 'sacred,' and *sacrae litterae* (used for more than letters narrowly defined) and similar terms became standard formulations." Simon Corcoran, "State Correspondence in the

Roman Empire," in *State Correspondence in the Ancient World: From New Kingdom Egypt to the Roman Empire*, ed. Karen Radner (New York: Oxford University Press, 2014), 177.

7. Gratian was the last emperor to bear the title, which was probably dropped in the course of the controversy over the altar of Victory at the senate house. The title became *pontifex inclitus* ("famous priest") instead. See Alan Cameron, "*Pontifex Maximus*: From Augustus to Gratian – and Beyond," *Collegium: Studies across Disciplines in the Humanities and Social Sciences* 20 (2016): 139–59.

8. For example, there is a Visigothic reworking of Gaius's *Institutes*. Also, in the mid-sixth century, Julianus, a law professor in Constantinople, produced what is known as the *Epitome Juliani*, a summary of Justinian's novels for his Latin-speaking students. See Max Conrat Cohn, *Die Entstehung des westgothischen Gaius* (Amsterdam: Johannes Müller, 1905); Wolfgang Kaiser, *Die Epitome Iuliani: Beiträge zum römischen Recht im frühen Mittelalter und zum byzantinischen Rechtsunterricht* (Frankfurt: Vittorio Klostermann, 2004). The general principles on *res sacrae* that I describe in part I were not "general" because they were obligatory or binding across a wide geographic scope but rather because they were taught to students of law across the Mediterranean.

9. Like *res sacrae*, *res religiosae* (places where human corpses are interred) could not be alienated according to the rules (see chapters 1 and 2), yet there are multiple pieces of evidence that such practices did take place. See, for example, Esen Öğüş, "The 'Sacrilegious, Accursed and Tomb-breaker': Sarcophagus Re-use at Aphrodisias," in *Questions, Approaches, and Dialogues: Studies in Honor of Marie-Henriette and Charles Gates*, ed. Ekin Kozal et al. (Münster: Ugarit-Verlag, 2017), 647–65. As with all rules, the very fact that they were promulgated demonstrates that their violation must have been occurring on the ground.

10. Among the major publications that generated this "legal turn," see Jill Harries, *Law and Empire in Late Antiquity* (Cambridge: Cambridge University Press, 1999); John F. Matthews, *Laying Down the Law: A Study of the Theodosian Code* (New Haven, CT: Yale University Press, 2000); and Caroline Humfress, *Orthodoxy and the Courts in Late Antiquity* (New York: Oxford University Press, 2007).

11. Igor Kopytoff, "The Cultural Biography of Things: Commoditization as Process," in *The Social Life of Things: Commodities in Cultural Perspective*, ed. Arjun Appadurai (New York: Cambridge University Press, 1986), 73–77.

12. On the tension between the concepts of "gift" and "commodity," see Arjun Appadurai, "Introduction: Commodities and the Politics of Value," in *Social Life of Things*, ed. Appadurai, 11–13; Mark Osteen, "Gift or Commodity?," in *The Question of the Gift: Essays across Disciplines*, ed. Osteen (London: Routledge, 2002), 229–47; Gadi Algazi, "Introduction: Doing Things with Gifts," in *Negotiating the Gift: Pre-Modern Figurations of Exchange*, ed. Algazi, Valentin Groebner, and Bernhard Jussen (Göttingen: Vandenhoeck and Ruprecht, 2003), 18–19; and Kenneth Hayes Lokensgard, *Blackfoot Religion and the Consequences of Cultural Commoditization* (Farnham: Ashgate, 2010).

CHAPTER 1. *RES SACRAE*

1. For Constantius II's use of the title, see Alan Cameron, "*Pontifex Maximus*: From Augustus to Gratian – and Beyond," *Collegium: Studies across Disciplines in the Humanities*

and Social Sciences 20 (2016): 143–44. Ludwig Voelkl compares entries in the *Liber pontificalis* with *leges templorum* to show that contracts similar to those for temples were drawn up for the consecration of Christian temples, i.e., churches. An important part of a *dedicatio* was the *leges templorum*, which were contract documents read by the *pontifex maximus* and repeated by the magistrate. The dedication was festively completed through the consecration. Ludwig Voelkl, *Die Kirchenstiftungen des Kaisers Konstantin im Lichte des römischen Sakralrechts*, Arbeitsgemeinschaft für Forschung des Landes Nordrhein-Westfalen 117 (Cologne: Westdeutscher Verlag, 1964), 19. Cf. Vitalijs Permjakovs, "'Make This the Place Where Your Glory Dwells': Origins and Evolution of the Byzantine Rite for the Consecration of a Church" (PhD diss., University of Notre Dame, 2012), 66–67.

2. Athanasius, *Apol. Const.* 18. Translation adapted from Philip Schaff and Henry Wace, eds., *A Select Library of Nicene and Post-Nicene Fathers of the Christian Church*, 2nd series, vol. 4 (1891; repr., Grand Rapids, MI: Eerdmans Publishing, 1978–79), 245. Since the Caesareum had been a site for the imperial cult since Emperor Augustus, Athanasius's reference to purifying it in advance likely refers to a ritual for exorcizing a pagan site before converting it to a Christian one.

3. For the history of how Christian practices came to be legal in the time of Constantine, see Noel Lenski, "The Significance of the Edict of Milan," in *Constantine: Religious Faith and Imperial Policy*, ed. A. Edward Siecienski (Abingdon: Routledge, 2017), 27–56.

4. The Council of Chalcedon in 451 is one example. Imperial officials presided over all the sessions, except the third. See the notes on the presidency of the council in TTH 45.1:41–42.

5. For studies on the *episcopalis audientia*, see Noel Lenski, *Constantine and the Cities* (Philadelphia: University of Pennsylvania Press, 2016), 197–200; Caroline Humfress, "Bishops and Law Courts in Late Antiquity: How (Not) to Make Sense of the Legal Evidence," *JECS* 19 (2011): 375–400; and John C. Lamoreaux, "Episcopal Courts in Late Antiquity," *JECS* 3 (1995): 143–67. For an evaluation of the state of the question, see Maria Doerfler, "Law and Order: Monastic Formation, Episcopal Authority, and Conceptions of Justice in Late Antiquity" (PhD diss., Duke University, 2013), 80–106. To a considerable degree, episcopal rule-making in synodal settings came to be largely modeled after Roman juristic practices. See Michael E. Moore, "The Spirit of the Gallican Councils, AD 314–506," *Annuarium Historiae Conciliorum* 39 (2007): 1–52.

6. Ramsay MacMullen, *Voting about God in Early Church Councils* (New Haven, CT: Yale University Press, 2006), 2–7. There are of course margins of error associated with Ramsay MacMullen's calculations. For instance, the calculation assumes semi-annual meetings, but Chalcedon, 451, c. 19 shows that although synods were supposed to meet twice a year, they did not.

7. For an evaluation of the merits of studying other literature for legal evidence, see Caroline Humfress, "Patristic Sources," in *The Cambridge Companion to Roman Law*, ed. David Johnston (New York: Cambridge University Press, 2015), 97–118.

8. I use the term "codex" rather than "code" for the same reason as that named in Simon Corcoran, "The Codex of Justinian: The Life of a Text through 1,500 Years," in *The Codex of Justinian: A New Annotated Translation, with Parallel Latin and Greek Text, Based on a Translation by Justice Fred H. Blume*, vol. 1, ed. Bruce W. Frier (Cambridge: Cambridge University Press, 2016), civ. The word "code" suggests completeness, comprehensiveness, and a

codified body of material, whereas the late antique term applied to the collection, "codex," refers to the format of publication only and does not share the wider connotation of "code."

9. The Gregorian and Hermogenian codices, collected in the third century, preceded that of Theodosius II and were used as sources for Theodosius's Codex, but have not been transmitted independently.

10. For the making of the Theodosian Codex, especially the editorial practices of the compilers, see John F. Matthews, *Laying Down the Law: A Study of the Theodosian Code* (New Haven, CT: Yale University Press, 2000). For a short discussion, see Corcoran, ci–civ.

11. Matthews, 121–67; Mark Vessey, "The Origins of the *Collectio Sirmondiana*: A New Look at the Evidence," in *The Theodosian Code: Studies in the Imperial Law of Late Antiquity*, ed. Jill Harries and Ian Wood (London: Duckworth, 1993), 178–99.

12. Corcoran, ci.

13. Rudolf Schoell and Guilelmus Kroll, eds., *Corpus Iuris Civilis*, vol. 3 (1895; repr., Berlin: Apud Weidmannos, 1954); Peter Sarris, "Introduction: The Novels of the Emperor Justinian," in *The Novels of Justinian: A Complete Annotated English Translation*, vol. 1, ed. David J. D. Miller and Peter Sarris (Cambridge: Cambridge University Press, 2018), 1–51.

14. Timothy G. Kearley, "The Creation and Transmission of Justinian's Novels," *Law Library Journal* 102 (2010): 381.

15. I consulted the following editions: Charles Joseph Hefele, *Histoire des conciles d'après les documents originaux*, vols. 1–2, trans. and ed. Henri Leclercq (Paris: Letouzey et Ané, 1907–8); Périclès-Pierre Joannou, ed., *Discipline generale antique*, 2 vols. (Rome: Grottaferrata, 1962–64); Charles Munier, ed., *Concilia Africae, a. 345–a. 525*, CCSL 149 (Turnhout: Brepols, 1974); Charles Munier, ed., *Concilia Galliae, a. 314–a. 506*, CCSL 148 (Turnhout: Brepols, 1963); Caroli de Clercq, ed., *Concilia Galliae, a. 511–a. 695*, CCSL 148A (Turnhout: Brepols, 1963); José Vives, Tomás Marín Martínez, and Gonzalo Martínez Díez, eds. and trans., *Concilios visigóticos e hispano-romanos*, España Cristiana, Textos 1 (Barcelona: Consejo Superior de Investigaciones Científicas, 1963); Gonzalo Martínez Díez and Félix Rodríguez, ed., *La colección canónica Hispana*, vol. 4 (Madrid: Consejo Superior de Investigaciones Científicas, Instituto Enrique Flórez, 1984).

16. Heinz Ohme, "Sources of the Greek Canon Law to the Quinisext Council (691/2): Councils and Church Fathers," in *The History of Byzantine and Eastern Canon Law to 1500*, ed. Wilfried Hartmann and Kenneth Pennington (Washington, DC: Catholic University of America Press, 2012), 24–114; Hubert Kaufhold, "Sources of Canon Law in the Eastern Churches," in Hartmann and Pennington, 215–342.

17. Wilhelm Riedel and Walter E. Crum, eds. and trans., *The Canons of Athanasius of Alexandria: The Arabic and Coptic Versions* (London: Williams and Norgate, 1904).

18. Alfred Pernice, "Zum römischen Sacralrechte," *Sitzungsberichte der königlich preussischen Akademie der Wissenschaften zu Berlin* 2 (1885): 1143–69; Moritz Voigt, "Die römische Klassifikation von Ius divinum und humanum," *Berichte über die Verhandlungen der königlich sächsischen Gesellschaft der Wissenschaften zu Leipzig, philologisch-historische Klasse* 54 (1902): 185–94; Georg von Hertling, *Konsekration und res sacrae im römischen Sakralrecht* (Munich: K. Hof- und Universitäts-Buchdruckerei Dr. C. Wolf und Sohn, 1911); Rudolf Düll, "Rechtsprobleme im Bereich des römischen Sakralrechts," *Aufstieg und Niedergang der römischen Welt* I.2 (1972): 283–94; Yan Thomas, "La valeur des choses: Le droit romain hors la religion," *Annales. Histoire, Sciences Sociales* 6 (2002): 1431–62; John Scheid,

"Oral Tradition and Written Tradition in the Formation of Sacred Law in Rome," in *Religion and Law in Classical and Christian Rome*, ed. Clifford Ando and Jörg Rüpke (Stuttgart: Franz Steiner Verlag, 2006), 14–33; James Rives, "Control of the Sacred in Roman Law," in *Law and Religion in the Roman Republic*, ed. Olga Tellegen-Couperus (Leiden: Brill, 2012), 165–80.

19. Johann Baptist Braun, *Das kirchliche Vermögen von der ältesten Zeit bis auf Justinian I* (Giefsen: Ferber, 1860); August Rivet, *Le régime des biens de l'église avant Justinien* (Lyons: Imprimerie Emmanuel Vitte, 1891); William K. Boyd, *The Ecclesiastical Edicts of the Theodosian Code*, Studies in History, Economics, and Public Law, vol. 24, no. 2 (New York: Columbia University Press, 1905); Jean Gaudemet, *L'Église dans l'empire romain (IVᵉ–Vᵉ siècles)* (Paris: Sirey, 1958), 288–315; Pier Giovanni Caron, "La proprietà ecclesiastica nel diritto del tardo impero," in *Atti dell'accademia romanistica costantiniana, IX convegno internazionale* (Naples: Edizioni Scientifiche Italiane, 1993), 217–30; Béatrice Caseau, "A Case Study for the Transformation of Law in Late Antiquity: The Legal Protection of Churches," in *Confrontation in Late Antiquity: Imperial Presentation and Regional Adaptation*, ed. Linda Jones Hall (Cambridge: Orchard Academic, 2003), 61–77; Susan Wood, *The Proprietary Church in the Medieval West* (Oxford: Oxford University Press, 2006), 1–108. Susan Wood (16) acknowledges the legal category of *res sacra*, but she dismisses it on account of (what I consider) patrons' reactions to it.

The only notable exceptions are as follows: Andrea Galante, *La condizione giuridica delle cose sacre*, part 1 (Milan: Torino, Unione Tipografico-Editrice, 1903); Gaetano Scherillo, *Lezioni di diritto romano: le cose*, part 1 (Milan: Dott. A. Giuffrè-Editore, 1945), 37–67; and Bernard Stolte, "Law for Founders," in *Founders and Refounders of Byzantine Monasteries*, ed. Margaret Mullett (Belfast: Belfast Byzantine Enterprises, 2007), 126. To my knowledge, Andrea Galante only published the first part of the announced project. In the first part, he restricted the scope to legal material only, postponing research on canonical sources to a future volume. Though I maintain a clear distinction between legal and canonical material, I interweave discussions of them in order to show how the two grew and morphed together in various kinds of relationships. As for Gaetano Scherillo, his short study on *res sacrae* is also limited strictly to legal sources—namely, the classical pedagogical material and Justinian's codification project. Bernard Stolte acknowledges the fact that *res sacrae* belonged to no one, but he does not offer a comprehensive account of late antique jurisprudence on this topic. Instead, he examines founders' private documents for the establishment of a monastery or another institution in an effort to determine what was happening on the ground.

20. Otto Grashof, "Die Gesetze der römischen Kaiser über die Immunitäten der Kirche hinsichtlich ihres Vermögens," *Archiv für katholisches Kirchenrecht* 35 (1876): 321–35; Grashof, "Die Gesetzgebung der römischen Kaiser über die Güter und Immunitäten der Kirche und des Klerus nebst deren Motiven und Principien," *Archiv für katholisches Kirchenrecht* 36 (1876): 3–51; François Chamard, "De l'immunité ecclésiastique et monastique," *Revue des questions historiques* 22 (1877): 428–64; Ch. Mury, "Immunités des biens d'église et du clergé sous les Empereurs romains," *Revue catholique des institutions et du droit* 10 (1877): 241–55; August Knecht, *System des Justinianischen Kirchenvermögensrechtes* (Stuttgart: Verlag von Ferdinand Enke, 1905); Boyd, 82–86; Giannino Ferrari dalla Spade, *Immunità ecclesiastiche nel diritto romano imperiale* (Venice: Premiate Officine Grafiche Carlo Ferrari, 1939); John Emmanuel Downs, *The Concept of Clerical Immunity* (Washington, DC: Catholic University

of America Press, 1941), 6–20; Biondo Biondi, *Il diritto romano cristiano*, 3 vols (Milan: Dott. A. Giuffrè editore, 1952 and 1954), 1:360–94; Gaudemet, *L'Église dans l'empire romain*; Lucio Bove, "Immunità fondiaria di chiese e chierici nel Basso Impero," in *Synteleia: Vincenzo Arangio-Ruiz*, vol. 2, ed. Antonio Guarino and Luigi Labruna (Naples: Jovene 1964), 886–902; Carles Buenacasa Pérez, "Accroissement et consolidation du patrimoine ecclésiastique dans le *Code Théodosien* XVI," in *Empire chrétien et église aux IVe et Ve siècles: Intégration ou «concordat»? Le témoinage du Code Théodosien*, ed. Jean-Noël Guinot and François Richard (Paris: Les éditions du Cerf, 2008), 259–75; Roland Delmaire, "Église et fiscalité: le *privilegium christianitatis* et ses limites," in Guinot and Richard, 285–93.

21. Joseph von Zhishman, *Das Stifterrecht in der morgenländischen Kirche* (Vienna: K. K. Hof- und Universitäts-Buchhändler, 1888); Voelkl, *Die Kirchenstiftungen des Kaisers Konstantin*; Hans Liermann, *Handbuch des Stiftungsrechts*, vol. 1 (Tübingen: J. C. B. Mohr, 1963), 24–46.

22. Arthur Desjardins, "De l'aliénation et de la prescription des biens de l'église dans le droit du bas-empire et dans le droit des capitulaires," *Revue historique de droit français et étranger* 16 (1860): 254–65; Otto Grashof, "Die Gesetze der römischen Kaiser über die Verwaltung und Veräusserung des kirchlichen Vermögens," *Archiv für katholisches Kirchenrecht* 36 (1876): 193–214; Joseph F. Cleary, *Canonical Limitations on the Alienation of Church Property: An Historical Synopsis and Commentary* (Washington, DC: Catholic University of America, 1936), 15–39; Giorgio Barone-Adesi, "Il sistema Giustinianeo delle proprietà ecclesiastiche," in *La proprietà e le proprietà*, ed. Ennio Cortese (Milan: Dott. A. Giuffrè editore, 1988), 75–120.

23. Biondi, 2:397–401; Fabrizio Fabbrini, *La manumissio in ecclesia* (Milan: Dott. A. Giuffrè editore, 1965).

24. Biondi, 3:445–46; Hans Langenfeld, *Christianisierungspolitik und Sklavengesetzgebung der römischen Kaiser von Konstantin bis Theodosius II* (Bonn: Habelt, 1977); Anne Ducloux, *Ad ecclesiam confugere: Naissance du droit d'asile dans les églises (IVe–milieu du Ve s.)* (Paris: De Boccard, 1994); Christian Traulsen, *Das sakrale Asyl in der Alten Welt* (Tübingen: Mohr Siebeck, 2004), 267–310. These studies take the unfavorable rhetoric of church historians on laws regarding asylum at face value. For this reason, they claim that asylum was not practiced in churches until the fifth century, but I argue in chapter 3 that such laws did not forbid the practice of ecclesial asylum altogether; rather, they imposed limitations on it.

25. Tony Honoré summarizes the procedure that the commission followed. See Tony Honoré, *Tribonian* (London: Duckworth, 1978), 139–86. For further detail, see also Honoré, *Justinian's Digest: Character and Compilation* (New York: Oxford University Press, 2010).

26. Gaius's *Institutes* have been transmitted independently, while Ulpian's *Institutes* are known only from the excerpts quoted in Justinian's *Digest*.

27. Gaius, *Institutes* 2.2; Francis de Zulueta, ed., *The Institutes of Gaius*, vol. 1 (Oxford: Clarendon Press, 1946), 66.

28. Gaius, *Institutes* 2.1; de Zulueta, 1:66.

29. Gaius, *Institutes* 2.1–8; de Zulueta, 1:66. James Rives offers a reflection as to how elite control of the sacred might have given rise to the tripartite distinction between *sacra, religiosa,* and *sancta* in "Control of the Sacred," 165–80. On *res sanctae*, see David J. Bloch, "*Res Sanctae* in Gaius and the Founding of the City," *Roman Legal Tradition* 3 (2006): 48–64.

30. Gaius, *Institutes* 2.4; de Zulueta, 1:66.

31. Gaius, *Institutes* 2.5; de Zulueta, 1:66. Cf. Stephan Brassloff, *Studien zur römischen Rechtsgeschichte, 1. Teil: Die Befugnis zur Dedikation (Zwei Fragen aus der Lehre von der res sacra)* (Vienna: Verlagsbuchhandlung Carl Fromme, 1925), 1–34.

32. Gaius, *Institutes* 2.1 and 10–11; de Zulueta, 1:66. The notion *nullius in bonis* crosses the categories of divine and human law but is used in different ways in each case. Things in a bequest belong to no one (*nullius in bonis*) until someone claims them. Public things belong to no one (*nullius in bonis*) because they belong to everyone. According to Gaius, (1) nothing under divine law can belong to anyone, (2) public things under human law cannot belong to anyone, (3) but there is a difference in the meaning of "*nullius in bonis*" in (1) and (2). Public things "belong to no one" in the sense that they do not belong to a particular individual but to a corporate body, while divine things "belong to no one" in the sense that they belong neither to individuals nor to a corporate body.

The latter fact, that divine things do not belong to a corporate body, can be deduced from Gaius's note on whether there are such things as *res sacrae, religiosae,* or *sanctae* in provincial lands. The Roman people or the emperor own provincial lands; individuals only have possession of it (2.7). For this reason, in the provinces, there is no such thing as *res divini iuris* per se; instead, there are lands that "are considered" *sacrae* or *religiosae* (2.7 and 7a), though in point of fact they are not, since they are owned by the Roman people (a corporate body) or the emperor (a representative of the corporate body).

33. D. 1.1.1.2; Paul Krueger and Theodor Mommsen, eds., *Corpus Iuris Civilis*, vol. 1 (1867–70; repr., Berlin: Apud Weidmannos, 1962), 1.

34. D. 1.1.1.2; Krueger and Mommsen, 1:1.

35. D. 1.1.1.3–4; Krueger and Mommsen, 1:1.

36. Scholars, such as Alfred Pernice, Georg Wissowa, and a more recent writer, Yan Thomas, generalize Ulpian's framework over all other jurists in their accounts of how Roman law treats cultic objects. See Pernice, 1143; Georg Wissowa, *Religion und Kultus der Römer* (Munich: C. H. Beck'sche Verlagsbuchhandlung, 1902), 318; Yan Thomas, 1434. If indeed Ulpian's framework was widely adopted, it is surprising that the jurists who compiled Justinian's *Institutes* did not set forth Ulpian's categorization in the updated textbook. It is in fact Ulpian who is sometimes compelled to operate with distinctions like those of Gaius and Justinian, not vice versa. Richard John Hebein argues that the subordination of *ius sacrum* to *ius publicum* was the exception, not the rule. See Richard John Hebein, "St. Ambrose and Roman Law" (PhD diss., St. Louis University, 1970), 63–64.

37. Justinian, *Institutes* 2.1.pr; J. A. C. Thomas, ed., *The Institutes of Justinian: Text, Translation, and Commentary* (Amsterdam: North-Holland Publishing Company, 1975), 65. Justinian's *Institutes* is generally thought to be a rewriting of Gaius's *Institutes*, but I show in appendix A that the section 2.1.pr-10 is made up largely of verbatim excerpts from D. 1.8.2–9. See appendix A for a chart of the sources and a synopsis.

38. Justinian, *Institutes* 2.1.7; J. A. C. Thomas, 65.

39. Justinian, *Institutes* 2.1.8; J. A. C. Thomas, 65.

40. See the discussions of Justinian's Novel 7, Novel 37, and Edict 1 in chapter 2.

41. D. 1.8.9.pr.

42. D. 1.8.9.1. The terms "dedication" and "consecration" were synonymous by Ulpian's time, though at an earlier point in history there was a fine distinction. See L. Koep,

"Dedicatio," in *Reallexikon für Antike und Christentum*, vol. 3, ed. Theodor Klauser (Stuttgart: Anton Hiersemann, 1957), columns 643–49 and Koep, "Consecratio," in Klauser, 3:269–83.

43. D. 50.12.2.

44. D. 17.2.63.10.

45. Epaon, 517, c. 25; Braga, 572, c. 5.

46. NJust 67.

47. NJust 67.pr. Translation from Miller and Sarris, 1:491.

48. NJust 67.1–2.

49. In fact, the Council of Braga in 561 decided on a punishment for junior clerics (i.e., nonbishops) who dared to consecrate churches: they would be defrocked (c. 19).

50. Orange, 441, c. 9.

51. Orleans, 538, c. 16.

52. Orleans, 549, c. 8.

53. Carthage, 401, c. 6. Cf. Carthage, 438, c. 7.

54. As chapter 2 shows, jurists also used analogies between things and persons to justify regulatory principles applied to things.

55. Orleans, 511, c. 10.

56. Epaon 517, c. 33.

57. Saragossa, 592, c. 3.

58. Antioch, 330, c. 25. The canons of the Council of Antioch were formerly thought to belong to the Dedication Council of 341 but are now considered the canons of a council held in 330. See Ohme, 44–45.

59. Canons of the Apostles 38. The Statuta Ecclesiae Antiqua, a late fifth-century Gallic collection of disciplinary writings, explicitly says that the bishop does not own ecclesial property, but is rather entrusted with it (*Statuta Ecclesiae Antiqua*, ch. 31).

60. Canons of the Apostles 41.

61. Canons of the Apostles 40.

62. Toledo, 589, c. 3.

63. CJ 1.3.41.

64. Chalcedon, 451, c. 22, 25, and 26.

65. Chalcedon, 451, c. 26.

66. CJ 1.3.41 and NJust 123.23.

67. NJust 123.25.

68. For the types of clerics and their roles, see the following study on Asia Minor: Sabine Hübner, *Der Klerus in der Gesellschaft des spätantiken Kleinasiens* (Stuttgart: Steiner, 2005).

69. Ancyra, 314, c. 15.

70. CJ 1.3.41.

71. Arles, 554, c. 6.

72. The appellation "murderer of the poor" (*necator pauperum*) has been noted in scholarship, but no one, to my knowledge, explains what it entailed as a penalty. See, for example, Michael E. Moore, "The Ancient Fathers: Christian Antiquity, Patristics and Frankish Canon Law," *Millenium* 7 (2010): 321–23; Barbara H. Rosenwein, *Negotiating Space: Power, Restraint, and Privileges of Immunity in Early Medieval Europe* (Ithaca, NY: Cornell University Press, 1999), 42–47.

73. Narbonne, 589, c. 8.

74. Chalcedon, 451, c. 17.

75. Lyons, 518–23, c. 4.

76. Antioch, 330, c. 25.

77. Constantinople, 382, c. 6.

78. In most cases, a woman would be represented by her male kin. On the limited extent to which women could serve as independent plaintiffs, see Jane F. Gardner, *Women in Roman Law and Society* (Beckenham: Croom Helm, 1986). Cf. Jill Harries, *Law and Empire in Late Antiquity* (Cambridge: Cambridge University Press, 1999), 106.

79. Chalcedon, 451, c. 21.

80. CJ 1.4.29.

81. On the subject of fees for services tendered and for accession to office, see Sabine R. Hübner, "Currencies of Power: The Venality of Offices in the Later Roman Empire," in *The Power of Religion in Late Antiquity*, ed. Andrew Cain and Noel Lenski (Burlington, VT: Ashgate, 2009), 167–79.

82. On these types of foundations, see especially Kim Bowes, *Private Worship, Public Values, and Religious Change in Late Antiquity* (New York: Cambridge University Press, 2008) and John Philip Thomas, *Private Religious Foundations in the Byzantine Empire* (Washington, DC: Dumbarton Oaks Research Library and Collection, 1987).

83. NJust 67.1.

84. Chalcedon, 451, c. 4.

85. TTH 45.2:241n63 and 242.

86. Orleans, 541, c. 33.

87. Gangra, ca. 340, epilogue.

88. Gangra, ca. 340, c. 6 and anathema 6.

89. Orleans, 541, c. 7.

90. CTh 16.2.33.

91. Laodicea, ca. 375–400, c. 58.

92. Agde, 506, c. 21; Clermont, 535, c. 15.

93. Dovin, Armenia, 527, c. 16.

94. Auxerre, 561–605, c. 3.

95. NJust 58.

96. NJust 131.8.

97. Denis Roques, *Études sur la Correspondance de Synésios de Cyrène* (Brussels: Latomus, Revue d'études latines, 1989), 47–64.

98. Synesius of Cyrene, *Ep.* 66.8. Cf. Antonio Garzya, ed., and Denis Roques, trans., *Synésios de Cyrène*, vol. 3 (Paris: Les belles lettres, 2000), 310n7.

99. Synesius of Cyrene, *Ep.* 66. On this letter, see Ewa Wipszycka, "Le lettere di Sinesio come fonte per la storia del patriarcato alessandrino," in *Christianity in Egypt: Literary Production and Intellectual Trends*, ed. Paola Buzi and Alberto Camplani, Studia Ephemeridis Augustinianum 125 (Rome: Institutum Patristicum Augustinianum, 2011), 613–20.

100. Constantinople, 382, c. 6.

101. Synesius of Cyrene, *Ep.* 66.186–90.

102. Synesius of Cyrene, *Ep.* 66.220–26.

103. Synesius of Cyrene, *Ep.* 66.9–42.

104. Synesius of Cyrene, *Ep.* 66.129–220.

105. Synesius of Cyrene, *Ep.* 66.220–61.

106. Synesius of Cyrene, *Ep.* 66.261–74.

107. Synesius of Cyrene, *Ep.* 66.43–128. Synesius's epistolary report to Theophilus constitutes our only record of the case and its provisional resolution. We do not have the documentation that Synesius forwarded to Theophilus or records of Theophilus's actions on receipt of Synesius's letter.

108. As mentioned above, the Third Council of Orleans, Gaul in 538 (c. 16) by contrast prescribed a one-year suspension to any bishop who consecrated a church outside his jurisdiction.

109. The fortress probably became ruined in the earthquake of 365. Garzya and Roques, 3:315n47.

110. Synesius of Cyrene, *Ep.* 66.61–110. Cf. Garzya and Roques, 3:311n15. According to Synesius, the people of Palaebisca and Hydrax claimed that certain churches (including the disputed building on the hill) belonged originally to Erythrum. Under Bishop Orion of Erythrum, the churches split from Erythrum. While Orion was quite old yet still alive, Siderius was elected, though Synesius believes his "election was positively unlawful" (lines 78–79; translation from Augustine FitzGerald, *The Letters of Synesius of Cyrene* [London: Humphrey Milford, Oxford University Press, 1926], 151). Athanasius of Alexandria transferred Siderius from Paleabisca to Erythrum, and Siderius died in Erythrum (lines 91–100; Siderius probably died in 401, according to Garzya and Roques, 3:311n15). The people claimed that Theophilus agreed to place Palaesbica and Hydrax back in the jurisdiction of Erythrum (lines 100–103). Apparently, Theophilus later changed his mind (probably in 412 according to Garzya and Roques, 3:311n15). Synesius blames Theophilus for not settling the issue once and for all when Siderius died (lines 111–20).

111. Synesius of Cyrene, *Ep.* 66.152; Garzya and Roques, 3:179.

112. Synesius of Cyrene, *Ep.* 66.175; Garzya and Roques, 3:179.

113. It is conceivable that Paul may have tried to claim long uncontested use of the church. As mentioned above, the council that would meet in Chalcedon in 451 would decide that bishops could retain areas they held uncontested for a prescriptive period of thirty years (Chalcedon, 451, c. 17). Paul was elected bishop of Erythrum in 401 (Garzya and Roques, 3:310n9), so even if he held the site at that time, by 412 he would have been able to claim eleven years of uncontested use at most. Unfortunately, Synesius only mentions that he read aloud Paul's letter to Theophilus during the ecclesiastical inspection, but he does not ennumerate the grounds of Paul's appeal of the provincial synod of Ptolemais's decision.

114. Synesius of Cyrene, *Ep.* 66.161–66. Translation from FitzGerald, 154.

115. Synesius of Cyrene, *Ep.* 66.167–69.

116. Orange, 441, c. 9 and Orleans, 538, c. 16.

117. D. 18.1.4 (Pomponius) and 62 (Modestinus). For further context, see chapter 2.

118. Synesius of Cyrene, *Ep.* 66.177–86. Translation from FitzGerald, 154. My emphasis.

119. Synesius of Cyrene, *Ep.* 66.191; Garzya and Roques, 3:180.

120. Synesius of Cyrene, *Ep.* 66.190–204. Translation from FitzGerald, 155.

121. Synesius of Cyrene, *Ep.* 66.213–20.

122. Synesius of Cyrene, *Ep.* 66.220–26. Translation from FitzGerald, 155–56.

123. Synesius of Cyrene, *Ep.* 66.230–33. Translation from FitzGerald, 156.

124. Synesius of Cyrene, *Ep.* 66.247–51.

125. Synesius of Cyrene, *Ep.* 66.261–66. Synesius does not always distinguish in his letter between the arguments regarding the consecration that he made at the ecclesiastical inspection and negotiation process and the ones he is personally sharing with Theophilus via the letter. It is possible that Synesius expressed to Theophilus reasons for invalidating Paul's consecration of the building in order to justify the sale of the property that took place.

126. Synesius of Cyrene, *Ep.* 66.183; Garzya and Roques, 3:180.

127. On the legal designations "heretic" and "schismatic," see Maureen A. Tilley, "When Schism Becomes Heresy in Late Antiquity: Developing Doctrinal Deviance in the Wounded Body of Christ," *JECS* 15 (2007): 1–21; Alfred Schindler, "Die Unterscheidung von Schisma und Häresie in Gesetzgebung und Polemik gegen den Donatismus (mit einer Bemerkung zur Datierung von Augustins Schrift: Contra Epistulam Parmeniani)," in *Pietas: Festschrift für Bernhard Kötting,* ed. Ernst Dassmann and K. Suso Frank, Jahrbuch für Antike und Christentum Ergänzungsband 8 (Münster: Aschendorffsche Verlagsbuchhandlung, 1980), 228–36.

128. CTh 16.1.2. On this constitution, see Wilhelm Enßlin, *Die Religionspolitik des Kaisers Theodosius d. Gr.* (Munich: Verlag der Bayerischen Akademie der Wissenschaften, 1953), 5–28; Pedro Barceló and Gunther Gottlieb, "Das Glaubensedikt des Kaisers Theodosius vom 27. Februar 380: Adressaten und Zielsetzung," in *Klassisches Altertum, Spätantike und frühes Christentum,* ed. Karlheinz Dietz, Dieter Hennig, and Hans Kaletsch (Würzburg: Seminars für Alte Geschichte der Universität Würzburg, 1993), 409–23.

129. Theodor Mommsen and Paul M. Meyer, eds., *Theodosiani Libri XVI cum Constitutionibus Sirmondianis,* vol. 2 (Berlin: Apud Weidmannos, 1905), 833.

130. *Statuta ecclesiae antiqua,* ch. 81.

131. CTh 16.5.57; Mommsen and Meyer, 2:875. Translation from Clyde Pharr, Theresa S. Davidson, and Mary Pharr, *The Theodosian Code and Novels and the Sirmondian Constitutions* (Princeton, NJ: Princeton University Press, 1952), 461.

132. CTh 16.5.65.

133. CJ 1.5.5; John Noël Dillon, ed. and trans., "First Book," in *The Codex of Justinian: A New Annotated Translation, with Parallel Latin and Greek Text, Based on a Translation by Justice Fred H. Blume,* vol. 1, ed. Bruce W. Frier (Cambridge: Cambridge University Press, 2016), 192–93.

134. CJ 1.5.10; Dillon, 1:200–201.

135. CJ 1.5.10; Dillon, 1:200–201.

136. D. 1.8.6.3.

137. Justinian, *Institutes* 2.1.8; J. A. C. Thomas, 65.

138. The churches of schismatics were sometimes recognized as churches. For example, in 326, Constantine wrote to Bassus, prefect of Rome, that Novatians could possess the churches they established after the schism, but no churches that existed prior to it (CTh 16.5.2). John Philip Thomas (33 and 33n117) lists the types of localities in which confiscations took place. For an assessment of how such policies were used to reward imperially-endorsed social identity and punish the rest, see Michele Renee Salzman, "The Evidence for the Conversion of the Roman Empire to Christianity in Book 16 of the 'Theodosian Code,'" *Historia: Zeitschrift für Alte Geschichte* 42 (1993): 362–78.

139. Orleans, 511, c. 10 and Saragossa, 592, c. 3 required the reconsecration of heretics' churches, while Epaon, 517, c. 33 did not permit their use.

140. CTh 16.5.3; CTh 16.6.2; CTh 16.5.8; CTh 16.5.12; CTh 16.5.21; CTh 16.5.34; CTh 16.5.36; CTh 16.5.30; CTh 16.5.33; CTh 16.6.4; CTh 16.5.40; CTh 16.5.45; CTh 16.5.58; CJ 1.5.8; CJ 1.5.10.

141. CTh 16.5.3; CTh 16.6.2; CTh 16.5.4; CTh 16.5.6; CTh 16.1.3; Sirm. 12 = CTh 16.5.43; CTh 16.5.54; CTh 16.5.52; CTh 16.5.57; CTh 16.5.65; NJust 37; NJust 131.

142. CTh 9.42.11; Roland Delmaire, *Largesses sacrées et* Res privata: *L'Aerarium impérial et son administration du IVᵉ au VIᵉ siècle* (Rome: École française de Rome, 1989), 600–601.

143. Delmaire, *Largesses sacrées*, 601 and 606.

144. Delmaire, 606.

145. CTh 10.9.1 = CJ 10.10.3.

146. CTh 16.5.3. On laws against Manichaeans, see Erich-Hans Kaden, "Die Edikte gegen die Manichäer von Diokletian bis Justinian," in *Festschrift Hans Lewald* (Basel: Verlag Helbing und Lichtenhahn, 1953), 55–68.

147. CTh 16.6.2.

148. CTh 16.5.4.

149. CTh 16.5.33.

150. CTh 16.2.37 = CJ 1.3.15.

151. CTh 16.6.4.

152. CTh 16.5.40.

153. CTh 16.5.45.

154. Sirm. 12 = CTh 16.5.43. Cf. Emilienne Demougeot, "Sur les lois du 15 novembre 407," *Revue historique de droit français et étranger* 27 (1949): 403–12.

155. CTh 16.5.52.

156. CTh 16.5.54.

157. CTh 16.5.6 = CJ 1.1.2 and CTh 16.1.3.

158. CTh 16.5.8 and CTh 16.5.12.

159. CTh 16.5.21. Translation from Pharr, Davidson, and Pharr, 454.

160. CTh 16.5.34 and CTh 16.5.36.

161. CTh 16.5.34.

162. CTh 16.5.57. Translation from Pharr, Davidson, and Pharr, 461.

163. CTh 16.5.58.

164. CTh 16.5.30 = CJ 1.5.3.

165. CTh 16.5.34.

166. CTh 16.5.30.

167. CTh 16.5.65.

168. CTh 16.5.21.

169. CJ 1.5.8.

170. CJ 1.5.10; Dillon, 1:200. Translation adapted from Dillon, 1:201.

171. NJust 131.8.

172. Laodicea, ca. 375–400, c. 9. Because corpses were interred in martyria, they fell under the category of *res religiosae*; if the martyrium was consecrated, then it would also be a *res sacra*. Note, however, that the use of the term "martyrium" in late antiquity did not always mean what the term designates in English today. As A. H. M. Jones wrote, "The word μαρτύριον is equivalent simply to 'church' and does not imply the presence of relics

or even dedication to a martyr." See A. H. M. Jones, "Inscriptions from Jerash," *Journal of Roman Studies* 18 (1928): 168n35. Ewa Wipszycka indicates that "martyrium" could refer to a private church. See Ewa Wipszycka, *Les ressources et les activiteés économiques des églises en Égypte du IVe au VIIIe siècle* (Brussels: Fondation Égyptologique Reine Élisabeth, 1972), 26–27.

173. Carthage, 418, c. 10.

174. Carthage, 418, c. 11.

175. Carthage, 418, c. 13.

176. Toledo, 589, c. 9.

177. CTh 16.5.21.

178. The fine of ten pounds of gold was not an uncommon penalty against an official or department that failed to enforce a law. I call attention here, not to ten pounds of gold as a unique fine altogether, but as extraordinary in the history of its application to clerics in North Africa.

179. Marlia Mundell Mango, "Artistic Patronage in the Roman Diocese of Oriens, 313–641 AD" (PhD diss., Cambridge University, 1984), 88 and 453a.

180. CTh 16.6.4 and 16.6.5. See further Erika T. Hermanowicz, *Possidius of Calama: A Study of the North African Episcopate at the Time of Augustine* (New York: Oxford University Press, 2008), 102–20.

181. By "petition" here and throughout, I mean that bishops used the means at their disposal to procure a law from the emperor.

The year 395/6 is when Seranus, the civil authority addressed in this petition, is thought to have served as vicar of Africa. See J. R. Martindale, *The Prosopography of the Later Roman Empire*, vol. 2 (Cambridge: Cambridge University Press, 1980), 992. For the backstory of what led Augustine to use councils as the forum in which to confront Donatist rivals, see Jane Merdinger, "On the Eve of the Council of Hippo, 393: The Background to Augustine's Program for Church Reform," *Augustinian Studies* 40 (2009): 27–36.

182. On the meaning of *ecclesia catholica* as "public church," see Ewa Wipszycka, "Καθολική et les autres épithètes qualifiant le nom ἐκκλησία," *Journal of Juristic Papyrology* 24 (1994): 191–212.

183. Augustine of Hippo, *C. litt. Petil.* 2.83.184.

184. Augustine of Hippo, *Ep.* 66. Translation from FC 12:314–16. For the date, see FC 12:xii and 314.

185. Augustine of Hippo, *C. litt. Petil.* 2.83.184.

186. Augustine of Hippo, *Ep.* 66.

187. Augustine of Hippo, *Ep.* 66. *Cur non valeat iussio regalis in provincia, si tantum valuit iussio provincialis in villa? Si personas compares, tu possessor, ille imperator. Si loca compares, tu in fundo, ille in regno. Si causas compares, ille ut divisio resarciatur, tu ut unitas dividatur* (PL 33:236). "Why should an imperial order not have such force in a province if a provincial order has such force in a town? If you compare the persons, you are only a landowner; he is the emperor. If you compare the places, you are in charge of a rural town; he is in charge of an empire. If you compare the causes, he was acting to mend a division; you were acting to divide a unity." The translation here is from Roland J. Teske, *Letters*, ed. Boniface Ramsey, The Works of St. Augustine: A Translation for the 21st Century, part 2, vol. 1 (Hyde Park, NY: New City Press, 2001), 258.

188. Jennifer V. Ebbeler, *Disciplining Christians: Correction and Community in Augustine's Letters* (New York: Oxford University Press, 2012), 172.

189. Augustine of Hippo, *Serm.* 162A responds to Crispinus's reaction to the proconsul's ruling and is dated to 404, so the trial must have occurred before Augustine preached his sermon. A. Kunzelman, "Die Chronologie der Sermones des hl. Augustinus," *Miscellanea Agostiniana* 2 (1931): 440.

190. Augustine of Hippo, *Cresc.* 3.47.51 and *Serm.* 162A.8.

191. Scholars, such as Erika T. Hermanowicz (102–20), assume that Bishop Crispinus was sentenced for personal injuries that one of his presbyters, who was also called Crispinus, committed against Possidius (Augustine of Hippo, *Cresc.* 3.46.50 and Possidius, *Life of Augustine* 12). One of the charges that Bishop Possidius named against his rival bishop of Calama, Crispinus, may well have concerned the injurious incident. However, it could not have been the charge that resulted in Crispinus's fine of ten pounds of gold because Theodosius I's law only enjoins the penalty against heretics who style themselves "cleric" and perform "forbidden practices" on landholdings. Crispinus, therefore, was fined ten pounds of gold for the baptisms he performed on the imperial farmland that he held by emphyteusis.

192. Possidius, *Life of Augustine* 12.

193. Noel Lenski, "Imperial Legislation and the Donatist Controversy: From Constantine to Honorius," in *The Donatist Schism: Controversy and Contexts*, ed. Richard Miles (Liverpool: Liverpool University Press, 2016), 212–13 (no. 84).

194. *Reg. eccl. carthag. excerpta* 93.

195. *Reg. eccl. carthag. excerpta* 93. Cf. the different explanation that Augustine retrospectively provides in his epistle 185.25, which was sent around 417 to Boniface, *comes* of Africa. Augustine claims that the synod only wished to apply the law against those Donatist clergy who committed acts of violence against Catholic clergy. Cf. Hermanowicz, 147.

196. CTh 16.6.4 and 16.6.5.

197. CTh 16.6.4. Translation from Pharr, Davidson, and Pharr, 464.

198. CTh 16.6.4.

199. CTh 16.6.5. Translation from Pharr, Davidson, and Pharr, 465.

200. Victor of Vita quotes the edict in his *History of the Vandal Persecution* 3.3–14. Cf. Eric Fournier, "Victor of Vita and the Conference of 484: A Pastiche of 411?," *Studia Patristica* 62 (2013): 395–408.

201. Victor of Vita, *History of the Vandal Persecution*, 3.7; CSEL 7:74. Translation from TTH 10:66.

202. Victor of Vita, *History of the Vandal Persecution*, 3.8.

203. NJust 37.

204. NJust 37.5 and 8. Translation from Miller and Sarris, 1:355 and 356.

205. Edict 2. Translation from Miller and Sarris, 2:1035. My emphasis.

CHAPTER 2. PROTECTED PLACES

1. Translation from TTH 4:95.

2. Gregory of Tours, *Glory of the Martyrs* 102. Jonathan Bardill argues that the story does refer accurately to a gilded wooden ceiling that was probably installed in Saint Polyeuktos: Jonathan Bardill, "A New Temple for Byzantium: Anicia Juliana, King Solomon,

and the Gilded Ceiling of the Church of St. Polyeuktos in Constantinople," in *Social and Political Life in Late Antiquity*, ed. William Bowden, Adam Gutteridge, and Carlos Machado (Leiden: Brill, 2006), 339–70.

3. Gaius, *Institutes* 2.1.9; Francis de Zulueta, ed., *The Institutes of Gaius*, vol. 1 (Oxford: Clarendon Press, 1946), 66.

4. D. 1.1.1.2.

5. Justinian, *Institutes* 2.1.7; J. A. C. Thomas, ed., *The Institutes of Justinian: Text, Translation, and Commentary* (Amsterdam: North-Holland Publishing Company, 1975), 65.

6. D. 41.2.30.1; Paul Krueger and Theodor Mommsen, eds., *Corpus Iuris Civilis*, vol. 2 (1867–70; repr., Berlin: Apud Weidmannos, 1962), 512. Translation from Alan Watson, *The Digest of Justinian*, vol. 4 (Philadelphia: University of Pennsylvania Press, 1985), 512.

7. D. 41.3.9.

8. D. 44.7.1.9. Translation from Watson, 4:640. My emphasis.

9. D. 45.1.83.5. Translation from Watson, 4:663.

10. D. 45.1.83.5. Translation from Watson, 4:662.

11. Cf. D. 48.13.1 and 4.

12. Justinian, *Institutes* 3.19.1–2.

13. D. 30.1.39.8–9.

14. D. 18.1.73.

15. D. 11.7.36.

16. D. 18.1.4. Translation from Watson, 2:514.

17. D. 18.1.62.

18. D. 18.1.22. Translation from Watson, 2:516.

19. D. 18.1.23.

20. D. 18.1.24.

21. D. 1.8.9.5.

22. D. 43.6.1; Krueger and Mommsen, 2:573. Translation from Watson, 4:573.

23. D. 39.1.1.1. Translation from Watson, 3:374.

24. D. 43.8.2.17–19. Translation from Watson, 4:574. My emphasis.

25. Justinian, *Institutes* 4.15.1 and 4.15.17.

26. Justinian, *Institutes* 4.6.19.

27. Justinian, *Institutes* 3.27.7.

28. CJ 1.3.55. Translation adapted from John Noël Dillon, "First Book," in *The Codex of Justinian: A New Annotated Translation, with Parallel Latin and Greek Text, Based on a Translation by Justice Fred H. Blume*, vol. 1, ed. Bruce W. Frier (Cambridge: Cambridge University Press, 2016), 147.

29. For the types of benevolent acts that were supported with laws, see chapter 3.

30. On the administrator of donations, see CJ 1.3.33; Gangra, ca. 340, c. 7 and 8; Orleans, 511, c. 15; and Orleans, 538, c. 5. On the procedure and incentives for making donations, see CJ 1.2.19; NJust 67; and CJ 1.2.22. On the proper purpose and use of donations, see CJ 1.3.41; Orleans, 511, c. 5; Tarragona, 516, c. 8; Dovin, 527, c. 23. On the transfer of donations, see CJ 1.2.15; CJ 1.2.23; NJust 131; NJust 111 = Edict 5; NJust 37; Orleans, 538, c. 25; Orleans, 549, c. 13 and 16; Vaison, 442, c. 4 (cf. Arles, 442–506, c. 47 and Macon, 581, c. 4); *Statuta Ecclesiae Antiqua*, ch. 95; Agde, 506, c. 4 (cf. Orleans III, 538, c. 25 and Orleans V, 549, c. 13 and c. 16); Clermont, 535, c. 14; Orleans, 541, c. 14 and 19; Eauze, 551, c. 6; Lyons, 567, c. 2; NMaj. 10;

CJ 1.3.28; CJ 1.2.14; CJ 1.2.25 (reiterated in NJust 131.9); CJ 1.3.48 (reiterated in NJust 131.11); CJ 1.3.45; and NJust 131.

31. On nontestamentary donations acquired by default, see Carthage, 419, c. 32; Hippo, 427, c. 5; Agde, 506, c. 6; Epaon, 517, c. 8; Dovin 527, c. 1; CJ 1.3.33; NJust 123.19; and CJ 1.3.41. On testamentary donations acquired by default, see Carthage, 401, c. 16 (cf. Carthage, 438, c. 14); CTh 5.3.1; and NJust 131. On compulsory donations, see CJ 1.3.38; CJ 1.3.40; Tarragona, 516, c. 10; Braga, 572, c. 5; Rome, 595, c. 3; CJ 1.3.44; CJ 1.3.53; NJust 123.43; CJ 1.3.54; and NJust 123.

32. On injurious acquisitions, see NJust 131. On the diminution of bequests, see NJust 7; CJ 1.3.45; and CJ 1.3.55.

33. Carthage, 419, c. 26.

34. CTh 16.8.25.

35. According to François Nau, "Deux épisodes de l'histoire juive sous Théodose II (423 et 438) d'après la vie de Barsauma le syrien," *Revue des études juives* 83 (1927): 184–93, this law was directed at the actions of Barsauma the Syrian. Cf. Amnon Linder, *The Jews in Roman Imperial Legislation* (Detroit: Wayne State University Press, 1987), 287–89. On Barsauma, see Johannes Hahn and Volker Menze, eds., *The Wandering Holy Man: The Life of Barsauma, Christian Asceticism, and Religious Conflict in Late Antique Palestine* (Oakland: University of California Press, 2020).

36. CJ 1.5.10. Translation from Dillon, 1:201.

37. CJ 1.2.14. Translation from Dillon, 1:51.

38. CJ 1.2.17.

39. On the history of legislation on pious houses, see Giorgio Barone-Adesi, "Dal dibattito cristiano sulla destinazione dei beni economici alla configurazione in termini di persona delle *venerabiles domus* destinate *piis causis*," in *Atti dell'accademia romanistica costantiniana, IX convegno internazionale* (Naples: Edizioni Scientifiche Italiane, 1993), 231–65.

40. CJ 1.2.21; Dillon, 1:60.

41. CJ 1.3.41.

42. CJ 1.2.21.

43. NJust 7.

44. NJust 7.1. Translation from David J. D. Miller and Peter Sarris, *The Novels of Justinian: A Complete Annotated English Translation*, vol. 1 (Cambridge: Cambridge University Press, 2018), 116.

45. NJust 7.11. Translation from Miller and Sarris, 1:123–24.

46. NJust 7.ep. Translation from Miller and Sarris, 1:125.

47. NJust 37.

48. NJust 7.8. Cf. CJ 1.2.21.

49. NJust 7.2.

50. Justinian here refers to the legal benefits of *res sacrae* as privileges of imperial patronage. In fact, he even considers his laws to be *res sacrae*, offerings consecrated to God. NJust 37 says "the present most pious law, to be valid in perpetuity," is "dedicated to almighty God" (translation from Miller and Sarris, 1:356). Edict 1 requires of bishops that the law "be taken indoors and deposited in the most holy church along with the holy vessels, as being, like them, dedicated to God and laid down for the salvation of mankind, which came to be by him" (τηνικαῦτα ληφθεὶς ἔνδον ἀποκείσθω ἐν τῇ ἁγιωτάτῃ ἐκκλησίᾳ

μετὰ τῶν ἱερῶν σκευῶν, οἷα καὶ αὐτὸς ἀνατεθειμένος θεῷ καὶ πρὸς σωτηρίαν τῶν ὑπ' αὐτοῦ γενομένων ἀνθρώπων γεγραμμένος). See Rudolf Schoell and Guilelmus Kroll, eds., *Corpus Iuris Civilis*, vol. 3 (1895; repr., Berlin: Weidmann, 1954), 79. Translation adapted from Miller and Sarris, 1:143.

51. NJust 46.
52. NJust 54.
53. NJust 55.
54. NJust 67.
55. NJust 120.
56. NJust 131.
57. Agde, 506, c. 7.
58. Agde, 506, c. 22.
59. Clermont, 535, c. 5.
60. Toledo, 589, c. 3.
61. Orleans, 538, c. 25.
62. Paris, 556–73, c. 7.
63. Orleans, 541, c. 11.
64. Orleans, 549, c. 13.
65. Hippo, 427, c. 4.
66. Toledo, 589, c. 4.
67. Tours, 567, c. 25.

68. Origen and Augustine, for example, interpreted Psalm 108 as a prophecy of Judas's betrayal of Christ. See excerpts of their writings in Quentin F. Wesselschmidt, *Ancient Christian Commentary on Scripture: Psalms 51–150*, Old Testament 8 (Downers Grove, IL: InterVarsity Press, 2007), 258–60.

69. On the significance of Psalm 108 in curses, see Lester K. Little, *Benedictine Maledictions: Liturgical Cursing in Romanesque France* (Ithaca, NY: Cornell University Press, 1993), 23 and 63–65.

70. CJ 1.3.41.
71. NJust 131.
72. Agde, 506, c. 33. Likewise, Ps-Agde, c. 48 and 51.
73. Epaon, 517, c. 17.
74. NJust 7.
75. NJust 54.
76. Orleans, 541, c. 9.
77. Chalcedon, 451, c. 17.
78. Orleans, 511, c. 23.
79. Epaon, 517, c. 18. Cf. Ps-Agde, c. 59.
80. NJust 7 and 55.
81. Carthage, 419, c. 33.
82. On this council, see the case study below.
83. Epaon, 517, c. 7.
84. Orleans, 538, c. 26.
85. Orleans, 541, c. 11.
86. Carthage, 401, c. 4. Epaon, 517, c. 12.

87. Carthage, 419, c. 26.

88. The canon is reiterated in Hippo, 427, c. 9, but "presbyters" is changed to "primates."

89. *Statuta Ecclesiae Antiqua*, ch. 32.

90. Carthage, 419, c. 26.

91. Agde, 506, c. 45.

92. Rome, 595, c. 6.

93. Orleans, 549, c. 8.

94. Epaon, 517, c. 8.

95. Orleans, 538, c. 13.

96. Orleans, 541, c. 35.

97. Orleans, 511, c. 6.

98. Riez, 439, c. 6.

99. Valencia, 529, c. 2.

100. A *domus ecclesiae* was not, as is commonly understood, a private home converted into a church. See Kristina Sessa, "*Domus Ecclesiae*: Rethinking a Category of *Ante-Pacem* Christian Space," *JTS*, n.s., 60 (2009): 90–108.

101. Orleans, 533, c. 6.

102. Tarragona, 516, c. 12. Cf. Rachel L. Stocking, *Bishops, Councils, and Consensus in the Visigothic Kingdom, 589–633* (Ann Arbor: University of Michigan Press, 2000), 38–41.

103. Lerida, 546, c. 16. Cf. Stocking, 38–41.

104. On this penalty, see Ralph W. Mathisen, "The *communio peregrina* in Late Antiquity: Origin, Purpose, Implementation," *Studia Patristica* 40 (2006): 49–54.

105. Valencia, 529, c. 3.

106. North Britain, early fifth century, c. 3. Cf. monastic rules like Shenoute, Canon 1, Rule 13 (Bentley Layton, *The Canons of Our Fathers* [New York: Oxford University Press, 2014], 94–95) and the Irish penitentials (Ludwig Bieler, *The Irish Penitentials* [Dublin: Dublin Institute for Advanced Studies, 1963], 85, 87, 93, 119, and 127).

107. Agde, 506, c. 5.

108. Orleans, 538, c. 25.

109. Orleans, 541, c. 25.

110. Orleans, 549, c. 14.

111. Antioch, 330, c. 25; Carthage, 419, c. 26; Hippo, 427, c. 5.

112. From his study of conciliar acts, Carlo de Clercq discerns four types of activities in which synods engaged: dogmatic, legislative, judicial, and electoral. See Carlo de Clercq, "Les Conciles de Constantinople de 326 à 715," *Apollinaris* 34 (1961): 345.

113. Quoted in the Acts of the Council of Chalcedon. Greek edition ACO 2.1:385. Latin edition ACO 2.3:471. Translation from TTH 45.2:286–87.

114. Cf. "Certain other articles were discussed *orally* and also settled." My emphasis. Quoted in the Acts of the Council of Chalcedon. Greek edition ACO 2.1:375. Latin edition ACO 2.3:458. Translation from TTH 45.2:263.

115. Johannes Flemming, ed., and George Hoffmann, trans., *Akten der ephesinischen Synode vom Jahre 449* (Berlin: Weidmann, 1917), 56–57. Translation from S. G. F. Perry, *The Second Synod of Ephesus* (Dartford: Orient Press, 1881), 126. I have modified the punctuation of the synod's acclamation here (from dashes between the acclamations to periods).

116. As Olivia Robinson has shown, Christian prioritization of blasphemy over sacrilege actually inverts traditional Roman practice, in which legal action could be taken against sacrilege, but not necessarily blasphemy. See Olivia Robinson, "Blasphemy and Sacrilege in Roman Law," *Irish Jurist* 8 (1973): 356–71.

117. Fergus Millar, "The Syriac Acts of the Second Council of Ephesus (449)," in *Chalcedon in Context: Church Councils 400–700*, ed. Richard Price and Mary Whitby (Liverpool: Liverpool University Press, 2009), 45–67.

118. Cf. Constantinople, 382, c. 6.

119. See the quotations of the proceedings before Domnus in the Acts of the Council of Chalcedon (Greek: *Eleventh Session* 47–51; Latin: *Tenth Session* 47–51).

120. Flemming and Hoffmann, 58–59. Translation from Perry, 130–31.

121. See chapter 3.

122. Ambrose of Milan also had to defend himself against the charge of sacrilege for melting down sacred vessels to redeem captives. For the details, see chapter 5.

123. Acts of the Council of Chalcedon (Greek: *Eleventh Session* 73; Latin: *Tenth Session* 73). Latin edition ACO 2.3:468–71. The charges are numbered here according to the Latin proceedings. The Greek numeration is different. See TTH 45.2:283n57.

124. Flemming and Hoffmann, 14–16. Translation from Perry, 44–45.

125. Flemming and Hoffmann, 16. Translation from Perry, 47.

126. Flemming and Hoffmann, 8. Translation from Perry, 51–53.

127. Flemming and Hoffmann, 22. Translation from Perry, 62.

128. Flemming and Hoffmann, 24–26. Translation from Perry, 69.

129. Flemming and Hoffmann, 34–36. Translation from Perry, 90.

130. Flemming and Hoffmann, 38. Translation from Perry, 95.

131. Cf. TTH 45.3:93. On the compilation of a numbered list of canons, see TTH 45.3:92.

132. Greek edition ACO 2.1:374–75. Latin edition ACO 2.3:458. Translation from TTH 45.2:263.

133. Joannou 1.1:89–90.

134. Greek edition ACO 2.1:216. Latin edition ACO 2.3:294. Translation from TTH 45.2:58.

135. Cf. Richard Price and Michael Gaddis's comment in TTH 45.2:58n77.

136. Greek edition ACO 2.1:217–18. Latin edition ACO 2.3:295–96. Translation from TTH 45.2:60.

137. For the extraordinary circumstances of Dioscorus's trial and deposition *in absentia*, see the discussion in TTH 45.2:29–35.

138. NJust 7.

139. NJust 120.

140. Richard A. Epstein, "The Economic Structure of Roman Property Law," in *The Oxford Handbook of Roman Law and Society*, ed. Paul J. du Plessis, Clifford Ando, and Kaius Tuori (New York: Oxford University Press, 2016), 519–20.

141. Dennis P. Kehoe, "Tenure of Land and Agricultural Regulation," in du Plessis et al., 655–56.

142. CJ 1.2.14.

143. NJust 7.

144. NJust 131.

145. Agde, 506, c. 7

146. Toledo, 527, c. 4.

147. Lyons, 567, c. 5.

148. Orleans, 541, c. 34.

149. CJ 1.2.24. The recipient of the law is unknown. The date is uncertain. See Gustav Pfannmüller, *Die kirchliche Gesetzgebung Justinians hauptsächlich auf Grund der Novellen* (Berlin: C. A. Schwetschke und Sohn, 1902), 8–10 for commentary on CJ 1.2.24.

150. NJust 7.

151. NJust 55.

152. NJust 120.

153. NJust 131.

154. NJust 123.

155. NJust 123.6.

156. NJust 123.6. Translation from Miller and Sarris, 2:807.

157. Sirm. 14 and CTh 16.2.31. For an analysis of the circumstances and episcopal petitions that occasioned this law, see María Victoria Escribano Paño, "Bishops, Judges and Emperors: CTh 16.2.31/CTh 16.5.46/Sirm. 14 (409)," in *The Role of the Bishop in Late Antiquity: Conflict and Compromise*, ed. Andrew Fear, José Fernández Ubiña, and Mar Marcos (London: Bloomsbury, 2013), 105–26.

158. CJ 1.12.5.

159. NJust 123.31–32.

160. Paris, 556, c. 2.

161. CJ 1.12.7.

162. CJ 1.12.8.

163. Initially, however, Theodoric tried not to involve himself in the dispute, but insisted that ecclesiastics resolve it.

164. Scholars identify the nature of the document in different ways. L. Duchesne calls it a "decree;" W. T. Townsend, an "edict of Odoacer;" Julia Hillner, a "senatorial statement;" and Kristina Sessa, a "testamentary provision." See L. Duchesne, "Les schismes romains au VIᵉ siècle," *Mélanges d'archéologie et d'histoire* 35 (1915): 221–56; W. T. Townsend, "Councils Held under Pope Symmachus," *Church History* 6 (1937): 233–59; Julia Hillner, "Families, Patronage, and the Titular Churches of Rome, c. 300–c. 600," in *Religion, Dynasty, and Patronage in Early Christian Rome, 300–900*, ed. Kate Cooper and Julia Hillner (Cambridge: Cambridge University Press, 2007), 225–61; and Kristina Sessa, *The Formation of Papal Authority in Late Antique Italy: Roman Bishops and the Domestic Sphere* (New York: Cambridge University Press, 2012), 208–39. I argue that the document was composed in response to a testamentary provision and, given the evidence of Theoderic's *responsum* discussed below, the document was a *senatus consultum*.

165. Eckhard Wirbelauer, *Zwei Päpste in Rom: Der Konflikt zwischen Laurentius und Symmachus (498–514)* (Munich: Tuduv Verlagsgesellschaft, 1993), 18.

166. *Liber pontificalis* (Laurentian Fragment) 53.6. L. Duchesne, ed., *Le Liber pontificalis: Texte, introduction et commentaire*, vol. 1 (Paris: E. de Boccard, 1955), 44. Translation from TTH 6:96.

167. *Liber pontificalis* 53. Cf. Jeffrey Richards, *The Popes and the Papacy in the Early Middle Ages 476–752* (London: Routledge and Kegan Paul, 1979), 80–81.

168. Richards, 72–73.

169. MGH AA 12:438–55. For a summary and discussion of the proceedings, see Townsend, 252–57.

170. MGH AA 12:445. For a discussion of the "mandate" as a legal contract in Roman law, see Andrew Borkowski, *Textbook on Roman Law* (London: Blackstone Press Limited, 1994), 269–70.

171. This would not be the first time that Symmachus would convene a council to make a *"post factum* justification" for his actions. On March 1, 499 he had convened a council to state the procedure for the election of popes, which named the procedure under which Symmachus was elected in 498. See Richard I. Harper, "Theodoric and the Laurentian Schism: An Aspect of Fifth-Century Church and State," *Southern Quarterly* 4 (1966): 130–31.

172. Ennodius, *Libellus adversus eos qui contra synodum scribere praesumpserunt*. MGH AA 7:48–67.

173. Greek edition ACO 2.1:468. The session on Photius and Eustathius is not transmitted in the Latin proceedings. Translation from TTH 45.2:181.

174. Five to seven years is a long time for a *responsum* to be issued (from the date of Symmachus's synod to Theodoric's *responsum*, 501/2–507/8). Perhaps the end of the schism or Laurentius's death explains the lag in time. For example, perhaps the *suggestio* was not sent until the schism ended. Alternatively, the *responsum* may concern another, unknown council more recent to the years 507/8. In any case, the issues raised (alienation and usufruct) are the same as those of the synod in 501/2.

175. MGH AA 12:392.

176. Copies of Cyril of Alexandria and Simplicius of Rome's actual testaments are no longer extant, but only references to their dying wishes in conciliar documents. In fact, few testaments of late antique bishops survive and the authenticity of most is questioned. The most notable (and perhaps the sole authentic one) is that of Gregory of Nazianzus. See Joëlle Beaucamp, "Le testament de Grégoire de Nazianze," in *Fontes Minores*, vol. 10, ed. Ludwig Burgmann (Frankfurt: Löwenklau, 1998), 1–100.

CHAPTER 3. PROTECTING PLACES

1. Augustine of Hippo, *Civ*. 1.1. Translation from FC 8:19. My emphasis. *Qui tamen etiam ipsi alibi truces atque hostili more saeuientes posteaquam ad loca illa ueniebant, ubi fuerat interdictum quod alibi belli iure licuisset, et tota feriendi refrenabatur inmanitas et captiuandi cupiditas frangebatur.* CCSL 47:2.

2. CJ 1.3.30.

3. CJ 1.3.30. John Noël Dillon, ed. and trans., "First Book," in *The Codex of Justinian: A New Annotated Translation, with Parallel Latin and Greek Text, Based on a Translation by Justice Fred H. Blume*, vol. 1, ed. Bruce W. Frier (Cambridge: Cambridge University Press, 2016), 90–91.

4. Dillon, 1:90.

5. Reuven Yaron shows that in other places alienation and manumission appear to be conflated owing to a reader's insertion. Reuven Yaron, "Alienation and Manumission," *Revue internationale des droits de l'antiquité*, 3rd series, 2 (1955): 381–87.

6. CJ 1.13.1. Translation adapted from Dillon, 1:257. Since Licinius was probably ruling Serdica at the time of the constitution's date of issue, questions have been raised as to whether "Protogenes" should be identified with the bishop of Serdica of the same name. Questions have also been raised about the date of issue. For a discussion of these matters, see Kyle Harper, *Slavery in the Late Roman World, AD 275–425* (Cambridge: Cambridge University Press, 2011), 475–76.

7. CTh 4.7.1 = CJ 1.13.2.

8. Since Sozomen refers to three laws of Constantine on the manumission of slaves in churches (*HE* 1.9.6), scholars have debated the order in which the two known laws and the unknown one were issued. See Harper, 474–75.

9. CTh 16.6.4.

10. CJ 1.3.54.

11. *Reg. eccl. carthag. excerpta* 64 and 82.

12. CTh 16.6.4.

13. Nimes, 394/396, c. 7.

14. Orange, 441, c. 6; Orleans, 549, c. 7.

15. Arles, 442–506, c. 34.

16. Orleans, 541, c. 9.

17. Toledo, 589, c. 6.

18. Ps-Agde, c. 49.

19. Orleans, 541, c. 9.

20. CJ 1.13.1 (to Protogenes); CTh 4.7.1 = CJ 1.13.2 (to Hosius).

21. Epaon, 517, c. 8.

22. Orleans, 541, c. 30.

23. CJ 1.3.54.

24. Scholars approach the issue of ecclesial asylum by asking the question, "to what extent did civil authorities recognize ecclesial asylum?" Such a question does not lend equal weight to both sides of the dialogue and negotiation that took place between civil and ecclesiastical authorities. It is also the reason why scholars claim that asylum only began to be recognized in churches in the year 431 (for example, Hans Langenfeld, *Christianisierungspolitik und Sklavengesetzgebung der römischen Kaiser von Konstantin bis Theodosius II* [Bonn: Habelt, 1977], 155). I argue that the issue is best approached by considering the strategies each kind of authority (civil and ecclesiastical) used to employ coercion or to petition for ecclesial asylum to be defined with their respective interests in view. The laws and canons do not question whether churches count as places of asylum; rather, they regulate how and to what extent churches may serve in such a capacity.

25. Serdica, 343, c. 8.

26. Hess, 216–17.

27. Agde, 506, c. 29. Macon, 585, c. 8.

28. CCSL 148A:243.

29. Orleans, 511, c. 1.

30. CCSL 149:193–94.

31. Orleans, 441, c. 5.

32. Orleans, 511, c.1.

33. Orleans, 541, c. 21.

34. Orleans, 549, c. 22.

35. Orleans, 511, c. 1 and 3; Epaon, 517, c. 39; Orleans 541, c. 24; and Orleans, 549, c. 22.

36. Epaon, 517, c. 39.

37. Orleans, 511, c. 3.

38. Orleans, 511, c. 1.

39. Orleans, 538, c. 14. For an attempt to place this and other canons regarding Jews within the larger context of evidence regarding Jews in Gaul, see F. J. E. Boddens Hosang, *Establishing Boundaries: Christian-Jewish Relations in Early Council Texts and the Writings of Church Fathers* (Leiden: Brill, 2010), 125–65.

40. Orleans, 549, c. 22.

41. Orange, 441, c. 5.

42. Orleans, 511, c. 2.

43. Orleans, 541, c. 30.

44. Adolf Berger, "Appellatio," in *Encyclopedic Dictionary of Roman Law*, ed. Berger, Transactions of the American Philosophical Society, n.s., vol. 43, pt. 2 (Philadelphia: American Philosophical Society, 1953), 364–65.

45. CTh 14.3.11.

46. CTh 9.45.1.

47. CTh 16.5.6.

48. CTh 16.5.6; Theodor Mommsen and Paul M. Meyer, eds., *Theodosiani Libri XVI cum Constitutionibus Sirmondianis*, vol. 1.2 (Berlin: Apud Weidmannos, 1905), 857.

49. CTh 9.45.2.

50. CTh 9.45.2; Mommsen and Meyer, 1.2:519. Cf. Volker Dautzenberg, "Die Gesetze des Codex Theodosianus und des Codex Justinianus für Ägypten im Spiegel der Papyri" (PhD diss., University of Cologne, 1971), 29–31.

51. CTh 11.36.31. Translation from Clyde Pharr, Theresa S. Davidson, and Mary Pharr, *The Theodosian Code and Novels and the Sirmondian Constitutions* (Princeton, NJ: Princeton University Press, 1952), 339.

52. CTh 9.40.15; Mommsen and Meyer, 1.2:504.

53. E. Herman, "Asile dans l'église orientale, le droit d," in *Dictionnaire de droit canonique*, vol. 1, ed. R. Naz (Paris: Librarie Letouzey et Ané, 1935), column 1085; Christian Traulsen, *Das sakrale Asyl in der Alten Welt* (Tübingen: Mohr Siebeck, 2004), 281n191. Christian Traulsen argues that it could not be the law for which Eutropius advocated because it conflicts with the accounts of ecclesiastical historians. The historiographical reports conflict with one another as well, and it is more likely that they exaggerate the implications of Eutropius's law to suit their rhetorical purposes.

54. CTh 9.40.16. Translation from Pharr, Davidson, and Pharr, 257. Cf. SC 531:202n4.

55. CTh 9.45.3; Mommsen and Meyer, 1.2:519.

56. According to Henri Leclercq, CTh 16.2.34 (addressed to Sapidianus, Vicar of Africa on June 25, 399) may have been Honorius's response to the conciliar request; it does not mention asylum at all but simply delimits a fine of five pounds of gold for violations of the privileges of the churches. Hefele-Leclercq 2.1:120–21.

57. CTh 16.6.4.

58. CTh 9.45.2.

59. SC 497:406.

60. CTh 16.8.23.

61. Sirm. 13.

62. Roland Delmaire and Claude Lepelley argue that Sirm. 13 responds to the episco-pal petition mentioned in Augustine's new letters 15*, 16*, and 23*. Roland Delmaire and Claude Lepelley, "Du nouveau sur Carthage: Le temoignage des lettres de saint Augustin decouvertes par Johannes Divjak," *Opus* 2 (1983): 473–87.

63. Letters 15*, 16*, and 23A*.

64. Sirm. 13; Mommsen and Meyer, 1.2:917.

65. CTh 9.45.4 = CJ 1.12.3. Collections of the Acts of the Council of Ephesus 431 record a Greek translation of the complete text of the law of which CTh 9.45.4 and CJ 1.12.3 are excerpts. Eduard Schwartz hypothesizes that this law, alongside three other documents, must have been at the end of a manuscript that largely contained the Acts of the Council of Ephesus 431. Later copyists assumed they were documents from the council and con-tinued to include them. Eduard Schwartz, "Βασιλικὸς νόμος περὶ τῶν προσφευγόντων ἐν ἐκκλησίαι," in Friedrich von Woeß, *Das Asylwesen Ägyptens in der Ptolermäerzeit* (Munich: C. H. Becksche Verlagsbuchhandlung Oskar Beck, 1923), 253–72. See also Fergus Millar, *A Greek Roman Empire: Power and Belief under Theodosius II (408–450)* (Berkeley: Univer-sity of California Press, 2006), 142–45.

66. Schwartz, 258.

67. CTh 9.45.4 = CJ 1.12.3; Mommsen and Meyer, 1.2:520.

68. CTh 16.8.19 of 409 does not permit forcible seizure of asylum-seekers (cf. CTh 9.45.3 of 398); however, Pharr, Davidson, and Pharr do not include this line in their translation because it is considered an interpolation. See also Herman, column 1086; Giovanni de Bonfils, "L'imperatore Onorio e la difesa dell'ortodossia cristiana contro celicoli ed ebrei," *Vetera Christianorum* 41 (2004): 267–94.

69. Henri Leclercq, "Droit d'asile," in *Dictionnaire d'archéologie chrétienne et de liturgie*, vol. 4.2, ed. Fernand Cabrol and Henri Leclercq (Paris: Librarie Letouzey et Ané, 1921), columns 1555–58.

70. CTh 9.45.5 = CJ 1.12.3.

71. CTh 9.45.5 = CJ 1.12.3; Mommsen and Meyer, 1.2:526. Translation from Pharr, Davidson, and Pharr, 266.

72. CJ 1.3.22.

73. CJ 1.12.6.

74. CTh 9.45.1.

75. CJ 1.12.6. Translation from Dillon, 1:251.

76. NJust 17.7. Translation from David J. D. Miller and Peter Sarris, *The Novels of Justin-ian: A Complete Annotated English Translation*, vol. 1 (Cambridge: Cambridge University Press, 2018), 200.

77. *Serm.* 302. On this sermon, see Júlio César Magalhães de Oliveira, "Le 'pouvoir du peuple:' une émeute à Hippone au début du Ve siècle connue par le sermon 302 de saint Augustin pour la fête de saint Laurent," *Antiquité Tardive* 12 (2004): 309–24.

78. *Serm.* 302. *Dico caritati vestrae: ad ecclesiam et iniqui fugiunt a facie iuste viventium, et iuste viventes fugiunt a facie iniquorum, et aliquando ipsi iniqui fugiunt a facie iniquo-rum. Tria sunt genera fugientium. Boni a bonis non fugiunt, soli iusti iustos non fugiunt; sed aut iniusti fugiunt iustos, aut iusti fugiunt iniustos, aut iniusti iniustos. Sed si voluerimus*

discernere, ut tollantur de ecclesia qui male faciunt, non erit ubi se abscondant qui bene faciunt: si voluerimus permittere ut hinc tollantur nocentes, non erit quo fugiant innocentes. Melius est ergo ut et nocentes in ecclesia muniantur, quam innocentes de ecclesia rapiantur. D. C. Lambot, ed., *Sancti Augustini Hipponensis Episcopi: Sermones Selecti Dvodeviginti*, Stromata Patristica et Mediaevalia 1 (Utrecht: In Aedibus Spectrum, 1950), 111.

"I'm telling your graces: Even the crooks take refuge in the Church from those who live upright lives, and those who live upright lives take refuge from the crooks; and sometimes, the very crooks take refuge from crooks. There are three sorts of people who take refuge here. The good don't take refuge from the good, only the just don't flee from the just. But either the unjust flee from the just, or the just flee from the unjust, or the unjust from the unjust. But if we wanted to sort them out, so that the evildoers could be removed from the Church, there would be nowhere for those who do good to hide themselves; if we wished to allow noxious criminals to be removed from here, there would be nowhere for the innocent to flee to. So it's better that noxious criminals too should be protected by the Church, than that the innocent should be snatched from the Church" (Edmund Hill, trans., *Sermons*, ed. John E. Rotelle, The Works of St. Augustine: A Translation for the 21st Century 3.8 [Hyde Park, NY: New City Press, 1994], 311).

79. CTh 9.45.1 and 9.40.15.

80. NJust 17.6; Rudolf Schoell and Guilelmus Kroll, eds., *Corpus Iuris Civilis*, vol. 3 (1895; repr., Berlin: Apud Weidmannos, 1954), 121.

81. NJust 17 (the instructions to governors) and NJust 117.

82. NJust 117; Schoell and Kroll, 3:566. Translation from Miller and Sarris, 2:765.

83. NJust 37.

84. NJust 37.10. Translation from Miller and Sarris, 1:356.

85. Edict 2.1. Translation adapted from Miller and Sarris, 2:1034.

86. Edict 10.

87. Edict 13.

88. Edict 13.10. Translation from Miller and Sarris, 2:1085.

89. In fact, William Thurman concludes that asylum was a kind of insurance policy for civil authorities who otherwise conducted their responsibilities at their own risk. The abuse of such insurance led to Justinian's policies on asylum and his requirement that the officials be carefully screened before appointment. See William S. Thurman, "A Law of Justinian Concerning the Right of Asylum," *Transactions and Proceedings of the American Philological Association* 100 (1969): 593–606.

90. Sirm. 13. Translation from Pharr, Davidson, and Pharr, 483.

91. The redemption of captives became an issue of increasing importance from the fifth century onward. See Noel Lenski, "Captivity among the Barbarians and Its Impact on the Fate of the Roman Empire," in *The Cambridge Companion to the Age of Attila*, ed. Michael Maas (New York: Cambridge University Press, 2014), 230–46. For the increased overall role of bishops as protectors of cities, see Peter Brown, *The Rise of Western Christendom*, 2nd ed. (Malden, MA: Blackwell, 2003), 106–10.

92. Orleans, 511, c. 5. Several of the canons attributed to the first synod meeting in Ireland in 457 under the presidency of Patrick, Auxilius, and Isserninus speak to the issue of the ransom of captives, and in particular to the collections of funds made without the bishop's permission and the embezzlement of funds. The authenticity of the document is

contested, and dates from the middle of the sixth century to the ninth century have been suggested. M. J. Faris, ed., *The Bishop's Synod ("The First Synod of St. Patrick"): A Symposium with Text, Translation, and Commentary* (Liverpool: Francis Cairns, 1976).

93. Sirm. 16.

94. CJ 1.3.28, CJ 1.3.48, and NJust 131. Cf. chapter 2.

95. Financial reserve of late antique wealth often took the form of metal objects (as opposed to coinage), which could be melted down for cash when needed. Ruth E. Leader-Newby, *Silver and Society in Late Antiquity: Functions and Meanings of Silver Plate in the Fourth to Seventh Centuries* (Burlington, VT: Ashgate, 2004), 2–3.

96. CJ 1.3.45.

97. CJ 1.3.45. Translation from Dillon, 1:121.

98. NJust 7.8.

99. NJust 120.

100. Sozomen, *HE* 4.25.2–4; Theodoret, *HE* 2.22–23.

101. Theodore of Mopsuestia's *Against Eunomius* as a whole has not survived; only a summary report in a fragment of a historical epitome written in the seventh or eighth century remains. See Ernest Bihain, "Le 'Contre Eunome' de Théodore de Mopsueste: Source d'un passage de Sozomène et d'un passage de Théodoret concernant Cyrille de Jérusalem," *Le Muséon* 75 (1962): 347–49.

102. Socrates, *HE* 2.40.38–40.

103. Sozomen, *HE* 4.25.

104. Sozomen, *HE* 4.25; SC 418:334.

105. Theodoret, *HE* 2.23.

106. Peter van Nuffelen dismisses Theodoret's account of an imperial donation as "fanciful." See Peter van Nuffelen, "The Career of Cyril of Jerusalem (*c.* 348–87): A Reassessment," *JTS*, n.s., 58 (2007): 134–46.

107. Bihain, 345–46.

108. René Henry, ed. and trans., *Photius: Bibliothèque*, vol. 1 (Paris: Les belles lettres, 1959), 52–57.

109. Photius calls Isaac a bishop, but as Timothy Barnes and George Bevan note, Isaac was a monk, not a bishop. TTH 60:157n24.

110. Henry, 1:52–57.

111. Peter van Nuffelen argues that Photius read a pro-Johannite version of the acts that created a "sense of chaos" so as to "generate the impression that the Synod of the Oak was not a serious gathering and went about its affairs without any order" (Peter van Nuffelen, "Theophilus against John Chrysostom: The Fragments of a Lost *Liber* and the Reasons for John's Deposition," *Adamantius* 19 [2013]: 141). However, van Nuffelen's argument is based on the assumed premise that the judges were obligated to investigate the charges in the order in which they were leveled. That is not true. As discussed in chapter 2, in the context of Ibas of Edessa's trials, the president chose the order in which charges were to be addressed.

112. Henry, 1:56: Ἕλληνας πολλὰ κακὰ τοῖς Χριστιανοῖς διαθεμένους ὑπεδέξατο καὶ ἔχει ἐν τῇ ἐκκλησίᾳ καὶ προΐστatαι αὐτῶν.

113. Cf. *Homily on Eutropius*, the sermon that John Chrysostom preached as Eutropius was present at the altar as a refugee, discussed below.

114. For attempts to identify the orator, see Martin Wallraff, ed., Cristina Ricci, trans., *Oratio funebris in laudem sancti Iohannis Chrysostomi: Epitaffio attribuito a Martirio di Antiochia* (Spoleto: Centro italiano di studi sull'alto medioevo, 2007), 15–17.

115. Florent van Ommeslaeghe, "Que vaut le témoignage de Pallade sur le procès de saint Jean Chrysostome?" *Analecta Bollandiana* 95 (1997): 410.

116. Ps-Martyrius, *Oratio funebris in laudem sancti Iohannis Chrysostomi* 74; Wallraff and Ricci, 126.

117. Ps-Martyrius, *Oratio funebris in laudem sancti Iohannis Chrysostomi* 74; Wallraff and Ricci, 126 and 128.

118. Palladius, *Dialogue on the Life of John Chrysostom* 3; SC 341:76.

119. Palladius, *Dialogue on the Life of John Chrysostom* 3; SC 341:76 and 78.

120. Palladius, *Dialogue on the Life of John Chrysostom* 3; SC 341:76 and 78. See also chapter 10, where Palladius argues that it was by divine providence that the ecclesial valuables did not burn in the church fire so that John Chrysostom would be exonerated from the charge that he alienated ecclesial property (τὰ κειμήλια αὐτὸν ἐκβεβληκέναι). SC 341:212.

The inventory itself probably took place as part of a measure of confiscation. Since legislation was passed against John Chrysostom's supporters, John's church must have been confiscated. The Theodosian Codex only records a piece of legislation that released John's supporters who had been accused of arson (burning down the church), but the excerpt makes reference to confiscatory edicts that targeted John's supporters (CTh 16.2.37). Confiscatory procedure (see above) would have required an official civil inventory of the ecclesial property.

121. The orator seems to have been aware of charges that were orally leveled against John Chrysostom but not recorded in the acts of the council. In paragraph 77, he refutes a charge that "they did not dare to put in writing" (γράμμασι μὲν οὐκ ἐτόλμησαν ἐνθεῖναι). Wallraff and Ricci, 130.

122. Ps-Martyrius, *Oratio funebris in laudem sancti Iohannis Chrysostomi* 62–65.

123. Ps-Martyrius, *Oratio funebris in laudem sancti Iohannis Chrysostomi* 62.

124. Ps-Martyrius, *Oratio funebris in laudem sancti Iohannis Chrysostomi* 61. Translation from TTH 60:75.

125. Ps-Martyrius, *Oratio funebris in laudem sancti Iohannis Chrysostomi* 62. Translation from TTH 60:76.

126. Ps-Martyrius, *Oratio funebris in laudem sancti Iohannis Chrysostomi* 64.

127. Ps-Martyrius, *Oratio funebris in laudem sancti Iohannis Chrysostomi* 75.

128. Ps-Martyrius, *Oratio funebris in laudem sancti Iohannis Chrysostomi* 74–75.

129. Ps-Martyrius, *Oratio funebris in laudem sancti Iohannis Chrysostomi* 5; Wallraff and Ricci, 128.

130. Palladius, *Dialogue on the Life of John Chrysostom* 5; SC 341:122.

131. Palladius, *Dialogue on the Life of John Chrysostom* 6. Isidore of Pelusium also accused Theophilus of lithomania (*Epistle* 1.152). Cf. Tomasz Polański, "The Three Young Men in the Furnace and the Art of Ecphrasis in the Coptic Sermon by Theophilus of Alexandria," in *Christian Art in Oriental Literatures. Greek, Syriac and Coptic Sources from the 4th to the 7th Century* (Salzburg: Horn, 2013), 113.

132. Palladius, *Dialogue on the Life of John Chrysostom* 13. Translation from Robert T. Meyer, *Palladius: Dialogue on the Life of St. John Chrysostom* (New York: Newman Press, 1985), 87.

133. Facundus, *Defense of the Three Chapters* 6.5.23.

134. Facundus, *Defense of the Three Chapters* 6.5.17; SC 479:378.

135. Cf. van Nuffelen, "Lost *Liber*," 149.

136. CTh 9.40.16 and 9.45.3.

137. John Chrysostom, *Homily on Eutropius* 3; PG 52:393–94.

138. Socrates, *HE* 6.5; Sozomen, *HE* 8.7. Cf. Wendy Mayer, "John Chrysostom as Crisis Manager: The Years in Constantinople," in *Ancient Jewish and Christian Texts as Crisis Management Literature: Thematic Studies from the Centre for Early Christian Studies*, ed. David C. Sim and Pauline Allen, Library of New Testament Studies 445 (London: T&T Clark, 2012), 137–38.

139. John Chrysostom, *Homily on Eutropius* 1 and 3. For a study that situates John Chrysostom's ecclesial images here within his broader ecclesiology, see Daniel R. Salyers, "'Clutching the Altar with Chattering Teeth:' Exploring the Ancient Custom of Asylum-Seeking through the Lens of John Chrysostom" (PhD diss., Fuller Theological Seminary, 2020), 147–207.

140. John Chrysostom, *Homily on Eutropius* 3; PG 52:393–94.

141. John Chrysostom, *Homily on Eutropius* 3.

142. John Chrysostom, *Homily on Eutropius* 5; PG 52:396. In his sixth sermon on Lazarus and the rich man, John Chrysostom describes the church as a place of transformation. Here Eutropius enters as a suppliant and, John Chrysostom hopes, will be transformed into an ornament for the altar. Earlier, during his priesthood in Antioch, John Chrysostom would say, "The Church has received irrational human beings, and does not merely save them, but also changes them. [. . .] The Church receives a raven and sends forth a dove; it receives a wolf and sends forth a sheep" (Sixth Sermon on Lazarus and the Rich Man). Translation from Catherine P. Roth, *John Chrysostom: On Wealth and Poverty* (Crestwood, NY: St. Vladimir's Seminary Press, 1981), 113–14.

143. John Chrysostom, *Homily on the* Comes *John*; PG 52:395–414. On this homily, see Mayer, 138–39.

144. Early editors identified the homily in question as another homily concerning Eutropius's asylum, but Alan Cameron argues that the homily concerns the *comes* John (Alan Cameron, "A Misidentified Homily of Chrysostom," *Nottingham Medieval Studies* 32 [1988]: 34–48). According to Sever Voicu, only the first two sections of the homily are authentic. See Sever Voicu, "La volontà e il caso: La tipologia dei primi spuri di Crisostomo," in *Giovanni Crisostomo: Oriente e occidente tra IV e V secolo, XXXIII Incontro di studiosi dell' antichità cristiana, Roma, 6–8 maggio 2004*, vol. 1, Studia Ephemeridis Augustinianum 93 (Rome: Institutum Patristicum Augustinianum, 2005), 111–12.

145. John Chrysostom, *Homily on the* Comes *John* 1.

146. John Chrysostom, *Homily on the* Comes *John* 1 and 2.

147. John Chrysostom, *Homily on the* Comes *John* 1; PG 52:397.

148. The letter has been transmitted in manuscripts of Palladius's *Dialogue on the Life of John Chrysostom*. The relevant phrases read: "which was most contrary to both the canons and the laws" (ὃ μάλιστα καὶ παρὰ κανόνας καὶ παρὰ πάντας νόμους ἦν); "which were entirely contrary to ordinance, both the canons and procedure" (ἅπερ ἅπαντα παρὰ θεσμὸν καὶ κανόνα καὶ

ἀκολουθίαν ἦν); and "in fact, all that had proceeded by them transgressed procedure and every law and ecclesiastical canon" (τὰ γὰρ νῦν γεγενημένα παρ᾽ αὐτῶν πάσης ἐκτός ἐστιν ἀκολουθίας καὶ παντὸς νόμου καὶ κανόνος ἐκκλησιαστικοῦ). SC 342:74, 76, and 92.

149. John Chrysostom, *Letter to Innocent of Rome*, line 110; SC 342:80.

150. John Chrysostom, *Letter to Innocent of Rome*, lines 149, 152–53, and 158–59; SC 342:82 and 84.

151. PG 52:537–38.

152. For the exception clauses, see chapter 2.

CHAPTER 4. DEDICATIONS

1. *Parietes faciunt Christianos?* Marius Victorinus quoted in Augustine, *Conf.* 8.2.4. James J. O'Donnell, ed., *Augustine: Confessions*, vol. 1 (Oxford: Clarendon Press, 1992), 89.

2. Prudentius, *Peristephanon liber* 2. Prudentius was not the first to celebrate Laurentius's martyrdom. For the relationship between Prudentius's poem and earlier extant accounts (such as those of Damasus of Rome and Ambrose of Milan), see Anne-Marie Palmer, *Prudentius on the Martyrs* (Oxford: Clarendon Press, 1989), 243–45. See also Anna Benvenuti and Elena Giannarelli, *Il diacono Lorenzo tra storia e leggenda* (Florence: Edizioni della Meridiana, 1998).

3. Prudentius, *Peristephanon liber* 2.121–32.

4. Prudentius, *Peristephanon liber* 2.170–76. Translation from H. J. Thomson, ed. and trans., *Prudentius*, vol. 2, Loeb Classical Library 398 (Cambridge, MA: Harvard University Press, 1953), 119.

5. Prudentius, *Peristephanon liber* 2.179–81.

6. Prudentius, *Peristephanon liber* 2.293–312. Translation from Thomson, 2:125 and 127.

7. Prudentius, *Peristephanon liber* 2.314–15.

8. Igor Kopytoff, "The Cultural Biography of Things: Commoditization as Process," in *The Social Life of Things: Commodities in Cultural Perspective*, ed. Arjun Appadurai (New York: Cambridge University Press, 1986), 64–91.

9. See chapter 3.

10. Kenneth Lokensgard argues that anthropologists have failed to take seriously the ontology of gifts, and he shows that among the Blackfeet, gifts were persons. See Kenneth Hayes Lokensgard, *Blackfoot Religion and the Consequences of Cultural Commoditization* (Farnham: Ashgate, 2010), 77–88. Unfortunately, there is no historical evidence that outlines donors' views. However, on the basis of bishops' emphasis on *res sacrae* as *res*, we may infer that they were addressing a perspective that understood sacralization as effecting an ontological shift from thing to person.

11. See the mosaic pavement designated as 11B in Peter Baumann, *Spätantike Stifter im Heiligen Land* (Wiesbaden: Reichert Verlag, 1999), 86, overview 1, and plate 3.

12. Januarius's inscription lies on the mosaic pavement of the northern room of the ecclesial complex at Aquileia, the earliest known archaeological site of a consecrated church. See Tomas Lehmann, "Die ältesten erhaltenen Bilder in einem Kirchenbau. Zu den frühchristlichen Kirchenbauten und ihren Mosaiken unter dem Dom von Aquileia," *Das Altertum* 54 (2009): 115n25.

13. Rudolph Cohen, "The Marvelous Mosaics of Kissufim," *Biblical Archaeology Review* 6.1 (1980): 16–23; Cohen, "A Byzantine Church and Its Mosaic Floors at Kissufim," in *Ancient*

Churches Revealed, ed. Yoram Tsafrir (Jerusalem: Israel Exploration Society, 1993): 277–82; Rachel Hachlili, *Ancient Mosaic Pavements: Themes, Issues, and Trends* (Leiden: Brill, 2009), 160, fig. VII–4.

14. Hachlili, plate VII.18a.

15. See the discussion in Baumann, 46–48 as to why and when the tessarae of figures' faces and bodies were removed and replaced. What the church was called in antiquity is unknown, but it is referred to as the "Church of Bishop Sergius," after an inscription that commemorates the mosaic program's completion in September 587 under Bishop Sergius's episcopacy (Baumann, 90–92).

16. Jean-Pierre Caillet, *L'Évergétisme monumental chrétien en Italie et à ses marges* (Rome: École française de Rome, 1993), 446–47.

17. Caillet, 27 and 29–30. The names are mentioned in descending order of the number of feet contributed, from the deacon Marinianus who paid for three hundred feet to Euresius who paid for sixty-five feet. Several names are still readable after that of Euresius, but the numbers associated with their names are not extant. Cf. Ann Marie Yasin, *Saints and Church Spaces in the Late Antique Mediterranean: Architecture, Cult, and Community* (Cambridge: Cambridge University Press, 2009), 124–25, fig. 3.8.

18. Graziano Marini, ed., *I Mosaici della basilica di Aquileia* (Aquileia: Ciscra, 2003), 77. The mosaic program has been the subject of many publications, especially among German and Italian scholars, who have been divided over the interpretation of the hall and its mosaics. For a summary of the respective views and arguments both for and against them, see Lehmann, 98 and 112.

19. Marini, 48–49.

20. Marini, 28–29. Cf. Peter Brown, *Through the Eye of a Needle: Wealth, the Fall of Rome, and the Making of Christianity in the West, 350–550 AD* (Princeton, NJ: Princeton University Press, 2012), 39–40.

21. Elsewhere I have shown that the nave floor was interpreted by liturgical commentators as the worldly (as opposed to celestial) realm. See Mary K. Farag, "The Mosaic Map of Madaba and Late Antique Discourse on Ecclesial Space," in ϲⲩⲛⲁⲝⲓⲥ ⲕⲁⲑⲟⲗⲓⲕⲏ: *Beiträge zu Gottesdienst und Geschichte der fünf altkirchlichen Patriarchate für Heinzgerd Brakmann zum 70. Geburtstag*, ed. Diliana Atanassova and Tinatin Chronz (Münster: LIT Verlag, 2014), 175–96. Perhaps donor images of everyday activities contributed to this interpretation.

22. My purpose here is not to review the evidence for or against the installation of images in churches, but to point out the kind of images that were identified as pedagogically beneficial. The literature on the former subject is vast. For a brief overview, see Thomas F. X. Noble, "Art, Icons, and Their Critics and Defenders before the Age of Iconoclasm," in *Images, Iconoclasm, and the Carolingians* (Philadelphia: University of Pennsylvania Press, 2009), 10–45.

23. Nilus of Ancyra, *Ep.* 62; Baumann, 187–88. Cf. Henry Maguire, *Nectar and Illusion: Nature in Byzantine Art and Literature* (New York: Oxford University Press, 2012), 24.

24. Nilus of Ancyra, *Ep.* 62; PG 79:577.

25. Nilus of Ancyra, *Ep.* 62; PG 79:577.

26. Nilus's letter may have been redacted during the iconoclastic controversy in the eighth century. It is possible he only advised crosses, not scriptural scenes as well. See Hans Georg Thümmel, "Neilos von Ancyra über die Bilder," *Byzantinische Zeitschrift* 71 (1978): 10–21.

27. οἱ μὴ εἰδότες γράμματα, μηδὲ δυνάμενοι τὰς θείας ἀναγινώσκειν Γραφὰς τῇ θεωρίᾳ τῆς ζωγραφίας, μνήμην τε λαμβάνωσιν τῆς τῶν γνωσίως τῷ ἀληθινῷ θεῷ δεδουλευκότων ἀνδραγαθίας, καὶ πρὸς ἄμιλλαν διεγείρωνται τῶν εὐκλεῶν καὶ ἀοιδίμων ἀριστευμάτων [. . .]. Nilus of Ancyra, *Ep.* 62; PG 79:577 and 580. Translation from Cyril Mango, *The Art of the Byzantine Empire 312–1453* (Toronto: University of Toronto Press, 1986), 33. Gregory the Great echoes the idea that pictures supply educational "texts" to the illiterate in a letter to Serenus, the bishop of Marseilles (*Ep.* 11.13). For a discussion of how such a notion creates a hierarchy of value in which text occupies a superior place in relation to image, see Robin Margaret Jensen, *Understanding Early Christian Art* (Abingdon: Routledge, 2000), 2–3.

28. Paulinus of Nola, *Carm.* 27.542–44. Translation from P. G. Walsh, *The Poems of St. Paulinus of Nola* (New York: Newman Press, 1975), 290.

29. Paulinus of Nola, *Carm.* 27.580. Translation from Walsh, 291–92.

30. Choricius of Gaza, *Marc.* I.33. Translation from R. W. Hamilton, "Two Churches of Gaza, as Described by Choricius of Gaza," in *Palestine Exploration Fund: Quarterly Statement for 1930* (London: Fund's Office, 1930), 181–82.

31. Richard Foerster and Eberhard Richtsteig, eds., *Choricii Gazaei Opera* (Leipzig: B. G. Teubner, 1929), 11.

32. My emphasis. For a photograph of the mosaic, see Yale University Art Gallery, "Mosaic Floor with Views of Alexandria and Memphis," accessed April 8, 2021, http://artgallery.yale.edu/collections/objects/51363. For a catalog entry, see Lisa Brody, "Floor Mosaic Depicting the Cities of Memphis and Alexandria," in *Byzantium and Islam: Age of Transition*, ed. Helen C. Evans and Brandie Ratliff (New York: Metropolitan Museum of Art, 2012), 12.

33. Kopytoff, 73–77.

34. Kopytoff, 71.

35. Kopytoff, 74.

36. Gaius, *Institutes* 2.2–4 and 9. *Summa itaque rerum divisio in duos articulos diducitur: nam aliae sunt divini iuris, aliae humani. Divini iuris sunt veluti res sacrae et religiosae. Sacrae sunt, quae diis superis consecratae sunt* [. . .]. *Quod autem divini iuris est, id nullius in bonis est.* Francis de Zulueta, ed., *The Institutes of Gaius*, vol. 1 (Oxford: Clarendon Press, 1946), 66.

37. Justinian, *Institutes* 2.1.7–8. *Nullius autem sunt res sacrae* [. . .]: *quod enim divini iuris est, id nullius in bonis est. Sacra sunt, quae rite et per pontifices Deo consecrata sunt, veluti aedes sacrae et dona quae rite ad ministerium Dei dedicata sunt.* J. A. C. Thomas, ed., *The Institutes of Justinian: Text, Translation, and Commentary* (Amsterdam: North-Holland Publishing Company, 1975), 65.

38. See chapters 2 and 3, respectively.

39. Kopytoff, 69.

40. For example, see Stephen D. White, *Custom, Kinship, and Gifts to Saints: The Laudatio Parentum in Western France, 1050–1150* (Chapel Hill: University of North Carolina Press, 1988); Barbara H. Rosenwein, *To Be the Neighbor of Saint Peter: The Social Meaning of Cluny's Property, 909–1049* (Ithaca, NY: Cornell University Press, 1989).

41. Cäcilia Davis-Weyer, "Das Traditio-Legis Bild und seine Nachfolge," *Münchner Jahrbuch der Bildenden Kunst* 12 (1961): 34; P. Bloch, "Dedikationsbild," in *Lexikon der christlichen Ikonographie*, vol. 1, ed. Engelbert Kirschbaum (Rome: Herder, 1968), columns 491–94; Elizabeth Lipsmeyer, "The Donor and His Church Model in Medieval Art from Early

Christian Times to the Late Romanesque Period" (PhD diss., Rutgers University, 1981), 17–18; Ida Malte Ploumis, "Gifts in the Late Roman Iconography," in *Patron and Pavements in Late Antiquity*, ed. Signe Isager and Birte Poulsen (Odense: Odense University Press, 1997), 138 and 138n81; Ann Terry and Henry Maguire, *Dynamic Splendor: The Wall Mosaics in the Cathedral of Euphrasius at Poreč*, vol. 1 (University Park: Pennsylvania State University Press, 2007), 4; Ann Marie Yasin, "Making Use of Paradise: Church Benefactors, Heavenly Visions, and the Late Antique Commemorative Imagination," in *Looking Beyond: Visions, Dreams, and Insights in Medieval Art and History*, ed. Colum Hourihane (Princeton, NJ: Princeton University, 2010), 45; Deborah M. Deliyannis, "Ecclesius of Ravenna as Donor in Text and Image," in *Envisioning the Bishop: Images and the Episcopacy in the Middle Ages*, ed. Sigrid Danielson and Evan A. Gatti (Turnhout: Brepols, 2014), 41.

42. Joachim Poeschke, *Italian Mosaics, 300–1300*, trans. Russell Stockman (New York: Abbeville Press Publishers, 2010), plate 24.

43. Poeschke, 18, fig. 9.

44. Poeschke, 33, fig. 30.

45. The depiction of Felix is the product of seventeenth-century restorative work, but it is thought that he and his church model were a constitutive part of the original mosaic program.

46. Poeschke, plate 60.

47. With the exception of Ida Malte Ploumis (138 and 138n81), who argues that Saint Vitalis offers his martyr's crown in homage to Christ.

48. Yasin, "Making Use of Paradise," 45. Deliyannis, 42.

49. Theodor Klauser, "*Aurum Coronarium*," *Mitteilungen des deutschen archaeologischen Instituts, Roemische Abteilung* 59 (1944): 129–53; Clifford Ando, *Imperial Ideology and Provincial Loyalty in the Roman Empire* (Berkeley: University of California Press, 2000), 175–90. See also Ploumis.

50. Kurt Weitzmann, ed., *Age of Spirituality: Late Antique and Early Christian Art, Third to Seventh Century* (New York: Metropolitan Museum of Art, 1979), 33–35 (no. 28). Cf. K. Wessel, "Das Diptychon Barberini," in *Akten des XI. internationalen Byzantinistenkongresses, München, 1958*, ed. Franz Dölger and Hans-Georg Beck (Munich: C. H. Beck, 1960), 668 and 670.

51. Linda Safran, "Points of View: The Theodosian Obelisk Base in Context," *Roman and Byzantine Studies* 34 (1993): 409–35.

52. Poeschke, plate 38.

53. Gilbert Dagron, "From the *Mappa* to the *Akakia*: Symbolic Drift," in *From Rome to Constantinople: Studies in Honour of Averil Cameron*, ed. Hagit Amirav and Bas ter Haar Romeny (Leuven: Peeters, 2007), 213–15.

54. Richard Brilliant, *Gesture and Rank in Roman Art: The Use of Gestures to Denote Status in Roman Sculpture and Coinage* (New Haven, CT: Connecticut Academy of Arts and Sciences, 1963), 172–73.

55. Richard Delbrueck, *Die Consulardiptychen und verwandte Denkmäler* (Berlin: Walter de Gruyter, 1929), 69, fig. 25.

56. Thomas F. Mathews's *The Clash of the Gods: A Reinterpretation of Early Christian Art* (Princeton, NJ: Princeton University Press, 1993) argues that early Christian art did not rely on the visual language of imperial imagery. Artists producing Christian items may not have

relied exclusively on imperial imagery, but it would certainly have been a major source for generating Christian images that convey athletic success and military triumph. See Peter Brown's important review of the book in *Art Bulletin* 77 (1995): 499–502.

57. Architectural plan in Iva Perčić, *Poreč: The Euphrasius Basilica* (Belgrade: Jugoslavija, 1969), inside back cover.

58. Terry and Maguire, 2:101.

59. Terry and Maguire, 2:110.

60. Antonio Muñoz, *La basilica di s. Lorenzo fuori le mura* (Rome: Fratelli Palombi, 1944), plates 82, 83, and 85. Color reproduction in Poeschke, 18, fig. 9.

61. My emphasis. *Demovit dominus tenebras luce creata His quondam latebris sic modo fulgor inest angustos aditus venerabile corpus habebat Huc ubi nunc populum largior aula capit fruta planities sub monte reciso est Namque remota gravi mole ruina minax presule pelagio martir laurentius olim Templa sibi statuit tam preciosa dari Mira fides gladios hostiles inter et iras pontificem meritis haec cebrasse suis Tu modo sanctorum cui crescere constat honores fac sub pace coli tecta dicata tibi.* Ioannes Bapt. de Rossi, ed., *Inscriptiones Christianae Urbis Romae*, vol. 2 (Rome: Ex Officina Libraria Philippi Cuggiani, 1888), 63–64, no. 10. For a photograph of the inscription, see Muñoz, plate 83.

62. De Rossi, 2:64.

63. Eusebius, *Life of Constantine* IV.7. ἃ δὴ παρὰ τῶν κομιζόντων ὑποδεχόμενος καὶ ἐντάττων, ἀντεδίδου τοσαῦτα βασιλεύς, ὡς ὑφ' ἕνα καιρὸν πλουσιωτάτους ἀποφῆναι τοὺς κομιζομένους. Ivar A. Heikel, ed., *Eusebius Werke*, Die griechischen christlichen Schriftsteller der ersten drei Jahrhunderte 1 (Leipzig: J.C. Hinrichs'sche Buchhandlung, 1902), 120.

64. Koep, "Dedicatio," columns 643–49.

65. Koep, "Consecratio," columns 269–83.

66. For example, Ancyra, 314, c. 15.

67. For example, Hippo, 427, c. 5.

68. For example, Augustine of Hippo, *Serm.* 336.

69. Barbara Burrell, *Neokoroi: Greek Cities and Roman Emperors* (Leiden: Brill, 2004), 1.

70. B. Pick, "Die templeltragenden Gottheiten und die Darstellung der Neokorie auf den Münzen," *Jahreshefte des österreichischen archäologischen Institutes in Wien* 7 (1904): 6, fig. 5. Barbara Burrell (9–10) does not include this coin because Lesbos is not known to have had the title *neokoros*.

71. The patera is not visible in Pick, 6, fig. 5, but similar coins do show Commodus with a spear in his left hand and a patera in the right. Cf. Warwick Wroth, *Catalogue of the Greek Coins of Troas, Aeolis, and Lesbos*, A Catalog of the Greek Coins in the British Museum (London: Trustees of the British Museum, 1894), 169–70, nos. 3 and 5.

72. Burrell, 94 and plate 80.

73. Pick, 11, fig. 14. Burrell, 283 and plate 189.

74. Al-Anba Matā'us, *Ṭaqs sir al-zawāj al-muqadas* (Wadī al-Natrūn: Dayr al-Suryān, 2000), 30.

75. In what follows, I analyze the visual series as a narrative, specifically the "participatory mode" of visual narrative theorized in Henry Maguire, "Two Modes of Narration in Byzantine Art," in *Byzantine East, Latin West: Art-Historical Studies in Honor of Kurt Weitzmann*, ed. Christopher Moss and Katherine Kiefer (Princeton, NJ: Department of Art and Archaeology, Princeton University, 1995), 385–95.

76. Robin S. Cormack, *The Church of Saint Demetrios: The Watercolours and Drawings of W. S. George* (Thessaloniki: Vafopoulio Cultural Center and the British Council, 1985). Cormack, "The Mosaic Decoration of S. Demetrios, Thessaloniki: A Re-Examination in Light of the Drawings of W. S. George," *Annual of the British School at Athens* 64 (1969): 17–52 and plates 1–15.

77. Maguire, "Two Modes of Narration," 390.

78. Maguire, "Two Modes of Narration," 391. Henry Maguire uses scenes of Christ's passion to illustrate the "participatory mode" of narration, so his text refers to Christ's accessibility. Here, I am arguing that the scenes of Saint Demetrios's interaction with an unnamed family illustrate the same type of accessibility.

79. For studies on this gesture, see Albrecht Dieterich, "Der Ritus der verhüllten Hände," in *Kleine Schriften* (Leipzig: B. G. Teubner, 1911), 440–48, and Franz Cumont, "L'Adoration des Mages et l'Art triomphal de Rome," *Atti della pontificia academia romana di archeologia, Memorie* 3 (1932): 81–132.

80. Brilliant, 165–70.

81. Translation from Cormack, *Church of Saint Demetrios*, 71.

82. Leslie Brubaker, "Elites and Patronage in Early Byzantium: The Evidence from Hagios Demetrios at Thessalonike," in *The Byzantine and Early Islamic Near East*, vol. 6, *Elites Old and New in the Byzantine and Early Islamic Near East*, ed. John Haldon and Lawrence Conrad (Princeton, NJ: Darwin Press, 2004), 73.

83. Translation from Cormack, *Church of Saint Demetrios*, 71.

84. Translation from Cormack, *Church of Saint Demetrios*, 71.

85. *Succedunt meliora sibi miranda tuenti. Quae leopardi labor cura et vigilantia fec Sumptibus haec ppriis ornaū moenia xpī. Respice et ingressu placido noua quaeq: reuisa. Caelestis manus ecce dei praemia reddit. Quae cumulata uides digna in aecclesia xpī.* De Rossi, 2:155. Cf. Richard Krautheimer, Wolfgang Frankl, and Spencer Corbett, *Corpus Basilicarum Christianarum Romae: The Early Christian Basilicas of Rome (IV–IX Cent.)*, vol. 2 (Vatican City: Pontificio istituto di archeologia cristiana, 1959), 8. Concerning this inscription, see Louise Ropes Loomis, *The Book of the Popes* (New York: Columbia University Press, 1916), 89n3.

86. Peter Grossmann, *Abū Mīnā I: Die Gruftkirche und die Gruft*, Archäologische Veröffentlichungen 44 (Mainz: Verlag Philipp von Zabern, 1989), 69–70, fig. 14 and plate 55a.

87. In the poem Paulinus of Nola delivered at the consecration of the renovated church (on Saint Felix's *dies natalis* in January 403), Paulinus expresses succinctly how saintly intercession results in divine largesse and ends in triumph: "What words of heart or tongue could I utter in my poverty, foolishness, and insignificance that would be worthy of so great a blessing? Felix himself must now provide me with the boon (*munus*) I need for this. He must obtain from Christ resources to bestow on me so that I can thank him in worthy fashion. If only a living spring of eternal water would emanate from my belly, so that I could announce my joy not by my tongue but through Christ's gift (*munus*)! For it is through His gift that joy floods my tranquil heart to unprecedented depths, and my affection which invests Felix's birthday is redoubled. Today I witness Nicetas in the flesh smiling upon me, and when I behold the father for whom above all others my love prevails, I myself become a Nicetas, not in blessed name but in heart now triumphant (*mente gerens, quae nunc uoto*

uictore triumphat), since my prayer has succeeded" (*Carm.* 27.169–83; CSEL 30:269–70; translation from Walsh, 276). As P. G. Walsh notes, the theme of triumph emerges from a wordplay on the Greek name of the visiting bishop Nicetas, meaning "victorious" (Walsh, 406n21). Nevertheless, this section of the poem explains the dynamic among supplication, intercession, divine largesse, and triumph, which permeates dedicatory epigraphy. For more on Paulinus's consecratory poem, see chapter 5.

88. Quoted from a fifth-century regulative text purporting to record a dialogue between Cyril and two deacons in Ewa Wipszycka, *The Alexandrian Church: People and Institutions*, Journal of Juristic Papyrology Supplement 25 (Warsaw: University of Warsaw and the Raphael Taubenschlag Foundation, 2015), 351.

89. See chapter 3.

90. For anthropological discussions of the tension between gift and commodity, see Lokensgard, and Mark Osteen, "Gift or Commodity?," in *The Question of the Gift: Essays across Disciplines*, ed. Osteen (London: Routledge, 2002), 229–47.

91. Ruth E. Leader-Newby, *Silver and Society in Late Antiquity: Functions and Meanings of Silver Plate in the Fourth to Seventh Centuries* (Burlington, VT: Ashgate, 2004), 61. Ruth Leader-Newby posits that furnishing a church constituted "pious disposal" of wealth: a more honorable use of wealth than hoarding it, but less honorable than giving it to charity. What I am arguing here is that donors did not see themselves as "disposing" their wealth at all; there was always a return expected, and therefore "investment" captures what donors were doing when they commissioned gifts for the sake of their soul or for other reasons.

92. Leader-Newby, 66–72.

93. Ammianus Marcellinus, *Rerum Gestarum* 16.8.8.

94. Similar stories across cultures abound. For example, Volpp shows how a sixteenth-century novel of late Ming fiction includes stories about the illegal circulation of the python robe. According to Sophie Volpp, when the robes are "out-of-place," the consistent result in the novel is "social disorder." See Sophie Volpp, "The Gift of a Python Robe: The Circulation of Objects in 'Jin Ping Mei,'" *Harvard Journal of Asiatic Studies* 65 (2005): 133–58. Likewise, when objects come to be "out of place" by sliding in the wrong direction of an implied hierarchy, late antique stories record negative outcomes. Compare the hierarchy named in the Mishnah (Megillah 3.1) from synagogues to books of the law. An item high on the hierarchy may be sold to purchase something immediately lower on the scale, but not vice versa. For an English translation, see Herbert Danby, trans., *The Mishnah* (Oxford: Clarendon Press, 1933), 204.

95. Ambrose, *Off.* 2.137. Translation from Ivor J. Davidson, *Ambrose: De officiis*, vol. 1 (New York: Oxford University Press, 2001), 345.

96. Translation from Robert Doran, *Stewards of the Poor: The Man of God, Rabbula, and Hiba in Fifth-Century Edessa* (Kalamazoo, MI: Cistercian Publications, 2006), 77.

97. Translation from Doran, 77.

98. *Life of Caesarius of Arles* 1.32. Translation from TTH 19:189. Later, Jacob of Edessa would find a way to allow sacred vessels to be used for the redemption of captives and yet not be melted down. He decided that sacred vessels should be exchanged with another pious house for their cash equivalent. The cash, not the sacred vessel itself, could then fund the ransom of captives. See Arthur Vööbus, ed. and trans., *The Synodicon in the West Syrian Tradition*, 2 vols., CSCO Scriptores Syri 161–62 (Louvain: Secrétariat du CorpusSCO,

1975), 1:245 (no. 27) and 2:225 (no. 27). On the matter of exchanges between pious houses, see chapter 2 above.

CHAPTER 5. CONSECRATIONS

1. 1 Cor 3:16–17. Translation adapted from RSV.

2. A church building was often referred to as an *oikos*, a "house" (i.e., a celestial being's house), or a *naos*, a "temple."

3. Festivals in general were widely attended. Ramsay MacMullen argues that a preacher's audience in Antioch and its environs in the late fourth century would be most representative of the city's demographics at festivals. See Ramsay MacMullen, "The Preacher's Audience (AD 350–400)," *JTS*, n.s., 40 (1989): 506–7. For some of John Chrysostom's remarks on the number of attendees at festivals for martyrs in Antioch, see Christine Shepardson, *Controlling Contested Spaces: Late Antique Antioch and the Spatial Politics of Religious Controversy* (Berkeley: University of California Press, 2014), 179. As Kenneth Holum and Gary Vikan note, the dedication of churches counted among the events that "affected the entire community," and therefore merited inclusion in the consular chronicles of Constantinople. See Kenneth G. Holum and Gary Vikan, "The Trier Ivory, 'Adventus' Ceremonial, and the Relics of St. Stephen," *DOP* 33 (1979): 116. Ian Wood studies the fragments of Avitus of Vienna's homilies for the consecration of churches to describe the elite demographic, which Avitus names or to which he alludes, in "The Audience of Architecture in Post-Roman Gaul," in *The Anglo-Saxon Church: Papers in History, Architecture and Archaeology in Honour of Dr. H. M. Taylor*, ed. L. A. S. Butler and R. K. Morris (London: Council for British Archaeology, 1986), 75–76.

4. Gaudentius of Brescia, *Tractatus* 17.2; Choricius of Gaza, *Marc.* I.93; Venantius Fortunatus, *Carmen* 3.6.11.

5. Famously, the Dedication Council of Antioch in 341. Several councils (in 418, 419, 421, and 535) were held in the Basilica Fausti in Carthage, either in the basilica proper or the *secretarium*. For literary references to the location of these councils, see Liliane Ennabli, *Carthage: Une métropole chrétienne du IVe à la fin du VIIe siècle* (Paris: CNRS Éditions, 1997), 28. For archaeological evidence of the *secretarium*, see Heimo Dolenz, "Two Annex Buildings to the Basilica Damous-el-Karita in Carthage: A Summary of the Excavations in 1996 and 1997," *Antiquités africaines* 36 (2000): 151. As Susan Holman notes, Basil of Caesarea uses the word "synod" to describe not just councils, but even a martyr's festival. Like festivals for the dedication of a church, festivals for martyrs also occasioned visits of bishops. See Susan Holman, *The Hungry Are Dying: Beggars and Bishops in Roman Cappadocia* (New York: Oxford University Press 2001), 99.

6. Athanasius of Alexandria, *Apol. Const.* 14. Neil McLynn explains the tensions that complicated imperial churchgoing, such as how emperor and bishop should together occupy the ceremonial space of a church. See Neil McLynn, "The Transformation of Imperial Churchgoing in the Fourth Century," in *Approaching Late Antiquity: The Transformation from Early to Late Empire*, ed. Simon Swain and Mark Edwards (Oxford: Oxford University Press, 2006), 235–70. The first emperor known to have attended the consecration of a church is Constantius II (Athanasius reports Constantius II's presence at the dedication of the Great Church of Antioch in 341 in *De Syn.* 25.1).

7. The general description here and above corresponds well with how other Christian festivals were conducted in late antiquity, such as the *dies natali* of saints and martyrs. See Johan Leemans et al., *"Let Us Die That We May Live:" Greek Homilies on Christian Martyrs from Asia Minor, Palestine, and Syria c. AD 350–AD 450* (London: Routledge, 2003), 15–22.

8. See chapter 6.

9. R. Coquin, "La consécration des églises dans le rite copte; ses relations avec les rites syrien et byzantin," *L'Orient syrien* 9 (1964): 166n40; Vitalijs Permjakovs, "'Make This the Place Where Your Glory Dwells': Origins and Evolution of the Byzantine Rite for the Consecration of a Church" (PhD diss., University of Notre Dame, 2012), 107–11 and 117–30.

10. For example, Ambrose of Milan's dedication of the Basilica of the Apostles included the deposition of relics. See Neil B. McLynn, *Ambrose of Milan: Church and Court in a Christian Capital* (Berkeley: University of California Press, 1994), 230. On the *adventus* ceremony in general, see Sabine G. MacCormack, *Art and Ceremony in Late Antiquity* (Berkeley: University of California Press, 1981). For a detailed description of a relic *adventus*, see Holum and Vikan, 116–20.

11. See appendix D.

12. For a brief summary, see Permjakovs, 594–95.

13. Choricius of Gaza, *Marc.* I.88.

14. Procopius of Caesarea, *Buildings* I.i.4–5.

15. While the literature on gift exchange is vast to the point that it is irreducible to one footnote, that on regifting is limited. Marcel Mauss cites Bronislaw Malinowski's descriptions of cultures in which gift exchange was not marked by the reciprocity of person A to person B and vice versa, but by the continuous motion of a gift from A to B to C to D, and so on. Annette Weiner and Maurice Godelier revisit Malinowski's conclusions by calling attention to the importance of the alienability of any given object. Lewis Hyde argues that this model of gift exchange captures the purpose and appropriate use of the arts. More recently, William Miller enacts his own regifting by playfully placing it within the context of celebrated Old Norse stories. Finally, it is worth noting here that the Jerusalem Talmud Megillah III.2 names the point at which a gift may be regifted (i.e., repurposed): once the name of the donor has been forgotten from communal memory. In a similar vein, a modern study on regifting shows that it becomes a more acceptable practice when the receiver's perception of the giver is changed. Marcel Mauss, *The Gift: Forms and Functions of Exchange in Archaic Societies*, trans. Ian Cunnison (Mansfield Center, CT: Martino Publishing, 2011); Bronislaw Malinowski, *Argonauts of the Western Pacific* (1922; repr., Prospect Heights, IL: Waveland Press, 1984); Annette B. Weiner, *Inalienable Possessions: The Paradox of Keeping-While-Giving* (Berkeley: University of California Press, 1992); Maurice Godelier, "Some Things You Give, Some Things You Sell, but Some Things You Must Keep for Yourselves: What Mauss Did Not Say about Sacred Objects," trans. Nora Scott, in *The Enigma of Gift and Sacrifice*, ed. Edith Wyschogrod, Jean-Joseph Goux, and Eric Boynton (New York: Fordham University Press, 2002), 19–37; Maurice Godelier, *The Enigma of the Gift*, trans. Nora Scott (Chicago: University of Chicago Press, 1999); Lewis Hyde, *The Gift: Imagination and the Erotic Life of Property* (New York: Random House, 1983); William Ian Miller, "Is a Gift Forever?," *Representations* 100 (2007): 13–22; Moïse Schwab, trans., *Le Talmud de Jérusalem*, vol. 4 (Paris: Éditions G.-P. Maisonneuve, 1960), 238; Gabrielle S. Adams, Francis

J. Flynn, and Michael I. Norton, "The Gifts We Keep on Giving: Documenting and Destig-matizing the Regifting Taboo," *Pyschological Science* 23 (2012): 1145–50.

16. The term "regifting" has no equivalent in the languages of Roman late antiquity. Of course, there were other circumlocutions. For example, the *Life of Antony* quotes Antony's verbal bequest of the sheepskin Athanasius had originally given Antony back to Athanasius. In her analysis of this passage, Thelma Thomas correctly, in my view, labels this "regift-ing." See Thelma Thomas, "The Honorific Mantle as Furnishing for the Household Memory Theater in Late Antiquity: A Case Study from the Monastery of Apa Apollo at Bawit," in *Catalogue of the Textiles in the Dumbarton Oaks Byzantine Collection*, ed. Gudrun Bühl and Elizabeth Dospěl Williams (Washington, DC: Dumbarton Oaks, 2019), accessed March 5, 2020, https://www.doaks.org/resources/textiles/essays/thomas. The most common meta-phor used among Christian writers of late antiquity to capture the importance of what I call here "regifting" is that of debt repayment. Examples abound, but I cite here Origen's exege-sis of Psalm 36:21 as a paradigmatic case (Homily 3.11 on Psalm 36). Origen interprets the line, "the sinner borrows and will not repay, but the righteous has compassion and gives," to mean that God gives to all in abundance by way of loan. Sinners use the loan for themselves and do not repay it, while the righteous not only repay the loan but return it with interest at a high rate. The return of the loan with interest is imagined in the manner of Luke 19:16 (the Parable of the Talents), but concretely refers, according to Origen, to spreading the true word of God *to others* and living an exemplary life *to others* in accordance with the word of God. On the face of it, the analogy to debt could lead one to see God as practicing usury, but the dynamic described is not simply one of reciprocal giving but circular giving. For an edition of the Greek text, see Lorenzo Perrone, ed., *Origenes Werke*, vol. 13 (Berlin: Walter de Gruyter, 2015), 153–55; for an edition of the Latin, see SC 411:168–75.

17. This chapter analyzes evidence primarily from consecratory festivities, but it is worth noting here that Gregory Nazianzen pinpoints the "ministry of souls" (θεραπεία τῶν ψυχῶν) as the purpose of festivals in general. In the context of an oration delivered to shore up sup-port for the construction of Basil of Caesarea's leprosarium, Gregory calls attention to the attendance of lepers at festivals. Gregory explains what he means by "festival" (*panēgyris*) with this line: "I am referring, of course, to those religious festivals (πανηγύρεις) that we have organized for the public as a way of ministering to souls (θεραπείᾳ τῶν ψυχῶν)." *Oration* 14.12; PG 35:873. Translation from FC 107:47.

18. An important topic in social anthropology has been the problem of distinguish-ing gift from commodity. In my preference here for "regifting" over "recommoditization," I am assuming the perspective of the bishops. Since "recommoditization" implies a former state of singularity (which "regifting" does not necessarily entail), it characterizes donors' perspective on the transaction (see chapter 4). On the issues of differentiating gift exchange too starkly from commodity circulation, see Arjun Appadurai, "Introduction: Commodi-ties and the Politics of Value," in *The Social Life of Things: Commodities in Cultural Per-spective*, ed. Appadurai (New York: Cambridge University Press, 1986), 3–63; Kenneth Hayes Lokensgard, *Blackfoot Religion and the Consequences of Cultural Commoditization* (Farnham: Ashgate, 2010).

19. Hyde, 16.

20. I rely on Weiner, 131–44 to describe the Kula exchange.

21. Bronislaw Malinowski, "Kula: The Circulating Exchange of Valuables in the Archipelagoes of Eastern New Guinea," *Man* 20 (1920): 97–105; Malinowski, *Argonauts of the Western Pacific.*

22. Mauss; Weiner; Godelier, *Enigma of the Gift*; Hyde.

23. Weiner, 140.

24. Vincent Déroche, *Études sur Léontios de Néapolis*, Acta Universitatis Upsaliensis, Studia Byzantina Upsaliensia 3 (Uppsala: Uppsala Universitet, 1995), 238–54; Daniel Caner, "Towards a Miraculous Economy: Christian Gifts and Material 'Blessings' in Late Antiquity," *JECS* 14 (2006): 329–77; Caner, "Alms, Blessings, Offerings: The Repertoire of Christian Gifts in Early Byzantium," in *The Gift in Antiquity*, ed. Michael L. Satlow (Malden, MA: Wiley-Blackwell, 2013), 25–44.

25. Caner, "Miraculous Economy," 330 (my emphasis). For further studies on circular giving based primarily on monastic sources, see the following: Daniel Caner, *Wandering, Begging Monks: Spiritual Authority and the Promotion of Monasticism in Late Antiquity* (Berkeley: University of California Press, 2002); Susan Ashbrook Harvey, "Praying Bodies, Bodies at Prayer: Ritual Relations in Early Syriac Christianity," in *Prayer and Spirituality in the Early Church*, vol. 4, *The Spiritual Life*, ed. Wendy Mayer, Pauline Allen, and Lawrence Cross (Strathfield: St. Paul's Publications, 2006), 149–67.

26. Deborah Deliyannis notes that the imperial couple never visited Ravenna. See Deborah Mauskopf Deliyannis, *Ravenna in Late Antiquity* (New York: Cambridge University Press, 2010), 241. Irina Andreescu-Treadgold and Warren Treadgold have shown that the bishop depicted is Victor, who was expected to consecrate the church but who died before the festival took place. The inscription names his successor Maximianus, who in fact consecrated San Vitale. See Irina Andreescu-Treadgold and Warren Treadgold, "Procopius and the Imperial Panels of S. Vitale," *Art Bulletin* 79 (1997): 719. Natalia Teteriatnikov makes a case for identifying the procession as taking place on the Feast of the Resurrection. See Natalia Teteriatnikov, "Gender and Ritual: Mosaic Panels of Justinian and Theodora in San Vitale," in *ANAΘHMATA EOPTIKA: Studies in Honor of Thomas F. Mathews*, ed. Joseph D. Alchermes, Helen C. Evans, and Thelma K. Thomas (Mainz: Verlag Philipp von Zabern, 2009), 301–3. However, given that the original bishop depicted was Victor (in anticipation of his consecration of the church), it is more likely that the procession imagined is that of the consecratory festival. Of course, this does not preclude the possibility that the inauguration took place on the Feast of the Resurrection.

27. Holum and Vikan (127–32) argue that the scene specifically portrays the consecration of the Church of Saint Stephen in Constantinople founded by the empress Pulcheria in 421. Not all scholars agree with their interpretation and a consensus has yet to be reached. For different interpretations, see, most recently, Paroma Chatterjee, "Iconoclasm's Legacy: Interpreting the Trier Ivory," *Art Bulletin* 100 (2018): 28–47. By all accounts, however, the scene depicts a relic *adventus* ceremony, real or imagined.

28. Holum and Vikan, 116–20. According to Holum and Vikan, an *adventus* ceremony can be divided into three stages: the *synantesis* when dignitaries are met and received by the populace, the *propompe*, a procession of the dignitaries and populace to the church, and the *apothesis*, the entrance into the church to deposit gifts. The ivory depicts the second stage.

It was not yet required that relics be deposited in order for a church to be consecrated. Rules would not be written to this effect until the seventh or eighth century, depending on the region. The second canon of a council held in Gaul sometime after 614 required relics to be deposited in a church in order for its altar to be consecrated (CCSL 148A:287). Canon 7 of the Second Council of Nicaea held in 787 prescribed that all new churches required relics to be consecrated and all churches that had already been consecrated without relics had to acquire relics (Joannou, 1.1:260–261).

29. An image of Christ is represented on the gate, which was added in the seventh century at the earliest. Holum and Vikan, 125.

30. According to Holum and Vikan (121n40), the emperor is wearing "the diadem and chlamys, the full-length cloak secured on the right shoulder with an elaborate jeweled fibula."

31. Holum and Vikan, 122.

32. Holum and Vikan, 122.

33. Holum and Vikan, 124.

34. George Galavaris, *The Illustrations of the Liturgical Homilies of Gregory Nazianzus* (Princeton, NJ: Princeton University Press, 1969), plate II.4 (Moscow, State Historical Museum, Cod. 146, fol. 23v, eleventh century); plate VI.28 (Turin, University Library, Cod. C.I.6, fol. 16r, eleventh century); plate LXXVII.380, (Sinai, Monastery of St. Catherine, Cod. Gr. 339, fol. 42v, twelfth century); plate CIV.457 (Paris, Bibliothèque Nationale, Cod. Gr. 543, fol. 51v, fourteenth century).

35. Orators would "lead" the listeners "around," a rhetorical strategy known by its ancient name of *periēgēsis*. Christine Smith, "Christian Rhetoric in Eusebius' Panegyric at Tyre," *Vigiliae Christianae* 43 (1989): 228; Ruth Webb, "The Aesthetics of Sacred Space: Narrative, Metaphor, and Motion in *Ekphraseis* of Church Buildings," *DOP* 53 (1999): 59–74.

36. Choricius of Gaza does explicitly refer to the church and its ornamentation as a gift. For example, he writes that Emperor Justinian (together with Archon Stephanus and Bishop Marcian) gifted (ἐδωρήσατο) the church to the citizens (*Marc.* I.30). Richard Foerster and Eberhard Richtsteig, eds., *Choricii Gazaei Opera* (Leipzig: B. G. Teubner, 1929), 10.

37. Choricius of Gaza, *Marc.* I.45.

38. On the πανήγυρις, see Speros Vryonis, "The Panēgyris of the Byzantine Saint: A Study in the Nature of a Medieval Institution, Its Origins and Fate," in *The Byzantine Saint: University of Birmingham Fourteenth Spring Symposium of Byzantine Studies*, ed. Sergei Hackel, Studies Supplementary to Sobornost 5 (London: Fellowship of St. Alban and St. Sergius, 1981): 196–227; Anna Usacheva, "The Term πανήγυρις in the Holy Bible and Christian Literature of the Fourth Century and the Development of Christian Panegyric Genre," *Studia Patristica* 62 (2013): 57–68. For a study of how the meaning of spectacles at festivals transformed in Christian late antiquity, see Byron MacDougall, "Spectatorship in City and Church in Late Antiquity: Theoria Returns to the Festival," in *From Constantinople to the Frontier: The City and the Cities*, ed. Nicholas S. M. Matheou, Theofili Kampianaki, and Lorenzo M. Bondioli (Leiden: Brill, 2016), 127–41.

39. Fotios K. Litsas, "Choricius of Gaza and His Descriptions of Festivals at Gaza," *Jahrbuch der österreichischen Byzantinistik* 32 (1982): 427.

40. Choricius of Gaza, *Marc.* I.1. Translation from Fotios K. Litsas, "Choricius of Gaza: An Approach to His Work: Introduction, Translation, Commentary" (PhD diss., University

of Chicago, 1980), 111. In ancient Greece, the *theoros* was a representative sent to attend the religious festival. See the section below on the practice of *theōria*.

41. Choricius of Gaza, *Marc.* I.83.

42. Choricius of Gaza, *Marc.* I.10. Translation from Litsas, "Choricius of Gaza: An Approach to His Work," 113.

43. For encomia, see Choricius of Gaza, *Marc.* I.4–9 and 78. For epideictic speeches, see Choricius of Gaza, *Marc.* I.16ff.

44. Choricius of Gaza, *Marc.* I.84.

45. Choricius of Gaza, *Marc.* I.83 and 85; Foerster and Richtsteig, 23. Translation from Litsas, "Choricius of Gaza: An Approach to His Work," 130.

46. Choricius of Gaza, *Marc.* I.86. Translation from Litsas, "Choricius of Gaza: An Approach to His Work," 131.

47. Choricius of Gaza, *Marc.* I.87.

48. Choricius of Gaza, *Marc.* I.93.

49. Choricius of Gaza, *Marc.* II.2.

50. Choricius of Gaza, *Marc.* II.9.

51. Choricius of Gaza, *Marc.* II.58.

52. Choricius of Gaza, *Marc.* II.60.

53. Choricius of Gaza, *Marc.* II.61.

54. Choricius of Gaza, *Marc.* II.62–63.

55. Choricius of Gaza, *Marc.* II.64–65.

56. Choricius of Gaza, *Marc.* II.66, 69.

57. Choricius of Gaza, *Marc.* II.72.

58. Choricius of Gaza, *Marc.* II.75. Translation from Litsas, "Choricius of Gaza: An Approach to His Work," 152. The postfestival report on return was a key duty of the *theoros* in ancient Greece. See the section below on the practice of *theōria*.

59. Choricius of Gaza, *Marc.* II.78.

60. Luigi Canetti discusses these celestial-earthly social ties generated by gift giving—namely, what I here call the "circle of sanctity." *Pace* Canetti, the celestial patrons do not become the legal owners of ecclesial property; rather, they protect the property. See Luigi Canetti, "Christian Gift and Gift Exchange from Late Antiquity to the Early Middle Ages," in *Gift Giving and the "Embedded" Economy in the Ancient World*, ed. Filippo Carlà and Maja Gori (Heidelberg: Universitätsverlag Winter, 2014), 343–44.

61. See chapter 4.

62. For a discussion of how Anicia Juliana's church building activities functioned in her and her husband Areobindus's bid for imperial power, see Diliana N. Angelova, *Sacred Founders: Women, Men, and Gods in the Discourse of Imperial Founding, Rome through Early Byzantium* (Oakland: University of California Press, 2015), 225–32.

63. For a study on the anthology, see Alan Cameron, *The Greek Anthology: From Meleager to Planudes* (New York: Oxford University Press, 1992).

64. Carolyn L. Connor, "The Epigram in the Church of Hagios Polyeuktos in Constantinople and Its Byzantine Response," *Byzantion* 69 (1999): 484 and 495–96; Mary Whitby, "The St Polyeuktos Epigram (*AP* 1.10): A Literary Perspective," in *Greek Literature in Late Antiquity: Dynamism, Didacticism, Classicism*, ed. Scott Johnson (Burlington, VT: Ashgate, 2006), 161–65.

65. On the church and its remains. see R. M. Harrison, *A Temple for Byzantium: The Discovery and Excavation of Anicia Juliana's Palace-Church in Istanbul* (Austin: University of Texas Press, 1989). On the monumental inscription and its remains, see Cyril Mango and Ihor Ševčenko, "Remains of the Church of St. Polyeuktos at Constantinople," *DOP* 15 (1961): 243–47. According to Carolyn Connor, "the ceremony of dedication of the church very likely included a reading of the epigram, for it sums up the history, incentive and pretentions that led to its creation," and she suggests that Anicia Juliana herself probably composed the epigram. See Connor, 506 and 516. On the "oralized reading" of Greek epigrams and their reception by various kinds of audiences, see Gianfranco Agosti, "*Saxa loquuntur?* Epigrammi epigrafici e diffusione della *paideia* nell'oriente tardoantico," *Antiquité Tardive* 18 (2010): 163–80. A number of studies have focused on the explicit claim in line 48 of surpassing Solomon and the resonance of this claim with the construction of structures competing for greater magnificence. See Georg Scheja, "Hagia Sophia und Templum Salomonis," *Istanbuler Mitteilungen* 12 (1962): 44–58; R. M. Harrison, "The Church of St. Polyeuktos in Istanbul and the Temple of Solomon," *Harvard Ukrainian Studies* 7 (1983): 276–79; Jonathan Bardill, "A New Temple for Byzantium: Anicia Juliana, King Solomon, and the Gilded Ceiling of the Church of St. Polyeuktos in Constantinople," in *Social and Political Life in Late Antiquity*, ed. William Bowden, Adam Gutteridge, and Carlos Machado (Leiden: Brill, 2006), 339–70; Peter N. Bell, "Hagia Sophia: Ideology in Stone— A Case Study," in *Social Conflict in the Age of Justinian* (Oxford: Oxford University Press, 2013), 319–36.

66. Connor, 481. Carolyn Connor argues that Anicia Juliana composed the epigram herself, while Mary Whitby, following Francesco Tissoni (who in turn took up a suggestion by F. Baumgarten), argues that Christodorus of Coptus composed it. See Connor, 515–16, and Whitby, 180–85.

67. Translation from Connor, 519.

68. Translation from Connor, 519.

69. Translation from Whitby, 163.

70. J. Josephus Overbeck, ed., *S. Ephraemi Syri, Rabulae Episcopae Edesseni, Balaei Aliorum Opera Selecta* (Oxford: Clarendon Press, 1865), 251–58.

71. Translation from Kathleen E. McVey, "The Sogitha on the Church of Edessa in the Context of Other Early Greek and Syriac Hymns for the Consecration of Church Buildings," *ARAM* 5 (1993): 361–62.

72. Kathleen McVey shows that it is possible Balai knew Eusebius's homily (see below), since the *Ecclesiastical History* was transmitted in Syriac translation probably quite early (our earliest attestation of the text in Syriac dates to AD 462). See McVey, 338.

73. Translation from McVey, 361–62 (my emphasis).

74. Paulinus of Nola, *Carm.* 27.639–47; CSEL 30:290–91. Translation from P. G. Walsh, *The Poems of St. Paulinus of Nola* (New York: Newman Press, 1975), 293. On the cult of Saint Felix and Paulinus's role in shaping it, see Dennis E. Trout, *Paulinus of Nola: Life, Letters, and Poems* (Berkeley: University of California Press, 1999), 160–97.

75. Paulinus asks this question in a poem he composed for the consecration of a baptistery for the Basilica of Saint Felix in 404, one year after the renovated basilica itself was consecrated, and again on Saint Felix's *dies natalis*. *Carm.* 28.279–81; CSEL 30:303. Translation from Walsh, 304.

76. Andrea Wilson Nightingale, "The Philosopher at the Festival: Plato's Transformation of Traditional *Theōria*," in *Pilgrimage in Graeco-Roman and Early Christian Antiquity: Seeing the Gods*, ed. Jaś Elsner and Ian Rutherford (New York: Oxford University Press, 2005), 171.

77. Nightingale, 155–58. For a book-length study of this topic, see Ian Rutherford, *State Pilgrims and Sacred Observers in Ancient Greece: A Study of* Theōria *and* Theōroi (Cambridge: Cambridge University Press, 2013).

78. Nightingale, 165.

79. Nightingale, 166–67.

80. Nightingale, 171.

81. Nightingale, 170.

82. For a study of, for example, Gregory Nazianzen's use of festivals to model the practice of *theōria*, see Byron MacDougall, "Gregory of Nazianzus and Christian Festival Rhetoric" (PhD diss., Brown University, 2015); MacDougall, "Spectatorship in City and Church," 134–41. Johan Leemans collects a number of passages in which fourth-century orators comment on the educational value of the homilies preached and the images viewed at festivals for martyrs. See Johan Leemans, "'Schoolrooms for Our Souls.' The Cult of the Martyrs: Homilies and Visual Representations as a Locus for Religious Education in Late Antiquity," *Paedagogica Historica: International Journal of the History of Education* 36 (2000): 112–27.

83. Jeremy M. Schott, "Eusebius' *Panegyric on the Building of Churches* (*HE* 10.4.2–72): Aesthetics and the Politics of Christian Architecture," in *Reconsidering Eusebius: Collected Papers on Literary, Historical, and Theological Issues*, ed. Sabrina Inowlocki and Claudio Zamagni (Leiden: Brill, 2011), 193–95.

84. W. R. Paton, ed. and trans., *The Greek Anthology*, vol. 1, revised by Michael A. Tueller, Loeb Classical Library 67 (Cambridge, MA: Harvard University Press, 2014), 32–33 (my emphasis).

85. Translation adapted from Cyril Mango, *The Art of the Byzantine Empire* (Toronto: University of Toronto Press, 1986), 129 (my emphasis).

86. These are not the only homilies and hymns composed for specific church consecrations to survive from late antiquity. Others exist, too, such as those of Avitus of Vienne, Ennodius of Pavia, and Venantius Fortunatus. As Ian Wood notes with regard to Gallic and Italian sources, it is not always possible to determine whether a homily was delivered at the consecration of a church or at anniversary celebration of the occasion (Wood, 74). On Venantius Fortunatus's poems, see Wilhelm Meyer, *Der Gelegenheitsdichter Venantius Fortunatus* (Berlin: Weidmannsche Buchhandlung, 1901). On Ennodius of Pavia, see C. Sotinel, "L'évergétisme dans le royaume gothique: le témoignage d'Ennode de Pavie," in *Homenatge a F. Giunta: Committenza e committenti tra antichità e alto medioevo*, ed. Marc Mayer Olivé and Mònica Miró Vinaixa (Barcelona: PPU—Littera—Departament Filologia Llatina UB, 1996), 213–22. On Avitus of Vienne, see Wood.

87. Leemans et al., viii.

88. Ambrose of Milan, *Ep.* 77.22; Gaudentius of Brecia, *Tractatus* 17.1.

89. Eusebius, *HE* 10.4.65. Translation from FC 29:265–66.

90. Eusebius, *HE* 10.4.63. Translation from FC 29:265.

91. Eusebius, *HE* 10.4.63. Translation from FC 29:265.

92. Eusebius, *HE* 10.4.64. Translation from FC 29:265.

93. Eusebius, *HE* 10.4.66.

94. Eusebius, *HE* 10.4.68. Translation from FC 29:266.

95. Cf. FC 29:266n100. We do not know what the Cathedral of Tyre looked like at the time of Eusebius's homily, so it is impossible to know what sort of painted programs may have covered the interior walls. The "Basilica of Quarter Sand" was identified with the Cathedral of Tyre, but Sophie Garreau-Forrest and Ali Khalil Badawi have recently made the case that the "Basilica of Quarter Sand" actually corresponds to sixth-century descriptions of a church named "Saint Mary of Swamp." See Sophie Garreau-Forrest and Ali Khalil Badawi, "La cathédrale de Paulin de Tyr décrite par Eusèbe de Césarée: mythe ou réalité?" *Antiquité Tardive* 22 (2014): 111–23.

It is not inconceivable that the artists conveyed visibly what Eusebius describes verbally, since Eusebius was not the first or the last to use architectural features as metaphors for human souls. In a temple of Zeus in Agrigento, Italy, for example, sculpted human bodies did serve as structural features. See Slobodan Ćurčić, "Architecture as Icon," in *Architecture as Icon: Perception and Representation of Architecture in Byzantine Art*, ed. Slobodan Ćurčić and Evangelia Hadjitryphonos (Princeton, NJ: Princeton University Art Museum, 2010), 11. More examples could be cited from Athens and Palmyra. See John Mitchell, "The Painted Decoration of San Salvatore de Brescia in Context," in *Dalla corte regia al monastero di San Salvatore—Santa Giulia de Brescia*, ed. Gian Pietro Brogiolo and Francesca Morandini (Mantua: SAP Società Archeologica, 2014), 174n38.

Late antique paintings in the Red Monastery Church sanctuary in Sohag, Egypt depict biblical and episcopal saints as architectural piers. See Elizabeth S. Bolman, "The Iconography of Salvation," in *The Red Monastery Church: Beauty and Asceticism in Upper Egypt*, ed. Bolman (New Haven, CT: Yale University Press, 2016), 128–49, figs. 10.19, 22–24, and 26–28. See also Mitchell, 174–76 for a discussion of how painted clipeate bust portraits over columns at San Salvatore de Brescia may have invoked (or evoked) similar associations.

96. Eusebius, *HE* 10.4.22. Translation from FC 29:251.

97. Eusebius, *HE* 10.4.55. Translation from FC 29:262.

98. Eusebius, *HE* 10.4.55.

99. Translation from McVey, 353–59.

100. As disparate as the examples appear to be, André Grabar offers an explanation as to how they cohere. See André Grabar, "Le témoignage d'une hymne syriaque sur l'architecture de la cathédrale d'Édesse au VIᵉ siècle et sur la symbolique de l'édifice chrétien," *Cahiers archéologiques* 2 (1947): 55.

101. Translation from McVey, 356.

102. W. E. Crum, "Inscriptions from Shenoute's Monastery," *JTS*, o.s., 5 (1904): 554–55.

103. Shenoute of Atripe, Canon 7.7 (*This Great House*). Stephen Emmel, "The Historical Circumstances of Shenoute's Sermon *God is Blessed*," θΕΜΕΛΙΑ: *Spätantike und koptologische Studien Peter Grossmann zum 65. Geburtstag*, ed. Martin Krause and Sofia Schaten (Wiesbaden: Reichert Verlag, 1998), 83. Caroline T. Schroeder has drawn forth in great detail the work that Shenoute does in *This Great House* and related homilies to map exemplary asceticism onto the contours of the church building. See Caroline T. Schroeder, "The Church Building as Symbol of Ascetic Renunciation," in *Monastic Bodies: Discipline and Salvation in Shenoute of Atripe* (Philadelphia: University of Pennsylvania Press, 2007), 90–125. My purpose here is to situate Shenoute's *This Great House* among several examples of

consecratory homilies that produce theological and moral reflection, which in turn produces a ritual economy distinct from the legal economy.

104. Shenoute of Atripe, Canon 7.7.46.

105. Shenoute of Atripe, Canon 7.7.54.

106. Shenoute of Atripe, Canon 7.7.54. Translation adapted from a provisional draft by Frederik Wisse.

107. Cf. Schroeder, 109–11. Caroline Schroeder shows how Shenoute, in other homilies of Canon 7, creates and explains hierarchical relationships. Most telling for my purposes here is the following excerpt Schroeder translates from *God is Holy*: "every adornment that is in the house of God in wood, in stone, in walls, in every place in it, and everything that is of any sort or any color, they are good, and it is possible for us to bring them to the spiritual, since they are fleshly things, like water that became wine in Cana of Galilee" (110–11).

108. Augustine of Hippo, *Serm.* 337.2. Translation from Edmund Hill, *Sermons*, ed. John E. Rotelle, The Works of Saint Augustine: A Translation for the 21st Century part 3, vol. 9 (Hyde Park, NY: New City Press, 1994), 272. Augustine preached sermons 336, 337, and 338 at the consecration of churches. I cite 337 only, though all three are similar in content. See Finbarr G. Clancy, "Augustine's Sermons for the Dedication of a Church," *Studia Patristica* 38 (2001): 48–55; Jane E. Merdinger, "Building God's House: Augustine's Homilies at Episcopal Consecrations, Church Dedications, and Funerals," *Studia Patristica* 43 (2006): 195–200.

109. Augustine of Hippo, *Serm.* 337.1. Translation from Hill, 3.9:271.

110. Augustine of Hippo, *Serm.* 337.5. Translation from Hill, 3.9:274 (my emphasis).

111. TTH 19:xi.

112. Sermons 227, 228, and 229. Sermon 228 explicitly refers to the consecration of an altar. It is possible that sermons 227 and 229 were delivered at an anniversary celebration of a church's consecration.

113. Caesarius of Arles, *Serm.* 227.3.

114. Caesarius of Arles, *Serm.* 227.6 and 229.5.

115. Caesarius of Arles, *Serm.* 229.5. Translation from FC 66:177.

116. Caesarius of Arles, *Serm.* 229.1; CCSL 104:905. Translation from FC 66:173.

117. Caesarius of Arles, *Serm.* 228.1. Translation from FC 66:168.

118. Caesarius of Arles, *Serm.* 229.2. Translation from FC 66:174.

119. Bissera Pentcheva has described the phenomenological effect that glittery and reflective surfaces have as "liveliness" or "animation." Pentcheva's work is important to note for our purposes because it shows that Eusebius's, Caesarius's, and the anonymous composer of the kontakion's visual exemplars for what the invisible soul ought to "look" like was not the still, inanimate, lifeless view of a photograph, but the dynamic, animated, and lively performance of light on glittery and reflective surfaces. See Bissera V. Pentcheva, "The Performative Icon," *Art Bulletin* 88 (2006): 631–55; Pentcheva, "The Power of Glittering Materiality: Mirror Reflections between Poetry and Architecture in Greek and Arabic Medieval Culture," in *Istanbul and Water*, ed. Paul Magdalino and Nina Ergin, Ancient Near Eastern Studies Supplement 47 (Leuven: Peeters, 2015), 241–74; Pentcheva, "Glittering Eyes: Animation in the Byzantine *Eikōn* and the Western *Imago*," *Codex Aquilarensis* 32 (2016): 209–36.

120. On the dates of the festivities for the reconsecration of Hagia Sophia, see TTH 52:17–18. I am grateful to Sysse Gudrun Engberg for calling my attention to issues regarding the date(s) of the reconsecration festivities.

121. C. A. Trypanis, ed., *Fourteen Early Byzantine Cantica*, Wiener byzantinische Studien 5 (Vienna: Hermann Böhlaus Nachfolger, 1968), 141. Translation from Andrew Palmer, "The Inauguration Anthem of Hagia Sophia in Edessa: A New Edition and Translation with Historical and Architectural Notes and A Comparison with a Contemporary Constantinopolitan Kontakion," *Byzantine and Modern Greek Studies* 12 (1988): 140 (my emphasis).

122. The kontakion's association of virtues with luminosity may build on a tradition of associating specific jewels with particular virtues. As Michael Roberts has noted, "Virtues are regularly described as jewels." In fact, a story recorded in the *Life of Pachomius* describes how he interpreted each jewel on a painted crown in the monastic assembly room at Pboou as a different virtue (SBo 73). See Michael Roberts, *The Jeweled Style: Poetry and Poetics in Late Antiquity* (Ithaca, NY: Cornell University Press, 1989), 144. On the significance of the story in the *Life of Pachomius*, see Paul C. Dilley, "Textual Aesthetics: *Dipinti* and the Early Byzantine Epigraphic Habit," in Bolman, *The Red Monastery Church*, 178–79.

123. Translation from Palmer, 141.

124. Translation from Palmer, 142.

125. Translation from Palmer, 141–42.

126. Translation from Palmer, 141–42.

127. As noted previously, Bissera Pentcheva's work in demonstrating the importance of phenomenology is significant for the claims I make here. My interest lies in how the luminous performances of the cosmos and ecclesial architecture are used to create visual images of the invisible soul, but the soul-images of the kontakion I analyze here can only be fully understood in the context of Pentcheva's work on how the ecclesial architecture of Hagia Sophia recreates the effect of light on water. See Bissera V. Pentcheva, "Hagia Sophia and Multisensory Aesthetics," *Gesta* 50 (2011): 93–111; Pentcheva, *Hagia Sophia: Sound, Space, and Spirit in Byzantium* (University Park: Pennsylvania State University Press, 2017).

128. *Vita Caesarii* I.37–38; SC 536:198 and 200. Translation from TTH 19:27–28.

129. SC 536:198. Translation from TTH 19:28.

130. Antony Eastmond, "Consular Diptychs, Rhetoric and the Languages of Art in Sixth-Century Constantinople," *Art History* 33 (2010): 747. On the subject of silver plates as gifts, see J. M. C. Toynbee and K. S. Painter, "Silver Picture Plates of Late Antiquity: A.D. 300 to 700," *Archaeologia* 108 (1986): 15–65. J. M. C. Toynbee notes at the outset that silver flatware was probably more often that not hung on the walls as decorative plates.

131. *Vita Caesarii* I.38. Translation from TTH 19:28.

132. Bede, *HE* 3.14; Bertram Colgrave and R. A. B. Mynors, eds. and trans., *Bede's Ecclesiastical History of the English People* (Oxford: Clarendon Press, 1969), 258–59.

133. See chapter 4.

134. Amber Epp and Linda Price note that recommoditization is undertheorized and offer a detailed case study to extend Kopytoff's theory. See Amber M. Epp and Linda L. Price, "The Storied Life of Singularized Objects: Forces of Agency and Network Transformation," *Journal of Consumer Research* 36 (2010): 820–37. See also Filippo Carlà, "Exchange of the Saints: Gift-Giving and the Commerce of Relics," in Carlà and Gori, 429–30.

135. Among the many studies on this shift, see above all Peter Brown, *Through the Eye of a Needle: Wealth, the Fall of Rome, and the Making of Christianity in the West, 350–550 AD*

(Princeton, NJ: Princeton University Press, 2012). See also Michele Renee Salzman, "From a Classical to a Christian City: Civic Euergetism and Charity in Late Antique Rome," *Studies in Late Antiquity* 1 (2017): 65–85; Peter van Nuffelen, "Social Ethics and Moral Discourse in Late Antiquity," in *Reading Patristic Texts on Social Ethics: Issues and Challenges for Twenty-First Century Christian Social Thought*, ed. Johan Leemans, Brian J. Matz, and Johan Verstraeten (Washington, DC: Catholic University of America Press, 2011), 45–63.

136. Brown, 40. This is echoed in the Liturgy of John Chrysostom. See Stefano Parenti and Elena Velkovska, eds., *L'Eucologio Barberini Gr. 336 (ff. 1–263)* (Rome: C. L. V. Edizioni Liturgiche, 1995), 34.

137. See chapter 2.

138. Translation from Robert Doran, *Stewards of the Poor: The Man of God, Rabbula, and Hiba in Fifth-Century Edessa* (Kalamazoo, MI: Cistercian Publications, 2006), 76–77.

139. Cf. Acacius of Amida's reasons for melting down sacred vessels to redeem enemy captives according to Socrates (*HE* 7.21): "Our God, my brethren, needs neither dishes nor cups [. . .]." Cf. Hypatius of Ephesus's acknowledgment that God does not need gold or silver but his simultaneous recognition of the educational value of ecclesial adornment for visual learners (Mango, 116–17).

140. Doran, 77.

141. Doran, 90. Cf. Han J. W. Drijvers, "The Man of God of Edessa, Bishop Rabbula, and the Urban Poor: Church and Society in the Fifth Century," *JECS* 4 (1996): 241.

142. John Chrysostom, *In Matt. hom.* 50; PG 58:508.

143. Ysabel de Andia, "Liturgie des pauvres et théologie du corps du Christ chez saint Jean Chrysostome," *Proche-orient chrétien* 51 (2001): 247–60. Most recently, see Junghun Bae, *John Chrysostom on Almsgiving and Therapy of the Soul*, Patristic Studies in Global Perspective 1 (Paderborn: Brill / Ferdinand Schöningh, 2021).

144. John Chrysostom, *In 2 Cor. hom.* 20; PG 61:540. On the poor as altars in John Chrysostom's thought, see Catherine Broc-Schmezer, "De l'aumône faite au pauvre à l'aumône du pauvre: Pauvreté et spiritualité chez Jean Chrysostome," in *Les Pères de l'Église et la voix des pauvres: Actes du IIᵉ colloque de La Rochelle 2, 3, et 4 septembre 2005*, ed. Pascal-Grégoire Delage (La Rochelle: Histoire et Culture, 2006), 131–48. Earlier theological literature compared widows to altars. Much has been written on this subject. See Marianne Bjelland Kartzow, *Gossip and Gender: Othering Speech in the Pastoral Epistles* (Berlin: Walter de Gruyter, 2009), 167 and the references there.

145. Lucian, *The Hall*, or literally, "Concerning the House," in *Lucian*, vol. 1, trans. A. M. Harmon, Loeb Classical Library 14 (Cambridge, MA: Harvard University Press, 1913), 176–207.

146. Ruth Webb, "Sight and Insight: Theorizing Vision, Emotion, and Imagination in Ancient Rhetoric," in *Sight and the Ancient Senses*, ed. Michael Squire (Abingdon: Routledge, 2016), 205; Webb, *Ekphrasis, Imagination and Persuasion in Ancient Rhetorical Theory and Practice* (Farnham: Ashgate, 2009), 172–74.

147. *Paralipomena* 32, chapter 13 (cf. *Life of Pachomius* G² 46 and Am 632; Paradise of the Holy Fathers ch. 16). Translation from Armand Veilleux, *Pachomian Chronicles and Rules*, Pachomian Koinonia 2, Cistercian Studies Series 46 (Kalamazoo, MI: Cistercian Publications, 1981), 55–56. For a discussion of how the story may serve as an apology for faulty construction, see Schroeder, 121–22 and the references there.

148. For more examples of Christian reports in late antiquity and beyond of the repurposing of ecclesial gold, see Thomas Sternberg, "'Aurum utile': Zu einem Topos vom Vorrang der Caritas über Kirchenschätze seit Ambrosius," *Jahrbuch für Antike und Christentum* 39 (1996): 128–48.

149. Ambrose of Milan, *Off.* 2.111; Ivor J. Davidson, ed. and trans., *Ambrose: De Officiis*, vol. 1 (New York: Oxford University Press, 2001), 329–31.

150. Ambrose of Milan, *Off.* 2.143. Translation from Davidson, 1:349. Ivor Davidson argues that Ambrose probably melted down golden vessels that had been acquired during the episcopacy of his *homoian* predecessor Auxentius, but, as Michael Williams shows, this reasoning falls into the trap of Ambrose's rhetorical strategy to lump (and thereby dismiss) all his critics into the category of "Arian." See Michael Stuart Williams, *The Politics of Heresy in Ambrose of Milan: Community and Consensus in Late-Antique Christianity* (Cambridge: Cambridge University Press, 2017), 172–73. Davidson further argues that the vessels must not yet have been consecrated (2:790–91), but this is not necessarily the case. Ambrose is at pains from sections 136 to 143 to explain when ecclesiastical leaders ought to repurpose even *consecrated* vessels.

151. Ambrose of Milan, *Off.* 2.138. Translation from Davidson, 1:345.

152. Ambrose of Milan, *Off.* 2.139. Translation from Davidson, 1:344–45.

153. Nor are they the only ones to comment on the spiritual significance of church architecture. Liturgical commentaries, for instance, also drew analogies between the human person, the church edifice, and the cosmos. For examples, see Mary K. Farag, "The Mosaic Map of Madaba and Late Antique Discourse on Ecclesial Space," in ⲤⲨⲚⲀⲌⲒⲤ ⲔⲀⲐⲞⲖⲒⲔⲎ: *Beiträge zu Gottesdienst und Geschichte der fünf altkirchlichen Patriarchate für Heinzgerd Brakmann zum 70. Geburtstag*, ed. Diliana Atanassova and Tinatin Chronz (Münster: LIT Verlag, 2014), 175–96. For other genres, see R. W. Thomson, "Architectural Symbolism in Classical Armenian Literature," *JTS*, n.s., 30 (1979): 102–14; Grabar, 54–61.

154. The first half of the poem was delivered at the imperial palace. Mary Whitby argues that the second half was delivered in the patriarchal palace, not the church. See Mary Whitby, "The Occasion of Paul the Silentiary's *Ekphrasis* of S. Sophia," *Classical Quarterly* 35 (1985): 216–17. As for hypotheses concerning the exact date of the Silentiary's speech, see TTH 52:17–18.

155. Lines 764–96; Paul Friedländer, ed., *Johannes von Gaza und Paulus Silentiarius: Kunstbeschreibungen Justinianischer Zeit* (Leipzig: B. G. Teubner, 1912), 248–49. On altar cloths in late antiquity more generally, see Sean V. Leatherbury, "Textiles as Gifts to God in Late Antiquity: Christian Altar Cloths as Cultic Objects," in *Textiles and Cult in the Ancient Mediterranean*, ed. Cecilie Brøns and Marie-Louise Nosch, Ancient Textiles Series 31 (Oxford: Oxbow Books, 2017), 243–57.

156. Lines 796–805; Friedländer, 249–50.

157. As noted by Mango and others before him, the textile described here has extant visual comparanda in two textiles from Egypt. See Josef Strzygowski, *Orient oder Rom* (Leipzig: J. C. Hinrichs'sche Buchhandlung, 1901), 88–126.

CHAPTER 6. ANNIVERSARIES

1. *Const. App.* 8.34.8–9, quoted in Stephen of Heracleopolis Magna, *A Panegyric on Apollo* 10; CSCO 394:18. Translation from CSCO 395:14.

2. See chapter 1.

3. The bibliography on the subject of pseudepigraphy is massive, but two contributions are worth noting here. They unpack the ways in which pseudepigraphy comments on (Victoria Wohl) or tests the limits of (Karen Ní Mheallaigh) an author-reader contract. See Victoria Wohl, "Plato avant la lettre: Authenticity in Plato's Epistles," *Ramus* 27 (1998): 60–93; Karen Ní Mheallaigh, "Pseudo-Documentarism and the Limits of Ancient Fiction," *American Journal of Philology* 129 (2008): 403–31. I show in this chapter that pseudepigraphy in two homilies functions to strengthen the speaker-audience contract, bonding the speaker and the audience in their shared opposition to the imperial government and in their distinctive claim to the authoritative past.

4. The term "monophysite" continues to be abused in scholarship. For a recent example, see Jennifer Pruitt, *Building the Caliphate: Construction, Destruction, and Sectarian Identity in Early Fatimid Architecture* (New Haven, CT: Yale University Press, 2020), 48. The term "miaphysite" has been proposed as a corrective. See, for example, Sebastian P. Brock, "Miaphysite, Not Monophysite!," *Cristianesimo nella storia: Ricerche storiche esegetiche teologiche* 37 (2016): 45–52. I prefer, however, to use designations that do not reduce the controversy to a theological core because the issues over the Council of Chalcedon in 451 were manifold, and included also administrative matters.

5. In general, scholars of liturgical studies have shown Jerusalem to be the source of many prayers and practices that migrated widely throughout the Mediterranean, following pilgrimage routes. See, for example, Juliette Day, *The Baptismal Liturgy of Jerusalem: Fourth- and Fifth-Century Evidence from Palestine, Syria, and Egypt* (Burlington, VT: Ashgate, 2007).

6. Neil McLynn shows that Constantine probably never entered any church at all until 337, when he attended the Easter vigil at the cathedral of Constantinople. See Neil McLynn, "The Transformation of Imperial Churchgoing in the Fourth Century," in *Approaching Late Antiquity: The Transformation from Early to Late Empire*, ed. Simon Swain and Mark Edwards (Oxford: Oxford University Press, 2006), 236–37. Timothy D. Barnes argues that Eusebius of Caesarea's "Oration in Praise of Constantine" was delivered at the dedication of the Church of the Holy Sepulchre in 335, and Ze'ev Rubin offers an explanation that resolves the major problems with this view, but Christine Smith maintains that Eusebius delivered the speech at Constantinople on the occasion of the emperor's tricennalia, soon after the dedication at Jerusalem. See Timothy D. Barnes, "Two Speeches by Eusebius," *Greek, Roman and Byzantine Studies* 18 (1977): 341–45; Ze'ev Rubin, "The Church of the Holy Sepulchre and the Conflict between the Sees of Caesarea and Jerusalem," in *The Jerusalem Cathedra: Studies in the History, Archaeology, Geography and Ethnography of the Land of Israel*, vol. 2, ed. Lee I. Levine (Detroit: Wayne State University Press, 1982), 79–105; Christine Smith, "Christian Rhetoric in Eusebius' Panegyric at Tyre," *Vigiliae Christianae* 43 (1989): 240–41. Cf. Christopher Beeley, *The Unity of Christ: Continuity and Conflict in Patristic Tradition* (New Haven, CT: Yale University Press, 2012), 56. Jeremy Schott refers to Eusebius's appended text as a combination of his homily at the Holy Sepulchre and the panegyric on Constantine for the occasion of his tricennial. See Jeremy M. Schott, "Eusebius' *Panegyric on the Building of Churches* (*HE* 10.4.2–72): Aesthetics and the Politics of Christian Architecture," in *Reconsidering Eusebius: Collected Papers on Literary, Historical, and Theological Issues*, ed. Sabrina Inowlocki and Claudio Zamagni (Leiden: Brill, 2011), 177.

Vitalijs Permjakovs notes reasons as to why the speech in question would not be a conse-cratory homily. See Vitalijs Permjakovs, "'Make This the Place Where Your Glory Dwells': Origins and Evolution of the Byzantine Rite for the Consecration of a Church" (PhD diss., University of Notre Dame, 2012), 84n273.

7. *Itineraria Egeriae* 48–49. Cf. Sozomen, *HE* 2.26.

8. Sophronius of Jerusalem, *Homily on the Exaltation of the Revered Cross and on the Holy Resurrection*. I thank John Duffy for sharing a draft of his edition and translation of this text.

9. Louis van Tongeren, *Exaltation of the Cross: Toward the Origins of the Feast of the Cross and the Meaning of the Cross in Early Medieval Liturgy* (Leuven: Peeters, 2000).

10. Anton Baumstark, *Festbrevier und Kirchenjahr des syrischen Jakobiten: Eine litur-giegeschichtliche Vorarbeit* (Paderborn: Ferdinand Schöningh, 1910), 168. Cf. Matthew Black, "The Festival of Encaenia Ecclesiae in the Ancient Church with Special Reference to Palestine and Syria," *Journal of Ecclesiastical History* 5 (1954): 78n2.

11. Baumstark, 168.

12. Juan Mateos, *Lelya-Ṣapra: Essai d'interprétation des matines chaldéennes*, Orienta-lia Christiana Analecta 156 (Rome: Pontificium Institutum Orientalium Studiorum, 1959), 290; Sylvester Pudichery, *Ramsa: An Analysis and Interpretation of the Chaldean Vespers* (Pachalam: Dharmaram College, 1972), 146–50. In the history of the East Syrian calendar, the mid-seventh century may be a *terminus ante quem* for the elongation of the feast to a period of four weeks. The *Exposition of the Offices of the Church*, attributed to Gīwargīs of Arbela, names Iso-Yahb III, Patriarch of Seleucia-Ctesiphon from 647 to 657, as the one who lengthened the feast to four weeks. The text explains the rationale for this emendation to the liturgical year: to draw a parallel between the four-week period and the four dedica-tions of tabernacles in the Old Testament. See R. H. Connolly, trans., *Anonymi Auctoris: Expositio Officiorum Ecclesiae, Georgio Arbelensi Vulgo Adscripta*, CSCO Scriptores Syri, series 2, vol. 91 (Paris: J. Gabalda, 1913), 25. As to the possible authors of the *Exposition*, see Connolly, 2–3. Cf. Anton Baumstark, *Nichtevangelische syrische Perikopenordnungen des ersten Jahrtausends im Sinne vergleichender Liturgiegeschichte* (Münster: Aschendorff, 1921), 58.

13. For a chart of the lections, see Arthur John Maclean, *East Syrian Daily Offices* (London: Rivington Percival, 1894), 280–81. Cf. John Moolan, *The Period of Annuncia-tion-Nativity in the East Syrian Calendar: Its Background and Place in the Liturgical Year* (Kottayam: Pontifical Oriental Institute of Religious Studies, 1985), 50–51. Cf. Baumstark, *Nichtevangelische syrische Perikopenordnungen*, 58–59.

14. Mateos, 291. Cf. Moolan, 51. Several different hypotheses as to the festal roots of this period have been propounded. The anniversary celebration of a specific church in Syriac-speaking lands may have been broadened and generalized. Arthur John Maclean briefly suggests the possibility of the Great Church of Seleucia-Ctesiphon (Maclean, xxv). Anton Baumstark also considers this possibility, but he rules it out. Since the general dedi-cation feast is shared by both the West and East Syrian traditions and derives from a com-mon source, it would be much more probable for the anniversary of the Great Church of Edessa to have been generalized in both traditions. An anniversary for the Great Church of Seleucia-Ctesiphon would not make its way into the West Syrian calendar. See Baumstark, *Festbrevier*, 167–69. The anniversary celebration of the consecration of the Holy

Sepulchre may have been placed at this point in the East Syrian liturgical year (November), not in September as elsewhere (Black, 78). A Christian rival festival to the Jewish season of Hanukkah, celebrating the dedication of all temples, may have developed. The readings for the feast according to the Armenian Lectionary (Heb 13:10–23 and Matt 23:13–22) and the timing (around the time of year when Jews would celebrate the Dedication of the Temple, 25 Kislev) suggest to Bernard Botte that the generic feast of the church was set at such a point in the liturgical year to coincide with the dedication of the temple at Jerusalem. See Bernard Botte, "Les Dimanches de la dédicace dans les églises syriennes," *L'Orient syrien* 2 (1957): 65–70. Sylvester Pudichery supports this view (Pudichery, 144–46).

15. Other than these three stories, I have only found one obscure reference to a "first-built" church of Mary. The Marian temple of the palace of Daphne in Constantinople is called πρωτοκτιστός—"first built"—in *The Book of Ceremonies* 1.1. See Ann Moffatt and Maxeme Tall, trans., *Constantine Porphyrogennetos: The Book of Ceremonies*, vol. 1 (Canberra: The Australian National University, 2012), 7. Kenneth Holum says that Pulcheria probably built this church. See Kenneth G. Holum, *Theodosian Empresses: Women and Imperial Dominion in Late Antiquity*, Transformation of the Classical Heritage 3 (Berkeley: University of California Press, 1982), 143.

16. Many editions of the synaxarium contain both the feasts of Koskam on 6 Hatūr and Philippi on 21 Paōni. Otto Meinardus, "A Comparative Study on the Sources of the Synaxarium of the Coptic Church," *Bulletin de la Société d'Archéologie Copte* 17 (1963–64): 121 (6 Hatūr) and 146–47 (21 Paōni). At least two *menologia*, however, contain the feast of Athribis on 21 Paōni, not Philippi, and Koskam on 6 Hatūr. See F. Nau, "Martyrologes et ménologes orientaux: Les ménologes évangéliaires coptes-arabes," *PO* 10 (1915): 205 and 215. To my knowledge, the only writer who reconciled two of the "firsts" by making one of them second is the thirteenth-century historian al-Makārim. However, only one of two editions of his *History of the Churches and Monasteries of Egypt* mentions the church of Mary in Athribis: Monk Ṣamū'īl al-Suryānī, ed., *Tārīkh al-Kanā'is wa al-'Adyurah fī al-Qarn al-Thānī 'Ashr al-Mīlādī li 'Abī al-Makārim* (Cairo: n.p., n.d.), fol. 30a. The church is not mentioned in the manuscript edited in B. T. A. Evetts, ed. and trans., *The Churches and Monasteries of Egypt and Some Neighbouring Countries attributed to Abû Ṣāliḥ the Armenian* (Oxford: Clarendon Press, 1895).

The feast of the dedication of a Marian church on 21 Paōni (June 15) is also attested in Greek and Syriac calendars. The Syriac calendar does not specify where the church is located. See F. Nau, "Martyrologes et ménologes orientaux: Un martyrologe et douze ménologes syriaques," *PO* 10 (1915): 42. In the Greek synaxarium of Constantinople, the third commemoration listed for June 15 is the "synaxis of the most-holy Theotokos, further [from the city] in Marinakiou." See Hippolyte Delehaye, *Synaxarium ecclesiae constantinopolitanae* (1902; repr., Brussels: Apud Socios Bollandianos, 1954), column 752. The typikon of the Monastery of Lips specifies that Marinakiou lies in the environs of Chalcedon. Nothing else is known of the district Marinakiou or the church of Mary there. See R. Janin, *Constantinople Byzantine*, 2nd ed. (Paris: Institut français d'études byzantines, 1964), 501 and the references there.

17. E. A. Wallis Budge, *The Miracles of the Blessed Virgin Mary and the Life of Ḥannâ (Saint Anne), and the Magical Prayers of 'Ahĕta Mîkâêl* (London: W. Griggs, 1900), ch. 34 (Athribis) and ch. 35 (Koskam).

18. Michel van Esbroeck argues that the Ps-Basil story was composed in the sixth century. See Michel van Esbroeck, "La Première église de la vierge bâtie par les apôtres," in *Aegyptus Christiana: Mélanges d'hagiographie égyptienne et orientale dédiés à la mémoire du P. Paul Devos Bollandiste*, ed. Ugo Zanetti and Enzo Lucchesi (Geneva: Patrick Cramer, 2004), 1–18. Paul Dilley agrees that it was likely composed in late antiquity sometime after the Council of Chalcedon. See Paul C. Dilley, "Homily on the Building of the First Church of the Virgin," in *New Testament Apocrypha: More Noncanonical Scriptures*, ed. Tony Burke and Brent Landau, vol. 1 (Grand Rapids, MI: Eerdmans, 2020), 192–93.

As for the story attributed to Theophilus, Leslie MacCoull suggests that it was composed in the eighth century. The existence of two recensions and the lack of a critical edition have made most scholars reticent to place the text's composition or redaction within specific historical circumstances. See Juan Pedro Monferrer-Sala, ed. and trans., *The Vision of Theophilus: The Flight of the Holy Family into Egypt* (Piscataway, NJ: Gorgias Press, 2015); Stephen J. Davis, *Coptic Christology in Practice: Incarnation and Divine Participation in Late Antique and Medieval Egypt* (New York: Oxford University Press, 2008), 135–39; Davis, "A Hermeneutic of the Land: Biblical Interpretation in the Holy Family Tradition," in *Coptic Studies on the Threshold of a New Millennium*, ed. Mat Immerzeel and Jacques van der Vliet, vol. 1 (Leuven: Peeters, 2004), 334–36; Davis, "Ancient Sources for the Coptic Tradition," in *Be Thou There: The Holy Family's Journey in Egypt*, ed. Gawdat Gabra (New York: American University in Cairo Press, 2001), 132–63; Leslie MacCoull, "Holy Family Pilgrimage in Late Antique Egypt: The Case of Qosqam," in *Akten des XII. internationalen Kongresses für christliche Archäologie* (Münster: Aschendorffsche Verlagsbuchhandlung, 1995), 987–92.

19. For overviews of the literature and context, see Phil Booth, "A Circle of Egyptian Bishops at the End of Roman Rule (*c.* 600): Texts and Contexts," *Le Muséon* 131 (2018): 21–72; Arietta Papaconstantinou, "Historiography, Hagiography, and the Making of the Coptic 'Church of the Martyrs' in Early Islamic Egypt," *DOP* 60 (2006): 65–86; David W. Johnson, "Anti-Chalcedonian Polemics in Coptic Texts, 451–641," in *The Roots of Egyptian Christianity*, ed. Birger A. Pearson and James E. Goehring (Philadelphia: Fortress, 1986), 216–34; C. Detlef G. Müller, "Die koptische Kirche zwischen Chalkedon und dem Arabereinmarsch," *Zeitschrift für Kirchengeschichte* 75 (1964): 271–308. In this chapter, I would like to highlight not the theological polemic, but the struggle over the holy places—that is, churches.

20. Vat. copt. 67.3. The text is classified under CPC 0073, CPG 2990, and BHO 73. Witnesses exist in Bohairic, Arabic, and Garshuni, but only the Bohairic text at the Vatican has been edited thus far. See M. Chaîne, "Catéchèse attribuée à saint Basile de Césarée," *ROC* 23 (1922–23): 150–59 and 271–302. Walter Crum published notes on two unedited fragments at Leipzig University (Cod. Tisch. XXIV.50 = Leipzig University 1086.50 and Cod. Tisch. XXV.21 = Leipzig University 1087.21) in "Hagiographica from Leipzig Manuscripts," *Proceedings of the Society of Biblical Archaeology* 29 (1907): 304. According to the CMCL database, both are thought to have originally belonged to the library of the Monastery of Saint Macarius in Wādī al-Naṭrūn (MACA.DI and MACA.EL). There are at least sixteen Arabic witnesses and two Garshuni: Georg Graf names eleven Arabic and two Garshuni in GCAL 1:323–24; Ugo Zanetti inventoried four copies at the library of Dayr Abu Maqar in *Les manuscrits de Dair Abû Maqâr: inventaire* (Geneva: P. Cramer, 1986); William F. Macomber mentions one in his *Catalogue of the Christian Arabic Manuscripts of the Franciscan Center*

of Christian Oriental Studies, Muski, Cairo (Cairo: Éditions du Centre franciscain d'études orientales chrétiennes, 1984), no. 213. An Ethiopic text has also been published. See Stefan Bombeck, ed. and trans., *Die Geschichte der heiligen Maria in einer alten äthiopischen Handschrift*, 2 vols. (Dortmund: Praxiswissen, 2004–10), 1:398–423 and 2:213–223.

In addition to Chaîne's French translation of a Coptic witness and Bombeck's of an Ethiopic one, an English translation of Chaîne's edition has appeared. See Dilley, "First Church." Michel van Esbroeck published a French translation of the Arabic text published in a twentieth-century collection of *mayamir* on the Virgin Mary cited in GCAL 1:323 in "La première église."

21. BnF copte 131.5, fol. 121 and 131.8, fol. 80. The text is classified under CPC 0416, CPG 2628, and CANT 56. On BnF copte 131.8, fol. 80, see Alin Suciu, "'Me, This Wretched Sinner': A Coptic Fragment from the Vision of Theophilus Concerning the Flight of the Holy Family to Egypt," *Vigiliae Christianae* 67 (2013): 436–50. Alin Suciu has since identified another fragment that belongs to the same codex (BnF copte 131.5, fol. 121), and I am grateful to him for sharing this information with me. The existence of a Coptic text is also attested in the colophon of fragments of an Arabic witness contained in Vat. ar. 1481; it is written there that the Arabic translation of the Coptic text was produced at the request of the superior of Dayr al-Muḥarraq in AD 1265. See Marcel Richard, "Les Écrits de Théophile d'Alexandrie," *Le Muséon* 52 (1939): 44. At least twenty-eight Arabic and two Garshuni witnesses exist. See GCAL 1:229–32; Wadī' al-Fransīskānī, "Mayāmir Riḥlat al-'Ā'ilah al-Muqaddasah: Al-Ṭabaʿāt wa al-Makhṭūṭāt," in *Kanīsat al-ʿAḏrāʾ bi-Rūḏ al-Faraj: Isbūʿ al-Qibṭayat al-Tāsaʿ* (n.p.: n.p., 2002), 90–95; Fatin Morris Guirguis, "The Vision of Theophilus: Resistance through Orality among the Persecuted Copts" (PhD diss., Florida Atlantic University, 2010), 92–129; Zanetti, 54 and 72; Monferrer-Sala, 35–82; Michelangelo Guidi, ed., "La omelia di Teofilo di Alessandria sul Monte Coscam nelle letterature orientali," *Rendiconti della reale accademia dei Lincei, classe di scienze morali, storiche e filologiche* 26 (1917): 381–469 and 30 (1921): 217–37. At least three Syriac witnesses exist. See A. Mingana, ed. and trans., *Woodbrooke Studies: Christian Documents in Syriac, Arabic, and Garshūni*, vol. 3 (Cambridge: W. Heffer and Sons, 1931), 1–92; Guidi, 391–440. At least two Ethiopic witnesses exist. See I. Guidi, ed. and trans., "Il discorso su Monte Coscam attribuito a Teofilo d'Alessandria nella versione Etiopica," *Rendiconti della reale accademia dei Lincei, classe di scienze morali, storiche e filologiche* 21 (1912): 395–471; Budge, ch. 35.

The task of telling the redaction history of the text has yet to be completed, but there were at least two recensions in circulation and the shorter one is likely an epitomized version of the longer one. See Wadī' al-Fransīskānī; Davis, *Coptic Christology in Practice*, 135n88; Monferrer-Sala, 11–34. Translations have appeared in Italian and English. See Michelangelo Guidi, "La omelia di Teofilo di Alessandria sul Monte Coscam nelle letterature orientali," *Rendiconti della reale accademia dei Lincei, classe di scienze morali, storiche e filologiche* 30 (1921): 274–315; I. Guidi, 442–71; Monferrer-Sala, 83–108; Mingana, 8–43; Budge, ch. 35.

22. There are many variants to the spelling of the geographic designation in Coptic, Greek, and Arabic. The Latinized form is *Cusae*. It was certainly an episcopal seat from at least the fourth century. The names of four bishops are known from late antiquity, including Theonas who attended the Council of Constantinople in 533. Constantine of Sioout is said to have transferred the relics of a bishop of Koskam. See Stefan Timm, *Das christlich-koptische Ägypten in arabischer Zeit*, vol. 5 (Wiesbaden: Dr. Ludwig Reichert Verlag, 1991),

2180–91; Klaas A. Worp, "A Checklist of Bishops in Byzantine Egypt (A.D. 325–c. 750)," *Zeitschrift für Papyrologie und Epigraphik* 100 (1994): 301; R. Janin, "Cusae," in *Dictionnaire d'histoire et de géographie ecclésiastiques*, ed. Alfred Baudrillart, A. de Meyer and Ét. van Cauwenbergh, vol. 13 (Paris: Librairie Letouzey et Ané, 1956), column 1117; Booth, 34.

23. Special hymns would be composed to commemorate this first consecration for use at the monastery church of Koskam itself (Dayr al-Muḥarraq) and perhaps also at the monasteries of Saint Mary in Wadī al-Natrūn (Dayr al-Suryān) and Saint Anthony at the Red Sea (Dayr al-Anba Antunyus). See Youhanna Nessim Youssef, "The Rite of the Consecration of the Church of Koskam," *Ancient Near Eastern Studies* 46 (2009): 72–92. The thirteenth-century historian al-Makārim also identifies the Church of Koskam as the place where the ritual of consecration was first learned. See Evetts, fol. 78b.

24. To my knowledge, there is no known *praepositus* in the first seven centuries with the exact name "Eumenius." The title had many uses, the most well-known being that of the head eunuch of the imperial household—the grand chamberlain (*praepositus sacri cubiculi*). The only near match I have found is Amantius, who was Emperor Anastasius I's *praepositus* (Evagrius, *HE* 4.2, and Procopius, *Secret History* 6.26), and who attempted to install another non-Chalcedonian emperor—namely, the count Theocritus—after Anastasius I died. However, the people and the army rejected Amantius's candidate, proclaiming instead Justin I as emperor. Justin I then had Amantius and Theocritus executed. See Rodolphe Guilland, *Recherches sur les institutions byzantines*, vol. 1 (Berlin: Akademie-Verlag, 1967), 178–79, 277, and 357. This marked a watershed in the history of the Byzantine Empire. Justin I was the first staunchly pro-Chalcedonian emperor to accede the throne after Marcian, and he became the first in an unending line of Chalcedonian emperors in Byzantine history. Regarding Amantius, see Shaun Tougher, *The Eunuch in Byzantine History and Society* (Abgindon, Oxon: Routledge, 2008), 40, 80, 101, 134, and 157. Cf. Booth, 27n35. On the title *praepositus* and all the offices to which it could refer, see Wilhelm Enßlin, "Praepositus," in *Paulys Realencyclopädie der classischen Altertumswissenschaft*, ed. Georg Wissowa, Wilhelm Kroll, and Karl Mittelhaus, Supplement 8 (Stuttgart: Alfred Druckenmüller Verlag, 1956), columns 556–67. On the *praepositus sacri cubiculi*, see Guilland, 1:338–80.

25. Vat. copt. 67 fols. 75v–76r.

26. Vat. copt. 67 fol. 80v; Chaîne, 280. The text is unique among all the other known claims to *acheiropoiēta*. Typically, textiles serve as the medium for an *acheiropoētos* image, not mosaics. The most comprehensive treatment of this topic remains Ernst von Dobschütz, *Christusbilder: Untersuchungen zur christlichen Legende* (Leipzig: J. C. Hinrichs'sche Buchhandlung, 1899). For some more recent studies, see Ernst Kitzinger, "The Cult of Images in the Age before Iconoclasm," *DOP* 8 (1954): 112–15; Averil Cameron, "The Sceptic and the Shroud," in *Continuity and Change in Sixth-Century Byzantium* (London: Variorum Reprints, 1981), no. V; James Trilling, "The Image Not Made by Hands and the Byzantine Way of Seeing," in *The Holy Face and the Paradox of Representation*, ed. Herbert L. Kessler and Gerhard Wolf (Rome: Bibliotheca Hertziana, 1998), 109–27; Charles Barber, *Figure and Likeness: On the Limits of Representation in Byzantine Iconoclasm* (Princeton, NJ: Princeton University Press, 2002), 24–37.

27. Vat. copt. 67 fol. 82r.

28. Vat. copt. 67 fol. 79v; Chaîne, 279.

29. Vat. copt. 67 fol. 78v; Chaîne, 278.

30. Vat. copt. 67 fol. 80v.

31. Vat. copt. 67 fols. 81v–82r.

32. Vat. ar. 698 fol. 123r.

33. See chapter 2 for the rules against acts of outrage in churches.

34. Vat. ar. 698 fols. 124–27.

35. Vat. ar. 698 fol. 109v. This list of how Theophilus prioritized the expenditure of imperial donations was surely composed with the Johannites' accusation of "lithomania" in mind (see the case study on Theophilus's prosecution of John Chrysostom in chapter 3). The composer lists "the poor" as the first beneficiaries of the assets Theophilus expended. The account also emphasizes that Theophilus's construction of martyria dedicated to John the Baptist and the Three Holy Children (of Daniel 3) took place prior to the acquisition of the imperial donations (107r). The details supplied regarding the construction of the martyrion to the Three Holy Children (including Theophilus's unsuccessful attempt to acquire their relics) show that the composer/redactor of the *maymar* on Koskam was likely aware of a *logos* (homily) also attributed to Theophilus concerning the Three Holy Children and/or related texts, on which see Mary K. Farag, "Relics vs. Paintings of the Three Holy Children: Coptic Responses to Chalcedonian Claims in Alexandria," *Analecta Bollandiana* 137 (2019): 261–76.

36. The feast of 21 Tūbi commemorated Mary's death not only on Egyptian calendars, but also on Syrian and Gallic ones, too. Arietta Papaconstantinou, "La liturgie stationale à Oxyrhynchos dans la première moitié du 6ᵉ siècle: Réédition et commentaire du POxy XI 1357," *Revue des études byzantines* 54 (1996): 147.

37. In fact, Coptic Museum Hist. 477 fols. 23a–35b and Vat. ar. 698 fols. 139–56 demonstrate that redactors of the story in Arabic balanced the two accounts of punishment (that of the merciless rich man and that of the sinful woman) with a long pericope on Abraham and Job as exemplars of mercy and righteousness.

38. Cf. the seventh-century Palestinian accounts analyzed by Derek Krueger in "Mary at the Threshold: The Mother of God as Guardian in Seventh-Century Palestinian Miracle Accounts," in *The Cult of the Mother of God in Byzantium: Texts and Images*, ed. Leslie Brubaker and Mary B. Cunningham (Burlington, VT: Ashgate, 2011), 31–38.

39. Vat. copt. 67 fols. 69v–70r. My emphasis.

40. Vat. ar. 698 fol. 104v.

41. Vat. ar. 698 fol. 103r.

42. Cornelia B. Horn and Robert R. Phenix, Jr., eds. and trans., *John Rufus: The Lives of Peter the Iberian, Theodosius of Jerusalem, and the Monk Romanus* (Atlanta: Society of Biblical Literature, 2008), liv; TTH 45.1:15; Jan-Eric Steppa, *John Rufus and the World Vision of Anti-Chalcedonian Culture*, 2nd ed. (Piscataway, NJ: Gorgias Press, 2005), 1–15. *Pace* Jan-Eric Steppa, Juvenal's "apostasy" was not merely the cost of his "determin[ation] to survive the Council of Chalcedon as Bishop of Jerusalem" (Steppa, 5), but the price he was willing to pay for his elevation to patriarch. See Ernest Honigmann, "Juvenal of Jerusalem," *DOP* 5 (1950): 240–46; Siméon Vailhé, "L'Érection du patriarchat de Jérusalem, 451," *ROC* 4 (1899): 44–57.

43. Leo cited two related reasons as to why Jerusalem ought not to have been elevated. First, the Council of Nicaea in 325 had already resolved that Jerusalem should remain subordinate to Caesarea. (By the fifth century, the decisions of Nicaea had acquired the most

authoritative status and could not be changed.) Second, Leo, as an archdeacon, and the then Pope Celestine had already disapproved of one of Juvenal's former attempts, when Juvenal had sought to secure Cyril of Alexandria's sanction of his presidency over all Palestine in 431. Leo even states that he possesses the original copies of the correspondence regarding the matter (*Ep.* 119.4). See Honigmann, 217 and Bronwen Neil, *Leo the Great* (London: Routledge, 2009), 14n27.

44. Honigmann, 233–56.

45. For arguments as to why Palestine became Chalcedonian, see John Binns, *Ascetics and Ambassadors of Christ: The Monasteries of Palestine 314–631* (Oxford: Clarendon Press, 1994), 183–217.

46. Giorgio Fedalto lists one Severus of Jerusalem as the non-Chalcedonian bishop from 590 to 635. See Giorgio Fedalto, "Liste vescovili del patriarcato di Gerusalemme. I. Gerusalemme e Palestina prima," *OCP* 49 (1983): 24; Fedalto, *Hierarchia Ecclesiastica Orientalis*, vol. 2 (Padua: Messaggero, 1988), 1005. Giorgio Fedalto cites J.-B. Chabot's publication of a list of non-Chalcedonian bishops of Antioch appended to the Syriac manuscript of Michael the Syrian's *Chronicle*, which mentions that Severus, metropolitan of Jerusalem, laid hands on Athanasius, surnamed Gamala, of Samosata, monk of Qenneshre, ordaining him patriarch of Antioch. *Pace* Fedalto, no dates are given for Severus's episcopacy. It is Athanasius that the document says died in the year 635 and served as patriarch for forty-five years, not Severus. See J.-B. Chabot, "Les évêques Jacobites du VIIIe au XIIIe siècle," *ROC* 4 (1899): 447. This is the only document that mentions a "Severus, metropolitan of Jerusalem," and the account does not accord with Michael the Syrian, *Chronicle* 10.24, according to which Athanasius was ordained by a group of (unnamed) bishops. The same chapter mentions that Athanasius had a brother by the name of Severus, whom he ordained bishop of Samosata. See J.-B. Chabot, trans., *Chronique de Michel le Syrien*, vol. 2 (Paris: Ernest Leroux, 1901), 376–77. Perhaps the compiler of the appendix turned Severus of Samosata into a metropolitan of Jerusalem. In Chabot's view, the list is only "of value" because, for Patriarch Cyriacus (793) and each patriarch thereafter, the list also includes the names of bishops ordained by each patriarch (Chabot, "Les évêques Jacobites," 445). If there was in fact no "Severus, metropolitan of Jerusalem" who ordained Athanasius patriarch of Antioch, then the non-Chalcedonian episcopal vacancy in Jerusalem lasted about three centuries after Theodosius's expulsion in 453.

It is worth noting as well that Fedalto and others list Theodosius of Jerusalem (451–53) as the first in a line of Syrian non-Chalcedonian bishops of Jerusalem. Theodosius, however, is the first and only Palestinian non-Chalcedonian bishop of Jerusalem; so he ought to be named as the only one on a list of Palestininan non-Chalcedonian bishops of Jerusalem (instead of becoming an honorary Syrian, so to speak).

47. Averil Cameron, "The Theotokos in Sixth-Century Constantinople," *JTS*, n.s., 29 (1978): 79–108; Bissera V. Pentcheva, *Icons and Power: The Mother of God in Byzantium* (University Park: Pennsylvania State University Press, 2006), 2.

48. Vered Shalev-Hurvitz, *Holy Sites Encircled: The Early Byzantine Concentric Churches of Jerusalem* (New York: Oxford University Press, 2015), 166; Stephen J. Shoemaker, *Ancient Traditions of the Virgin Mary's Dormition and Assumption* (New York: Oxford University Press, 2002), 68–69; Shoemaker, "The Cult of Fashion: The Earliest 'Life of the Virgin' and Constantinople's Marian Relics," *DOP* 62 (2008): 53–74; Cameron, "The Theotokos in

Sixth-Century Constantinople"; Cameron, "The Virgin's Robe: An Episode in the History of Early Seventh-Century Constantinople," *Byzantion* 49 (1979): 42–56.

49. Cameron, "The Virgin's Robe," 43–48. While the bibliography on the political role of Mary in the Greek literature of the Byzantine empire is large, much less has been produced on her role in other eastern literatures, especially Coptic and Arabic. Angie Heo has recently published a monograph with a strong focus on Mary's role in mediating relationships between Christians and Muslims in contemporary Egypt, but the long history of her role from late antiquity to the present in Egypt has yet to be told. See Angie Heo, *The Political Lives of Saints: Christian-Muslim Mediation in Egypt* (Oakland: University of California Press, 2018).

50. For an argument about how the holy places of Palestine rose to such significance, see, for example, the following article and the references therein: Pablo Argárate, "L'Influence de Constantin sur l'émergence de la notion de 'lieux saints' au IVᵉ siècle," in *Les Pères de l'Église et le pouvoir*, ed. Pascal-Grégoire Delage (Royan: CaritasPatrum, 2014), 233–37.

51. Among the most famous are Theodosius of Jerusalem, Peter the Iberian, and Severus of Antioch. See Alois Grillmeier, et al., *Christ in Christian Tradition*, vol. 2, pt. 3: *The Churches of Jerusalem and Antioch*, trans. Marianne Ehrhardt (Oxford: Oxford University Press, 2013), 40–43.

52. Despite their loss of Palestine, sixth-century non-Chalcedonians did not consider themselves "second-rate" Christians anymore than earlier diaspora Jews perceived themselves as subpar by comparison to those in Jerusalem. See Daniel R. Schwartz, "Humbly Second-Rate in the Diaspora? Philo and Stephen on the Tabernacle and the Temple," in *Envisioning Judaism: Studies in Honor of Peter Schäfer on the Occasion of His Seventieth Birthday*, ed. Ra'anan S. Boustan et al., vol. 1 (Tübingen: Mohr Siebeck, 2013), 81–89. For fifth-century non-Chalcedonian responses to Chalcedonian possession of the churches in Palestine, see Cornelia B. Horn, *Asceticism and Christological Controversy in Fifth-Century Palestine: The Career of Peter the Iberian* (Oxford: Oxford University Press, 2006), 320–28.

53. Vat. ar. 698 fol. 104v; M. Guidi, 1917:443. My emphasis.

54. Vat. ar. 698 fols. 105v–106r.

55. According to Revelation 12:6, the woman was in the wilderness for 1,260 days (the equivalent of three-and-a-half years), and verse 14 repeats the time-frame as "a time and times and half a time."

56. Vat. ar. 170 fol. 211v. The text of Vat. ar. 698 is not complete; I use Vat. ar. 170 to supply the remaining text. See M. Guidi, 1921:234. As mentioned in a previous footnote, the *maymar* on the Church of Koskam survives in a long and a short recension, and the latter is likely an epitome of the former. According to Wadīʿ al-Fransīskānī (90–95), Vat. ar. 698 is a witness to the long recension, whereas Vat. ar. 170 transmits the short recension. Unfortunately, the only other known witnesses to the long recension belong to libraries in Egypt, and I was unable to access them (with the exception of two detached leaves in Vat. ar. 1481, which transmit only the final exhortation of the homily). Therefore, I can only use witnesses that transmit the short recension to read the end of the text. However, it is worth noting that according to Guirguis's chart, which summarizes and compares the contents of seven versions of the text (three manuscripts, one modern edition of a manuscript, and three modern retellings), one witness to the long recension, Dayr al-Muḥarraq 12/42, includes a pericope like the one I quote here from Vat. ar. 170. See Guirguis, 125.

57. Already by the late fourth century, it is clear that traditions regarding the flight of the Holy Family were in circulation. Hermopolis was the first site to be associated with the flight. Eventually, the tradition grew to the point that the exact itinerary of the Holy Family's journey would be traced, generating an Egyptian Holy Land that extends along the entire Nile River. I argue that non-Chalcedonian responses to dispossession of the holy places in Palestine contributed to the dramatic expansion of the tradition. For an excellent overview of the history of the tradition, see Davis, "Ancient Sources for the Coptic Tradition"; Davis, *Coptic Christology in Practice*, 125–52. The literature on this topic is vast. Some significant volumes include Gabriele Giamberardini, *Il Culto Mariano in Egito*, 2nd ed., 3 vols. (Jerusalem: Franciscan Printing Press, 1975); Lucette Valensi, *La Fuite en Égypte: Histoires d'orient et d'occident* (Paris: Éditions du Seuil, 2002); Ashraf Sadek and Bernadette Sadek, "Un Fleuve d'eau vive: Trilogie sur l'Entrée du Christ en Égypte," *Le Monde Copte* 34, 35 (2011, 2017). Sadek and Sadek's third volume (*Le Monde Copte* 36) has been announced, but it has not yet appeared.

58. CSCO 394:x–xii.

59. Stephen of Heracleopolis Magna, *Panegyric on Apollo* 8; CSCO 394:14. Translation from CSCO 395:10–11. Stephen was not the first in Egypt to have interpreted Revelation for a heresiological purpose. According to Eusebius of Caesarea, *HE* 7.10, Dionysius of Alexandria interpreted Revelation 13:5 as a prophecy against Emperor Valerian and his advisor "the teacher and *archisynagōgos* of the *magoi* from Egypt" in his correspondence with Hermammon. Most significantly, as Elaine Pagels has shown, Athanasius of Alexandria interpreted the "whore" of Revelation 17–18 as a personification of "heresy" (a feminine noun in Greek) in his campaigns against the "Melitians" and "Arians" in the fourth century. See Elaine Pagels, *Revelations: Visions, Prophecy, and Politics in the Book of Revelation* (New York: Viking, 2012), 141–45 and 160–65; Pagels, "How Athanasius, Subject to Christian Emperors, Read John's Apocalypse into His Canon," in Boustan et al., 2:799–808.

60. Stephen of Heracleopolis Magna, *Panegyric on Apollo* 9–10; CSCO 394:14–15 and 17. Translation from CSCO 395:11 and 13.

61. J. Mark Sheridan, ed. and trans., *Rufus of Shotep: Homilies on the Gospels of Matthew and Luke* (Rome: C. I. M., 1998), 12–14.

62. Sheridan, 67 and 131.

63. Sheridan, 67 and 131.

64. Cf. Wendy Mayer's suggestion concerning homilies pseudonymously attributed to John Chrysostom: "subjects that are superficially innocuous—the historic persecution of the apostles and of the Christian church—take on contemporary significance and are intentionally adduced to frame the Johannite cause." See Wendy Mayer, "Media Manipulation as a Tool in Religious Conflict: Controlling the Narrative Surrounding the Deposition of John Chrysostom," in *Religious Conflict from Early Christianity to the Rise of Islam*, ed. Wendy Mayer and Bronwen Neil, Arbeiten zur Kirchengeschichte 121 (Berlin: De Gruyter, 2013), 166. To borrow some of Mayer's phrases, the "superficially innocuous" story of the Holy Family's flight into Egypt from Mary's perspective "take[s] on contemporary significance" by strengthening a non-Chalcedonian resistance.

65. Thomas Schmidt, "The Last Book: Revelation, Commentaries, and the Making of the New Testament" (PhD diss., Yale University, 2020), 168–71. I am grateful to Thomas

Schmidt for sharing this excerpt of his dissertation with me. On the thirteenth-century exegete, see Benedict Englezakis, *Studies on the History of the Church of Cyprus, 4th–20th Centuries*, trans. Norman Russell, ed. Silouan Ioannou and Misael Ioannou (Aldershot: Variorum, 1995), 105–45. Other interpreters generally identified the woman as a symbol of the church (see Hippolytus, *On the Christ and the Antichrist* 61 and Quodvultdeo, *De Symbolo* III.1). Interpretations of the woman as Mary can be found only in non-Chalcedonian literature. See Oecumenius, *Commentary on the Apocalypse* 6; Ps-Theophilus, *Maymar on the Church of Koskam;* and an *Encomion Interpreting Part of the Apocalypse of John the Apostle of Christ Jesus* attributed to Cyril of Alexandria in Morgan Library M591 fols. 11v–33r (Hyvernat's foliation) or pp. 22–65 (Coptic pagination), at fol. 29v or p. 58. For a facsimile edition of this manuscript, see Henri Hyvernat, ed., *Bibliothecae Pierpont Morgan: Codices Coptici Photographice Expressi*, vol. 25 (Rome: n.p., 1922), 24–67; for an Italian translation, see Tito Orlandi, *Omelie copte: Scelte e tradotte, con una introduzione sulla letterature copta* (Turin: Società editrice internazionale, 1981), 123–44. It is worth noting that the encomion attributed to Cyril identifies the woman as Mary, quoting Revelation 12:2 as saying that she was "in travail though *not* having pain" (p. 57, my emphasis; ⲉⲥⲉⲉⲧ ⲉⲥϯⲛⲁⲁⲕⲉ ⲉⲥϯⲧⲕⲁⲥ ⲁⲛ). To my knowledge, no known Greek or Coptic attestations of this verse contain this variant. In addition, Ps-Cyril says that the desert to which the woman fled is unknown to everyone in the flesh (p. 59).

66. Vat. copt. 67 fol. 69r; Chaîne, 153–54.

67. George W. Horner, *The Coptic Version of the New Testament in the Northern Dialect* (Oxford: Clarendon Press, 1905), 514.

68. Vat. copt. 67 fol. 80r; Chaîne, 279.

69. Vat. copt. 67 fol. 80r; Chaîne, 279.

70. Vat. copt. 67 fol. 82r; Chaîne, 281.

71. Vat. copt. 67 fol. 84v; Chaîne, 283.

72. Mark 8:27–30 has a shorter version of the story, but by the sixth century the Matthean version was most well-known and Matthew had already grown to be the preferred gospel, regularly being the first gospel copied in codices of evangelia.

73. Michel van Esbroeck also entertains the possibility that the text geographically conflates Caesarea Philippi with Philippi. He conjectures that the text responds to rivalry between Philippi and Jerusalem, both equally ancient sites of Christianization. However, this hypothesis does not explain Basil of Caesarea's significance or role in the presumed rivalry. Van Esbroeck, 16.

74. Gérard Godron, ed. and trans., *Textes coptes relatifs à Saint Claude d'Antioche*, PO 35.4 (Turnhout: Brepols, 1970), 614 and 615.

75. Sheridan, 13n7 and Tito Orlandi in CSCO 350:vii n9. Cf. Booth, 36.

76. E. A. Wallis Budge, ed., *The Martyrdom and Miracles of Saint George of Cappadocia* (London: D. Nutt, 1888), 101.

77. Budge, *George of Cappadocia*, 168.

78. Hippolyte Delehaye, *Les origines du culte des martyrs* (Brussels: Bureaux de la société des Bollandistes, 1912), 202; Delehaye, *Les légends grecques des saints militaires* (Paris: Librairie Alphonse Picard et fils, 1909), 78–79. Cf. Sophie Métivier, *La Cappadoce, IVᵉ–VIᵉ siècle: Une histoire provinciale de l'empire romain d'orient* (Paris: Publications de la Sorbonne, 2005), 307n382.

79. Georg Graf, Michel van Esbroeck, and Paul Dilley have all puzzled over the geographic conundrum as well. Graf tries to distinguish among stories that name "Caesarea," "Philippi," or no location in GCAL 1:323–24. As mentioned in a footnote above, van Esbroeck argues that Caesarea Philippi is conflated with Philippi. Dilley claims that "we cannot rule out a conflation of Caesarea Philippi and Caesarea in Cappadocia, Basil's episcopal see" (Dilley, 192).

80. Honigmann, 215.

81. A. H. M. Jones, *Cities of the Eastern Roman Provinces*, 2nd ed. (Oxford: Clarendon Press, 1971), 182–83. Philip Rousseau, *Basil of Caesarea* (Berkeley: University of California Press, 1994), 41 and 169–70.

82. Sozomen, *HE* 6.16. Cf. Benoît Gain, "Conflit de Basile de Césarée avec l'autorité imperiale d'après Grégoire de Nazianze," in Delage, 153–75.

83. Shoemaker, *Ancient Traditions*, 101.

84. Susan Graham, "Justinian and the Politics of Space," in *Constructions of Space II: The Biblical City and Other Imagined Spaces*, ed. Jon L. Berquist and Claudia V. Camp (New York: T&T Clark, 2008), 61.

85. Procopius, *Buildings* 5.6.18–22; H. B. Dewing, ed. and trans., *Procopius*, vol. 7, Loeb Classical Library 343 (Cambridge, MA: Harvard University Press, 1940), 346 and 367.

86. Oren Gutfeld, *Jewish Quarter Excavations in the Old City of Jerusalem*, vol. 5 (Jerusalem: Israel Exploration Society, 2012), 228 (fig. 5.9) and 243–45. Oren Gutfeld calculates that the height of the extraordinarily large columns must have been 17.75m.

87. Irfan Shahîd, "Justinian and the Christianization of Palestine: The Nea Ecclesia in Jerusalem," in *Klētorion in Memory of Nikos Oikonomides*, ed. Florentia Evangelatou-Notara and Triantafyllitsa Maniati-Kokkini (Athens: University of Athens, 2005), 381.

88. Vat. copt. 67 fols. 84v and 80v, respectively; Chaîne, 284 and 280.

89. Anastasius of Sinai, *Questions and Answers* 69; Marcel Richard and Joseph A. Munitiz, eds., *Anastasii Sinaitae: Quaestiones et Responsiones* (Turnhout: Brepols, 2006), 121.

90. Translation from Joseph A. Munitiz, *Anastasios of Sinai: Questions and Answers* (Turnhout: Brepols, 2011), 184–85. Cf. Jack Tannous, *The Making of the Medieval Middle East: Religion, Society, and Simple Believers* (Princeton, NJ: Princeton University Press, 2018), 62–63.

91. See chapter 3.

92. In the late seventh century, the non-Chalcedonian Jacob of Edessa would explicitly approve the pedagogical value of the noble lie, even claiming that the patristic heroes Athanasius of Alexandria and Basil of Caesarea made use of it themselves (Jacob of Edessa, *Letter 2, to John, the Stylite of Litharb*). Quoted in Tannous, 70.

93. Graf mentions thirteen Arabic and eight Garshuni manuscripts in GCAL 1:255 and 2:489. Budge edited and translated two Ethiopic texts in *Miracles*, ch. 34. This section is based on my reading of a digital copy of BnF ar. 154 fols. 165–78; the manuscript was produced in the year 1607.

94. However, it is worth noting that the detailed description of the church given on BnF ar. 154 fols. 165v–166r accords remarkably well with archaeological finds. Archaeological remains confirm the destruction of a major church in Athribis by the ninth century. A rubble dump included marble, marble-like stucco, gilded marble, and mosaic tesserae. See Barbara Ruszczyc, *Kościół pod wezwaniem Świętej Dziewicy w Tell Atrib* (Warsaw: Polska Akademia Nauk, 1997). While Barbara Ruszczyc identifies the remains with what is known

as the Church of Mary in Athribis from literary evidence, Tomasz Górecki questions the matter on the grounds that the name or image of Mary is not attested in the archaeological data and also because the description in the miracle story of Athribis is "idealized." However, Górecki was dependent on E. Amélineau's inaccurate French paraphrase of the description in BnF ar. 154. See E. Amélineau, *La Géographie de l'Égypte à l'époque copte* (Paris: Imprimerie nationale, 1894), 67–68; Tomasz Górecki, "Remnants of a Byzantine Church at Athribis," in *Christianity and Monasticism in Northern Egypt*, ed. Gawdat Gabra and Hany N. Takla (New York: American University in Cairo Press, 2017), 239–52. According to the *History of the Patriarchs of Alexandria*, marauding Madalgah destroyed the Church of Mary in Athribis during the patriarchate of Shenouti I (the fifty-fifth patriarch, who served from 858 to 880).

The miracle story features a white dove that carries the message of al-Ma'mūn's annulment from Baghdad to Athribis. The historians al-Shābushtī and al-Maqrīzī (quoting al-Shābushtī) also mention the significance of a white dove in relation to the monastery at Athribis, saying that the dove visits the monastery yearly on its feast day (21 Paōnī). See Aziz Suryal Atiya, "Some Egyptian Monasteries according to the Unpublished Ms. of al-Shābushtī's '*Kitāb al-Diyārāt*,'" *Bulletin de la Société d'Archéologie Copte* 5 (1939): 23 and 28; F. Wüstenfeld, *Macrizi's Geschichte der Copten* (Göttingen: Dieterich'sche Buchhandlung, 1845), 108.

95. On the significance of primacy in the late antique Egyptian context, cf. Papaconstantinou, "The Making of the Coptic 'Church of the Martyrs,'" 79–80.

96. *Life of Longinus* 31; Tito Orlandi, ed., *Vite dei monaci Phif e Longino* (Milan: Cisalpino-Goliardica, 1975), 82. For a short study of the *Life of Longinus* and an English translation, see Tim Vivian, *The Life of Longinus*, special issue, *Coptic Church Review* 20 (1999).

97. In fact, it is possible that the house/tomb of Mary in the Valley of Josaphat was considered the "first" church of Mary in Jerusalem. The other early Marian foundation in Palestine, the Kathisma, might have been consecrated before the house/tomb of Mary in the Valley of Josaphat, but was located farther away from Jerusalem, midway between Jerusalem and Bethlehem. On both churches, see Ute Verstegen, "Byzantine Jerusalem," in *Routledge Handbook of Jerusalem*, ed. Suleiman A. Mourrad, Naomi Koltun-Fromm, and Bedross Der Matossian (Abingdon: Routledge, 2019), 71; Shalev-Hurvitz, 117–67; and Shoemaker, *Ancient Traditions*, 78–141.

98. See chapter 2 for rules against outrage committed in church buildings.

99. *Panegyric of Macarius of Tkōou* 8.2; CSCO 415:54.

100. Perhaps this is why Basil reluctantly learns to trust Mary in the story about Philippi. If the completion of Justinian's massive undertaking in founding the Nea proves Mary's support of Chalcedonians, then non-Chalcedonians would have reason to begin to distrust her. Like non-Chalcedonians, Basil learns to trust Mary.

101. On this story, see Samuel Moawad, *Untersuchungen zum Panegyrikos auf Makarios von Tkōou und zu seiner Überlieferung* (Wiesbaden: Reichert, 2010), 187–93.

CONCLUSION

1. CTh 16.2.25. *Qui divinae legis sanctitatem aut nesciendo confundunt aut neglegendo violant et offendunt, sacrilegium committunt.* Theodor Mommsen and Paul M. Meyer, eds., *Theodosiani Libri XVI cum Constitutionibus Sirmondianis*, vol. 2 (Berlin: Apud Weidmannos,

1905), 843. Translation from Clyde Pharr, Theresa S. Davidson, and Mary Pharr, *The Theodosian Code and Novels and the Sirmondian Constitutions* (Princeton, NJ: Princeton University Press, 1952), 444.

2. See chapter 5.

3. See chapter 3.

4. CTh 16.5.57. See chapter 1.

5. Ps-Theophilus, *Maymar on the Church of Koskam* (Vat. ar. 698 fol. 123r). See chapter 6.

6. Roland Betancourt, "Icon, Eucharist, Relic: Negotiating the Division of Sacred Matter in Byzantium" (paper presented at the Byzantine Materiality Conference, St. Vladimir's Orthodox Theological Seminary, Yonkers, NY, 2019); Charles Barber, "Leo of Chalcedon, Euthymios Zigabenos, and the Return to the Past," in *Contesting the Logic of Painting: Art and Understanding in Eleventh-Century Byzantium* (Leiden: Brill, 2007), 131–57; Annemarie Weyl Carr, "Leo of Chalcedon and the Icons," in *Byzantine East, Latin West: Art-Historical Studies in Honor of Kurt Weitzmann*, ed. Christopher Moss and Katherine Kiefer (Princeton, NJ: Department of Art and Archaeology, Princeton University, 1995), 579–84; Pelopidas Stephanou, "La Doctrine de Léon de Chalcédoine et de ses adversaires sur les images," *OCP* 12 (1946): 177–99; Stephanou, "Le procès de Léon de Chalcédoine," *OCP* 9 (1943): 5–64. The fact that the repurposing of *res sacrae* was against the law was not lost on Stephanou (see p. 7 of the latter article).

7. PG 127:981A.

8. See chapter 2.

APPENDIX D. LATE ANTIQUE LECTIONS FOR THE CONSECRATORY RITUAL

1. This is my translation of the French translation in Athanase Renoux, *Le Codex arménien Jérusalem 121*, PO 35.2 (Turnhout: Brepols, 1971), 367. Abbreviations to scriptural books have been adapted.

2. Athanase Renoux, *Le Codex arménien Jérusalem 121*, PO 35.1 (Turnhout: Brepols, 1969), 196–97.

3. F. C. Burkitt, *The Early Syriac Lectionary System* (London: Humphrey Milford, Oxford University Press, 1923), 13. Abbreviations to scriptural books have been adapted.

4. Bernard Botte, "Les Dimanches de la dédicace dans les églises syriennes," *L'Orient syrien* 2 (1957): 65–70. The readings for the feast according to the Armenian Lectionary (Heb 13:10–23 and Matt 23:13–22) and the timing (around the time of year when Jews would celebrate the Dedication of the Temple, 25 Kislev) suggest to Bernard Botte that the generic feast of the church was set at such a point in the liturgical year as to coincide with the dedication of the temple at Jerusalem. Botte argues that the reason why no date is attached to the entry in the Armenian lectionary is because the feast took place on 25 Kislev, which would fall on a different day each year on the Syrian calendar.

BIBLIOGRAPHY

PRIMARY SOURCES

Acts of the Council of Chalcedon, 451.

Price, Richard, and Michael Gaddis, trans. *The Acts of the Council of Chalcedon*. Translated Texts for Historians 45. 3 vols. Liverpool: Liverpool University Press, 2005.

Schwartz, Eduard, ed. *Concilium Universale Chalcedonense*, 1.1–1.3 and 3.1–3.3. Acta Conciliorum Oecumenicorum 2.1 and 2.3. Berlin: Walter de Gruyter, 1933–37.

Acts of the Council of Ephesus, 449.

Flemming, Johannes, ed., and Georg Hoffman, trans. *Akten der ephesinischen Synode vom Jahre 449*. Berlin: Weidmann, 1917.

Perry, S. G. F., trans. *The Second Synod of Ephesus*. Dartford: Orient Press, 1881.

Acts of the Synod of 1091 at the Blachernae, Constantinople. In *Patrologia Graeca*, edited by Jacques-Paul Migne, 971–84. Vol. 127. Paris: n.p., 1864.

African Councils.

Munier, Charles, ed. *Concilia Africae a. 345–a. 525*. Corpus Christianorum, Series Latina 149. Turnhout: Brepols, 1974.

Al-Makārim. *History of the Churches and Monasteries of Egypt*.

Al-Suryānī, Monk Ṣamū'īl, ed. *Tārīkh al-Kana'is wa al-'Adyurah fī al-Qarn al-Thānī 'Ashr al-Mīlādī li 'Abī al-Makārim*. Cairo: n.p., n.d.

Evetts, B. T. A., ed. and trans. *The Churches and Monasteries of Egypt and Some Neighbouring Countries attributed to Abû Ṣâliḥ the Armenian*. Oxford: Clarendon Press, 1895.

Al-Maqrīzī. *Akhbār Qibṭ Maṣr*.

Wüstenfeld, F., ed. and trans. *Macrizi's Geschichte der Copten*. Göttingen: Dieterich'sche Buchhandlung, 1845.

Al-Shābushtī. *Kitāb al-Diyārāt.*
>   Atiya, Aziz Suryal, ed. and trans. "Some Egyptian Monasteries according to the Un-published Ms. of al-Shābushtī's '*Kitāb al-Diyārāt*.'" *Bulletin de la Société d'Archéologie Copte* 5 (1939): 1–28.
Ambrose of Milan. *On Duties.*
>   Davidson, Ivor J., ed. and trans. *Ambrose: De officiis.* 2 vols. New York: Oxford University Press, 2001.
Anastasius of Sinai. *Questions and Answers.*
>   Munitiz, Joseph A., trans. *Anastasios of Sinai: Questions and Answers.* Turnhout: Brepols, 2011.
>   Richard, Marcel, and Joseph A. Munitiz, eds. *Anastasii Sinaitae: Quaestiones et Respon-siones.* Turnhout: Brepols, 2006.
Athanasius of Alexandria. *Apology to Constantius.* In *A Select Library of Nicene and Post-Nicene Fathers of the Christian Church,* edited by Philip Schaff and Henry Wace, 238–53. 2nd series, vol. 4. Grand Rapids, MI: Eerdmans Publishing, 1978–79. First published 1891 by Eerdmans.
Augustine of Hippo. *The City of God.*
>   Dombart, B., and A. Kalb, eds. *De Civitate Dei, Libri I–X.* Corpus Christianorum, Series Latina 47. Turnhout: Brepols, 1955.
>   Zema, Demetrius B., and Gerald G. Walsh, trans. *Saint Augustine: The City of God, Books I–VII.* The Fathers of the Church 8. Washington, DC: Catholic University Press, 1949.
———. *Confessions.*
>   O'Donnell, James J., ed. *Augustine: Confessions.* Vol. 1. Oxford: Clarendon Press, 1992.
———. *Epistle 66.*
>   Migne, Jacques-Paul, ed. *Patrologia Latina.* 33: 236. Paris: Apud Garnieri Fratres, 1865.
>   Parsons, Wilfrid, trans. *Saint Augustine: Letters.* 1: 314–16. The Fathers of the Church 12. Washington, DC: Catholic University of America Press, 1951.
>   Teske, Roland J., trans. *Letters,* pp. 258–59. The Works of St. Augustine: A Translation for the 21st Century, part 2, vol. 1, edited by Boniface Ramsey. Hyde Park, NY: New City Press, 2001.
———. *Sermon 302.*
>   Hill, Edmund, trans. *Sermons,* pp. 301–13. The Works of St. Augustine: A Translation for the 21st Century, part 3, vol. 8, edited by John E. Rotelle. Hyde Park, NY: New City Press, 1994.
>   Lambot, D. C., ed. *Sancti Augustini Hipponensis Episcopi: Sermones Selecti Dvodeviginti,* pp. 100–111. Stromata Patristica et Mediaevalia 1. Utrecht: In Aedibus Spectrum, 1950.
———. *Sermon 337.*
>   Hill, Edmund, trans. *Sermons,* pp. 272–76. The Works of Saint Augustine: A Translation for the 21st Century, part 3, vol. 9, edited by John E. Rotelle. Hyde Park, NY: New City Press, 1994.
>   Migne, Jacques-Paul, ed. *Patrologia Latina.* 38: 1475–78. Paris: Apud Garnieri Fratres, 1863.
Balai. *Madrasha on the Church at Qenneshrin.*
>   McVey, Kathleen E., trans. "The Sogitha on the Church of Edessa in the Context of Other Early Greek and Syriac Hymns for the Consecration of Church Buildings." *ARAM* 5 (1993): 329–70.

Overbeck, J. Josephus, ed. *S. Ephraemi Syri, Rabulae Episcopae Edesseni, Balaei Aliorum Opera Selecta*, pp. 251–58. Oxford: Clarendon Press, 1865.

Basil of Caesarea, Pseudo. *Catachesis on the Church of Mary.*

Bombeck, Stefan, ed. and trans. *Die Geschichte der heiligen Maria in einer alten äthiopischen Handschrift.* 1: 398–423 and 2: 213–23. Dortmund: Praxiswissen, 2004–10.

Chaîne, M., ed. and trans. "Catéchèse attribuée à saint Basile de Césarée." *Revue de l'orient chrétien* 23 (1922–23): 150–59 and 271–302.

Coptic Museum History 477 fols. 23a–35b.

Van Esbroeck, Michel, trans. "La Première église de la vierge bâtie par les apôtres." In *Aegyptus Christiana: Mélanges d'hagiographie égyptienne et orientale dédiés à la mémoire du P. Paul Devos Bollandiste*, edited by Ugo Zanetti and Enzo Lucchesi, 1–18. Geneva: Patrick Cramer, 2004.

Vatican Arabic 698 fols. 139–56.

Bede. *Ecclesiastical History.*

Colgrave, Bertram, and R. A. B. Mynors, ed. and trans. *Bede's Ecclesiastical History of the English People.* Oxford: Clarendon Press, 1969.

Book of Ceremonies 1.

Moffatt, Ann, and Maxeme Tall, trans. *Constantine Porphyrogennetos: The Book of Ceremonies.* Vol. 1. Canberra: Australian National University, 2012.

Caesarius of Arles. *Sermons* 227–29.

Morin, Germain, ed. *Sancti Caesarii Arelatensis Sermones.* Part 2. Corpus Christianorum, Series Latina 104, pp. 897–910.Turnhout: Brepols, 1953.

Mueller, Mary Magdeleine, trans. *Saint Caesarius of Arles: Sermons.* 3: 164–79. The Fathers of the Church 66. Washington, DC: Catholic University of America Press, 1973.

Choricius of Gaza. *Laudatio Marciani* I and II.

Foerster, Richard, and Eberhard Richtsteig, eds. *Choricii Gazaei Opera*, pp. 1–47. Leipzig: B. G. Teubner, 1929.

Hamilton, R. W., trans. "Two Churches of Gaza as Described by Choricius of Gaza." In *Palestine Exploration Fund: Quarterly Statement for 1930*, 178–91. London: Fund's Office, 1930.

Litsas, Fotios K., trans. "Choricius of Gaza: An Approach to His Work: Introduction, Translation, Commentary," pp. 111–32 and 134–53. PhD diss., University of Chicago, 1980. ProQuest (AAT T-27791).

Collection of Councils Normative for the Greek-Speaking East. In *Discipline generale antique*, edited by Périclès-Pierre Joannou. 2 vols. Rome: Grottaferrata, 1962–64.

Constantine of Sioout. *Second Panegyric on Claudius of Antioch.* In *Textes coptes relatifs à Saint Claude d'Antioche*, edited and translated by Gérard Godron. Patrologia Orientalis. 35.4: 171–247. Turnhout: Brepols, 1970.

Council of Dovin, Armenia, 527. In *Histoire des conciles d'après les documents originaux*, translated and edited by Henri Leclercq, 1077–80. Vol. 2, part 2. By Charles Joseph Hefele. Paris: Letouzey et Ané, 1908.

Council of Rome, 501/2. In *Cassiodori Senatoris Variae*, edited by Theodor Mommsen, 438–55. Monumenta Germaniae Historica, Auctorum Antiquissimorum 12. Berlin: Apud Weidmannos, 1894. First printed 1861 by Apud Weidmannos.

Council of Serdica, 343. In *The Early Development of Canon Law and the Council of Serdica*, edited by Hamilton Hess, 213–55. New York: Oxford University Press, 2002.

Council of Toledo, 589.

Rodriguez, Felix, ed. "El Concilio III de Toledo." In *Concilio III de Toledo: XIV Centenario, 589–1989*, edited by Felix Rodriguez, 13–38. Toledo: Caja Toledo, 1991.

Councils of Hispania.

Martínez Díez, Gonzalo, and Félix Rodríguez, eds. *La colección canónica Hispana*. Vol. 4, *Concilios Galos, Concilios Hispanos: Primera parte*. Monumenta Hispaniae Sacra, Serie Canónica 4. Madrid: Consejo Superior de Investigaciones Científicas, Instituto Enrique Flórez, 1984.

Vives, José, Tomás Marín Martínez, and Gonzalo Martínez Díez, eds. and trans. *Concilios visigóticos e hispano-romanos*. España Cristiana, Textos 1. Barcelona: Consejo Superior de Investigaciones Científicas, 1963.

Cyril of Alexandria, Pseudo. *Encomion Interpreting Part of the Apocalypse of John the Apostle of Christ Jesus*.

Hyvernat, Henri, ed. *Bibliothecae Pierpont Morgan: Codices Coptici Photographice Expressi*. 25: 24–67. Rome: n.p., 1922.

Morgan Library M591 fols. 11v–33r (Hyvernat's foliation) or pp. 22–65 (Coptic pagination).

Orlandi, Tito, trans. *Omelie copte: Scelte e tradotte, con una introduzione sulla letterature copta*, pp. 123–44. Turin: Società editrice internazionale, 1981.

Dioscorus of Alexandria, Pseudo. *Panegyric of Macarius of Tkōou*.

Johnson, David W., ed. and trans. *A Panegyric on Macarius, Bishop of Tkôw, Attributed to Dioscorus of Alexandria*. Corpus Scriptorum Christianorum Orientalium 415–16, Scriptores Coptici 41–42. Louvain: Secrétariat du CorpusSCO, 1980.

Ennodius. *Libellus adversus eos qui contra synodum scribere praesumpserunt*. In *Magni Felicis Ennodi Opera*, edited by Friedrich Vogel. Monumenta Germaniae Historica, Auctores Antiquissimorum. 7: 48–67. Berlin: Apud Weidmannos, 1885.

Eusebius of Caesarea. *Ecclesiastical History*.

Bardy, Gustave, ed. and trans. *Eusèbe de Césarée: Histoire ecclésiastique*. Sources chrétiennes 31, 41, 55, and 73. Paris: Éditions du Cerf, 1952–60.

Defarrari, Roy J., trans. *Ecclesiastical History*. The Fathers of the Church 19 and 29. Washington, DC: Catholic University of America Press, 1953–55.

———. *Life of Constantine*. In *Eusebius Werke*, edited by Ivar A. Heikel, 1–148. Die griechischen christlichen Schriftsteller der ersten drei Jahrhunderte 1. Leipzig: J. C. Hinrichs'sche Buchhandlung, 1902.

Facundus of Hermiane. *Defense of the Three Chapters*.

Clément, J.-M., and R. Vander Plaetse, eds. *Facundus d'Hermiane: Défense des trois chapitres (à Justinien)*. Translated by Anne Fraïsse-Bétoulières. Sources chrétiennes 471, 478–79, 484, and 499. Paris: Éditions du Cerf, 2002–6.

Gaius. *Institutes*.

De Zulueta, Francis, ed. and trans. *The Institutes of Gaius*. 2 vols. Oxford: Clarendon Press, 1946 and 1953.

Gallic Councils.

De Clercq, Caroli, ed. *Concilia Galliae, a. 511–a. 695*. Corpus Christianorum, Series Latina 148A. Turnhout: Brepols, 1963.

Munier, Charles, ed. *Concilia Galliae, a. 314–a. 506*. Corpus Christianorum, Series Latina 148. Turnhout: Brepols, 1963.

Gaudentius of Brescia. *Tractatus* 17.

    Boehrer, Stephen L., trans. "Gaudentius of Brescia: Sermons and Letters," pp. 190–201. PhD diss., Catholic University of America, 1965. ProQuest (AAT 6604756).

    Migne, Jacques-Paul, ed. *Patrologia Latina*. 20: 959–71. Paris: Apud Garnieri Fratres, 1845.

Gīwargīs of Arbela. *Exposition of the Offices of the Church*.

    Connolly, R. H., trans. *Anonymi Auctoris: Expositio Officiorum Ecclesiae, Georgio Arbelensi Vulgo Adscripta*. Corpus Scriptorum Christianorum Orientalium, Scriptores Syri. Series 2, vol. 91. Paris: J. Gabalda, 1913.

Greek Anthology, Book 1. In *The Greek Anthology*, edited and translated by W. R. Paton. Revised by Michael A. Tueller. 1: 4–81. Loeb Classical Library 67. Cambridge, MA: Harvard University Press, 2014.

Gregory Nazianzen. *Oration* 14.

    Migne, Jacques-Paul, ed. *Patrologia Graeca*. 35: 857–910. Paris: n.p., 1857.

    Vinson, Martha, trans. *St. Gregory of Nazianzus: Select Orations*, pp. 39–71. The Fathers of the Church 107. Washington, DC: Catholic University of America Press, 2003.

Gregory the Great, *Letter* 5.57a. In *The Letters of Gregory the Great*, translated by John R. C. Martyn. 2: 388–92. Toronto: Pontifical Institute of Medieval Studies, 2004.

Gregory of Tours. *Glory of the Martyrs*.

    Van Dam, Raymond, trans. *Gregory of Tours: Glory of the Martyrs*. Translated Texts for Historians 4. Liverpool: Liverpool University Press, 2004. First published 1988 by Liverpool University Press.

John Chrysostom. *Homily 20 on 2 Corinthians*. In *Patrologia Graeca*, edited by Jacques-Paul Migne. 61: 533–40. Paris: n.p., 1862.

———. *Homily on the* Comes John. In *Patrologia Graeca*, edited by Jacques-Paul Migne. 52: 395–414. Paris: n.p., 1862.

———. *Homily on Eutropius*. In *Patrologia Graeca*, edited by Jacques-Paul Migne. 52: 391–96. Paris: n.p., 1862.

———. *Homily 50 on Matthew*. In *Patrologia Graeca*, edited by Jacques-Paul Migne. 58: 503–10. Paris: n.p., 1862.

———. *Letter to Innocent of Rome*. In *Palladios: Dialogue sur la vie de Jean Chrysostome*, edited and translated by Anne-Marie Malingrey, 47–95. Sources chrétiennes 342. Paris: Éditions du Cerf, 1988.

———. *Sixth Sermon on Lazarus and the Rich Man*. In *John Chrysostom: On Wealth and Poverty*, translated by Catherine P. Roth, 97–124. Crestwood, NY: St. Vladimir's Seminary Press, 1981.

Justinian. *Codex*, Book 1.

    Dillon, John Noël, ed. and trans. "First Book." In *The Codex of Justinian: A New Annotated Translation, with Parallel Latin and Greek Text, Based on a Translation by Justice Fred H. Blume*, edited by Bruce W. Frier, 14–405. Vol. 1. Cambridge: Cambridge University Press, 2016.

———. *Digest*.

    Krueger, Paul and Theodor Mommsen, eds. *Corpus Iuris Civilis*. Vols. 1–2. Berlin: Apud Weidmannos, 1962. First published 1867–70 by Apud Weidmannos.

    Watson, Alan, trans. *The Digest of Justinian*. 4 vols. Philadelphia: University of Pennsylvania Press, 1985.

———. *Institutes*.

Thomas, J. A. C., ed. and trans. *The Institutes of Justinian: Text, Translation, and Commentary*. Amsterdam: North-Holland Publishing Company, 1975.

———. *Novels* and *Edicts*.

Miller, David J. D., and Peter Sarris, trans. *The Novels of Justinian: A Complete Annotated English Translation*. 2 vols. Cambridge: Cambridge University Press, 2018.

Schoell, Rudolf, and Guilelmus Kroll, eds. *Corpus Iuris Civilis*. Vol. 3. Berlin: Apud Weidmannos, 1954. First published 1895 by Apud Weidmannos.

Kontakion for the Reconsecration of Hagia Sophia in AD 562.

Palmer, Andrew, trans. "The Inauguration Anthem of Hagia Sophia in Edessa: A New Edition and Translation with Historical and Architectural Notes and A Comparison with a Contemporary Constantinopolitan Kontakion." *Byzantine and Modern Greek Studies* 12 (1988): 117–67.

Trypanis, C. A., ed. *Fourteen Early Byzantine Cantica*, pp. 141–47. Wiener byzantinische Studien 5. Vienna: Hermann Böhlaus Nachfolger, 1968.

Liber Pontificalis.

Davis, Raymond, trans. *The Book of Pontiffs* (Liber Pontificalis*): The Ancient Biographies of First Ninety Roman Bishops to AD 715*. Translated Texts for Historians 6. 3rd ed. Liverpool: Liverpool University Press, 2010.

Duchesne, L., ed. *Le Liber pontificalis: Texte, introduction et commentaire*. 3 vols. Paris: E. de Boccard, 1955–57.

Life of Caesarius of Arles.

Morin, G., and Marie-José Delage, eds. *Vie de Césaire d'Arles*. Sources chrétiennes 536. Paris: Les Éditions du Cerf, 2010.

Klingshirn, William E., trans. *Caesarius of Arles: Life, Testament, Letters*. Translated Texts for Historians 19. Liverpool: Liverpool University Press, 1994.

Life of Longinus. In *Vite dei monaci Phif e Longino*, edited and translated by Tito Orlandi, 46–93. Milan: Cisalpino-Goliardica, 1975.

Life of Rabbula of Edessa. In *Stewards of the Poor: The Man of God, Rabbula, and Hiba in Fifth-Century Edessa*, translated by Robert Doran, 65–105. Kalamazoo, MI: Cistercian Publications, 2006.

Liturgy of John Chrysostom. In *L'Eucologio Barberini Gr. 336 (ff. 1–263)*, edited by Stefano Parenti and Elena Velkovska, pp. 24–42. Rome: C. L. V. Edizioni Liturgiche, 1995.

Lucian. *The Hall*. In *Lucian*, edited and translated by A. M. Harmon. 1: 176–207. Loeb Classical Library 14. Cambridge, MA: Harvard University Press, 1913.

Martyrius, Pseudo. *Funeral Speech for John Chrysostom.*

Barnes, Timothy D., and George Bevan, trans. *The Funerary Speech for John Chrysostom*. Translated Texts for Historians 60. Liverpool: Liverpool University Press, 2013.

Wallraff, Martin, ed., and Cristina Ricci, trans. *Oratio funebris in laudem sancti Iohannis Chrysostomi: Epitaffio attribuito a Martirio di Antiochia*. Spoleto: Centro italiano di studi sull'alto medioevo, 2007.

Michael the Syrian. *Chronicle*, Book 10. In *Chronique de Michel le Syrien*, translated by J.-B. Chabot, 282–399. Vol. 2. Paris: Ernest Leroux, 1901.

Miracle of St. Mary at Athribis.

Bibliothèque nationale de France arabe 154 fols. 165–78.

Budge, E. A. Wallis, ed. and trans. *The Miracles of the Blessed Virgin Mary and the Life of Ḥannâ (Saint Anne), and the Magical Prayers of 'Aheta Mîkâêl*. Ch. 34. London: W. Griggs, 1900.

Miracle of St. Mary at Koskam. In *The Miracles of the Blessed Virgin Mary and the Life of Ḥannâ (Saint Anne), and the Magical Prayers of 'Aheta Mîkâêl*, edited and translated by E. A. Wallis Budge, ch. 35. London: W. Griggs, 1900.

Miracles of St. Demetrios.

 LeMerle, Paul, ed. *Les plus anciens recueils des miracles de saint Démétrius*. Paris: Éditions du centre national de la recherche scientifique, 1979.

Nilus of Ancyra. *Epistle* 62.

 Mango, Cyril, trans. *The Art of the Byzantine Empire 312–1453*. Toronto: University of Toronto Press, 1986.

 Migne, Jacques-Paul, ed. *Patrologia Graeca*. 79: 577–80. Paris: n.p., 1865.

Origen, *Homily* 3.11 on Psalm 36.

 Perrone, Lorenzo, ed. *Origenes Werke*. 13: 153–55. Berlin: Walter de Gruyter, 2015.

 Prinzivalli, Emanuela, ed., and Henri Crouzel and Luc Brésard, trans. *Origène: Homélies sur les Psaumes 36 à 38*, pp. 168–75. Sources chrétiennes 411. Paris: Éditions du Cerf, 1995.

Palladius. *Dialogue on the Life of John Chrysostom*.

 Malingrey, Anne-Marie, ed. and trans. *Palladios: Dialogue sur la vie de Jean Chrysostome*. Sources chrétiennes 341. Paris: Éditions du Cerf, 1988.

 Meyer, Robert T., trans. *Palladius: Dialogue on the Life of St. John Chrysostom*. New York: Newman Press, 1985.

Paralipomena. In *Pachomian Chronicles and Rules*, Pachomian Koinonia 2, translated by Armand Veilleux. Cistercian Studies Series 46. Kalamazoo, MI: Cistercian Publications, 1981.

Paul the Silentiary. *Ekphrastic Poem on Hagia Sophia*. In *Johannes von Gaza und Paulus Silentiarius: Kunstbeschreibungen Justinianischer Zeit*, edited by Paul Friedländer, 227–56. Leipzig: B. G. Teubner, 1912.

Paulinus of Nola. *Carmina* 27, 28, and 30.

 De Hartel, Guilelmus, ed. *Sancti Pontii Meropii Paulini Nolani*, pp. 262–305 and 307. Corpus Scriptorum Ecclesiasticorum Latinorum 30. Vienna: Verlag der österreichischen Akademie der Wissenschaften, 1999.

 Walsh, P. G., trans. *The Poems of St. Paulinus of Nola*, pp. 270–305 and 308. New York: Newman Press, 1975.

Photius of Constantinople. *Bibliothēkē*.

 Henry, René, ed. and trans. *Photius: Bibliothèque*. 9 vols. Paris: Les belles lettres, 1959–91.

Procopius of Caesarea. *Buildings*, Book 5. In *Procopius*, edited and translated by H. B. Dewing, 316–61. Vol 7. Loeb Classical Library 343. Cambridge: Harvard University Press, 1940.

Prudentius. *Peristephanon liber* 2. In *Prudentius*, edited and translated by H. J. Thomson, 108–43. Vol. 2. Loeb Classical Library 398. Cambridge, MA: Harvard University Press, 1953.

Rufus of Shotep. Homilies on the Gospel of Matthew. In *Rufus of Shotep: Homilies on the Gospels of Matthew and Luke*, edited and translated by J. Mark Sheridan, 61–164. Rome: C. I. M., 1998.

Socrates. *Ecclesiastical History*.

 Hansen, G. C., ed. *Socrate de Constantinople: Histoire ecclésiastique*. Translated by Pierre Périchon and Pierre Maraval. Sources chrétiennes 493. Paris: Éditions du Cerf, 2005.

Sozomen. *Ecclesiastical History*.

 Bidez, J., ed. *Sozomène: Histoire ecclésiastique*. Translated by André-Jean Festugière. Sources chrétiennes 306, 418, and 495. Paris: Éditions du Cerf, 1996.

Stephen of Heracleopolis Magna. *Panegyric on Apollo, Archimandrite of the Monastery of Isaac.*

    Kuhn, K. H., ed. and trans. *A Panegyric on Apollo, Archimandrite of the Monastery of Isaac by Stephen, Bishop of Heracleopolis Magna.* Corpus Scriptorum Christianorum Orientalium 394–95, Scriptores Coptici 39–40. Louvain: Secrétariat CorpusSCO, 1978.

Synesius of Cyrene. *Epistle 67.*

    FitzGerald, Augustine, trans. *The Letters of Synesius of Cyrene*, pp. 149–60. London: Humphrey Milford, Oxford University Press, 1926.

    Garzya, Antonio, ed. *Synésios de Cyrène.* Translated by Denis Roques. 3: 173–86. Paris: Les belles lettres, 2000.

Theodoret. *Ecclesiastical History.*

    Parmentier, L., and G. C. Hansen, eds. *Théodoret de Cyr: Histoire ecclésiastique.* Translated by Pierre Canivet, Jean Bouffartigue, and Annick Martin. Sources chrétiennes 501 and 530. Paris: Éditions du Cerf, 2006 and 2009.

Theodoric. *Praeceptum.* In *Cassiodori Senatoris Variae*, edited by Theodor Mommsen, 392. Monumenta Germaniae Historica, Auctorum Antiquissimorum 12. Berlin: Apud Weidmannos, 1894. First printed 1861 by Apud Weidmannos.

Theodosius. *Codex.*

    Mommsen, Theodor, and Paul M. Meyer, eds. *Theodosiani Libri XVI cum Constitutionibus Sirmondianis.* 3 vols. Berlin: Apud Weidmannos, 1905.

    Pharr, Clyde, Theresa S. Davidson, and Mary Pharr, trans. *The Theodosian Code and Novels and the Sirmondian Constitutions.* Princeton, NJ: Princeton University Press, 1952.

Theodotus of Ancyra. *Encomium on Saint George.* In *The Martyrdom and Miracles of Saint George of Cappadocia*, edited and translated by E. A. Wallis Budge, 83–173 and 274–331. London: D. Nutt, 1888.

Theophilus of Alexandria, Pseudo. *Maymar on the Church of Koskam.*

    Guidi, I., ed. and trans. "Il discorso su Monte Coscam attribuito a Teofilo d'Alessandria nella versione Etiopica." *Rendiconti della reale accademia dei Lincei, classe di scienze morali, storiche e filologiche* 21 (1912): 395–471.

    Guidi, Michelangelo, ed. and trans. "La omelia di Teofilo di Alessandria sul Monte Coscam nelle letterature orientali." *Rendiconti della reale accademia dei Lincei, classe di scienze morali, storiche e filologiche* 26 (1917): 381–469, 30 (1921): 217–37 and 274–315.

    Mingana, A., ed. and trans. *Woodbrooke Studies: Christian Documents in Syriac, Arabic, and Garshūni.* 3: 1–92. Cambridge: W. Heffer and Sons, 1931.

    Suciu, Alin, ed. and trans. "'Me, This Wretched Sinner': A Coptic Fragment from the Vision of Theophilus Concerning the Flight of the Holy Family to Egypt." *Vigiliae Christianae* 67 (2013): 436–50.

Victor of Vita. *History of the Vandal Persecution.*

    Moorhead, John, trans. *Victor of Vita: History of the Vandal Persecution.* Translated Texts for Historians 10. Liverpool: Liverpool University Press, 1992.

    Petschenig, Michael, ed. *Victoris Episcopi Vitensis: Historia Persecutionis Africanae Provinciae.* Corpus Scriptorum Ecclesiasticorum Latinorum 7. Vienna: Apud C. Geroldi Filium Bibliopolam Academiae, 1881.

SECONDARY SOURCES

Adams, Gabrielle S., Francis J. Flynn, and Michael I. Norton. "The Gifts We Keep on Giving: Documenting and Destigmatizing the Regifting Taboo." *Pyschological Science* 23 (2012): 1145–50.

Agosti, Gianfranco. "*Saxa loquuntur?* Epigrammi epigrafici e diffusione della *paideia* nell'oriente tardoantico." *Antiquité Tardive* 18 (2010): 163–80.

Al-Fransīskānī, Wadī'. "Mayāmir Riḥlat al-'Ā'ilah al-Muqaddasah: Al-Ṭaba'āt wa al-Makhṭūṭāt." In *Kanīsat al-'Aḏrā' bi-Rūḏ al-Faraj: Isbū' al-Qibṭayat al-Tāsa'*, 85–104. N.p.: n.p., 2002.

Algazi, Gadi. "Introduction: Doing Things with Gifts." In *Negotiating the Gift: Pre-Modern Figurations of Exchange*, edited by Gadi Algazi, Valentin Groebner, and Bernhard Jussen, 9–27. Göttingen: Vandenhoeck and Ruprecht, 2003.

Amélineau, E. *La Géographie de l'Égypte à l'époque copte*. Paris: Imprimerie nationale, 1894.

Ando, Clifford. *Imperial Ideology and Provincial Loyalty in the Roman Empire*. Berkeley: University of California Press, 2000.

Andreescu-Treadgold, Irina, and Warren Treadgold. "Procopius and the Imperial Panels of S. Vitale." *Art Bulletin* 79 (1997): 708–23.

Angelova, Diliana N. *Sacred Founders: Women, Men, and Gods in the Discourse of Imperial Founding, Rome through Early Byzantium*. Oakland: University of California Press, 2015.

Appadurai, Arjun. "Introduction: Commodities and the Politics of Value." In *The Social Life of Things: Commodities in Cultural Perspective*, edited by Arjun Appadurai, 3–63. New York: Cambridge University Press, 1986.

Argárate, Pablo. "L'Influence de Constantin sur l'émergence de la notion de 'lieux saints' au IVe siècle." In *Les Pères de l'Église et le pouvoir*, edited by Pascal-Grégoire Delage, 233–37. Royan: CaritasPatrum, 2014.

Bae, Junghun. *John Chrysostom on Almsgiving and Therapy of the Soul*. Patristic Studies in Global Perspective 1. Paderborn: Brill / Ferdinand Schöningh, 2021.

Barber, Charles. *Figure and Likeness: On the Limits of Representation in Byzantine Iconoclasm*. Princeton, NJ: Princeton University Press, 2002.

———. "Leo of Chalcedon, Euthymios Zigabenos, and the Return to the Past." In *Contesting the Logic of Painting: Art and Understanding in Eleventh-Century Byzantium*, 131–57. Leiden: Brill, 2007.

Barceló, Pedro, and Gunther Gottlieb. "Das Glaubensedikt des Kaisers Theodosius vom 27. Februar 380: Adressaten und Zielsetzung." In *Klassisches Altertum, Spätantike und frühes Christentum*, edited by Karlheinz Dietz, Dieter Hennig, and Hans Kaletsch, 409–23. Würzburg: Seminars für Alte Geschichte der Universität Würzburg, 1993.

Bardill, Jonathan. "A New Temple for Byzantium: Anicia Juliana, King Solomon, and the Gilded Ceiling of the Church of St. Polyeuktos in Constantinople." In *Social and Political Life in Late Antiquity*, edited by William Bowden, Adam Gutteridge, and Carlos Machado, 339–70. Leiden: Brill, 2006.

Barnes, Timothy D. "The Date of the Council of Gangra." *Journal of Theological Studies*, n.s., 40 (1989): 121–24.

———. "Two Speeches by Eusebius." *Greek, Roman and Byzantine Studies* 18 (1977): 341–45.

Barone-Adesi, Giorgio. "Dal dibattito cristiano sulla destinazione dei beni economici alla configurazione in termini di persona delle *venerabiles domus* destinate *piis causis*."

In *Atti dell'accademia romanistica costantiniana, IX convegno internazionale*, 231–65. Naples: Edizioni Scientifiche Italiane, 1993.

———. "Il sistema Giustinianeo delle proprietà ecclesiastiche." In *La proprietà e le proprietà*, edited by Ennio Cortese, 75–120. Milan: Dott. A. Giuffrè editore, 1988.

Baumann, Peter. *Spätantike Stifter im Heiligen Land*. Wiesbaden: Reichert Verlag, 1999.

Baumstark, Anton. *Festbrevier und Kirchenjahr des syrischen Jakobiten: Eine liturgiegeschichtliche Vorarbeit*. Paderborn: Ferdinand Schöningh, 1910.

———. *Nichtevangelische syrische Perikopenordnungen des ersten Jahrtausends im Sinne vergleichender Liturgiegeschichte*. Münster: Aschendorff, 1921.

Beaucamp, Joëlle. "Le testament de Grégoire de Nazianze." In *Fontes Minores*, edited by Ludwig Burgmann, 1–100. Vol. 10. Frankfurt: Löwenklau, 1998.

Beeley, Christopher. *The Unity of Christ: Continuity and Conflict in Patristic Tradition*. New Haven, CT: Yale University Press, 2012.

Bell, Peter N. "Hagia Sophia: Ideology in Stone—A Case Study." In *Social Conflict in the Age of Justinian*, 319–36. Oxford: Oxford University Press, 2013.

———. *Three Political Voices from the Age of Justinian*. Translated Texts for Historians 52. Liverpool: Liverpool University Press, 2009.

Benvenuti, Anna, and Elena Giannarelli. *Il diacono Lorenzo tra storia e leggenda*. Florence: Edizioni della Meridiana, 1998.

Berger, Adolf. "Appellatio." In *Encyclopedic Dictionary of Roman Law*, 364–65. Transactions of the American Philosophical Society, n.s., vol. 43, part 2. Philadelphia: American Philosophical Society, 1953.

Betancourt, Roland. "Icon, Eucharist, Relic: Negotiating the Division of Sacred Matter in Byzantium." Paper presented at the Byzantine Materiality Conference, St. Vladimir's Orthodox Theological Seminary, Yonkers, NY, 2019.

Bieler, Ludwig. *The Irish Penitentials*. Dublin: Dublin Institute for Advanced Studies, 1963.

Bihain, Ernest. "Le 'Contre Eunome' de Théodore de Mopsueste: Source d'un passage de Sozomène et d'un passage de Théodoret concernant Cyrille de Jérusalem." *Le Muséon* 75 (1962): 331–55.

Binns, John. *Ascetics and Ambassadors of Christ: The Monasteries of Palestine 314–631*. Oxford: Clarendon Press, 1994.

Biondi, Biondo. *Il diritto romano cristiano*. 3 vols. Milan: Dott. A. Giuffrè editore, 1952 and 1954.

Black, Matthew. "The Festival of Encaenia Ecclesiae in the Ancient Church with Special Reference to Palestine and Syria." *Journal of Ecclesiastical History* 5 (1954): 78–85.

Bloch, David J. "*Res Sanctae* in Gaius and the Founding of the City." *Roman Legal Tradition* 3 (2006): 48–64.

Bloch, P. "Dedikationsbild." In *Lexikon der christlichen Ikonographie*, edited by Engelbert Kirschbaum, 491–94. Vol. 1. Rome: Herder, 1968.

Bolman, Elizabeth S. "The Iconography of Salvation." In *The Red Monastery Church: Beauty and Asceticism in Upper Egypt*, edited by Elizabeth S. Bolman, 128–49. New Haven, CT: Yale University Press, 2016.

Booth, Phil. "A Circle of Egyptian Bishops at the End of Roman Rule (*c.* 600): Texts and Contexts." *Le Muséon* 131 (2018): 21–72.

Borkowski, Andrew. *Textbook on Roman Law*. London: Blackstone Press Limited, 1994.

Botte, Bernard. "Les Dimanches de la dédicace dans les églises syriennes." *L'Orient syrien* 2 (1957): 65–70.

Bove, Lucio. "Immunità fondiaria di chiese e chierici nel Basso Impero." In *Synteleia: Vincenzo Arangio-Ruiz*, edited by Antonio Guarino and Luigi Labruna, 886–902. Vol. 2. Naples: Jovene 1964.

Bowes, Kim. *Private Worship, Public Values, and Religious Change in Late Antiquity*. New York: Cambridge University Press, 2008.

Boyd, William K. *The Ecclesiastical Edicts of the Theodosian Code*. Studies in History, Economics, and Public Law, vol. 24, no. 2. New York: Columbia University Press, 1905.

Brassloff, Stephan. *Studien zur römischen Rechtsgeschichte, 1. Teil: Die Befugnis zur Dedikation (Zwei Fragen aus der Lehre von der res sacra)*. Vienna: Verlagsbuchhandlung Carl Fromme, 1925.

Braun, Johann Baptist. *Das kirchliche Vermögen von der ältesten Zeit bis auf Justinian I*. Giefsen: Ferber, 1860.

Brilliant, Richard. *Gesture and Rank in Roman Art: The Use of Gestures to Denote Status in Roman Sculpture and Coinage*. New Haven, CT: Connecticut Academy of Arts and Sciences, 1963.

Brock, Sebastian P. "Miaphysite, Not Monophysite!" *Cristianesimo nella storia: Ricerche storiche esegetiche teologiche* 37 (2016): 45–52.

Broc-Schmezer, Catherine. "De l'aumône faite au pauvre à l'aumône du pauvre: Pauvreté et spiritualité chez Jean Chrysostome." In *Les Pères de l'Église et la voix des pauvres: Actes du IIe colloque de La Rochelle 2, 3, et 4 septembre 2005*, edited by Pascal-Grégoire Delage, 131–48. La Rochelle: Histoire et Culture, 2006.

Brody, Lisa. "Floor Mosaic Depicting the Cities of Memphis and Alexandria." In *Byzantium and Islam: Age of Transition*, edited by Helen C. Evans and Brandie Ratliff, 12. New York: Metropolitan Museum of Art, 2012.

Brown, Peter. Review of *The Clash of the Gods: A Reinterpretation of Early Christian Art*, by Thomas F. Mathews. *Art Bulletin* 77 (1995): 499–502.

———. *The Rise of Western Christendom*. 2nd ed. Malden, MA: Blackwell, 2003.

———. *Through the Eye of a Needle: Wealth, the Fall of Rome, and the Making of Christianity in the West, 350–550 AD*. Princeton, NJ: Princeton University Press, 2012.

Brubaker, Leslie. "Elites and Patronage in Early Byzantium: The Evidence from Hagios Demetrios at Thessalonike." In *The Byzantine and Early Islamic Near East*. Vol. 6, *Elites Old and New in the Byzantine and Early Islamic Near East*, edited by John Haldon and Lawrence Conrad, 63–90. Princeton, NJ: Darwin Press, 2004.

Burkitt, F. C. *The Early Syriac Lectionary System*. London: Humphrey Milford, Oxford University Press, 1923.

Burrell, Barbara. *Neokoroi: Greek Cities and Roman Emperors*. Leiden: Brill, 2004.

Caillet, Jean-Pierre. *L'Évergétisme monumental chrétien en Italie et à ses marges*. Rome: École française de Rome, 1993.

Cameron, Alan. *The Greek Anthology: From Meleager to Planudes*. New York: Oxford University Press, 1992.

———. "A Misidentified Homily of Chrysostom." *Nottingham Medieval Studies* 32 (1988): 34–48.

———. "*Pontifex Maximus*: From Augustus to Gratian – and Beyond." *Collegium: Studies across Disciplines in the Humanities and Social Sciences* 20 (2016): 139–59.

Cameron, Averil. "The Sceptic and the Shroud." In *Continuity and Change in Sixth-Century Byzantium*, no. V. London: Variorum Reprints, 1981.

———. "The Theotokos in Sixth-Century Constantinople." *Journal of Theological Studies*, n.s., 29 (1978): 79–108.

———. "The Virgin's Robe: An Episode in the History of Early Seventh-Century Constantinople." *Byzantion* 49 (1979): 42–56.

Caner, Daniel. "Alms, Blessings, Offerings: The Repertoire of Christian Gifts in Early Byzantium." In *The Gift in Antiquity*, edited by Michael L. Satlow, 25–44. Malden, MA: Wiley-Blackwell, 2013.

———. "Towards a Miraculous Economy: Christian Gifts and Material 'Blessings' in Late Antiquity." *Journal of Early Christian Studies* 14 (2006): 329–77.

———. *Wandering, Begging Monks: Spiritual Authority and the Promotion of Monasticism in Late Antiquity*. Berkeley: University of California Press, 2002.

Canetti, Luigi. "Christian Gift and Gift Exchange from Late Antiquity to the Early Middle Ages." In *Gift Giving and the "Embedded" Economy in the Ancient World*, edited by Filippo Carlà and Maja Gori, 337–51. Heidelberg: Universitätsverlag Winter, 2014.

Carlà, Filippo. "Exchange of the Saints: Gift-Giving and the Commerce of Relics." In *Gift Giving and the "Embedded" Economy*, edited by Filippo Carlà and Maja Gori, 403–37. Heidelberg: Universitätsverlag Winter, 2014.

Caron, Pier Giovanni. "La proprietà ecclesiastica nel diritto del tardo impero." In *Atti dell'accademia romanistica costantiniana, IX convegno internazionale*, 217–30. Naples: Edizioni Scientifiche Italiane, 1993.

Carr, Annemarie Weyl. "Leo of Chalcedon and the Icons." In *Byzantine East, Latin West: Art-Historical Studies in Honor of Kurt Weitzmann*, edited by Christopher Moss and Katherine Kiefer, 579–84. Princeton, NJ: Department of Art and Archaeology, Princeton University, 1995.

Caseau, Béatrice. "A Case Study for the Transformation of Law in Late Antiquity: The Legal Protection of Churches." In *Confrontation in Late Antiquity: Imperial Presentation and Regional Adaptation*, edited by Linda Jones Hall, 61–77. Cambridge: Orchard Academic, 2003.

Chabot, J.-B. "Les évèques Jacobites du VIIIᵉ au XIIIᵉ siècle." *Revue de l'orient chrétien* 4 (1899): 444–51 and 495–511.

Chaîne, M. "Catéchèse attribuée à saint Basile de Césarée." *Revue de l'orient chrétien* 23 (1922–23): 150–59 and 271–302.

Chamard, François. "De l'immunité ecclésiastique et monastique." *Revue des questions historiques* 28 (1877): 428–64.

Chatterjee, Paroma. "Iconoclasm's Legacy: Interpreting the Trier Ivory." *Art Bulletin* 100 (2018): 28–47.

Clancy, Finbarr G. "Augustine's Sermons for the Dedication of a Church." *Studia Patristica* 38 (2001): 48–55.

Cleary, Joseph F. *Canonical Limitations on the Alienation of Church Property: An Historical Synopsis and Commentary*. Washington, DC: Catholic University of America, 1936.

Cohen, Rudolph. "A Byzantine Church and Its Mosaic Floors at Kissufim." In *Ancient Churches Revealed*, edited by Yoram Tsafrir, 277–82. Jerusalem: Israel Exploration Society, 1993.

———. "The Marvelous Mosaics of Kissufim." *Biblical Archaeology Review* 6.1 (1980): 16–23.

Cohn, Max Conrat. *Die Entstehung des westgothischen Gaius*. Amsterdam: Johannes Müller, 1905.

Connor, Carolyn L. "The Epigram in the Church of Hagios Polyeuktos in Constantinople and Its Byzantine Response." *Byzantion* 69 (1999): 479–527.

Coquin, R. "La consécration des églises dans le rite copte; ses relations avec les rites syrien et byzantine." *L'Orient syrien* 9 (1964): 144–87.

Corcoran, Simon. "The Codex of Justinian: The Life of a Text through 1,500 Years." In *The Codex of Justinian: A New Annotated Translation, with Parallel Latin and Greek Text, Based on a Translation by Justice Fred H. Blume*, edited by Bruce W. Frier, 1: xcvii–clxiv. Cambridge: Cambridge University Press, 2016.

———. "State Correspondence in the Roman Empire." In *State Correspondence in the Ancient World: From New Kingdom Egypt to the Roman Empire*, edited by Karen Radner, 172–209. New York: Oxford University Press, 2014.

Cormack, Robin S. *The Church of Saint Demetrios: The Watercolours and Drawings of W. S. George*. Thessaloniki: Vafopoulio Cultural Center and The British Council, 1985.

———. "The Mosaic Decoration of S. Demetrios, Thessaloniki: A Re-Examination in Light of the Drawings of W. S. George." *Annual of the British School at Athens* 64 (1969): 17–52 and plates 1–15.

Crum, Walter E. "Hagiographica from Leipzig Manuscripts," *Proceedings of the Society of Biblical Archaeology* 29 (1907): 289–96 and 301–7.

———. "Inscriptions from Shenoute's Monastery." *Journal of Theological Studies*, o.s., 5 (1904): 552–69.

Cumont, Franz. "L'Adoration des Mages et l'Art Triumphal de Rome." *Atti della pontificia academia romana di archeologia, Memorie* 3 (1932): 81–132.

Ćurčić, Slobodan. "Architecture as Icon." In *Architecture as Icon: Perception and Representation of Architecture in Byzantine Art*, edited by Slobodan Ćurčić and Evangelia Hadjitryphonos, 2–37. Princeton, NJ: Princeton University Art Museum, 2010.

Dagron, Gilbert. "From the *Mappa* to the *Akakia*: Symbolic Drift." In *From Rome to Constantinople: Studies in Honour of Averil Cameron*, edited by Hagit Amirav and Bas ter Haar Romeny, 203–19. Leuven: Peeters, 2007.

Dalla Spade, Giannino Ferrari. *Immunità ecclesiastiche nel diritto romano imperiale*. Venice: Premiate Officine Grafiche Carlo Ferrari, 1939.

Danby, Herbert, trans. *The Mishnah*. Oxford: Clarendon Press, 1933.

Dautzenberg, Volker. "Die Gesetze des Codex Theodosianus und des Codex Justinianus für Ägypten im Spiegel der Papyri." PhD diss., University of Cologne, 1971.

Davis, Stephen J. "Ancient Sources for the Coptic Tradition." In *Be Thou There: The Holy Family's Journey in Egypt*, edited by Gawdat Gabra, 132–63. New York: American University in Cairo Press, 2001.

———. *Coptic Christology in Practice: Incarnation and Divine Participation in Late Antique and Medieval Egypt*. New York: Oxford University Press, 2008.

———. "A Hermeneutic of the Land: Biblical Interpretation in the Holy Family Tradition." In *Coptic Studies on the Threshold of a New Millennium*, edited by Mat Immerzeel and Jacques van der Vliet, 329–36. Vol. 1. Leuven: Peeters, 2004.

Davis-Weyer, Cäcilia. "Das Traditio-Legis Bild und seine Nachfolge." *Münchner Jahrbuch der Bildenden Kunst* 12 (1961): 7–45.

Day, Juliette. *The Baptismal Liturgy of Jerusalem: Fourth- and Fifth-Century Evidence from Palestine, Syria, and Egypt*. Burlington, VT: Ashgate, 2007.

De Andia, Ysabel. "Liturgie des pauvres et théologie du corps du Christ chez saint Jean Chrysostome." *Proche-orient chrétien* 51 (2001): 247–60.

De Bonfils, Giovanni. "L'imperatore Onorio e la difesa dell'ortodossia cristiana contro celicoli ed ebrei." *Vetera Christianorum* 41 (2004): 267–94.

De Clercq, Carlo. "Les Conciles de Constantinople de 326 à 715." *Apollinaris* 34 (1961): 345–68.

Delbrueck, Richard. *Die Consulardiptychen und verwandte Denkmäler*. Berlin: Walter de Gruyter, 1929.

Delehaye, Hippolyte. *Les légends grecques des saints militaires*. Paris: Librairie Alphonse Picard et fils, 1909.

———. *Les origines du culte des martyrs*. Brussels: Bureaux de la société des Bollandistes, 1912.

———. *Synaxarium ecclesiae constantinopolitanae*. Brussels: Apud Socios Bollandianos, 1954. First published 1902 by Apud Socios Bollandianos.

Deliyannis, Deborah M. "Ecclesius of Ravenna as Donor in Text and Image." In *Envisioning the Bishop: Images and the Episcopacy in the Middle Ages*, edited by Sigrid Danielson and Evan A. Gatti, 41–61. Turnhout: Brepols, 2014.

———. *Ravenna in Late Antiquity*. New York: Cambridge University Press, 2010.

Delmaire, Roland. "Église et fiscalité: le *privilegium christianitatis* et ses limites." In *Empire chrétien et église aux IVe et Ve siècles: Intégration ou «concordat»? Le témoinage du Code Théodosien*, edited by Jean-Noël Guinot and François Richard, 285–93. Paris: Les éditions du Cerf, 2008.

———. *Largesses sacrées et Res privata: L'Aerarium impérial et son administration du IVe au VIe siècle*. Rome: École française de Rome, 1989.

Delmaire, Roland, and Claude Lepelley. "Du nouveau sur Carthage: Le temoignage des lettres de saint Augustin decouvertes par Johannes Divjak." *Opus* 2 (1983): 473–87.

Demougeot, Emilienne. "Sur les lois du 15 novembre 407." *Revue historique de droit français et étranger* 27 (1949): 403–12.

De Oliveira, Júlio César Magalhães. "Le 'pouvoir du peuple:' une émeute à Hippone au début du Ve siècle connue par le sermon 302 de saint Augustin pour la fête de saint Laurent." *Antiquité Tardive* 12 (2004): 309–24.

Déroche, Vincent. *Études sur Léontios de Néapolis*. Acta Universitatis Upsaliensis, Studia Byzantina Upsaliensia 3. Uppsala: Uppsala Universitet, 1995.

De Rossi, Ioannes Bapt., ed. *Inscriptiones Christianae Urbis Romae*. Vol. 2. Rome: Ex Officina Libraria Philippi Cuggiani, 1888.

Desjardins, Arthur. "De l'aliénation et de la prescription des biens de l'église dans le droit du bas-empire et dans le droit des capitulaires." *Revue historique de droit français et étranger* 16 (1860): 254–65.

Dieterich, Albrecht. "Der Ritus der verhüllten Hände." In *Kleine Schriften*, 440–48. Leipzig: B. G. Teubner, 1911.

Dilley, Paul C. "Homily on the Building of the First Church of the Virgin." In *New Testament Apocrypha: More Noncanonical Scriptures*, edited by Tony Burke and Brent Landau, 188–207. Vol. 1. Grand Rapids, MI: Eerdmans, 2020.

———. "Textual Aesthetics: *Dipinti* and the Early Byzantine Epigraphic Habit." In *The Red Monastery Church: Beauty and Asceticism in Upper Egypt*, edited by Elizabeth S. Bolman, 175–81. New Haven, CT: Yale University Press, 2016.

Doerfler, Maria. "Law and Order: Monastic Formation, Episcopal Authority, and Conceptions of Justice in Late Antiquity." PhD diss., Duke University, 2013. ProQuest (AAT 3559317).

Dolenz, Heimo. "Two Annex Buildings to the Basilica Damous-el-Karita in Carthage: A Summary of the Excavations in 1996 and 1997." *Antiquités africaines* 36 (2000): 147–59.

Doran, Robert. *Stewards of the Poor: The Man of God, Rabbula, and Hiba in Fifth-Century Edessa*. Kalamazoo, MI: Cistercian Publications, 2006.

Downs, John Emmanuel. *The Concept of Clerical Immunity*. Washington, DC: Catholic University of America Press, 1941.

Drijvers, Han J. W. "The Man of God of Edessa, Bishop Rabbula, and the Urban Poor: Church and Society in the Fifth Century." *Journal of Early Christian Studies* 4 (1996): 235–48.

Duchesne, L. "Les schismes romains au VIᵉ siècle." *Mélanges d'archéologie et d'histoire* 35 (1915): 221–56.

Ducloux, Anne. *Ad ecclesiam confugere: Naissance du droit d'asile dans les églises (IVᵉ–milieu du Vᵉ s.)*. Paris: De Boccard, 1994.

Düll, Rudolf. "Rechtsprobleme im Bereich des römischen Sakralrechts." *Aufstieg und Niedergang der römischen Welt* I.2 (1972): 283–94.

Eastmond, Antony. "Consular Diptychs, Rhetoric and the Languages of Art in Sixth-Century Constantinople." *Art History* 33 (2010): 743–65.

Ebbeler, Jennifer E. *Disciplining Christians: Correction and Community in Augustine's Letters*. New York: Oxford University Press, 2012.

Emmel, Stephen. "The Historical Circumstances of Shenute's Sermon *God is Blessed*." In *ΘΕΜΕΛΙΑ: Spätantike und koptologische Studien Peter Grossmann zum 65. Geburtstag*, edited by Martin Krause and Sofia Schaten, 81–96. Wiesbaden: Reichert Verlag, 1998.

Englezakis, Benedict. *Studies on the History of the Church of Cyprus, 4th–20th Centuries*. Translated by Norman Russell. Edited by Silouan and Misael Ioannou. Aldershot: Variorum, 1995.

Ennabli, Liliane. *Carthage: Une métropole chrétienne du IVᵉ à la fin du VIIᵉ siècle*. Paris: CNRS Éditions, 1997.

Enßlin, Wilhelm. *Die Religionspolitik des Kaisers Theodosius d. Gr.* Munich: Verlag der Bayerischen Akademie der Wissenschaften, 1953.

———. "Praepositus." In *Paulys Realencyclopädie der classischen Altertumswissenschaft*, edited by Georg Wissowa, Wilhelm Kroll, and Karl Mittelhaus, 556–67. Supplement 8. Stuttgart: Alfred Druckenmüller Verlag, 1956.

Epp, Amber M., and Linda L. Price. "The Storied Life of Singularized Objects: Forces of Agency and Network Transformation." *Journal of Consumer Research* 36 (2010): 820–37.

Epstein, Richard A. "The Economic Structure of Roman Property Law." In *The Oxford Handbook of Roman Law and Society*, edited by Paul J. du Plessis, Clifford Ando, and Kaius Tuori, 513–23. New York: Oxford University Press, 2016.

Fabbrini, Fabrizio. *La manumissio in ecclesia*. Milan: Dott. A. Giuffrè editore, 1965.

Farag, Mary K. "The Mosaic Map of Madaba and Late Antique Discourse on Ecclesial Space." In ϹΥΝΑϪΙϹ ΚΑΘΟΛΙΚΗ: *Beiträge zu Gottesdienst und Geschichte der fünf altkirchlichen Patriarchate für Heinzgerd Brakmann zum 70. Geburtstag*, edited by Diliana Atanassova and Tinatin Chronz, 175–96. Münster: LIT Verlag, 2014.

———. "Relics vs. Paintings of the Three Holy Children: Coptic Responses to Chalcedonian Claims in Alexandria." *Analecta Bollandiana* 137 (2019): 261–76.

Faris, M. J., ed. *The Bishop's Synod ("The First Synod of St. Patrick"): A Symposium with Text, Translation, and Commentary*. Liverpool: Francis Cairns, 1976.

Fedalto, Giorgio. *Hierarchia Ecclesiastica Orientalis*. Vol. 2. Padua: Messaggero, 1988.

———. "Liste vescovili del patriarcato di Gerusalemme. I. Gerusalemme e Palestina prima." *Orientalia Christiana Periodica* 49 (1983): 5–41.

Fournier, Eric. "Victor of Vita and the Conference of 484: A Pastiche of 411?" *Studia Patristica* 62 (2013): 395–408.

Gain, Benoît. "Conflit de Basile de Césarée avec l'autorité impériale d'après Grégoire de Nazianze." In *Les Pères de l'Église et le pouvoir*, edited by Pascal-Grégoire Delage. 153–75. Royan: CaritasPatrum, 2014.

Galante, Andrea. *La condizione giuridica delle cose sacre*. Part 1. Milan: Torino, Unione Tipografico-Editrice, 1903.

Galavaris, George. *The Illustrations of the Liturgical Homilies of Gregory Nazianzus*. Princeton, NJ: Princeton University Press, 1969.

Gardner, Jane F. *Women in Roman Law and Society*. Beckenham: Croom Helm, 1986.

Garreau-Forrest, Sophie, and Ali Khalil Badawi. "La cathédrale de Paulin de Tyr décrite par Eusèbe de Césarée: mythe ou réalité?" *Antiquité Tardive* 22 (2014): 111–23.

Gaudemet, Jean. *L'Église dans l'empire romain (IVᵉ–Vᵉ siècles)*. Paris: Sirey, 1958.

Giamberardini, Gabriele. *Il Culto Mariano in Egito*. 2nd ed. 3 vols. Jerusalem: Franciscan Printing Press, 1975.

Godelier, Maurice. *The Enigma of the Gift*. Translated by Nora Scott. Chicago: University of Chicago Press, 1999.

———. "Some Things You Give, Some Things You Sell, but Some Things You Must Keep for Yourselves: What Mauss Did Not Say about Sacred Objects." Translated by Nora Scott. In *The Enigma of Gift and Sacrifice*, edited by Edith Wyschogrod, Jean-Joseph Goux, and Eric Boynton, 19–37. New York: Fordham University Press, 2002.

Górecki, Tomasz. "Remnants of a Byzantine Church at Athribis." In *Christianity and Monasticism in Northern Egypt*, edited by Gawdat Gabra and Hany N. Takla, 239–52. New York: American University in Cairo Press, 2017.

Grabar, André. "Le témoignage d'une hymne syriaque sur l'architecture de la cathédrale d'Édesse au VIᵉ siècle et sur la symbolique de l'édifice chrétien." *Cahiers archéologiques* 2 (1947): 41–67.

Graf, Georg. *Geschichte der christlichen arabischen Literatur*. 5 vols. Vatican: Biblioteca Apostolica Vaticana, 1944–53.

Graham, Susan. "Justinian and the Politics of Space." In *Constructions of Space II: The Biblical City and Other Imagined Spaces*, edited by Jon L. Berquist and Claudia V. Camp, 53–77. New York: T&T Clark, 2008.

Grashof, Otto. "Die Gesetze der römischen Kaiser über die Immunitäten der Kirche hinsichtlich ihres Vermögens." *Archiv für katholisches Kirchenrecht* 35 (1876): 321–35.

———. "Die Gesetze der römischen Kaiser über die Verwaltung und Veräusserung des kirchlichen Vermögens." *Archiv für katholisches Kirchenrecht* 36 (1876): 193–214.

———. "Die Gesetzgebung der römischen Kaiser über die Güter und Immunitäten der Kirche und des Klerus nebst deren Motiven und Principien." *Archiv für katholisches Kirchenrecht* 36 (1876): 3–51.

Grillmeier, Alois, Theresa Hainthaler, Luise Abramowski, Tanios Bou Mansour, and Andrew Louth. *Christ in Christian Tradition.* Vol. 2, part 3, *The Churches of Jerusalem and Antioch*, translated by Marianne Ehrhardt. Oxford: Oxford University Press, 2013.

Grossmann, Peter. *Abū Mīnā I: Die Gruftkirche und die Gruft.* Archäologische Veröffentlichungen 44. Mainz: Verlag Philipp von Zabern, 1989.

Guilland, Rodolphe. *Recherches sur les institutions byzantines.* Vol. 1. Berlin: Akademie-Verlag, 1967.

Guirguis, Fatin Morris. "The Vision of Theophilus: Resistance through Orality among the Persecuted Copts." PhD diss., Florida Atlantic University, 2010. ProQuest (AAT 3405408).

Gutfeld, Oren. *Jewish Quarter Excavations in the Old City of Jerusalem.* Vol. 5. Jerusalem: Israel Exploration Society, 2012.

Hachlili, Rachel. *Ancient Mosaic Pavements: Themes, Issues, and Trends.* Leiden: Brill, 2009.

Hahn, Johannes, and Volker Menze, eds. *The Wandering Holy Man: The Life of Barsauma, Christian Asceticism, and Religious Conflict in Late Antique Palestine.* Oakland: University of California Press, 2020.

Harper, Kyle. *Slavery in the Late Roman World, AD 275–425.* Cambridge: Cambridge University Press, 2011.

Harper, Richard I. "Theodoric and the Laurentian Schism: An Aspect of Fifth-Century Church and State." *Southern Quarterly* 4 (1966): 123–43.

Harries, Jill. *Law and Empire in Late Antiquity.* Cambridge: Cambridge University Press, 1999.

Harrison, R. M. "The Church of St. Polyeuktos in Istanbul and the Temple of Solomon." *Harvard Ukrainian Studies* 7 (1983): 276–79.

———. *A Temple for Byzantium: The Discovery and Excavation of Anicia Juliana's Palace-Church in Istanbul.* Austin: University of Texas Press, 1989.

Harvey, Susan Ashbrook. "Praying Bodies, Bodies at Prayer: Ritual Relations in Early Syriac Christianity." In *Prayer and Spirituality in the Early Church.* Vol. 4, *The Spiritual Life*, edited by Wendy Mayer, Pauline Allen, and Lawrence Cross, 149–67. Strathfield: St. Paul's Publications, 2006.

Hebein, Richard John. "St. Ambrose and Roman Law." PhD diss., St. Louis University, 1970. ProQuest (AAT 7121392).

Hefele, Charles Joseph. *Histoire des conciles d'áprès les documents originaux.* Translated and edited by Henri Leclercq. 7 vols. Paris: Letouzey et Ané, 1907–11.

Heo, Angie. *The Political Lives of Saints: Christian-Muslim Mediation in Egypt*. Oakland: University of California Press, 2018.

Herman, E. "Asile dans l'église orientale, le droit d." In *Dictionnaire de droit canonique*, edited by R. Naz, 1084–89. Vol. 1. Paris: Librarie Letouzey et Ané, 1935.

Hermanowicz, Erika T. *Possidius of Calama: A Study of the North African Episcopate at the Time of Augustine*. New York: Oxford University Press, 2008.

Hillner, Julia. "Families, Patronage, and the Titular Churches of Rome, c. 300–c. 600." In *Religion, Dynasty, and Patronage in Early Christian Rome, 300–900*, edited by Kate Cooper and Julia Hillner, 225–61. Cambridge: Cambridge University Press, 2007.

Honoré, Tony. *Justinian's Digest: Character and Compilation*. New York: Oxford University Press, 2010.

———. *Tribonian*. London: Duckworth, 1978.

Holman, Susan. *The Hungry Are Dying: Beggars and Bishops in Roman Cappadocia*. New York: Oxford University Press 2001.

Holum, Kenneth G. *Theodosian Empresses: Women and Imperial Dominion in Late Antiquity*. Transformation of the Classical Heritage 3. Berkeley: University of California Press, 1982.

Holum, Kenneth G., and Gary Vikan. "The Trier Ivory, 'Adventus' Ceremonial, and the Relics of St. Stephen." *Dumbarton Oaks Papers* 33 (1979): 115–33.

Honigmann, Ernest. "Juvenal of Jerusalem." *Dumbarton Oaks Papers* 5 (1950): 209–79.

Horn, Cornelia B. *Asceticism and Christological Controversy in Fifth-Century Palestine: The Career of Peter the Iberian*. Oxford: Oxford University Press, 2006.

Horn, Cornelia B., and Robert R. Phenix Jr., eds. and trans. *John Rufus: The Lives of Peter the Iberian, Theodosius of Jerusalem, and the Monk Romanus*. Atlanta: Society of Biblical Literature, 2008.

Horner, George W. *The Coptic Version of the New Testament in the Northern Dialect*. Oxford: Clarendon Press, 1905.

Hosang, F. J. E. Boddens. *Establishing Boundaries: Christian-Jewish Relations in Early Council Texts and the Writings of Church Fathers*. Leiden: Brill, 2010.

Hübner, Sabine R. "Currencies of Power: The Venality of Offices in the Later Roman Empire." In *The Power of Religion in Late Antiquity*, edited by Andrew Cain and Noel Lenski, 167–79. Burlington, VT: Ashgate, 2009.

———. *Der Klerus in der Gesellschaft des spätantiken Kleinasiens*. Stuttgart: Steiner, 2005.

Humfress, Caroline. "Bishops and Law Courts in Late Antiquity: How (Not) to Make Sense of the Legal Evidence." *Journal of Early Christian Studies* 19 (2011): 375–400.

———. *Orthodoxy and the Courts in Late Antiquity*. New York: Oxford University Press, 2007.

———. "Patristic Sources." In *The Cambridge Companion to Roman Law*, edited by David Johnston, 97–118. New York: Cambridge University Press, 2015.

Hyde, Lewis. *The Gift: Imagination and the Erotic Life of Property*. New York: Random House, 1983.

Janin, R. *Constantinople Byzantine*. 2nd ed. Paris: Institut français d'études byzantines, 1964.

———. "Cusae." In *Dictionnaire d'histoire et de géographie ecclésiastiques*, edited by Alfred Baudrillart, A. de Meyer, and Ét. van Cauwenbergh, 1117. Vol. 13. Paris: Librairie Letouzey et Ané, 1956.

Jensen, Robin Margaret. *Understanding Early Christian Art*. Abingdon: Routledge, 2000.

Johnson, David W. "Anti-Chalcedonian Polemics in Coptic Texts, 451–641." In *The Roots of Egyptian Christianity*, edited by Birger A. Pearson and James E. Goehring, 216–34. Philadelphia: Fortress, 1986.

Jones, A. H. M. *Cities of the Eastern Roman Provinces*. 2nd ed. Oxford: Clarendon Press, 1971.

———. "Inscriptions from Jerash." *Journal of Roman Studies* 18 (1928): 144–78.

Jones, A. H. M, J. R. Martindale, and J. Morris, eds. *Prosopography of the Later Roman Empire*. 3 vols. Cambridge: Cambridge University Press, 1971–92.

Kaden, Erich-Hans. "Die Edikte gegen die Manichäer von Diokletian bis Justinian." In *Festschrift Hans Lewald*, 55–68. Basel: Verlag Helbing und Lichtenhahn, 1953.

Kaiser, Wolfgang. *Die Epitome Iuliani: Beiträge zum römischen Recht im frühen Mittelalter und zum byzantinischen Rechtsunterricht*. Frankfurt: Vittorio Klostermann, 2004.

Kartzow, Marianne Bjelland. *Gossip and Gender: Othering Speech in the Pastoral Epistles*. Berlin: Walter de Gruyter, 2009.

Kaufhold, Hubert. "Sources of Canon Law in the Eastern Churches." In *The History of Byzantine and Eastern Canon Law to 1500*, edited by Wilfried Hartmann and Kenneth Pennington, 215–342. Washington, DC: Catholic University of America Press, 2012.

Kearley, Timothy G. "The Creation and Transmission of Justinian's Novels." *Law Library Journal* 102 (2010): 377–97.

Kehoe, Dennis P. "Tenure of Land and Agricultural Regulation." In *The Oxford Handbook of Roman Law and Society*, edited by Paul J. du Plessis, Clifford Ando, and Kaius Tuori, 646–59. Oxford: Oxford University Press, 2016.

Kitzinger, Ernst. "The Cult of Images in the Age before Iconoclasm." *Dumbarton Oaks Papers* 8 (1954): 83–150.

Klauser, Theodor. "*Aurum Coronarium*." *Mitteilungen des deutschen archaeologischen Instituts, Roemische Abteilung* 59 (1944): 129–53.

Klingshirn, William. *Caesarius of Arles: Life, Testament, Letters*. Translated Texts for Historians 19. Liverpool: Liverpool University Press, 1994.

Knecht, August. *System des Justinianischen Kirchenvermögensrechtes*. Stuttgart: Verlag von Ferdinand Enke, 1905.

Koep, L. "Consecratio." In *Reallexikon für Antike und Christentum*, edited by Theodor Klauser, 269–83. Vol. 3. Stuttgart: Anton Hiersemann, 1957.

———. "Dedicatio." In *Reallexikon für Antike und Christentum*, edited by Theodor Klauser, 643–49. Vol. 3. Stuttgart: Anton Hiersemann, 1957.

Kopytoff, Igor. "The Cultural Biography of Things: Commoditization as Process." In *The Social Life of Things: Commodities in Cultural Perspective*, edited by Arjun Appadurai, 64–91. New York: Cambridge University Press, 1986.

Krautheimer, Richard, Wolfgang Frankl, and Spencer Corbett. *Corpus Basilicarum Christianarum Romae: The Early Christian Basilicas of Rome (IV–IX Cent.)*. Vol. 2. Vatican City: Pontificio istituto di archeologia cristiana, 1959.

Krueger, Derek. "Mary at the Threshold: The Mother of God as Guardian in Seventh-Century Palestinian Miracle Accounts." In *The Cult of the Mother of God in Byzantium: Texts and Images*, edited by Leslie Brubaker and Mary B. Cunningham, 31–38. Burlington, VT: Ashgate, 2011.

Kunzelman, A. "Die Chronologie der Sermones des hl. Augustinus." *Miscellanea Agostiniana* 2 (1931): 417–520.

Laird, Raymond. *Mindset, Moral Choice and Sin in the Anthropology of John Chrysostom*. Early Christian Studies 15. Sydney: Sydney College of Divinity Press, 2017. First published 2012 by St Paul's Publications.

Lamoreaux, John C. "Episcopal Courts in Late Antiquity." *Journal of Early Christian Studies* 3 (1995): 143–67.

Langenfeld, Hans. *Christianisierungspolitik und Sklavengesetzgebung der römischen Kaiser von Konstantin bis Theodosius II*. Bonn: Habelt, 1977.

Laniado, Avshalom. "Note sur la datation conserve en syriaque du Concile de Gangres." *Orientalia Christiana Periodica* 61 (1995): 195–99.

Layton, Bentley. *The Canons of Our Fathers*. New York: Oxford University Press, 2014.

Leader-Newby, Ruth E. *Silver and Society in Late Antiquity: Functions and Meanings of Silver Plate in the Fourth to Seventh Centuries*. Burlington, VT: Ashgate, 2004.

Leatherbury, Sean V. "Textiles as Gifts to God in Late Antiquity: Christian Altar Cloths as Cultic Objects." In *Textiles and Cult in the Ancient Mediterranean*, edited by Cecilie Brøns and Marie-Louise Nosch, 243–57. Ancient Textiles Series 31. Oxford: Oxbow Books, 2017.

Leclercq, Henri. "Droit d'asile." In *Dictionnaire d'archéologie chrétienne et de liturgie*, edited by Fernand Cabrol and Henri Leclercq, 1550–65. Vol. 4, part 2. Paris: Librarie Letouzey et Ané, 1921.

Leemans, Johan. "'Schoolrooms for Our Souls.' The Cult of the Martyrs: Homilies and Visual Representations as a Locus for Religious Education in Late Antiquity." *Paedagogica Historica: International Journal of the History of Education* 36 (2000): 112–27.

Leemans, Johan, Wendy Mayer, Pauline Allen, and Boudewijn Dehandschutter. *"Let Us Die That We May Live:" Greek Homilies on Christian Martyrs from Asia Minor, Palestine, and Syria c. AD 350–AD 450*. London: Routledge, 2003.

Lehmann, Tomas. "Die ältesten erhaltenen Bilder in einem Kirchenbau. Zu den frühchristlichen Kirchenbauten und ihren Mosaiken unter dem Dom von Aquileia." *Das Altertum* 54 (2009): 91–122.

Lenski, Noel. "Captivity among the Barbarians and Its Impact on the Fate of the Roman Empire." In *The Cambridge Companion to the Age of Attila*, edited by Michael Maas, 230–46. New York: Cambridge University Press, 2014.

———. *Constantine and the Cities*. Philadelphia: University of Pennsylvania Press, 2016.

———. "Imperial Legislation and the Donatist Controversy: From Constantine to Honorius." In *The Donatist Schism: Controversy and Contexts*, edited by Richard Miles, 172–226. Liverpool: Liverpool University Press, 2016.

———. "Note on the Dating of Constitutions." In *The Codex of Justinian: A New Annotated Translation, with Parallel Latin and Greek Text, Based on a Translation by Justice Fred H. Blume*, edited by Bruce W. Frier, 1: xciv–xcvi. Cambridge: Cambridge University Press, 2016.

———. "The Significance of the Edict of Milan." In *Constantine: Religious Faith and Imperial Policy*, edited by A. Edward Siecienski, 27–56. Abingdon: Routledge, 2017.

Liermann, Hans. *Handbuch des Stiftungsrechts*. Vol. 1. Tübingen: J. C. B. Mohr, 1963.

Linder, Amnon. *The Jews in Roman Imperial Legislation*. Detroit: Wayne State University Press, 1987.

Lipsmeyer, Elizabeth. "The Donor and His Church Model in Medieval Art from Early Christian Times to the Late Romanesque Period." PhD diss., Rutgers University, 1981. ProQuest (AAT 8122095).

Litsas, Fotios K. "Choricius of Gaza and His Descriptions of Festivals at Gaza." *Jahrbuch der österreichischen Byzantinistik* 32 (1982): 427–36.

Little, Lester K. *Benedictine Maledictions: Liturgical Cursing in Romanesque France*. Ithaca, NY: Cornell University Press, 1993.

Lokensgard, Kenneth Hayes. *Blackfoot Religion and the Consequences of Cultural Commod-itization*. Farnham: Ashgate, 2010.

Loomis, Louise Ropes, trans. *The Book of the Popes*. New York: Columbia University Press, 1916.

MacCormack, Sabine G. *Art and Ceremony in Late Antiquity*. Berkeley: University of California Press, 1981.

MacCoull, Leslie. "Holy Family Pilgrimage in Late Antique Egypt: The Case of Qosqam." In *Akten des XII. internationalen Kongresses für christliche Archäeologie*, 987–92. Münster: Aschendorffsche Verlagsbuchhandlung, 1995.

MacDougall, Byron. "Gregory of Nazianzus and Christian Festival Rhetoric." PhD diss., Brown University, 2015.

———. "Spectatorship in City and Church in Late Antiquity: Theoria Returns to the Festival." In *From Constantinople to the Frontier: The City and the Cities*, edited by Nicholas S. M. Matheou, Theofili Kampianaki, and Lorenzo M. Bondioli, 127–41. Leiden: Brill, 2016.

Maclean, Arthur John. *East Syrian Daily Offices*. London: Rivington and Percival, 1894.

MacMullen, Ramsay. "The Preacher's Audience (AD 350–400)." *Journal of Theological Studies*, n.s., 40 (1989): 503–11.

———. *Voting about God in Early Church Councils*. New Haven, CT: Yale University Press, 2006.

Macomber, William F. *Catalogue of the Christian Arabic Manuscripts of the Franciscan Center of Christian Oriental Studies, Muski, Cairo*. Cairo: Éditions du Centre franciscain d'études orientales chrétiennes, 1984.

Maguire, Henry. *Nectar and Illusion: Nature in Byzantine Art and Literature*. New York: Oxford University Press, 2012.

———. "Two Modes of Narration in Byzantine Art." In *Byzantine East, Latin West: Art-Historical Studies in Honor of Kurt Weitzmann*, edited by Christopher Moss and Katherine Kiefer, 385–95. Princeton, NJ: Department of Art and Archaeology, Princeton University, 1995.

Malinowski, Bronislaw. *Argonauts of the Western Pacific*. Prospect Heights, IL: Waveland Press, 1984. First published 1922 by E. P. Dutton.

———. "Kula: The Circulating Exchange of Valuables in the Archipelagoes of Eastern New Guinea," *Man* 20 (1920): 97–105.

Mango, Cyril. *The Art of the Byzantine Empire 312–1453*. Toronto: University of Toronto Press, 1986.

Mango, Cyril, and Ihor Ševčenko. "Remains of the Church of St. Polyeuktos at Constantinople." *Dumbarton Oaks Papers* 15 (1961): 243–47.

Mango, Marlia Mundell. "Artistic Patronage in the Roman Diocese of Oriens, 313–641 AD." PhD diss., Cambridge University, 1984.

Marini, Graziano, ed. *I Mosaici della basilica di Aquileia*. Aquileia: Ciscra, 2003.

Martindale, J. R. *Prosopography of the Later Roman Empire*. Vol. 2. Cambridge: Cambridge University Press, 1980.

Matā'us, Al-Anba. *Ṭaqs sir al-zawāj al-muqadas*. Wadī al-Natrūn: Dayr al-Suryān, 2000.

Mateos, Juan. *Lelya-Ṣapra: Essai d'interprétation des matines chaldéennes*. Orientalia Christiana Analecta 156. Rome: Pontificium Institutum Orientalium Studiorum, 1959.

Mathews, Thomas F. *The Clash of the Gods: A Reinterpretation of Early Christian Art*. Princeton, NJ: Princeton University Press, 1993.

Matthews, John F. *Laying Down the Law: A Study of the Theodosian Code*. New Haven, CT: Yale University Press, 2000.

Mathisen, Ralph W. "The *communio peregrina* in Late Antiquity: Origin, Purpose, Implementation." *Studia Patristica* 40 (2006): 49–54.

Mauss, Marcel. *The Gift: Forms and Functions of Exchange in Archaic Societies*. Translated by Ian Cunnison. Mansfield Center, CT: Martino Publishing, 2011.

Mayer, Wendy. "John Chrysostom as Crisis Manager: The Years in Constantinople." In *Ancient Jewish and Christian Texts as Crisis Management Literature: Thematic Studies from the Centre for Early Christian Studies*, edited by D. Sim and P. Allen, 129–43. Library of New Testament Studies 445. New York: T&T Clark, 2012.

———. "Media Manipulation as a Tool in Religious Conflict: Controlling the Narrative Surrounding the Deposition of John Chrysostom." In *Religious Conflict from Early Christianity to the Rise of Islam*, edited by Wendy Mayer and Bronwen Neil, 151–68. Arbeiten zur Kirchengeschichte 121. Berlin: De Gruyter, 2013.

McLynn, Neil. *Ambrose of Milan: Church and Court in a Christian Capital*. Berkeley: University of California Press, 1994.

———. "The Transformation of Imperial Churchgoing in the Fourth Century." In *Approaching Late Antiquity: The Transformation from Early to Late Empire*, edited by Simon Swain and Mark Edwards, 235–70. Oxford: Oxford University Press, 2006.

Meinardus, Otto. "A Comparative Study on the Sources of the Synaxarium of the Coptic Church." *Bulletin de la Société d'Archéologie Copte* 17 (1963–64): 111–55.

Merdinger, Jane E. "Building God's House: Augustine's Homilies at Episcopal Consecrations, Church Dedications, and Funerals." *Studia Patristica* 43 (2006): 195–200.

———. "On the Eve of the Council of Hippo, 393: The Background to Augustine's Program for Church Reform." *Augustinian Studies* 40 (2009): 27–36.

Métivier, Sophie. *La Cappadoce, IVe–VIe siècle: Une histoire provinciale de l'empire romain d'orient*. Paris: Publications de la Sorbonne, 2005.

Meyer, Wilhelm. *Der Gelegenheitsdichter Venantius Fortunatus*. Berlin: Weidmannsche Buchhandlung, 1901.

Millar, Fergus. *A Greek Roman Empire: Power and Belief under Theodosius II (AD 408–450)*. Berkeley: University of California Press, 2006.

———. "The Syriac Acts of the Second Council of Ephesus (449)." In *Chalcedon in Context: Church Councils 400–700*, edited by Richard Price and Mary Whitby, 45–67. Liverpool: Liverpool University Press, 2009.

Miller, William Ian. "Is A Gift Forever?" *Representations* 100 (2007): 13–22.

Mitchell, John. "The Painted Decoration of San Salvatore de Brescia in Context." In *Dalla corte regia al monastero di San Salvatore—Santa Giulia de Brescia*, edited by Gian

Pietro Brogiolo and Francesca Morandini, 169–201. Mantua: SAP Società Archeologica, 2014.

Moawad, Samuel. *Untersuchungen zum Panegyrikos auf Makarios von Tkōou und zu seiner Überlieferung*. Wiesbaden: Reichert, 2010.

Monferrer-Sala, Juan Pedro, ed. and trans. *The Vision of Theophilus: The Flight of the Holy Family into Egypt*. Piscataway, NJ: Gorgias Press, 2015.

Moolan, John. *The Period of Annunciation-Nativity in the East Syrian Calendar: Its Background and Place in the Liturgical Year*. Kottayam: Pontifical Oriental Institute of Religious Studies, 1985.

Moore, Michael E. "The Ancient Fathers: Christian Antiquity, Patristics, and Frankish Canon Law." *Millenium* 7 (2010): 293–342.

———. "The Spirit of the Gallican Councils, AD 314–506." *Annuarium Historiae Conciliorum* 39 (2007): 1–52.

Müller, C. Detlef G. "Die koptische Kirche zwischen Chalkedon und dem Arabereinmarsch." *Zeitschrift für Kirchengeschichte* 75 (1964): 271–308.

Muñoz, Antonio. *La basilica di s. Lorenzo fuori le mura*. Rome: Fratelli Palombi, 1944.

Mury, Ch. "Immunités des biens d'église et du clergé sous les Empereurs romains." *Revue catholique des institutions et du droit* 10 (1877): 241–55.

Nau, François. "Deux episodes de l'histoire juive sous Théodose II (423 et 438) d'après la vie de Barsauma le syrien." *Revue des études juives* 83 (1927): 184–93.

———. "Martyrologes et ménologes orientaux: Les ménologes évangéliaires coptes-arabes." *Patrologia Orientalis* 10 (1915): 166–244.

———. "Martyrologes et ménologes orientaux: Un martyrologe et douze ménologes syriaques," *Patrologia Orientalis* 10 (1915): 3–163.

Neil, Bronwen. *Leo the Great*. London: Routledge, 2009.

Nightingale, Andrea Wilson. "The Philosopher at the Festival: Plato's Transformation of Traditional *Theōria*." In *Pilgrimage in Graeco-Roman and Early Christian Antiquity: Seeing the Gods*, edited by Jaś Elsner and Ian Rutherford, 151–80. New York: Oxford University Press, 2005.

Ní Mheallaigh, Karen. "Pseudo-Documentarism and the Limits of Ancient Fiction." *American Journal of Philology* 129 (2008): 403–31.

Noble, Thomas F. X. "Art, Icons, and Their Critics and Defenders before the Age of Iconoclasm." In *Images, Iconoclasm, and the Carolingians*, 10–45. Philadelphia: University of Pennsylvania Press, 2009.

Öğüş, Esen. "The 'Sacrilegious, Accursed and Tomb-breaker': Sarcophagus Re-Use at Aphrodisias." In *Questions, Approaches, and Dialogues: Studies in Honor of Marie-Henriette and Charles Gates*, edited by Ekin Kozal, Murat Akar, Yağmur Heffron, Çiler Çilingiroğlu, Tevfik Emre Şerifoğlu, Canan Çakırlar, Sinan Ünlüsoy, and Eric Jean, 647–65. Münster: Ugarit-Verlag, 2017.

Ohme, Heinz. "Sources of the Greek Canon Law to the Quinisext Council (691/2): Councils and Church Fathers." In *The History of Byzantine and Eastern Canon Law to 1500*, edited by Wilfried Hartmann and Kenneth Pennington, 24–114. Washington, DC: Catholic University of America Press, 2012.

Orlandi, Tito, ed. and trans. *Constantini Episcopi Urbis Siout: Encomia in Athanasium Duo*. Corpus Scriptorum Christianorum Orientalium 349–50, Scriptores Coptici 37–38. Louvain: Secrétariat du CorpusSCO, 1974.

Osteen, Mark. "Gift or Commodity?" In *The Question of the Gift: Essays across Disciplines*, edited by Mark Osteen, 229–47. Routledge Studies in Anthropology 2. London: Routledge, 2002.

Pagels, Elaine. "How Athanasius, Subject to Christian Emperors, Read John's Apocalypse into His Canon." In *Envisioning Judaism: Studies in Honor of Peter Schäfer on the Occasion of His Seventieth Birthday*, edited by Ra'anan S. Boustan, Klaus Herrmann, Reimund Leicht, Annette Yoshiko Reed, and Giuseppe Veltri, 799–808. Vol. 2. Tübingen: Mohr Siebeck, 2013.

———. *Revelations: Visions, Prophecy, and Politics in the Book of Revelation*. New York: Viking, 2012.

Palmer, Anne-Marie. *Prudentius on the Martyrs*. Oxford: Clarendon Press, 1989.

Paño, María Victoria Escribano. "Bishops, Judges and Emperors: CTh 16.2.31/CTh 16.5.46/ Sirm. 14 (409)." In *The Role of the Bishop in Late Antiquity: Conflict and Compromise*, edited by Andrew Fear, José Fernández Ubiña, and Mar Marcos, 105–26. London: Bloomsbury, 2013.

Papaconstantinou, Arietta. "Historiography, Hagiography, and the Making of the Coptic 'Church of the Martyrs' in Early Islamic Egypt." *Dumbarton Oaks Papers* 60 (2006): 65–86.

———. "La liturgie stationale à Oxyrhynchos dans la première moitié du 6ᵉ siècle: Réédition et commentaire du POxy XI 1357." *Revue des études byzantines* 54 (1996): 135–59.

Pentcheva, Bissera V. "Glittering Eyes: Animation in the Byzantine *Eikōn* and the Western *Imago*." *Codex Aquilarensis* 32 (2016): 209–36.

———. "Hagia Sophia and Multisensory Aesthetics." *Gesta* 50 (2011): 93–111.

———. *Hagia Sophia: Sound, Space, and Spirit in Byzantium*. University Park: Pennsylvania State University Press, 2017.

———. *Icons and Power: The Mother of God in Byzantium*. University Park: Pennsylvania State University Press, 2006.

———. "The Performative Icon." *Art Bulletin* 88 (2006): 631–55.

———. "The Power of Glittering Materiality: Mirror Reflections between Poetry and Architecture in Greek and Arabic Medieval Culture." In *Istanbul and Water*, edited by Paul Magdalino and Nina Ergin, 241–74. Ancient Near Eastern Studies Supplement 47. Leuven: Peeters, 2015.

Perčić, Iva. *Poreč: The Euphrasius Basilica*. Belgrade: Jugoslavija, 1969.

Pérez, Carles Buenacasa. "Accroissement et consolidation du patrimoine ecclésiastique dans le *Code Théodosien XVI*." In *Empire chrétien et église aux IVᵉ et Vᵉ siècles: Intégration ou «concordat»? Le témoinage du Code Théodosien*, edited by Jean-Noël Guinot and François Richard, 259–75. Paris: Les éditions du Cerf, 2008.

Permjakovs, Vitalijs. "'Make This the Place Where Your Glory Dwells': Origins and Evolution of the Byzantine Rite for the Consecration of a Church." PhD diss., University of Notre Dame, 2012. ProQuest (AAT 3733713).

Pernice, Alfred. "Zum römischen Sacralrechte." *Sitzungsberichte der königlich preussischen Akademie der Wissenschaften zu Berlin* 2 (1885): 1143–69.

Pfannmüller, Gustav. *Die kirchliche Gesetzgebung Justinians hauptsächlich auf Grund der Novellen*. Berlin: C. A. Schwetschke und Sohn, 1902.

Pick, B. "Die templtragenden Gottheiten und die Darstellung der Neokorie auf den Münzen." *Jahreshefte des österreichischen archäologischen Institutes in Wien* 7 (1904): 1–41.

Ploumis, Ida Malte. "Gifts in the Late Roman Iconography." In *Patron and Pavements in Late Antiquity*, edited by Signe Isager and Birte Poulsen, 125–41. Odense: Odense University Press, 1997.

Poeschke, Joachim. *Italian Mosaics, 300–1300*. Translated by Russell Stockman. New York: Abbeville Press Publishers, 2010.

Polański, Tomasz. "The Three Young Men in the Furnace and the Art of Ecphrasis in the Coptic Sermon by Theophilus of Alexandria." In *Christian Art in Oriental Literatures. Greek, Syriac and Coptic Sources from the 4th to the 7th Century*, 111–24. Salzburg: Horn, 2013.

Pruitt, Jennifer. *Building the Caliphate: Construction, Destruction, and Sectarian Identity in Early Fatimid Architecture*. New Haven, CT: Yale University Press, 2020.

Pudichery, Sylvester. *Ramsa: An Analysis and Interpretation of the Chaldean Vespers*. Pachalam: Dharmaram College, 1972.

Renoux, Athanase. *Le Codex arménien Jérusalem 121*. Patrologia Orientalis 35.1–2. Turnhout: Brepols, 1969–71.

Richard, Marcel. "Les Écrits de Théophile d'Alexandrie." *Le Muséon* 52 (1939): 33–50.

Richards, Jeffrey. *The Popes and the Papacy in the Early Middle Ages 476–752*. London: Routledge and Kegan Paul, 1979.

Riedel, Wilhelm, and W. E. Crum, eds. and trans. *The Canons of Athanasius of Alexandria: The Arabic and Coptic Versions*. London: Williams and Norgate, 1904.

Rives, James. "Control of the Sacred in Roman Law." In *Law and Religion in the Roman Republic*, edited by Olga Tellegen-Couperus, 165–80. Leiden: Brill, 2012.

Rivet, August. *Le régime des biens de l'église avant Justinien*. Lyons: Imprimerie Emmanuel Vitte, 1891.

Roberts, Michael. *The Jeweled Style: Poetry and Poetics in Late Antiquity*. Ithaca, NY: Cornell University Press, 1989.

Robinson, Olivia. "Blasphemy and Sacrilege in Roman Law." *Irish Jurist* 8 (1973): 356–71.

Roques, Denis. *Études sur la Correspondance de Synésios de Cyrène*. Brussels: Latomus, Revue d'études latines, 1989.

Rosenwein, Barbara H. *Negotiating Space: Power, Restraint, and Privileges of Immunity in Early Medieval Europe*. Ithaca, NY: Cornell University Press, 1999.

———. *To Be the Neighbor of Saint Peter: The Social Meaning of Cluny's Property, 909–1049*. Ithaca, NY: Cornell University Press, 1989.

Rougé, Jean, trans. *Le code Théodosien, Livre XVI*. Sources chrétiennes 497. Paris: Cerf, 2005.

Rougé, Jean, and Roland Delmaire, trans. *Code Théodosien I–XV, Code Justinien, Constitutions Sirmondiennes*. Sources chrétiennes 531. Paris: Cerf, 2009.

Rousseau, Philip. *Basil of Caesarea*. Berkeley: University of California Press, 1994.

Rubin, Ze'ev. "The Church of the Holy Sepulchre and the Conflict between the Sees of Caesarea and Jerusalem." In *The Jerusalem Cathedra: Studies in the History, Archaeology, Geography and Ethnography of the Land of Israel*, vol. 2, edited by Lee I. Levine, 79–105. Detroit: Wayne State University Press, 1982.

Ruszczyc, Barbara. *Kościół pod wezwaniem Świętej Dziewicy w Tell Atrib*. Warsaw: Polska Akademia Nauk, 1997.

Rutherford, Ian. *State Pilgrims and Sacred Observers in Ancient Greece: A Study of* Theōria *and* Theōroi. Cambridge: Cambridge University Press, 2013.

Sadek, Ashraf, and Bernadette Sadek. "Un Fleuve d'eau vive: Trilogie sur l'Entrée du Christ en Égypte." *Le Monde Copte* 34 and 35 (2011 and 2017).

Safran, Linda. "Points of View: The Theodosian Obelisk Base in Context." *Roman and Byzantine Studies* 34 (1993): 409–35.

Salyers, Daniel R. "'Clutching the Altar with Chattering Teeth:' Exploring the Ancient Custom of Asylum-Seeking through the Lens of John Chrysostom." PhD diss., Fuller Theological Seminary, 2020. ProQuest (AAT 27955117).

Salzman, Michele Renee. "The Evidence for the Conversion of the Roman Empire to Christianity in Book 16 of the 'Theodosian Code.'" *Historia: Zeitschrift für Alte Geschichte* 42 (1993): 362–78.

———. "From a Classical to a Christian City: Civic Euergetism and Charity in Late Antique Rome." *Studies in Late Antiquity* 1 (2017): 65–85.

Sarris, Peter. "Introduction: The Novels of the Emperor Justinian." In *The Novels of Justinian: A Complete Annotated English Translation*, edited by David J. D. Miller and Peter Sarris, 1–51. Vol. 1. Cambridge: Cambridge University Press, 2018.

Scheid, John. "Oral Tradition and Written Tradition in the Formation of Sacred Law in Rome." In *Religion and Law in Classical and Christian Rome*, edited by Clifford Ando and Jörg Rüpke, 14–33. Stuttgart: Franz Steiner Verlag, 2006.

Scheja, Georg. "Hagia Sophia und Templum Salomonis." *Istanbuler Mitteilungen* 12 (1962): 44–58.

Scherillo, Gaetano. *Lezioni di diritto romano: le cose*. Part 1. Milan: Dott. A. Giuffrè-Editore, 1945.

Schindler, Alfred. "Die Unterscheidung von Schisma und Häresie in Gesetzgebung und Polemik gegen den Donatismus (mit einer Bemerkung zur Datierung von Augustins Schrift: Contra Epistulam Parmeniani)." In *Pietas: Festschrift für Bernhard Kötting*, edited by Ernst Dassmann and K. Suso Frank, 228–36. Jahrbuch für antike und Christentum Ergänzungsband 8. Münster: Aschendorffsche Verlagsbuchhandlung, 1980.

Schmidt, Thomas. "The Last Book: Revelation, Commentaries, and the Making of the New Testament." PhD diss., Yale University, 2020.

Schott, Jeremy M. "Eusebius' *Panegyric on the Building of Churches* (HE 10.4.2–72): Aesthetics and the Politics of Christian Architecture." In *Reconsidering Eusebius: Collected Papers on Literary, Historical, and Theological Issues,* edited by Sabrina Inowlocki and Claudio Zamagni, 177–97. Leiden: Brill, 2011.

Schroeder, Caroline T. "The Church Building as Symbol of Ascetic Renunciation." In *Monastic Bodies: Discipline and Salvation in Shenoute of Atripe*, 90–125. Philadelphia: University of Pennsylvania Press, 2007.

Schwab, Moïse, trans. *Le Talmud de Jérusalem*. Vol. 4. Paris: Éditions G.-P. Maisonneuve et Larose, 1960.

Schwartz, Daniel R. "Humbly Second-Rate in the Diaspora? Philo and Stephen on the Tabernacle and the Temple." In *Envisioning Judaism: Studies in Honor of Peter Schäfer on the Occasion of His Seventieth Birthday*, edited by Ra'anan S. Boustan, Klaus Herrmann, Reimund Leicht, Annette Yoshiko Reed, and Giuseppe Veltri, 81–89. Vol. 1. Tübingen: Mohr Siebeck, 2013.

Schwartz, Eduard. "Βασιλικὸς νόμος περὶ τῶν προσφευγόντων ἐν ἐκκλησίαι." In *Das Asylwesen Ägyptens in der Ptolermäerzeit*, by Friedrich von Woeß, 253–72. Munich: C. H. Beckesche Verlagsbuchhandlung Oskar Beck, 1923.

Sessa, Kristina. "*Domus Ecclesiae:* Rethinking a Category of *Ante-Pacem* Christian Space." *Journal of Theological Studies*, n.s., 60 (2009): 90–108.

———. *The Formation of Papal Authority in Late Antique Italy: Roman Bishops and the Domestic Sphere*. New York: Cambridge University Press, 2012.

Shahîd, Irfan. "Justinian and the Christianization of Palestine: The Nea Ecclesia in Jerusalem." In *Klētorion in Memory of Nikos Oikonomides*, edited by Florentia Evangelatou-Notara and Triantafyllitsa Maniati-Kokkini, 373–85. Athens: University of Athens, 2005.

Shalev-Hurvitz, Vered. *Holy Sites Encircled: The Early Byzantine Concentric Churches of Jerusalem*. New York: Oxford University Press, 2015.

Shepardson, Christine. *Controlling Contested Spaces: Late Antique Antioch and the Spatial Politics of Religious Controversy*. Berkeley: University of California Press, 2014.

Sheridan, J. Mark. *Rufus of Shotep: Homilies on the Gospels of Matthew and Luke*. Rome: C. I. M., 1998.

Shoemaker, Stephen J. *Ancient Traditions of the Virgin Mary's Dormition and Assumption*. New York: Oxford University Press, 2002.

———. "The Cult of Fashion: The Earliest 'Life of the Virgin' and Constantinople's Marian Relics." *Dumbarton Oaks Papers* 62 (2008): 53–74.

Smith, Christine. "Christian Rhetoric in Eusebius' Panegyric at Tyre." *Vigiliae Christianae* 43 (1989): 226–47.

Sotinel, C. "L'évergétisme dans le royaume gothique: le témoignage d'Ennode de Pavie." In *Homenatge a F. Giunta: Committenza e committenti tra antichità e alto medioevo*, edited by Marc Mayer Olivé and Mònica Miró Vinaixa, 213–22. Barcelona: PPU—Littera—Departament Filologia Llatina UB, 1996.

Stephanou, Pelopidas. "La Doctrine de Léon de Chalcédoine et de ses adversaires sur les images." *Orientalia Christiana Periodica* 12 (1946): 177–99.

———. "Le procès de Léon de Chalcédoine," *Orientalia Christiana Periodica* 9 (1943): 5–64.

Steppa, Jan-Eric. *John Rufus and the World Vision of Anti-Chalcedonian Culture*. 2nd ed. Piscataway, NJ: Gorgias Press, 2005.

Sternberg, Thomas. "'Aurum utile': Zu einem Topos vom Vorrang der Caritas über Kirchenschätze seit Ambrosius." *Jahrbuch für Antike und Christentum* 39 (1996): 128–48.

Stocking, Rachel L. *Bishops, Councils, and Consensus in the Visigothic Kingdom, 589–633*. Ann Arbor: University of Michigan Press, 2000.

Stolte, Bernard. "Law for Founders." In *Founders and Refounders of Byzantine Monasteries*, edited by Margaret Mullett, 121–39. Belfast: Belfast Byzantine Enterprises, 2007.

Strzygowski, Josef. *Orient oder Rom*. Leipzig: J. C. Hinrichs'sche Buchhandlung, 1901.

Suciu, Alin. "'Me, This Wretched Sinner': A Coptic Fragment from the Vision of Theophilus Concerning the Flight of the Holy Family to Egypt." *Vigiliae Christianae* 67 (2013): 436–50.

Tannous, Jack. *The Making of the Medieval Middle East: Religion, Society, and Simple Believers*. Princeton, NJ: Princeton University Press, 2018.

Terry, Ann, and Henry Maguire. *Dynamic Splendor: The Wall Mosaics in the Cathedral of Euphrasius at Poreč*. 2 vols. University Park: Pennsylvania State University Press, 2007.

Teteriatnikov, Natalia. "Gender and Ritual: Mosaic Panels of Justinian and Theodora in San Vitale." In *ΑΝΑΘΗΜΑΤΑ ΕΟΡΤΙΚΑ: Studies in Honor of Thomas F. Mathews*, edited by Joseph D. Alchermes, Helen C. Evans, and Thelma K. Thomas, 296–304. Mainz: Verlag Philipp von Zabern, 2009.

Thomas, John Philip. *Private Religious Foundations in the Byzantine Empire*. Washington, DC: Dumbarton Oaks Research Library and Collection, 1987.

Thomas, Thelma. "The Honorific Mantle as Furnishing for the Household Memory Theater in Late Antiquity: A Case Study from the Monastery of Apa Apollo at Bawit." In *Catalogue of the Textiles in the Dumbarton Oaks Byzantine Collection*, edited by Gudrun Bühl and Elizabeth Dospěl Williams. Washington, DC: Dumbarton Oaks Research Library and Collection, 2019. Accessed March 5, 2020. https://www.doaks.org/resources /textiles/essays/thomas.

Thomas, Yan. "La valeur des choses: Le droit romain hors la religion." *Annales. Histoire, Sciences Sociales* 6 (2002): 1431–62.

Thomson, R. W. "Architectural Symbolism in Classical Armenian Literature." *Journal of Theological Studies*, n.s., 30 (1979): 102–14.

Thümmel, Hans Georg. "Neilos von Ancyra über die Bilder." *Byzantinische Zeitschrift* 71 (1978): 10–21.

Thurman, William S. "A Law of Justinian Concerning the Right of Asylum." *Transactions and Proceedings of the American Philological Association* 100 (1969): 593–606.

Tilley, Maureen A. "When Schism Becomes Heresy in Late Antiquity: Developing Doctrinal Deviance in the Wounded Body of Christ." *Journal of Early Christian Studies* 15 (2007): 1–21.

Timm, Stefan. *Das christlich-koptische Ägypten in arabischer Zeit*. Vol. 5. Wiesbaden: Dr. Ludwig Reichert Verlag, 1991.

Tougher, Shaun. *The Eunuch in Byzantine History and Society*. Abingdon: Routledge, 2008.

Townsend, W. T. "Councils Held under Pope Symmachus." *Church History* 6 (1937): 233–59.

Toynbee, J. M. C., and K. S. Painter. "Silver Picture Plates of Late Antiquity: A.D. 300 to 700." *Archaeologia* 108 (1986): 15–65.

Traulsen, Christian. *Das sakrale Asyl in der Alten Welt*. Tübingen: Mohr Siebeck, 2004.

Trilling, James. "The Image Not Made by Hands and the Byzantine Way of Seeing." In *The Holy Face and the Paradox of Representation*, edited by Herbert L. Kessler and Gerhard Wolf, 109–27. Rome: Bibliotheca Hertziana, 1998.

Trout, Dennis E. *Paulinus of Nola: Life, Letters, and Poems*. Berkeley: University of California Press, 1999.

Usacheva, Anna. "The Term πανήγυρις in the Holy Bible and Christian Literature of the Fourth Century and the Development of Christian Panegyric Genre." *Studia Patristica* 62 (2013): 57–68.

Vailhé, Siméon. "L'Érection du patriarchat de Jérusalem, 451." *Revue de l'orient chrétien* 4 (1899): 44–57.

Valensi, Lucette. *La Fuite en Égypte: Histoires d'orient et d'occident*. Paris: Éditions du Seuil, 2002.

Van Esbroeck, Michel. "La Première église de la vierge bâtie par les apôtres." In *Aegyptus Christiana: Mélanges d'hagiographie égyptienne et orientale dédiés à la mémoire du P. Paul Devos Bollandiste*, edited by Ugo Zanetti and Enzo Lucchesi, 1–18. Geneva: Patrick Cramer, 2004.

Van Nuffelen, Peter. "The Career of Cyril of Jerusalem (c. 348–87): A Reassessment." *Journal of Theological Studies*, n.s., 58 (2007): 134–46.

————. "Social Ethics and Moral Discourse in Late Antiquity." In *Reading Patristic Texts on Social Ethics: Issues and Challenges for Twenty-First Century Christian Social Thought*, edited by Johan Leemans, Brian J. Matz, and Johan Verstraeten, 45–63. Washington, DC: Catholic University of America Press, 2011.

————. "Theophilus against John Chrysostom: The Fragments of a Lost *Liber* and the Reasons for John's Deposition." *Adamantius* 19 (2013): 139–55.

Van Ommeslaeghe, Florent. "Que vaut le témoignage de Pallade sur le procès de saint Jean Chrysostome?" *Analecta Bollandiana* 95 (1997): 389–414.

Van Tongeren, Louis. *Exaltation of the Cross: Toward the Origins of the Feast of the Cross and the Meaning of the Cross in Early Medieval Liturgy*. Leuven: Peeters, 2001.

Verstegen, Ute. "Byzantine Jerusalem." In *The Routledge Handbook of Jerusalem*, edited by Suleiman A. Mourrad, Naomi Kolton-Fromm, and Bedross Der Matossian, 64–76. Abingdon: Routledge, 2019.

Vessey, Mark. "The Origins of the *Collectio Sirmondiana*: A New Look at the Evidence." In *The Theodosian Code: Studies in the Imperial Law of Late Antiquity*, edited by Jill Harries and Ian Wood, 178–99. London: Duckworth, 1993.

Vivian, Tim. *The Life of Longinus*. Special Issue, *Coptic Church Review* 20 (1999).

Voelkl, Ludwig. *Die Kirchenstiftungen des Kaisers Konstantin im Lichte des römischen Sakralrechts*. Arbeitsgemeinschaft für Forschung des Landes Nordrhein-Westfalen 117. Cologne: Westdeutscher Verlag, 1964.

Voicu, Sever. "La volontà e il caso: La tipologia dei primi spuri di Crisostomo." In *Giovanni Crisostomo: Oriente e occidente tra IV e V secolo, XXXIII Incontro di studiosi dell' antichità cristiana, Roma, 6–8 maggio 2004*, 101–18. Vol. 1. Studia Ephemeridis Augustinianum 93. Rome: Institutum Patristicum Augustinianum, 2005.

Voigt, Moritz. "Die römische Klassifikation von Ius divinum und humanum." *Berichte über die Verhandlungen der königlich sächsischen Gesellschaft der Wissenschaften zu Leipzig, philologisch-historische Klasse* 54 (1902): 185–94.

Volpp, Sophie. "The Gift of a Python Robe: The Circulation of Objects in 'Jin Ping Mei.'" *Harvard Journal of Asiatic Studies* 65 (2005): 133–58.

Von Dobschütz, Ernst. *Christusbilder: Untersuchungen zur christlichen Legende*. Leipzig: J. C. Hinrichs'sche Buchhandlung, 1899.

Von Hertling, Georg. *Konsekration und res sacrae im römischen Sakralrecht*. Munich: K. Hof- und Universitäts-Buchdruckerei Dr. C. Wolf und Sohn, 1911.

Von Zhishman, Joseph. *Das Stifterrecht in der morgenländischen Kirche*. Vienna: K. K. Hof- und Universitäts-Buchhändler, 1888.

Vööbus, Arthur, ed. and trans. *The Synodicon in the West Syrian Tradition*. Corpus Scriptorum Christianorum Orientalium, Scriptores Syri 161 and 162. Louvain: Secrétariat du CorpusSCO, 1975.

Vryonis, Speros. "The Panēgyris of the Byzantine Saint: A Study in the Nature of a Medieval Institution, Its Origins and Fate." In *The Byzantine Saint: University of Birmingham Fourteenth Spring Symposium of Byzantine Studies*, edited by Sergei Hackel, 196–227. Studies Supplementary to Sobornost 5. London: Fellowship of St. Alban and St. Sergius, 1981.

Webb, Ruth. "The Aesthetics of Sacred Space: Narrative, Metaphor, and Motion in *Ekphraseis* of Church Buildings." *Dumbarton Oaks Papers* 53 (1999): 59–74.

———. *Ekphrasis, Imagination and Persuasion in Ancient Rhetorical Theory and Practice.* Farnham: Ashgate, 2009.

———. "Sight and Insight: Theorizing Vision, Emotion, and Imagination in Ancient Rhetoric." In *Sight and the Ancient Senses*, edited by Michael Squire, 205–19. Abingdon: Routledge, 2016.

Weiner, Annette B. *Inalienable Possessions: The Paradox of Keeping-While-Giving.* Berkeley: University of California Press, 1992.

Weitzmann, Kurt, ed. *Age of Spirituality: Late Antique and Early Christian Art, Third to Seventh Century.* New York: Metropolitan Museum of Art, 1979.

Wessel, K. "Das Diptychon Barberini." In *Akten des XI. internationalen Byzantinistenkongresses, München, 1958*, edited by Franz Dölger and Hans-Georg Beck, 665–70. Munich: C. H. Beck, 1960.

Wesselschmidt, Quentin F. *Ancient Christian Commentary on Scripture: Psalms 51–150.* Old Testament 8. Downers Grove, IL: InterVarsity Press, 2007.

Whitby, Mary. "The Occasion of Paul the Silentiary's *Ekphrasis* of S. Sophia." *Classical Quarterly* 35 (1985): 215–28.

———. "The St. Polyeuktos Epigram (*AP* 1.10): A Literary Perspective." In *Greek Literature in Late Antiquity: Dynamism, Didacticism, Classicism*, edited by Scott Johnson, 159–87. Burlington, VT: Ashgate, 2006.

White, Stephen D. *Custom, Kinship, and Gifts to Saints: The* Laudatio Parentum *in Western France, 1050–1150.* Chapel Hill: University of North Carolina Press, 1988.

Williams, Michael Stuart. *The Politics of Heresy in Ambrose of Milan: Community and Consensus in Late-Antique Christianity.* Cambridge: Cambridge University Press, 2017.

Wipszycka, Ewa. *The Alexandrian Church: People and Institutions.* Journal of Juristic Papyrology Supplement 25. Warsaw: University of Warsaw and Raphael Taubenschlag Foundation, 2015.

———. "Καθολική et les autres épithètes qualifiant le nom ἐκκλησία." *Journal of Juristic Papyrology* 24 (1994): 191–212.

———. "Le lettere di Sinesio come fonte per la storia del patriarcato alessandrino." In *Christianity in Egypt: Literary Production and Intellectual Trends*, edited by Paola Buzi and Alberto Camplani, 611–20. Studia Ephemeridis Augustinianum 125. Rome: Institutum Patristicum Augustinianum, 2011.

———. *Les ressources et les activités économiques des églises en Égypte du IVᵉ au VIIIᵉ siècle.* Brussels: Fondation Égyptologique Reine Élisabeth, 1972.

Wirbelauer, Eckhard. *Zwei Päpste in Rom: Der Konflikt zwischen Laurentius und Symmachus (498–514).* Munich: Tuduv Verlagsgesellschaft, 1993.

Wissowa, Georg. *Religion und Kultus der Römer.* Munich: C. H. Beck'sche Verlagsbuchhandlung, 1902.

Wohl, Victoria. "Plato avant la lettre: Authenticity in Plato's Epistles." *Ramus* 27 (1998): 60–93.

Wood, Ian. "The Audience of Architecture in Post-Roman Gaul." In *The Anglo-Saxon Church: Papers in History, Architecture and Archaeology in Honour of Dr. H. M. Taylor*, edited by L. A. S. Butler and R. K. Morris, 74–79. London: Council for British Archaeology, 1986.

Wood, Susan. *The Proprietary Church in the Medieval West*. Oxford: Oxford University Press, 2006.

Worp, Klaas A. "A Checklist of Bishops in Byzantine Egypt (A.D. 325–c. 750)." *Zeitchrift für Papyrologie und Epigraphik* 100 (1994): 283–318.

Wroth, Warwick. *Catalogue of the Greek Coins of Troas, Aeolis, and Lesbos*. A Catalog of the Greek Coins in the British Museum. London: Trustees of the British Museum, 1894.

Yale University Art Gallery. "Mosaic Floor with Views of Alexandria and Memphis." Accessed April 8, 2021. http://artgallery.yale.edu/collections/objects/51363.

Yaron, Reuven. "Alienation and Manumission." *Revue internationale des droits de l'antiquité*, 3rd series, 2 (1955): 381–87.

Yasin, Ann Marie. "Making Use of Paradise: Church Benefactors, Heavenly Visions, and the Late Antique Commemorative Imagination." In *Looking Beyond: Visions, Dreams, and Insights in Medieval Art and History*, edited by Colum Hourihane, 39–57. Princeton, NJ: Princeton University, 2010.

———. *Saints and Church Spaces in the Late Antique Mediterranean: Architecture, Cult, and Community*. Cambridge: Cambridge University Press, 2009.

Youssef, Youhanna Nessim. "The Rite of the Consecration of the Church of Koskam." *Ancient Near Eastern Studies* 46 (2009): 72–92.

Zanetti, Ugo. *Les manuscrits de Dair Abû Maqâr: inventaire*. Geneva: P. Cramer, 1986.

INDEX LOCORUM

Specific churches will be found by location; for instance, the Church of the Holy Sepulchre is listed under Jerusalem.

Cassian (deacon and supporter of John Chrysostom), 89
Cecropius (bishop of Sebastopolis), 68
Celestine of Rome, 262n43
Chabot, J.-B., 262n46
Chaereas (count and judge of Osrhoene), 59–60
Chalcedon, Council of (451): aftermath of, 166–67; on divine protection of res sacrae, 42, 53, 58, 60, 61, 65, 68, 69, 224nn113–14; legal concept of res sacrae at, 22, 23, 24, 25, 35, 209n4; non-Chalcedonian responses to, 157–59, 161; rift in church caused by, 158. See also Index Locorum for specific canons; non-Chalcedonian celebrations of anniversaries
Challoa and her children (connected to Daniel and Ibas of Edessa), 59
charity: bequests and donations for charitable purposes, 71; civic euergetism and, 253n135; donor resistance to alienation of church property for purposes of, 99–101, 126–28; as gift, 132, 147, 241n91; inalienability of church property versus, 99–100, 126–28; John Chrysostom's charitable building project, 89–90; repurposing of ecclesial property for 155. See also mercy.
Choricius of Gaza, 102, 103, 104, 105, 133, 135–37, 246n36
Christodorus of Coptus, 248n66
church, as building and community, 144
churches as protecting spaces, 71–97; acts of mercy, use of ecclesial property to perform, 85–93, 99–100, 126; asylum, 75–83, 85, 87–88, 91–92, 212n24, 228n24, 231n89; Augustine's City of God on, 71, 72; bribes/bribery undermining, 72; Cyril of Jerusalem, trial of, 85–86; donor resistance to, 99–101, 126–28; manumission of slaves, churches as public place of, 5, 72–75; redemption of captives, 83–85, 225n122; singularization and, 107; status as res sacrae and, 130
Cimitile, church of Saint Felix at, 104, 141, 248n75
circle of sanctity, 130, 131, 132, 137, 138–41, 143–44, 155, 247n60
circular giving, 131–32, 155, 244n16, 245n25
Circumcellions, 33
Claudius (archdeacon), 110fig., 110
Claudius of Antioch, 172
Clearchus (prefect of the City), 189table
clerics: accusations against, 24; administrative duties regarding res sacrae, 19, 23, 36–37, 46, 51–52, 54–56, 61–62; bishops, relationship to,

23, 26; bribery, corruption via, 72; property of, 45; support of, 22, 25–26; witnesses in the alienation of res sacrae 48.
Clicherius (count of the Orient), 188table
"codex" versus "code," 209–10n8
coins and coinage, 118–20, 119fig.
commoditization, 97, 105–6. See also recommoditization
commodity versus gift, 244n18
Commodus (emperor), 119fig., 239n71
conciliabula or conventicula ("meeting places" or "gathering places"), 31
conciliar activities, 57–58, 224n112. See also specific councils and synods in this index and in Index Locorum
confiscation as legal means of delegitimization, 11, 13, 30–36
Connor, Carolyn, 138, 248nn65–66
consecrations, 5, 129–56; assignment of ritual agents, 20; charitable purposes, using res sacrae for, 128; circle of sanctity at, 130, 131, 132, 137, 138–41, 143–44, 155, 247n60; contracts for pagan temples and Christian churches, 209n1; deconsecration, no legal or canonical means of, 12, 30; dedications versus, 213n42; devaluation of res sacrae compared to human souls, 130, 151–56; earthly versus celestial festivals of, 165–66; episcopal control of, 19; evidence and sources, 129, 130; festivals for, 129–30, 132–37, 133–36fig., 242n3, 245–46n28; gifts and gifting, centrality of, 132–37, 133–36fig.; homilies and orations at, 135–37, 141, 142–49, 150, 151, 153, 155, 242n3, 249n86; hymnic texts for, 138–40, 143–44, 145, 147–49, 151, 249n86; lectionary readings and liturgical traditions for, 130, 205–6; legal rules for consecration ritual, 19–21; as loss of possession, 43; prerequisites for, 19–20; reconsecrations, 20–21; regifting, 131–32, 148–56, 156chart, 243–44nn15–16; relics, deposition of, 130, 134, 135, 143, 243n10; religiophilosophical context in Roman world, 141–43; singularization and economies of exchange in, 101, 106, 150; taboo status of regifting in late antiquity and, 148–50; Ulpian's criterion for valid consecration, 32; use not tantamount to, 11, 28; validity if improperly performed, 20, 27–30. See also anniversaries non-Chalcedonian celebrations of anniversaries
Constantianus (Vicar of Pontus), 188table

Umm al-Rasas, church at, 102, 236n15
Uranius of Hemerium, 58, 59, 60
usucaption, 43, 46, 53–54
usufruct (detention) of *res sacrae*, 62–63, 68
usury, 244n16

Valens (emperor), 174, 187–88*table*
Valentinian I (emperor), 33, 35, 78, 187–88*table*
Valentinian II (emperor), 33, 35, 187–89*table*,
   191–92*table*
Valerian (emperor), 264n59
van Esbroeck, Michel, 258n18, 265n73, 266n79
van Nuffelen, Peter, 232n106, 232n111
Venantius Fortunatus, 242n4, 249n86
Venerius (presbyter), 87
Victor (bishop of Ravenna), 245n26
Victor of Vita, *History of the Vandal Persecution,* 13
Vikan, Gary, 242n3, 245nn27–30
Vincentius (bishop), 77
violence against or on church property,
   prohibitions on, 44–45, 46, 65–66. *See also*
   outrages against churches
Virgin Mary. *See* Saint Mary
virtues associated with jewels/luminosity, 148,
   252n122

Visigoths: Gaius's *Institutes,* reworking of, 208n8;
   sack of Rome by (410), 71
Saint Vitalis, 110, 111*fig.,* 238n47
Voelkl, Ludwig, 209n1
Voicu, Sever, 207nn1–2
Volpp, Sophia, 241n94

Wadiʿ al-Fransīskānī, 263n56
Wadī al-Natrūn: Monastery of Saint Macarius,
   161, 258n20; Monastery of Saint Mary,
   260n23
Weiner, Annette, 131–32, 243n15
western provinces, confiscation policies and
   practices in, 33
Whitby, Mary, 248n66, 254n154
Williams, Michael, 254n149
women: kidnappers of women seeking asylum,
   slavery as penalty for, 78; legal representation
   of, 215n78
Wood, Ian, 249n86
Wood, Susan, 211n19

Yaron, Reuven, 227n5

Zeno (emperor), 192*table*

Founded in 1893,
UNIVERSITY OF CALIFORNIA PRESS
publishes bold, progressive books and journals
on topics in the arts, humanities, social sciences,
and natural sciences—with a focus on social
justice issues—that inspire thought and action
among readers worldwide.

The UC PRESS FOUNDATION
raises funds to uphold the press's vital role
as an independent, nonprofit publisher, and
receives philanthropic support from a wide
range of individuals and institutions—and from
committed readers like you. To learn more, visit
ucpress.edu/supportus.